TO BELIEVE IN
WOMEN

Books by Lillian Faderman

Surpassing the Love of Men: Romantic Friendship and Love
Between Women from the Renaissance to the Present

Scotch Verdict: Miss Pirie and Miss Woods
v. Dame Cumming Gordon

Odd Girls and Twilight Lovers:
A History of Lesbian Life in Twentieth-Century America

Chloe Plus Olivia: An Anthology of Lesbian Literature
from the Seventeenth Century to the Present

To Believe in Women: What Lesbians
Have Done for America — A History

TO BELIEVE IN WOMEN

WHAT LESBIANS HAVE DONE FOR AMERICA — A HISTORY

Lillian Faderman

To you —

I know we both believe in women, and I believe in you — and always will! Here's to a future full of sharing and sisterhood!

With love always —

Barb

— Graduation 2001 —

HOUGHTON MIFFLIN COMPANY

Boston New York

1999

For information about permission to reproduce selections from this
book, write to Permissions, Houghton Mifflin Company,
215 Park Avenue South, New York, New York 10003.

Library of Congress Cataloging-in-Publication Data

Faderman, Lillian.
To believe in women : what lesbians have done for
America — a history / Lillian Faderman.
p. cm.
Includes bibliographical references and index.
ISBN 0-395-85010-X
1. Lesbian feminism — United States — History.
2. Lesbians — United States — History.
I. Title.
HQ75.6.U5F35   1999
305.48'9664'0973 — dc21   99-26209   CIP

Book design by Anne Chalmers
Typeface: Linotype-Hell Fairfield

Printed in the United States of America
QUM 10 9 8 7 6 5 4 3 2 1

To Phyllis — again

FOR EVERYTHING — AGAIN

I have forgotten everything I learned at Bryn Mawr, but I still see you standing in chapel and telling us to believe in women.

— from a letter to Bryn Mawr's president,
M. Carey Thomas, from an alumna

ACKNOWLEDGMENTS

It would be impossible to write a book of this nature without the help of the numerous archivists and special collections librarians who very kindly assisted me in finding the papers I needed and often led me to materials that were invaluable for my research. My thanks to the staff at the Swarthmore College Peace Collection, the Huntington Library, the Nantucket Historical Association, the Bancroft Library of the University of California at Berkeley, the Bryn Mawr College Archives, the American Philosophical Society Library, the Archives and Special Collections at the Allegheny University of the Health Sciences, the Sophia Smith Collection at Smith College, the Vassar College Special Collections, the Wellesley College Archives, the Cornell University Rare and Manuscript Collections, the Schlesinger Library of Radcliffe College, and the Mount Holyoke College Archives and Special Collections.

I am especially grateful to Patricia Albright of Mount Holyoke College, Wendy Chmielewski of the Swarthmore College Peace Collection, Amy Hague of Smith College, Wilma Slaight of Wellesley College, Ellen Shea of the Schlesinger Library, and Jeanne Tempesta, head of Interlibrary Loan at California State University, Fresno.

I want to thank the friends and colleagues who very generously gave me their time, insight, and encouragement, reading numerous drafts of my manuscript and/or patiently listening to me spin out my ideas. My special gratitude goes to Joyce Brotsky, Rosie Pegueros, Dana Shugar, Linda Garber, Barbara Blinick, Steve Yarbrough, and Priscilla Allen. Heather Phillips and Sara Cable kindly shared with me their work on Pauli Murray. Joan Organ shared her work on Florence Allen. Margaret Bacon shared her work on Mildred Olmsted. Phyllis Irwin's assistance with research and photography has been precious to me.

It would not have been possible for me to complete this book without the gift of time from my university and the help and understanding of the dean of the School of Arts and Humanities, Luis Costa.

I thank John Radziewicz, my editor, and his very patient assistant, Jenna Terry. As always during our twenty-year relationship, Sandra Dijkstra continues to be a wonderful agent and a good friend.

I thank Dawn Seferian for her early faith in this project and Steve Fraser for his good suggestions during the all-too-brief time I was fortunate to work with him. My special thanks go to my superb manuscript editor, Liz Duvall.

CONTENTS

Acknowledgments · ix

1. Introduction   1

I · How American Women Got Enfranchised

2. The Loves and Living Arrangements of
   Nineteenth-Century Suffrage Leaders   15

3. Bringing the Suffrage Movement into the
   Twentieth Century: Anna Howard Shaw   40

4. Victory: Carrie Chapman Catt   61

5. Two Steps Forward . . .   79

II · How America Got a Social Conscience

6. Mother-Hearts/Lesbian-Hearts   99

7. Social Housekeeping:
   The Inspiration of Jane Addams   115

8. Social Housekeeping Becomes
   a Profession: Frances Kellor   136

9. Poisoning the Source   154

III · How American Women Got Educated

10. "Mental Hermaphrodites":
    Pioneers in Women's Education   175

11. Making Women's Higher Education
    Even Higher: M. Carey Thomas   197

12. The Struggle to Maintain Women's
    Leadership: Mary Emma Woolley   217

13. The Triumph of Angelina:
    Education in Femininity   237

IV · How American Women Got into the Professions

14. "When More Women Enter Professions":
    Lesbian Pioneering in the Learned Professions 255

15. Making Places for Women in
    Medicine: Emily Blackwell   274

16. Carrying On: Martha May Eliot, M.D.   291

17. The Rush to Bake the Pies
    and Have the Babies   306

18. Conclusion: Legacies · 327

Notes · 351
Index · 410

TO BELIEVE IN
WOMEN

❧ 1 ❧

INTRODUCTION

Not-men, not-women, answerable to no function of either sex, whose careers were carried on, and how successfully, in whatever field they chose: They were educators, writers, editors, politicians, artists, world travellers,
and international hostesses, who lived in public and by
the public and played out their self-assumed roles in
such masterly freedom as only a few medieval queens
had equalled. Freedom to them meant precisely freedom
from men and their stuffy rules for women.

— Katherine Anne Porter, on nineteenth- and
early twentieth-century "lesbians"

THIS IS A BOOK about how millions of American women became
what they now are: full citizens, educated, and capable of earning a
decent living for themselves. It is also a book about how Americans
developed a social conscience and adapted the goals of various
reform movements into laws. But it departs from other such histories because it focuses on how certain late nineteenth- and early
twentieth-century women whose lives can be described as lesbian
were in the forefront of the battle to procure the rights and privileges that large numbers of Americans enjoy today.

For a variety of reasons, many of the women at the center of this
book would not have used the noun "lesbian" to describe their
identity, or even have been familiar with the word. However, using
materials such as their letters and journals as evidence, I argue that
that term used as an adjective accurately describes their committed
domestic, sexual, and/or affectional experiences. I also argue that
in their eras, lesbian arrangements freed these pioneering women

to pursue education, professions, and civil and social rights for themselves and others far more effectively than they could have if they had lived in traditional heterosexual arrangements.

Lesbians Before "Lesbian Identity"

The emotional and sexual lives of many of the women discussed in this book were often complex. Most of them lived before the days when sexual identity was defined by clear-cut labels, and the noun "lesbian" would not in any case have been entirely adequate to identify all of them. Mary Dreier, for example, shared her life with another woman in a relationship that was almost certainly sexual, but she was also in love with a man she could not marry, and she probably did not consummate her attraction to him. Mildred Olmsted was married for most of her life and had a child with her husband, yet she was sexually uninterested in him, and throughout her marriage she continued a relationship with a woman that was emotionally and erotically intense. Still others loved and lived with women only. They may or may not have had sexual relationships with those women, but regardless, they saw them as their domestic spouses, partners, or lifelong loves. The binary paradigm of homosexual/heterosexual would probably have been baffling to many of them even if they had known those terms. However, what all these people had in common was that beloved women were centrally implicated in their emotional lives, and to a greater or lesser extent, their intimate relationships with other women helped enable their achievements.

To Believe in Women will perhaps be seen as being in opposition to postmodernism, which does not recognize the possibility of reclaiming women of the past as lesbians. Academic postmodernists might point to the precarious status of identity — the instability, indecipherability, and unnameability of sexualities — and conclude that lesbianism cannot really be discussed, particularly in regard to history. With their epistemological doubts, they would be suspicious of any attempt to construct a coherent pattern out of complex human lives in order to create a "grand narrative" of history. Grand narratives — indeed, any such theoretical speculations, they would argue — must ultimately expose themselves as "passionate fictions."

I believe that such arguments have merit and serve as an important corrective to a simplistic temptation to name the "lesbians" in history. As the postmodernists claim, it is impossible — especially when dealing with historical figures — to make safe statements about identities, which are so slippery in their subjectivity and mutability. However, if enough material that reveals what people *do* and *say* is available, we can surely make apt observations about their *behavior.* That is what I have attempted to do in this book. I use the term "lesbian" as an *adjective* that describes intense woman-to-woman relating and commitment. Thus, I will admit at the outset that my subtitle is somewhat misleading. If there had been more space on the title page, and if the phrase had not been so aesthetically dismal, I might have subtitled this book, with greater accuracy, "What Women of the Late Nineteenth and Early Twentieth Centuries, Whose Chief Sexual and/or Affectional and Domestic Behaviors Would Have Been Called 'Lesbian' If They Had Been Observed in the Years after 1920, Have Done for America." When I slip into the shorthand of referring to these women as "lesbians," readers might keep my alternate subtitle in mind.

While most of these women appear not to have had what we in the later twentieth century have called a "lesbian identity," they somehow recognized each other. On what basis? Perhaps it was because they fought together to expand women's possibilities, they were usually not living with a husband, and, most important, they were ostensibly engaged in a romantic and committed relationship with another woman. They often knew each other well. Anna Howard Shaw, the suffrage leader, was close not only to other suffrage leaders such as Susan B. Anthony and the woman Anthony called her "lover," Emily Gross, but also to women such as M. Carey Thomas, the college president, and her partner, Mary Garrett. Thomas was also friends with Jane Addams, the social reformer, who, along with her partner, Mary Rozet Smith, was friends with the suffragist and politician Anne Martin and her partner, Dr. Margaret Long. When Addams and Smith visited Boston, they often dined or stayed with the writer Sarah Orne Jewett and her partner, Annie Fields.

These women seldom wrote to each other without also sending regards to the partner of the correspondent; "Love from both of us to both of you" was an oft-repeated phrase in their letters. When female couples traveled with other female couples, it was taken for granted that each woman would be sharing a room with her partner and not with another friend. Sleeping arrangements were understood to be as inviolate as they would be with husband and wife. Those qualities and lifestyles these women shared and recognized in each other apparently constituted an "identity" of sorts, though there is little evidence that they gave a name to it.

In the context of their day, the general absence of a name for their loves and lives is not surprising. I have found no articulated concepts of lesbianism in the late nineteenth and early twentieth centuries with which they would have been entirely comfortable. "Inverts" were seen by most sexologists as pathological, and since these women believed their discontent was not pathological but rationally based on the unjust treatment of females, they would not have dubbed themselves "sexual inverts," no matter how much sexologists' definitions of the invert fit them. The term "homosexual" too would probably have felt foreign to most of them, since regardless of whether their relationships were specifically sexual, they were also much more than sexual. Nor would other nineteenth-century views of lesbianism, such as the images of the *lesbienne* in French decadent fiction and poetry, have seemed acceptable to most of them.

However, though most of the women discussed here may not have articulated, even to themselves, that their choice of a female mate instead of a husband was "lesbian," sexologists writing at the end of the nineteenth century made the point emphatically, characterizing the leaders of the women's movement as "sexual inverts." In his 1897 work, Havelock Ellis even laid the blame for what he said was an increase in female homosexuality on the "modern movement of emancipation," which encouraged women's "intimacy with their own sex" and taught them "disdain" for women's conventional roles.

Ellis's supposition ran counter to a theory proposed several decades earlier and generally accepted by him that homosexuality was congenital. The true homosexual, sexologists insisted, suffered from a *hereditary* neurosis. But Ellis explained an apparent contradiction by asserting that the homosexuality of women who came to that "aberration" through the emancipation movement was only "a spurious imitation." However, he continued his argument, the *true* homosexual often assumed leadership in women's rights movements, where she made other women "spuriously" homosexual. She could intellectually seduce other females because her "congenital anomaly" of homosexuality "occurs with special frequency in women of high intelligence who, voluntarily or involuntarily, influence others." Despite the charm of this supposition, I will not argue as Ellis does that the leadership for women's rights and reform came from lesbians because of the "high intelligence" associated with their "anomaly." Rather, it seems that women of this time who formed domestic partnerships with other women were much more likely to be effective as social pioneers than women who lived with husbands.

The Virtues of Lesbian Domesticity

Almost all of the women discussed in the pages that follow had a primary relationship with another woman that lasted for twenty years or more. However, there was no one model of domestic and affectional arrangements among them. In some cases, such as that of Anna Shaw and Lucy Anthony, one member of the couple mostly kept the home fires burning while the other traveled the continent to procure women's rights. Lucy Anthony, who would surely have been called a "femme" if she had lived in the mid-twentieth century, had no interest in a public role for herself, yet she believed ardently in the women's movement and felt that by taking care of the charismatic and politically effective Shaw, she was contributing to the cause.

In contrast, other women worked together with their partners to advance women's position. Emily Blackwell and Elizabeth Cushier were both pioneering doctors in the New York infirmary that Emily founded. Frances Willard and Anna Gordon both led the Woman's Christian Temperance Union. Carrie Catt and Mollie Hay were both suffrage leaders on a national level. Tracy Mygatt and Frances Witherspoon both worked on issues of peace and civil rights.

In other cases, one woman made her considerable fortune available to the reform work in which her partner was engaged, thereby empowering the beloved partner while promoting a cause in which she too believed. Jane Addams was able to put Hull House on the map in part because of the many excellent projects that the generosity of her wealthy partner, Mary Rozet Smith, permitted her to pursue. M. Carey Thomas became one of the first female college presidents in 1894 because Mary Garrett, with whom Thomas lived until Garrett's death, in 1915, told the trustees that she would give Bryn Mawr a large yearly endowment if, and only if, Thomas headed the college. Miriam Van Waters became a powerful women's prison reformer with the help of the purse and political clout of Geraldine Thompson, with whom she had a long-term committed relationship.

In *Surpassing the Love of Men* and *Odd Girls and Twilight Lovers,* I traced how the successes of the women's rights movement by the late nineteenth century meant that so-called romantic friendships of earlier eras could become "Boston marriages": committed relationships between two women who, having gone to college and then found decent-paying jobs, could set up a household together rather than marry men out of economic need. In *To Believe in Women,* I will show how many of those women also shared the excitement of pioneering. They went where no women had gone before — not only into colleges and universities, but also into the polls, the operating rooms, the pulpits, the legislatures, the law courts. It was often their same-sex partnerships and commitments that made those exciting explorations possible.

Why were women who lived in committed relationships with

other women so apt to be the most effective early leaders in the movement to advance women and in many other reform movements? At the end of the long, strong first wave of the women's rights movement, in 1920, Crystal Eastman, who had had two husbands and numerous male lovers, characterized what she believed to be crucial differences between heterosexual relationships and female-female relationships. Heterosexual marriage, in her summation, posed a danger to certain women:

> Two business women can "make a home" together without either one being over-burdened or over-bored. It is because they both know how and both feel responsible. But it is the rare man who can marry one of them and continue the home-making partnership. Yet if there are not children, there is nothing essentially different in the combination. Two self-supporting adults decide to make a home together: If both are women, it is a pleasant partnership more often than work; if one is a man, it is almost never a partnership — the woman simply adds running the home to her regular outside job. Unless she is very strong, it is too much for her, she gets tired and bitter over it, and finally perhaps gives up her outside work and condemns herself to the tiresome half-jobs of housekeeping for two.

In our post–second-wave-of-feminism era, when egalitarian heterosexual relationships are not as rare as they were several generations ago, the fears of women such as Eastman may seem overwrought; but they clearly mirrored those of many of her cohorts and predecessors. For example, in a 1906 essay for *Harper's Bazaar,* "The Passing of Matrimony," Charlotte Perkins Gilman expressed great relief that women no longer had to strive desperately to find a husband and that more and more women were in fact choosing to remain single. As Gilman phrased it, they were "refusing to be yoked in marriage," which demanded that they "give up the dream of self-realization." While there were marriages that were exceptions to these complaints, even with cooperative and well-meaning husbands, women often felt conflicts over attempting to balance professional and domestic life.

Because many women's rights leaders believed that an unmarried woman could be more committed to the cause than one with a husband and children, they not infrequently hoped to encourage young women not to marry. As Susan B. Anthony phrased it on the occasion of her fiftieth birthday party, at which an army of movement women demonstrated how greatly they revered her, "I am so glad of it all because it will help teach the young girls that to be true to principle — to live to an idea — though an unpopular one — that is to live single — *without any man's name* — *may* be honorable." But did the loneliness of single life not appear formidable to many pioneering women? If a woman chose not to be "yoked in marriage," was she not condemned to solitude? The women who are the subjects of this book believed that through their intimate relationships with other women they found escape from loneliness while maintaining their "dreams of self-realization."

With regard to many of these women, it is impossible to determine which came first, the realization that it was important to remain single if they wanted to achieve or the desire to achieve because they knew they must since they did not want to marry. Did they fight for women's rights because they did not have the *opportunity* to marry? Or was their opportunity to marry foreclosed by their fight for women's rights? Or did they realize that they must fight for women's rights because they *preferred* not to marry? Whatever the case, their same-sex living arrangements permitted them far more time for social causes and other pursuits than was available to those who were busy running a multiperson household before the days of modern conveniences and with raising a family before effective birth control could limit the number of pregnancies. It is not surprising that in Frances Willard and Mary Livermore's biographical dictionary, *A Woman of the Century,* more than half of the 1470 biographies of women of achievement were of those who had never married or who were widowed young and never remarried. In the same vein, in her study of the twenty-six leading suffragists from 1890 to 1920, Aileen Kraditor talks about a number of women leaders who married "and then withdrew from activity because of family responsibility." It was not easy to be a wife and mother while one led a revolution in the nineteenth and early twentieth centuries.

Moreover, women in relationships that we would describe today as lesbian truly had a unique interest in the advancement of women and a psychological advantage in effecting that advancement: they were fighting for their lives, or at least for the quality of their lives. If no man was going to represent them at the polls or in politics, they needed the vote and they needed power to effect social changes. If no man was going to support them, they needed education and good jobs. They had the luxury as well as the necessity of greater female chauvinism than the woman whose "significant other" was a man. The 1970s lesbian feminist term "woman-identified woman" was cumbersome and unlovely, but it expressed something of the feeling not only of lesbian feminists of the second half of the twentieth century but also of many of the leading women's rights activists of the nineteenth century. Regardless of whether a woman became a pioneer by volition or necessity, if she had a relationship with another woman, not only could she escape the inevitable loneliness of the single life, but also such a relationship might have made her feel double the plight of females in her era; it might have enhanced her desire to stand shoulder to shoulder with other women in order to lessen that plight.

Women who knew they were not going to marry also had less fear of offending men than a woman whose burning ambition was to be a wife. They could afford to be more militant and more devoted to pioneering pursuits in the cause of women, since they did not have to care what men thought. Through their commitments to each other and their freedom from heterosexual dependence, they were in the best position to wage the necessary grueling and often brutal battles on behalf of women.

Gender Trouble

The individuals who are the subject of this book might all be said to have had "gender trouble," in the sense that they could not accept the restrictions inherent in the notion of gender: they were dissatisfied with the way the category "woman" was constructed, and they were frustrated by the limitations placed on them as forced members of that category. They desired the privileges that were associated with men. Such desires demanded that they break into the "masculine" public sphere, claim it for their own, and thereby neuter the notion of gender-appropriate spheres. However, many leaders who were particularly effective in the nineteenth century strategically disguised the fact that gender was a concept with which they wished to dispense. If, as Judith Butler has argued, all gender is performance, most of the heroes of this book can be said to have performed the role of "woman" while conducting their battles to invade the public spaces belonging to men.

These women also recognized that the category of gender was artificial and "as changeable as dress," as Carroll Smith-Rosenberg phrased it with regard to modernist women. But they were quite the reverse of certain female inverts of the working class in their day, who claimed men's privileges by literally changing their dress and traversing the world in men's drag. By donning women's drag (both literally and figuratively), many of the pioneers concealed their intent to claim male privileges. They believed that they must perform "woman" publicly in order to change what "woman" meant. Yet in private, traditional gender notions had little meaning for them.

It was in fact these women's secret understanding of the sham of gender roles that fueled the movements that eventually gave women the vote, the right to a higher education and a profession, and the power of influence over public policy. But because most of them believed — with justification — that their society was not ready for unalloyed radical approaches, they often argued that changes in woman's sphere were necessary not because women were just like men and gender was an absurd notion, but precisely because women were different from men. With essentialist arguments — which their own lives patently contradicted — their strategy was to proclaim that women's special gifts were desperately needed in the muddle of nineteenth- and early twentieth-century society. For example, they claimed a place for females in politics by insisting that women should have more say in public policy because they were "morally superior" to men. Though few of these leaders were biological mothers, they insisted that if the influence of the "mother-heart," which (they publicly declared) was intrinsic to all women, were expanded to spheres outside the home, everyone would profit.

They did not call attention to what they certainly understood: that once "woman" succeeded in moving into the public sphere, the constructed category of "woman" — as a domestic being — would be altered beyond recognition. The rights and privileges they were demanding in the name of "woman" and her "moral superiority" had the potential to revolutionize (and eventually did revolutionize) the way "woman" was conceptualized.

These women's refusal to characterize their discontent as gender trouble gave them one more reason not to identify with the sexologists' depiction of women like them as inverts. Nevertheless, case histories of female sexual inverts often described these pioneering women quite precisely, their public masquerade notwithstanding. As Krafft-Ebing depicted the female sexual invert, even in childhood she preferred "male" occupations, "the rocking horse, playing at soldiers, etc., to dolls and other girlish occupations. The toilet is neglected and tough boyish manners are affected." The sexologists could not move beyond their fixed notion of appropriate gender behavior and its inevitability, even in childhood, in those they deemed normal.

Thus they would surely have considered a woman such as Susan B. Anthony to be abnormal — "inverted" — since she envied male freedoms and resented the limitations foisted on women. Anthony bitterly complained that beginning in girlhood, the female was "sacrificed to clean clothes, glossy curls and fair complexions." She characterized this fictive yet autobiographical girl as wishing she could be "a boy like my brother, so I would wear long boots and thick pantaloons, romp on the lawn, play ball, climb trees." The sexologists made precisely such sentiments central to their definition of female sexual inversion. If they had seen Anthony's letters concerning her women "lovers," they would have had no doubt whatsoever that she was a textbook specimen of an invert.

Almost all of the women discussed in this book experienced

"inverted feelings" (as the sexologists would have dubbed them) such as Anthony's. If "sexual inversion" signified discontent with women's roles, envy of the broader possibilities that men had claimed for themselves, and love of other females who would succor them and help them fight their battles, these women were indeed sexual inverts. Yet they did not want to be men, as the sexologists claimed, as much as they wanted the rights and privileges their society had accorded to men alone.

Obviously, my valorization of these women's leadership is not meant to imply that there were no heterosexual women leaders in the nineteenth and early twentieth centuries. However, heterosexuality is almost always a tacit assumption we make about those whose actions have been socially useful or heroic. By emphasizing what I call the "lesbian presence" in movements that have bettered America, I aim to bring to the forefront what has been unfairly neglected and for too long unspoken.

PART I

HOW AMERICAN WOMEN
GOT ENFRANCHISED

2

THE LOVES AND LIVING ARRANGEMENTS OF NINETEENTH-CENTURY SUFFRAGE LEADERS

> I shall go to Chicago & visit my new lover — dear Mrs.
> [Emily] Gross — en route to Kansas. So with new hope
> & new life . . .
>
> — Susan B. Anthony

FROM ITS INCEPTION, women's fight for the vote was largely led by women who loved other women. It was a grueling battle. As Carrie Chapman Catt, the leading spokesperson at the time the Nineteenth Amendment was passed, summed it up, success was won only after 56 state referendum campaigns, 480 legislative campaigns for state suffrage amendments, 47 state constitutional conventional campaigns, 277 state party convention campaigns to get suffrage planks in the party platforms, and so forth and so on. What Catt did not say in her dry summation was how many female couples (including herself and her partner, Mollie Hay) were in the forefront of the struggle, and how their intimate relations helped them endure and stay focused on their elusive goal through years of discouragement.

In view of the distrust of marriage that was prevalent among so many of the woman suffrage pioneers, as well as their era's disdain for "illicit" heterosexual relationships and "illegitimate" pregnancy, which was a danger of loving a man out of wedlock, where could these leaders have turned for intimacy and succor if not to one another? To whom else could they have trusted themselves? Where could they lay down their shields? As Susan B. Anthony wrote to Anna Dickinson, her "Dear Anna Dicky Darly [sic]," she needed Anna to help soothe her when she was exhausted by the frays of her public battles. The relationship renewed her, she told Anna: "Somehow your very breath gives me new hope and new life." She understood that Anna too needed encouragement, and she coaxed the younger woman from her dark moods by sweet blandishments: "Ah, Anna, your *mission* will brighten and beautify every day if you will but keep the eye of your own spirit turned *within* . . . [where] that precious jewel of truth is to be sought — and *formed* — And darling — *you will find it & speak it, and live it* — and all men and women will call you blessed." Such often-reiterated support, which was frequently peppered with what we might today call sexy and reassuring flirtation, was vital to pioneering women who regularly faced the hostilities of those who saw them as "unsexed" or "grim." To know they were not so to each other gave them the emotional fuel to carry on the tiring and often lonely battle.

Overcoming "Real" Women

Throughout the woman suffrage movement, antisuffrage women insisted that *real* women neither wanted nor needed to be enfranchised. Even when both houses of Congress had already passed an amendment that required only state ratification before equal suffrage became the law of the land, the "antis" were still insisting, as the female officers of the Michigan Association Opposed to Woman Suffrage declared, that, "as women, we do not want the strife, bitterness, falsification and publicity which accompany political campaigns. We women are not suffering at the hands of our fathers, husbands, and brothers because they protect us in our homes. . . . Keep mother, wife, and sister in the protected home."

Unlike them, the women who are the focus of this book eschewed the "protected home" for themselves. They actively sought the strife of worldly engagement from which female antisuffragists, who typically presented themselves as the "true women," in keeping with the Victorian construction of that concept, claimed to wish to be sheltered. They relied on each other rather than on fathers, husbands, and brothers. Because they would never be represented in civil matters by a spouse, women's enfranchisement was crucial to them — indeed, a sine qua non, since all other progress for which they worked, such as higher education and entrance into the professions, would be meaningless if women continued to be second-class citizens.

In the hostile nineteenth-century media, these women were not described as lesbians but rather as females who were manlike, or "unsexed." Despite the pioneers' common ploy — their argument that women needed the vote to extend moral housekeeping and nurturance to society — the media often emphasized their "gender-inappropriate" wishes for a place at the polls alongside men. Newspapers and journals dramatized the point by accusing those whose appearance was not conventionally feminine of being male. For example, the *St. Louis Dispatch* meanly proclaimed that Sojourner Truth, an African-American abolitionist and women's rights advocate, "is the name of a man now lecturing in Kansas City." (Tired of such repeated slanders, Truth bared her breast on the lecture platform at a women's rights convention in Indiana.)

The accusation that suffragists were unsexed was intended to be a weapon of denigration that would discourage other women from joining the movement, but obviously it also revealed the widespread fear that suffrage would actually threaten a woman's biological capacities and thus — the argument expanded in geometric proportions — the future of the human race. The *New York Herald,* for example, used the term to indicate disgust with the minister Antoinette Brown and her cheering audience of five thousand at a national suffrage convention in 1853, "a gathering of unsexed women, unsexed in mind, all of them publicly propounding the doctrine that they should be allowed to step out of their appropriate sphere to the neglect of those duties which both human and divine law have assigned them." The reporter's tirade concluded with the hysterical question, "Is the world to be depopulated?" Such allegations would surely have been difficult for any woman to bear, but the sting must have been especially painful for heterosexual women whose very stock in trade was their ability to present themselves to men as womanly. It is possible that for a time many women turned away from the suffrage movement because they feared working with "unsexed" women and becoming "unsexed" themselves.

There were, of course, married women and women who hoped to be married in the suffrage movement from its inception. Some, such as Elizabeth Cady Stanton, were even among the most unladylike and unconventional of the suffragists; her husband and seven children notwithstanding, Stanton saucily declared in the mid-nineteenth century, "It is a settled maxim with me that the existing public sentiment on any subject is wrong." But for the most part, women who intended to make their lives with other women rather than placing themselves on the marriage market had greater freedom in asserting leadership within the suffrage movement: they could feel that they had much less to lose if they were called unsexed than the average woman, who depended for sustenance, emotional and otherwise, on men.

There were also, of course, men who actively supported suffrage for women and to whom such allegations would not have mattered. Yet the problems in being a heterosexual suffrage leader, even if married to a supportive man, remained complex. Nineteenth-century wifehood and motherhood were not compatible with work for the cause. For example, the suffragist leader Lucy Stone married Henry Blackwell when she was thirty-seven years old. Eight months later, the suffragist orator Antoinette Brown married Henry's brother, Samuel. Both of the women's careers in the suffrage movement came to a standstill for a long while.

They did not cease working because their husbands opposed suffrage. In fact, Henry Blackwell convinced Lucy Stone to marry him in 1855 by promising that he would work by her side for women's enfranchisement, and he was true to his word. Yet neither he nor Lucy could foresee her societally inculcated guilt, which the marriage brought to the surface. Lucy continued her active career in the suffrage movement right after her daughter, Alice, was born, in 1857. However, when she lost a second child in 1859, she became so anxious about Alice's well-being that she gave up her work for the next seven years in order to be a full-time mother. Though she was again an important figure in the suffrage movement by the end of the 1860s, Lucy's correspondence with her husband indicates that she felt uneasy because she was not a better homemaker. Henry Blackwell also felt guilty, as Alice reported after her mother died in 1893: "Papa . . . has been blaming himself for marrying mamma at all. He says he spoiled her career." Whether Henry Blackwell's guilt was at all merited, Alice, who also became a suffrage activist, apparently believed that there was some justice in his self-accusation. She herself chose other women as her loves and never married.

Susan B. Anthony (who declared to her diary when she was eighteen, "I think any female would rather live and die an old maid") was horrified when strong suffragists were lost to the cause through the effects of heterosexual marriage. When Antoinette Brown married Samuel Blackwell in 1856, her career as a lecturer for suffrage came to a halt for eighteen years while she busied herself bearing seven children and raising the five who survived infancy. Anthony foresaw such dangers to the movement; in terms that were only nominally joking, she wrote to Antoinette after the second pregnancy in 1858, "Not another baby, is my peremptory command." But obviously Susan Anthony had no control over what went on in the Blackwells' bedroom.

Similarly, when Ida Wells, the African-American woman suffrage and civil rights leader whom Anthony had befriended and supported, became Mrs. F. L. Barnett in 1895 and then had two babies, Anthony could not hide her distress. Wells reported in her autobiography that when she was Anthony's houseguest in the course of a lecture tour that took her to Rochester, New York, Anthony "would bite out my married name in addressing me." Finally Wells asked her, "Don't you believe in women getting married?" Anthony answered, "Oh yes, but not women like you who had a special call for special work. . . . You are distracted over the thought that maybe [your eleven-month-old baby] is not being looked after as he would if you were there, and that makes for a divided duty." The most consistently effective early suffrage leaders had no such divided duty.

"A Closer Union Than That of Most Marriages": Female Couples Among the Early Suffragists

Many of the early leaders of the suffrage cause began their careers as abolitionists. In 1840, eight women who had been involved in the American antislavery movement hoped to attend the World's Anti-Slavery Convention in London as delegates, but the convention voted to ban them from participating. The women claimed that the experience was an epiphany for them, making them understand that they, like the enslaved Africans whose freedom they worked to procure, had been kept socially and legally inferior to white men. They did not give up their abolitionist sentiments, but their frustration led two of the rejected delegates, Lucretia Mott and Elizabeth Cady Stanton, to call a convention of their own, devoted to women's rights, in 1848. Other frustrated female delegates to the world antislavery meeting, such as Mary Grew, joined them. Out of that meeting in Seneca Falls the women's rights movement was born.

Female same-sex love was common among this first generation of social activists, but regardless of whether such relationships were sexual, they were usually characterized as "romantic friendships." Mary Grew, for example, described her life with Margaret Burleigh in such terms in 1892, just after Burleigh's death, when Grew responded to a condolence letter from the younger suffragist Isabel Howland:

> Your words respecting my beloved friend touch me deeply. Evidently you understood her fine character; & you comprehended and appreciated, as few persons do, the nature of the relation which existed, which exists [still, despite the death of Burleigh's body] between her and myself. . . . To me it seems to have been a

closer union than that of most marriages. We know that there have been other such between two men, & also between two women. And why should there not be. Love is spiritual, only passion is sexual.

Since Howland was herself romantically involved with women, Grew's conviction that Howland "comprehended and appreciated" her relationship with Burleigh "as few persons do" may have conveyed a special recognition between them of an unnamed identity. Under the guise of romantic friendships, such relationships might still be widely condoned in the nineteenth century. They were acknowledged by many observers as an "affection passing the love of men."

Both Grew and Burleigh were revered among abolitionist and suffrage women. Grew was for many years a high official in antislavery societies. She was an especially powerful speaker for the cause and had successfully challenged the early prohibition within the movement — shared even by her abolitionist father — on women speaking in mixed gatherings. Like most female antislavery lecturers who were agents for the American Anti-Slavery Society, she never married in the conventional sense, but she lived most of her adult life with Margaret Burleigh, a schoolteacher. Burleigh also worked closely with Grew, both in the antislavery movement and for women's rights. After the Civil War, in 1865, they fought side by side against the move to disband the Pennsylvania Anti-Slavery Society, on whose executive committee they both served. Their argument was radical at the time: the society's work had not finished with the Emancipation Proclamation, they insisted, but needed to continue until the constitutional amendments granting the former slaves full citizenship were ratified.

To their abolitionist and suffrage acquaintances, Mary and Margaret made no secret of the fact that they shared both a home and a bed. Nor did they hide from their friends their general distrust of heterosexual relations and the married state. To young William Lloyd Garrison II, who was contemplating marriage, Mary preached, "When I say that I think you are qualified to be a good husband, I think I say a great deal, for that manner of man is rare." Even well-intentioned men failed at matrimony, she said, because of "the low ideal of a wife's position . . . [and] the marriage relation," a relation from which she believed she was saved through her "union" with Margaret Burleigh.

Once Grew turned to the cause of women's rights, she became a leading figure in that movement as well. She fought successfully for a married woman's property law in Pennsylvania. She was the founding president of the Pennsylvania Woman Suffrage Association in 1869 and continued as president until 1892, and she became the national president of the American Woman Suffrage Association in 1887. Almost until her death at the age of eighty-three, she was a dynamic and popular speaker for social causes. The suffragist Emily Howland (Isabel's aunt) spoke of the admiration of Grew's fellow workers in the movement in summing up her life on her eightieth birthday, in 1893: "The largesse of life is yours, dowered with a brain alive to the issues of your time and heart aglow with service for truth, blessed with a friendship as rare as the friend [Margaret Burleigh] was noble — your joy is all immortal." As much as the "old maid" was reviled outside the women's rights movement, those within believed that in a life such as Grew and Burleigh shared, nothing was missing.

How the Suffrage Movement Got Off the Ground: Susan B. Anthony

Susan B. Anthony began her public career as a lecturer for the American Anti-Slavery Society and the temperance movement. She turned to the cause of women's rights in 1852, after being denied permission to speak at a temperance rally because she was a woman. As a result of that experience, she helped form an all-women's temperance organization, and there began her close working relationship with Elizabeth Cady Stanton. Stanton led Anthony even further into women's rights issues as they began organizing state and national women's rights conventions and presenting formal demands to the New York legislature for improvement of that state's laws on married women's property. Before they could begin their daily work, however, Anthony had to help the overburdened Stanton with housekeeping and care of her seven children so they might, as Anthony described it, "sit up far into the night preparing our ammunition and getting ready to move on the enemy."

Their relationship was not simply a working one. Though a wife and mother, Stanton characterized it in terms that were almost romantic and revealed the depth of emotion that spurred them on in their shared work: "So closely interwoven have been our lives, our purposes, and experiences that [when] separated, we have a feeling of incompleteness." She provocatively quipped about her love for Susan Anthony, "I prefer a tyrant of my own sex, so I shall not deny the patent fact of my subjection; for I do believe that I have developed into much more of a woman under her jurisdiction."

Though Stanton was as committed to suffrage as Anthony, she was less mobile than her friend, who did not have responsibility for a husband and numerous children. Anthony could more easily travel for the cause. In the years after the Civil War, it was she who could invest the most time in working for an amendment to the Constitution that would grant suffrage to all American women and not just to the male freedmen.

In 1869, Anthony and Stanton called the first post–Civil War women's suffrage convention, which resulted in the formation of the National Woman Suffrage Association. Their organization quickly split with less radical women suffragists over the Fifteenth Amendment. "Do you believe the African race is composed entirely of males?" Anthony and Stanton asked those who said that "the negro's hour" to be enfranchised had come and that woman suffragists must hold in abeyance their demand for their own enfranchisement. Anthony was especially angry that regardless of their level of education, women were denied the vote, while the freedmen, who were largely illiterate, were enfranchised by virtue of being male. It was one more bitter reminder of women's devaluation. But the issue was not one of race for her; she maintained close relationships with African-American woman suffrage leaders such as Mary Church Terrell and Ida Wells, and she often raised the concerns of African-American women before her largely white suffrage organization.

Susan B. Anthony became the driving force of woman suffrage for the next four decades, traveling widely and constantly to promote the cause virtually until her death, in 1906, bringing one generation of younger women after another into the movement. She indisputably earned the posthumous honor of having the Nineteenth Amendment, which granted American women the vote, named after her.

Anthony was far more radical in her public pronouncements than many of the women's rights activists who followed her. Her speeches often gave vent to her fury at historical and contemporary heterosexual arrangements. In an 1857 lecture that she called "The True Woman," she complained that women had never been treated fairly by men. She decried the barbarism of the past, when women had been degraded to "merchantable property . . . fit only to minister to man's animal comforts, pleasures and passions." She revealed her disgust with her own era, in which "all the richly endowed colleges . . . are open to *young men alone*" and women, regardless of their abilities, were told, "'Rest content, we pray you, and be the *true woman,* — the teacher of children, the genial companion of man, the loving mother of sons.'" Anthony challenged the notion of the "true woman" as "the exponent of another." As unpopular as the idea was in her day, she threw her energy into the argument that a woman had a right to develop her talents for her own ends. The "true woman" of the future, she insisted, would not lean upon a husband, but rather would know that "bread and strength and happiness are sure only to the self-producer."

The average woman of the nineteenth century was little prepared for so heroic ("so selfish," they would have said) a view of female potential. Perhaps to counterbalance her fierce challenge to gender notions, Anthony attempted to appear ladylike on the platform, usually wearing a modest black silk dress. Yet despite her drag and though she was not at all masculine, her militancy inspired the antisuffragists to call her "a grim Old Gal with a manly air." In "The

New Century's Manly Woman" (1900), Anthony actually attempted to defuse such accusations against her and other suffragists by claiming and redefining the term "manly." She was among the first to insist on what we have come to view as a radical, postmodern understanding of the constructed nature of gender and its potential mutability. Anthony argued that the woman who had been called "manly" was simply the woman who was fully human. In the ideal future, such a woman would be considered entirely equal to men, and men would develop "womanly" qualities such as gentleness, sympathy, and affection. Despite those expressed hopes for the future, however, Anthony and many of her fellow suffragists preferred to love those who already had such excellent "womanly" qualities.

Elizabeth Stanton, perhaps wishing to explain away the fact of her friend's spinsterhood, remarked in *The History of Woman Suffrage* that "the outpourings of Miss Anthony's love element all flowed into the suffrage movement." However, Anthony's extant letters reveal the great degree to which her love element also flowed into other women. Though Anthony was hated by the antisuffragists and was often in conflict with those who made up the rival suffrage group, the American Woman Suffrage Association, she was adored by women throughout the country, certainly as a leader but also in a much more personal way. Anna Dickinson was one of several women who caused Anthony to reciprocate that affection intensely. The emotional, playful, and erotic letters between Anthony and Dickinson in the 1860s demonstrate that their relationship transcended by far their mutual political interests.

Throughout her life, Anna Dickinson was often the recipient of billets-doux from other women, who declared to her, "I have an irresistible desire all through this letter to make love to you," and "Sweet Anna, I shall hope to see you soon & kiss your soft, tender lips," and "I am so glad that I have got you for my darling that I can't find words to express my delight in my new love." But judging from Dickinson's letters to Susan B. Anthony, it appears to have been the younger woman who was the aggressor. She wrote Anthony a charmed and charming loverlike missive in 1862: "I want to see you very much indeed, to hold your hand in mine, to hear your voice, in a word, I want *you* — I can't have you? Well, I will at least put down a little fragment of my foolish self and send it to look up at you."

If we look at the existing correspondence between the two women, we cannot doubt that Anthony returned Dickinson's desire for personal contact and shared the mood of her 1862 letter. She addressed Dickinson as "My Dear Darling Anna" and "Dear Chick a dee dee." In these letters she often implored Dickinson to speak at various suffrage meetings, to "speak right out in words the deep, rich, earnest love for your own sex that I know lies in the inner courts of your being." These appeals were almost always punctuated with flirtations and intimacies. In a December 1866 letter, Anthony said that she was coming to Philadelphia, where she hoped "to snuggle you darling closer than ever." In a letter written several months later, she informed Dickinson that she was going to Kansas for a suffrage campaign, but "I cannot bear to go off without another precious look into your face — *my Soul.*" En route to Cincinnati three months later, she wrote, "Well, Anna Darling — I do wish I could take you in these strong arms of mine this very minute."

Dickinson, a star of the lyceum circuit, was often linked in 1860s gossip columns to eligible bachelors. Anthony was displeased both for her own part and for the sake of the movement. In an 1868 letter to "My Dear Chicky Dicky Darlint," she said she was writing to tell Dickinson not only that she loved her but also to "engage" her "not to *marry* a *man*" and instead to commit herself to "speak for Equal Rights." In several letters she invited Dickinson into her bed, which was "big enough and good enough to take you in." After such an invitation in one letter, she called Dickinson a "naughty Teaze" but promised that the younger woman wouldn't be scolded a single time if she would "share it [that is, Susan's bed] a few days." In a particularly provocative note of November 11, 1869, to "Dearly loved Anna," Anthony said how much she missed her and longed to see her "for more reasons than one," reiterating "I must see you & can't put it on paper — my heart is full."

In some of these letters, Anthony, who was twenty-two years

older than Dickinson, presented herself as being motherly. However, such a disclaimer notwithstanding — and while we cannot be sure of what actually happened between the two women when they were in Anthony's "big . . . good" bed — there can be no doubt of the flirtatious nature of their correspondence. Dickinson, who actually played pant roles on the stage later in her career, was Octavian to Anthony's Marschallin in these sparking letters.

Yet Anthony wanted more than occasional intimacies. Though she lived with her sister Mary for many years and often said that Mary "made my life-work possible," she felt that her sister was necessary but not sufficient to her, and she longed for another kind of partner to share her life and struggles. As she poignantly confessed to Elizabeth Stanton, "I have *very weak moments* — and long to lay my weary head somewhere & nestle my full soul close to that of another in full sympathy." The desire never went away. Much later in life, Anthony admitted to having confessed to her niece Lucy, the mate of the suffrage leader Reverend Anna Howard Shaw, "that I wanted what I feared I shouldn't find, that is a young woman who would be to me — in every way — what she is to the Rev. Anna Shaw." What did she mean to signify by those words "in every way"? While Lucy Anthony sometimes served as Anna Shaw's assistant in movement business, there can be no doubt that Susan Anthony was aware that her niece also played a more intimate role in Shaw's life. In 1897, for example, Lucy was to accompany her aunt to a convention where she would act as her secretary, and Shaw would join them at a later point. Rehearsing arrangements for the trip, Susan promised her niece, "I will try to get [you] a bedroom large enough for you to take in your Rev. Lady when she comes."

Perhaps in the later years of her life, Susan Anthony wistfully wanted a relationship such as Anna Shaw had with Lucy because she had come frustratingly close to one in her intimacy with Emily Gross, a Chicago woman who was the wife of a wealthy businessman, Samuel Gross. While no correspondence between Susan Anthony and Emily Gross has come to light, it is possible to trace their relationship through various sources, including letters that Anthony wrote to friends and relatives.

The two women may have met when Anthony addressed the

Congress of Representative Women at the Columbia Exposition in Chicago during the spring of 1893. That summer, Emily Gross went to visit Susan Anthony at her home in Rochester. Anna Shaw saw them there and wished for them what she herself had with Lucy, as she wrote in her diary:

> I am so thankful for the new friend for Aunt Susan. How nice it is! . . . Whenever anything like this good fortune comes to her, it is a great comfort to me. Whenever I come into [her] house it makes me feel sad, for it does need someone who can get out of a little rut and make it homelike. I wish it could be done. Aunt Mary is an angel but not a housekeeper except in the sense of great neatness and stiffness.

Though Emily Gross was not in a position to brighten Susan's home permanently as Lucy brightened Anna Shaw's, she apparently did bring joy and pleasure into Susan's life of duty. Susan was obviously ecstatic about the relationship, as she told both friends and relatives. To a niece, Jessie Anthony, she revealed the same exuberance she had to Isabel Howland in the letter that serves as an epigraph to this chapter, writing that before she would visit Jessie in California, she intended first to "call in Chicago — at my new *lover's* — Mrs. Gross — 48 Lake Shore Drive." It must be noted in this context that Susan B. Anthony encouraged many of the women to whom she was close in the suffrage movement to call her Aunt Susan, and she referred to them as her nieces. But "lover" was not a term she bandied about to describe the legions of women who admired her.

The spring 1895 reunion in Chicago between Susan and Emily must have been a success, as their visits during the two previous years had been. Now Susan impulsively invited Emily to accompany her to California, where they spent the rest of that spring and much of the summer together. That trip was so fulfilling that they repeated it the following year, Susan combining her leisure with suffrage work. When she was interviewed by a reporter for the *San Francisco Chronicle* on June 28, 1896, it was surely her relationship with Emily Gross that gave her the immediate impetus to brag, "I'm sure no man could have made me any happier than I have been. . . . I never found the man who was necessary to my happiness. I was very well as I was." From that point, Susan and Emily traveled regularly together.

Emily Gross is an elusive figure, though what she meant to Susan B. Anthony is less elusive. Gross supported woman suffrage, but she was not actively involved in the movement, and she made no name for herself outside her connection with Anthony. For this reason, Anthony's biographer Katherine Anthony (no relation) was puzzled by a mysterious picture that was sent to her for possible inclusion in her book. In the picture, "the great Susan B.," as Katherine Anthony calls her, is in the background. In the foreground is a woman whose face "looks slightly Jewish, and I remember that Mrs. Gross was a Jewess." The picture ostensibly disturbed the biographer. "What surprises me is that she (whoever she was) was so naive as to place herself in the foreground of a photograph which included Susan B. It was no doubt Miss Anthony's suggestion, but the lady in the photograph should have known better," Katherine Anthony concluded in a 1952 letter.

Was Katherine Anthony, herself a lesbian, whose life partner was the progressive educator Elisabeth Irwin, perhaps being disingenuous with her correspondent in order to save her beloved subject's reputation during homophobic times? As familiar as she was with Susan Anthony's life, she must have understood why Anthony would have been happy to place the woman she adored in the foreground of a picture. And there can be little doubt that Susan Anthony did adore the beautiful, wealthy Emily Gross. In an 1894 letter, Susan boasted of Emily's elegance and the grandeur of a party in her lavish home, where Susan stayed with her. "If you could have seen Mrs. Gross in her '*Worth*' made dress," she gushed. The following year, by Emily's side, Susan wrote to her niece Jessie that her beloved was "splendid as ever," and related their acquaintance with the lesbian sculptor Harriet Hosmer (whom they may have met through another sculptor, Bessie Potter, who created a statue of Susan and Emily in 1896).

Though they did not live together, the two women managed to be together for long periods of time. Anthony's death on March 13, 1906, affected her lover deeply, as a mutual friend wrote to Anna Shaw twelve days after Susan died: "Times are very hard with dear Mrs. Gross I fear." The last recorded trace of Emily Gross was in March 1919, around the thirteenth anniversary of Susan Anthony's death, when Shaw, visiting Chicago, paid her respects to Emily Gross in "a long talk."

Personal relations such as those between Susan B. Anthony and Emily Gross were mirrored everywhere among the suffragists. They were, of course, encouraged by their venerable leader, who understood the pressures on pioneers in a controversial movement and the exhausting loneliness if one could not "nestle [one's] full soul close to another in full sympathy." Thus, for example, when Isabel Howland became the devoted companion of Harriet May Mills, another suffragist lecturer, Anthony happily addressed them together in 1892 as "My Dear girls" and sent to them her "heart full of love and rejoicing over my two new young girls. . . . You are just lovely." She saw their "union" not only as good in itself but also as being important, because it would help them help the cause. When Isabel's father financed a trip to Nova Scotia for her and Harriet, Anthony expressed her delight, "for the trip will make you both all the better for the work before you." She knew too, from observation of Elizabeth Stanton and other women who had to juggle heterosexual domesticity with their commitment to the cause, that female couples made less emotionally torn suffragists because they were not distracted by the wifely duties and innumerable pregnancies that followed marriage.

How the Suffrage Movement Picked Up Steam: Frances Willard

The move to enfranchise women did not begin to gather great numbers of followers until the last years of the nineteenth century. Suffragism had long remained a minority movement because it was far too frightening to most women: it seemed to threaten to shove them into the public sphere and create an unaccustomed nonfamilial role. A movement such as temperance, which fought the "vices" that had often been blamed for domestic miseries, was far more popular among American women. Though many of the early suffragists supported temperance, the major temperance organization, the Woman's Christian Temperance Union, had no stance on suffrage for years. The suffragists were outnumbered by those women in the WCTU who feared that the franchise would indeed be "unsexing."

The lack of interest in the vote among the majority of WCTU members changed, however, when Frances Willard became president, in 1879. As a woman who would in today's parlance be called a lesbian, Willard had little personal fear of being "unsexed," since the gender categories were anyway artificial and annoying to her. She never married, and as she admitted in her autobiography, she had long-term, committed, passionate relationships exclusively with other women. Yet during the two decades that she headed the WCTU, until her death in 1898, she was phenomenally successful in bringing married women into the suffrage movement.

Her tactic was a brilliant response to the antisuffragists and a challenge to married women's complacency regarding their political powerlessness. She insisted to the conservative women of the WCTU that if they were enfranchised, they would be in a better position to protect their families, which were under attack by a terrifying array of enemies, including prostitution, opium, and especially the tyrannical demon of drink. They could vote such threats out of existence, she told them. In this way Willard co-opted the prime shibboleth of the antisuffragists, "home protection," and turned it to the uses of the suffrage movement. She was able to convince large numbers of otherwise conventional women that they would not only not be "unsexed" if they were enfranchised, but they could actually bring their womanly virtues to bear on the public sphere, uplifting it and making politics as "pure" as women were.

In 1881, the WCTU officially endorsed woman suffrage, at Willard's urging. By itself the endorsement was obviously not enough to make woman suffrage a fait accompli, but it was a tremendous coup for the suffrage movement. Willard virtually delivered the "average woman" to the suffrage cause through the organization she headed, which became the largest women's group in the United States, having grown to 200,000 members and millions of sympathizers.

Despite Willard's great charismatic appeal to ordinary women, a scrutiny of her life reveals a classic example of what the sexologists were describing as the sexual invert. The notion of appropriate gender behavior was infuriating to Willard, as it was to many of the other subjects of *To Believe in Women*, as well as to the subjects of the sexologists' case studies. She would not submit to the straitjacket of nineteenth-century gender roles. As an adolescent, Frank, as she wanted to be called in her youth and later by the women with whom she lived, loathed all things constructed as feminine, especially the pressure to learn to cook, sew, and iron. Carpentry, however, she adored, fashioning for herself sleds and whip handles and repairing her own guns while her sister did the dishes. Her childhood playmates were always boys, because she preferred their tree-climbing and stilt-walking to the tamer pursuits of girls.

Also like the sexologists' homosexual subjects, she admitted feeling deep discontent at having to become a woman as that creature was constructed in her day. "No girl went through a harder experience than I when my free, out-of-door life had to cease, and the long skirt and clubbed-up hair spiked with hair-pins, had to be endured," Willard recalled in her autobiography.

As a student at North Western Female College in Evanston, Illinois, Willard was often the object of romantic "smashes," and, she confessed, she reciprocated wholeheartedly. She had no interest in the men at neighboring Northwestern University. As she admitted to her journal, "I never hung upon any man's words or took any man's name into my prayer because I loved him." Though she was later briefly engaged to a man, she broke the engagement because she felt more emotion toward her friend Mary Bannister (whom she believed she had lost when Mary also became engaged) than she did toward her fiancé.

Yet even though Willard's early history as she herself recorded it might easily be found in the pages of a work such as Havelock Ellis's "Sexual Inversion in Women," once she attained a position of leadership, she cultivated and publicly performed a womanly, motherly image. For example, a *Boston Times-Democrat* reporter who observed her at length was enchanted, because despite Willard's executive abilities, her manner was "never . . . abrupt or angular" but rather gentle, sympathetic, kindly. The image may seem rather incredible in juxtaposition to the blustering Frank persona, which never died off in her. But it demonstrates her protean ability to play with gender rather than be imprisoned by it, as nineteenth-century women often were. That ability was shared by many of the androgynous female leaders of the late nineteenth and early twentieth centuries. Willard's slogan, "Womanliness first — afterwards what you will," says much about their *modus operandi.*

However, what appears obvious to the contemporary reader with regard to Willard's sexuality may not have been so to her. Her autobiography reveals little awareness of herself as a homosexual or a sexual invert. She made no attempt to hide even her lifelong attractions to other women, though she placed those attractions in the context of the universal rather than the odd (or what the twentieth century would call "queer"). Willard insisted that such attractions and the domestic arrangements to which they led were becoming ubiquitous in the nineteenth century. After admitting her love for Anna Gordon, a "lovely Boston girl" with whom she had been living for twelve years, Willard expounded in her autobiography, *Glimpses of Fifty Years,* what a more psychologically sophisticated individual might have thought necessary to hide:

> The loves of women for each other grow more numerous every day, and I have pondered much why these things were. That so little should be said about them surprises me, for they are everywhere. . . . In these days when any capable woman can honorably earn her own support, there is no village that has not its examples of "two heads in counsel," both of which are feminine. Oftentimes these joint proprietors have been unfortunately married, and so have failed to "better their condition" until, thus clasping hands, they have taken each other "for better or worse."

It would seem that despite the proliferation of sexological writing in the last decades of the nineteenth century, many women continued to believe that their same-sex relationships were (or would be seen by others as) romantic friendships, which were still largely socially condoned. Thus, perhaps as a sign of the relative innocence of her era, Willard felt free to confess not only her domestic relationship with Anna Gordon and a slew of earlier infatuations with other women, but also her role-playing relationship with Kate Jackson, a locomotive heiress, with whom she had formed a couple in 1864. In modern terms, their partnership would surely be described as butch/femme: Frank did the "masculine" outdoor jobs, obviously not because Kate could not afford to hire a man but rather because Frank loved, as she admitted, "chopping kindling, bringing in wood and coal, and doing the rougher work."

Kate, however, was hardly passive as a femme. She sought to occupy herself not as a housewife but in a career, generally as a teacher of language, even as she encouraged Frances Willard's professional advancement. When Frances became principal of the Grove School in Evanston, Illinois, Kate became a French teacher at the school so that, as Frances admitted in her autobiography, she might "be with me." She also accompanied Frances to subsequent jobs — when Frances became a preceptor in a school in Lima, New York, when she was made corresponding secretary of the American Methodist Ladies' Centenary Association ("Miss Jackson did much of the writing for me, and helped me in every way she could"), when Frances was made president of her alma mater, North Western Female College (where Kate became a professor).

From 1868 to 1870, the two went to Europe on an extended grand tour, which Kate could easily finance. That trip abroad was instrumental in bringing Willard an epiphany about how she must spend the rest of her life. In Paris, she grimly observed "the fate of women *as such,*" which, she believed, was everywhere unhappy. She concluded, with Kate's encouragement, that she would fight the battles to unfetter her sex.

Frances Willard's relationship with Kate Jackson continued until 1876, but Kate, who was unsympathetic to the philosophy of the temperance movement, felt alienated when Frances accepted the presidency of the Chicago WCTU in 1874. It was about that time that Frances met Anna Gordon, a woman fourteen years younger,

and thus began the domestic arrangement that continued virtually (though not always monogamously) until Frances's death. In
Glimpses of Fifty Years, Frances ingenuously described Anna as "my
loved and *last.*" Anna Gordon linked her life to Frances and through
her to the WCTU. While Frances lived, Anna was happy to take a
secondary role, doing the duties of wife, secretary, and — as her
hagiographic books, *The Beautiful Life of Frances E. Willard* (1898)
and *What Frances E. Willard Said* (1905), suggest — chief admirer
among a devoted throng. After Frances's death she became her
widow in the eyes of many in the WCTU and the suffrage movement. She was elected to step into Frances's role as head of the
WCTU and continued Frances's work for the vote through that
organization, acting as a mover and shaker in the suffrage community until the Nineteenth Amendment was finally ratified, in 1920.

How the Divided Suffrage Movement Got United: Alice Stone Blackwell

Despite her long history as an abolitionist, Susan B. Anthony broke
away from the American Equal Suffrage Association when it supported the Fifteenth Amendment, which enfranchised only male
freedmen. In 1869 she and Elizabeth Stanton founded the National
Woman Suffrage Association, which was committed to working
for a constitutional amendment that would enfranchise women.
A few months later, those suffragists who believed that women
would have a better chance of getting the vote through a state-by-
state strategy rather than a campaign for a federal amendment, or
who did not wish to grumble about the male "negro's hour" of enfranchisement, or who simply did not like Anthony and Stanton,
formed a rival organization, the American Woman Suffrage Association. Lucy Stone was named its chief.

The unfortunate split among suffragists lasted for many years
after male freedmen were given the vote. Finally, in 1890, through
forceful appeals to suffragists in both organizations, Alice Stone
Blackwell was able to unite the NWSA and the AWSA and create
the powerful National American Woman Suffrage Association

(NAWSA). As the editor of *Woman's Journal*, the leading publication of the women's rights movement in the nineteenth century, and the daughter of Lucy Stone, who had been a salient figure in the rift, Blackwell was a good choice to make amends, patch wounds, and effect the happy merger of two organizations whose crucial differences had essentially disappeared over the years. The large, united NAWSA could ultimately claim major responsibility for the passage of the Nineteenth Amendment.

Alice Stone Blackwell held her position as editor (and head writer, reporter, columnist, and so on) of *Woman's Journal* for thirty-five years. Her life was devoted to social causes, particularly those that affected women. Although she was not as flamboyant a character as her mother (married women who refused to take their husband's last name were called "Lucy Stoners"), she was a key figure not only in unifying the movement but also in promulgating its ideas well into the twentieth century.

Perhaps the unfortunate interruption of Lucy Stone's career to perform domestic duties and her subsequent ambivalence served as a cautionary tale for Alice Stone Blackwell, who followed her mother into the suffrage movement but had no desire to follow her into marriage. At an age when a woman of her era usually feared that she was becoming an old maid, Alice firmly decided that she did not want to encourage male attention. She went through a mild crisis when a Mr. Black sent her a "spoony" letter that "made my hair stand on end. . . . [It was] sentimental to the last degree." The situation cast her into "the doleful dumps," because she felt she should have been more explicit in the discouraging signals she had already sent him, and she concluded that "I am afraid the poor fellow is in for a heartache . . . [but I will] be as gentle as I can manage . . . so as not to hurt him." She seemed not even briefly to consider accepting his attentions.

To Blackwell, heterosexuality was a trap that could, and most likely would, vitiate women's power. When she read Wilkie Collins's novel *Man and Wife* in 1885, she shared with her aunt Dr. Emily Blackwell (whose life partner was Dr. Elizabeth Cushier) her annoyance over what later generations would call Collins's "heterosexism": "[Collins] harps . . . upon the same string in regard to every woman's needing a master, and being unhappy if she is 'in no direct way dependent on a man.' It riles me to the bottom of my soul. I think such novel-writers have a great deal to answer for in making girls silly."

Surrender to heterosexuality would have been impossibly problematic for Alice, but she had less reason to be guarded in her feelings for women. Though she lamented when she was in her late twenties, "I fell in love with Mrs. P. like a schoolgirl and feel rather ashamed of it," she kept falling in love with women throughout her life, and such romances apparently constituted the only affectional or erotic outlets that she could, in the long run, reconcile with her grand goals.

Alice Blackwell was surrounded from her earliest years by women who devoted their lives to changing the lot of women. Her unmarried aunts, Emily and Elizabeth Blackwell, were among the first female doctors in America. They demonstrated to her other paths to fulfillment than heterosexual marriage, and those were the paths she took. However, unlike her predecessors and role models, who were apparently unfamiliar with sexological writing, Blackwell read Havelock Ellis with some anguish. She generally refused to acknowledge herself in the sexologists' delineation of the invert, but despite her attempt at distancing, she was clearly disturbed. Well-read people of her generation were losing the innocence (whether real or pretended) of Mary Grew's and Frances Willard's generation. But as unsettling as it must have been to a woman like Alice Blackwell to know that others considered her most important life choices to be abnormal, she could not and would not alter those choices.

Her powerful erotic imagination was from the beginning acted out with other females. Her first — and indeed last — love, her Aunt Elizabeth's adopted daughter, Kitty Barry, was ten years older than she was. Kitty seems to have encouraged eroticism between them (though Alice needed little encouragement). Their correspondence when Kitty was in her twenties included an elaborate fantasy that was carried on for several years; in these sexually charged letters, Kitty (Kiddy) was Captain Robert Kidd and Alice was her/his bride. They often addressed each other as "Dear Betrothed" and spoke of their forthcoming marriage and honeymoon. In her Captain Kidd persona, Kitty played with the language of passion, erotic frustration, and threat: "Indeed, '*when* will the dream come true?' If you do not come to me I suppose that before the close of 1872 you will see the glitter of a well known blade." Alice faithfully mirrored the fantasies, reminding Kiddy that it would be in keeping with his/her character to "forcibly possess yourself of your bride. I wish you could." Occasionally the violent fantasies were combined with references to what may have actually been physical exchanges. For instance, Alice wrote to Kitty, who was in England, "Your stomach shall certainly be rubbed when I come across the ocean."

When Alice was seventeen and Kitty twenty-seven, Kitty's letters in her Captain Kidd persona were frequently signed "your faithful lover," but the two were often separated by the Atlantic, since Kitty lived in England with her adopted mother and Alice lived in Massachusetts. Alice repeatedly tried to entice Kitty to return to New England, writing, for example, on July 7, 1874, "Why don't you come back. . . . [On Cape Cod, where Alice was] you would be basking in the smiles of your betrothed, with a sea breeze to cool you if they proved to be too ardent!" Their game barely veiled serious feelings. In an 1877 letter, Kitty expressed the fear that she would inevitably lose Alice to a man, and she somberly admitted, "If I lost you, life wd have ceased to be worth anything to me."

Though the wilder fantasies of their relationship seemed to diminish in later years, affection and mutual dependence, and even a flirtatious tension, remained, as the correspondence demonstrates. Kitty addressed Alice often as "My dear Pie," and Alice expressed the desire to "wrap you in ermines and keep you in a crystal case."

Yet for a time Alice was enamored of several other women. Typically she confessed her passions to her cousin, leaving a long paper trail of her lesbian desires. In her mid-thirties, for instance, Alice wrote to her cousin about her feelings for a new acquaintance, the writer Eliza Sproat Turner, a Philadelphia widow: "I fell in love on this trip, madly, hopelessly, and head over ears. . . . Oh, why am I not a man! But she wouldn't have me; she is much too old and wise, and I couldn't hold a candle to her. . . . I lost my heart entirely."

Kitty too confessed to Alice her attraction to other women, admitting the justice in Florence Blackwell's accusation (Florence was one of Antoinette Brown Blackwell's daughters): "Florence says I'm given to falling in love with gentle, sensible, lady-like girls, but that my utter indifference to the male part of creation is something provocative."

Despite such confessions of infatuation, the voluminous correspondence suggests that Kitty remained the great emotional center of Alice's life, and vice versa. It was not until 1921, fifteen years before her death, however, that Kitty returned to the United States for good. During those years, as Alice wrote in her cousin's obituary, Kitty "made her home" with Alice. By then, in good part thanks to the efforts of NAWSA, American women could vote, and *Woman's Journal* had become *Woman Citizen*, the journal of the League of Women Voters.

Lesbian relationships among nineteenth-century suffragists were not always without the frustrations of infidelity or separation. Yet these women were committed to the conviction that unlike the relationships of heterosexuals, which distracted a woman's energy from the cause, their relationships helped contribute to it. Sometimes they could do no more for each other than to serve as an outlet for eroticism, whether expressly or through fantasy, so that it would not lead to what they saw as the slavery of wifehood. In other cases they created long-lasting same-sex "marriages," though a heterosexual marriage would have been unacceptable to them.

It remains impossible to tell in many instances which came first in these women's lives, their passions for other women or their desires for women's rights. But there is no question that those passions and desires fed each other. Whether a woman reduced the domestic or economic strains on her mate so she could work more effectively for woman suffrage, or enabled her to spend large amounts of energy on the movement merely by receiving her love, or struggled with her in the cause that was crucial to them both, there were not many heterosexual equivalents to such partnerships in the nineteenth century.

❧ 3 ❧

BRINGING THE SUFFRAGE MOVEMENT
INTO THE TWENTIETH CENTURY:
ANNA HOWARD SHAW

> The last day of the new year of the new century and I am
> alone from Lucy in a strange land. I hope it is the last
> time so long as we both live that I shall have to feel that I
> must leave her and go alone. With the new year will come
> a hope that before it closes we shall have fixed upon the
> spot where we will find rest and peace and grow old and
> good and useful together. God bless her.

> — Anna Howard Shaw, Kingston, Jamaica

"A True, Lovable Woman": Shaw's Masquerade

WHEN ANNA HOWARD SHAW DIED, in 1919 — shortly after the
United States Senate passed the amendment giving women the
vote, for which she had fought much of her life — her obituaries
depicted her as "the strongest force for the advancement of women
that the age has known." The *New York Times* printed a eulogy —
significantly, on Independence Day — comparing her to Abraham
Lincoln, praising her "measureless patience . . . deep and gentle
humor . . . and whimsical and tolerant philosophy." While other
suffragist leaders had been described by the media as grim, Shaw
was dubbed by the obituary writer for *The Nation* as "the ideal type
of reformer": "She was the despair of the anti-suffragists, because
she was so normal and sane, so sound and effective. . . . With a
mind that was a match for any man's in its cleverness and logic, her
feminine charm [italics are mine] never left her."

In the game of gender, Shaw preferred to play masculine, but for the sake of the cause she consciously constructed the "feminine charm" of her public persona after some irritating experiences. In the 1880s, early in her public career, she sported a distinctly mannish hairdo. When someone snidely asked in a roomful of people why she wore her hair so short, she retorted (intending to be clever, but unintentionally delivering a Krafft-Ebing-ism), "I will admit frankly that it is a birthmark. I was born with short hair." Despite the bravado of this retort, she grew her hair longer and arranged it in a decorous bun.

Her willingness to alter her style for the sake of the cause extended even to aspects of her life that were only semipublic. In 1895, Shaw and Lucy Anthony entertained a number of suffragists in Wianno, a seaside resort where they had a summer home, and all appeared on the public beach wearing knickerbockers or skirtless swimsuits. The *New York World* somehow discovered the unconventional sartorial habits of the bunch and sent a reporter, who wrote a long, sensational article for the Sunday edition, replete with numerous boldface headlines: "AN ADAMLESS EDEN OF WOMEN IN BLOOMERS," "Summer Suffragists Who Discard Skirts and Wear Bathing Suits Just Like a Man," "THE REV. ANNA SHAW'S INTERESTING COLONY AT SELECT WIANNO," "For Comfort's Sake They Go Crabbing and Walking in Costumes [Wianno] Founder Bradley Would Shudder At, But Are Not Dress Reformers." The article was accompanied by a drawing of Shaw (in a skirt) eyeing her young friends decked out in pants, their appearance undoubtedly calculated by the artist to elicit the shocked response, "Those girls look like boys!"

Shaw called the article "almost libelous" in her autobiography. Yet despite her perturbation, the experience confirmed that she needed to exercise care, even in such a setting. She believed that "no woman in public life can afford to make herself conspicuous by an eccentricity of dress and appearance. If she does so she suffers for it herself, which may not disturb her, and to a greater degree, for the cause she represents, which should disturb her." Shaw saw the suffrage cause as so crucial that she would make whatever concessions to conformity she was convinced she must make in public. As her correspondence indicates, however, at home, with Lucy and with other women who were her lovers at various times, she was as butch as she pleased.

Shaw crafted her appearance to conform to her audience's standard of decorum, but it was a superficial concession. In all other ways she undermined appropriate gender behavior. She was a forceful and dynamic public speaker at a time when virtuous women were supposed to be demure and silent. She was powerfully assertive when passivity was the norm for women. Shaw was convinced that if she presented herself as being as radical, as angry, as impatient as she truly was, she could do nothing for the cause. Therefore, as she grew older she cultivated a grandmotherly persona, which helped make her "esteemed by her countrymen, males as well as females."

However, a scrutiny of Shaw's life suggests that she, like Frances Willard, might in fact easily have stepped out of the pages of Havelock Ellis's "Sexual Inversion in Women." When Shaw's father left his invalid wife and children on 368 acres of land in the northern Michigan wilderness, Anna's sisters did the housework while she and her brothers did the outdoor work — "an arrangement that suited me very well," she admitted in her autobiography. She found all typical little-girl pursuits frivolous and from the youngest age loved playing with a hatchet and saw. She determined early that she would go to college, even though, "so far as I knew . . . no woman had gone to college." When she was forced, briefly, to sew for a living, she declared that she would have preferred "the digging of ditches or the shoveling of coal."

In her public life she was too shrewd to be a man-basher. "We will never win the battle by 'bully ragging,'" she warned a more plainspoken suffragist. But in her private life she had little use for the male of the species. To an old friend who expressed the desire to be married, Shaw wrote, "Just think of the men along your street" and enumerated each with his various faults. "If a human being or a god could conceive of a worse hell than being a wife of any one of them I would like to know what it could be." After delineating to her friend her own rich, full life without a man, she concluded, "I have seen nothing so far which does not make me say every night of my life, 'I thank thee for all good but for nothing more than that I have been saved from the misery of marriage.'"

Anna Shaw had a number of passionate relationships with women. In the early 1870s, for example, when she was an undergraduate at Albion College, she was writing vehemently to Clara Osburn: "My dear little girl, I love you so much and want so much to see you. I want you to come out here. I have set my heart on it and it does not seem as though I could be disappointed. Can't you come[?] I will help you, will you come if you can?" A more significant relationship began in 1876, with Persis Addy. After Shaw discovered her speaking talents at Albion, she decided to take a graduate degree in theology at Boston University, where she was the only woman in a class with forty-two men. As a divinity student she preached in several Cape Cod pulpits, and it was there that she met Persis, a young widow, who became her first mature love. Like Willard, Shaw did not hide her love for women in her 1915 autobiography: "[Persis] brought me at once the greatest happiness and [because of her early death] deepest sorrow of that period of my life," she confessed.

The pattern of most of Shaw's lesbian relationships was also like that of Willard, who was attracted to nurturing women who would support her work. Persis and Anna met during the summer. In the autumn of 1876, Persis returned with Anna to Boston, where they lived together while Anna finished divinity school. Persis's "coming opened windows into a new world. I was no longer lonely," Anna wrote openly. "For the first time, I had someone to come home to, someone to confide in, . . . listen to, and love." Persis, who was wealthy, virtually supported Anna and "gave me my first experience of an existence in which comfort and culture . . . were cheerful commonplaces." Anna called their dyad "a family of two."

Their relationship was short-lived, however. Persis died in 1878, and Anna apparently lived in solitude for ten years. But she was miserable alone. As she confided to a friend, "I would give years of my life and any celebrity which could come to know that in my later years I should have someone always with me who loved me." She was ultimately fortunate in that she managed to achieve it all: celebrity, a relatively long life, and someone always with her who loved her as well. But she never ceased mourning and memorializing Persis. Twenty-four years after Persis's death, Anna wrote in her diary that she wondered if Persis in the "other world" knew about her loving relationship with Lucy: "If she knows she will be glad of Lucy's loving care for me. I am sure she will love her for it," she concluded, comforting herself.

In view of Shaw's earlier concern over the accusation that she looked masculine and her quick determination to alter that appearance, her confessions about Persis in her autobiography may be surprising. She did not seem to fear the possibility that her readers might connect her love for Persis with sexual inversion. Her failure to censor herself surely demonstrates that when she wrote her autobiography, in 1915, she still believed that such relationships continued to be viewed through the lens of innocent romantic friendship. She was certain that love between women — the sexual possibilities of which perhaps continued to be discounted among the uninitiated — was perceived as unthreatening to her society; it was women's claims on male prerogatives, such as inverting *gender*, being "unsexed," that brought social disdain. Therefore, as long as she made a performance of femininity, she believed, she risked nothing by revealing her gentle love of a woman who was lost to Thanatos.

Shaw apparently counted so much on the public's refusal to acknowledge the possibility of anything more profound between women than romantic friendship that she dared to report, seemingly without self-consciousness, a joke that went around when she was a minister: there was "a charge [against her] never before made against a Cape Cod minister," to wit, "All the women in town are in love with Miss Shaw. Has that been charged against any other minister here?"

Shaw held a pulpit for seven years after Persis Addy's death, but she discovered that as a minister she was not able to deal directly enough with the problems of women, which were far more interesting to her than theology. Therefore, she studied for a medical degree (which she received from Boston University in 1886), working her way through medical school as a lecturer on suffragism and temperance and doing her internship among poor women. In 1887, while practicing as a doctor, she was hired as a lecturer for Lucy Stone's American Woman Suffrage Association. The following year she met Frances Willard, by then the president of the national WCTU, and Willard convinced her to become head of the suffrage department of that organization.

Willard must have recognized a kindred spirit in Anna Howard Shaw. Through the years, each sent greetings from her mate, Willard's Anna Gordon and Shaw's Lucy Anthony, in her correspondence. But some of their letters evince the flirtation and electricity between each other that were common among movement women. For example, Frances wrote to Anna, "You are dear to me and trusted by me always everywhere. I only wish I were less unworthy of your confidence. If you would 'take me in hand' and 'Deal with me in righteousness' as my clerical confessor I would try hard to improve."

Whatever the nature of their personal relationship actually was, it is clear that Shaw learned from Willard a skill that was to stand her in good stead as a lecturer throughout her life: how to mediate a message so as to convince a recalcitrant audience. Anna Shaw's success as a suffrage lecturer was rapid, and it made her decide to give up her career in medicine while it was still in its infancy. Finally she had found what she had hoped to find in the ministry and medicine, an occupation that permitted her to engage directly with her primary interest — working to alleviate the burdens suffered by those who were born female.

The social historian James McGovern has estimated that in the course of Shaw's career as a women's rights orator, lecturing steadily for more than thirty years in civic centers, churches, and colleges in every state of the union, she probably reached five million people. Her press reviews were raves. For example, the mass circulation *North American Magazine* opined that she was generally considered "the greatest woman speaker who ever lived," that many even believed her to be "without peer in either sex among orators of her day." The *Pomona Weekly Times*'s assessment of her as a lecturer in 1895 reveals the enthusiasm she met with even in small towns and testifies to how successful she was in convincing her audience that her assumed persona was authentic and admirable and that her cause was just:

> Miss Shaw occupied seventy minutes and devoted her time to the legal rights of women. Her facts were so evident, her arguments so forceful and logical, her diction so elegant, her satire so velvety, that when done many thought she had used up twenty minutes instead of seventy. Those who differ with the policies she advocates admit that as a good natured, polished, and convincing speaker she has no superior. And she is a woman — a true, lovable woman.

Though Shaw's lectures indicate little intellectual profundity, they evince something more important for a speaker attempting to convince large audiences to support an unpopular cause: an acute cognizance of where her audience is emotionally situated and how to move them forward step by step; how to disarm them with accessible, good-natured humor; and, that being accomplished, how to educate them toward her goal. For example, in a lecture of the early 1890s, "The New Man," Shaw hastened to allay fears that the "new woman" desired to rid herself of her femininity by "invad[ing men's] prerogative in dress. This is a useless fear," she quipped, "as the real new woman will always want to look as well as she can and no human being could look well in men's clothes, so the new woman will not wear them for that reason if for no other." After such levity, however, and some crucial assurances that she was not arguing for anything particularly radical (for instance, "The new woman is the same old woman, with a few modern improvements"), Shaw moved to the nugget of her message, which was indeed radical for her era: women have the right to the advantages of an education, to the opportunities for entering any trade or profession that suits them, to all the avenues that will bring them in contact with "the larger life of the world" and permit them to become "more broad-minded and better developed."

As an orator, Shaw was intent on getting her mass audiences to identify with her, which would enable her to bring them to her side. Thus, before she delivered her radical punch lines, she often disarmed her listeners by speaking in the voice of a heterosexual woman and seducing them with her folksy but womanly humor, which helped to distract them from meditating on her unsexed, spinsterish state. For example, in "The Fundamental Principle of a Republic," Shaw mocked antisuffragists who worried that women's enfranchisement would bring discord into the home through political disagreements. She argued that if there were never disagreements between two intelligent human beings, their relationship would stagnate. "Now it may be that the kind of man . . . the anti-suffragists live with [would prefer stagnation to occasional disagreements]," she suggested, "but they are not the kind we live with, and we could not do it. Great big overgrown babies! Cannot be disputed without having a row!" Her audiences howled at her poker-faced annoyance with the image of "big overgrown babies," and she would continue: "While we do not believe that men are saints, we do believe that the average American man is a fairly good sort of fellow."

The men in her audience would of course agree that they were the good sorts who could handle a little disagreement; none of the women would admit that she would tolerate being married to a big overgrown baby. Having captured her listeners thus far, Shaw lulled them further in domestic coziness before hitting them with her chief argument. She claimed to grant that of course "men and women must go through this world together from the cradle to the grave." But that being the case, just as you can't "build up homes without men," you can't "build up the state without women." Women's participation in the state, she concluded, must be "the fundamental principle of a republican form of government."

Such speeches were wildly popular, in the boondocks as well as in New York.

"My dear, dear Balance"

In 1888, Shaw shared a platform at the International Council of Women conference with Susan B. Anthony. Through her, Shaw met Lucy Anthony, Susan's niece, and the two Anthony women soon became the most important people in Shaw's life. By 1890, Susan Anthony, who was always looking for exceptional lecturers for the cause and believed she had found a most remarkable one in Shaw, convinced the younger woman to leave her work for the WCTU and travel with her as national lecturer for the National American Woman Suffrage Association, just created through the efforts of Alice Stone Blackwell.

In her autobiography, Shaw claimed that Susan Anthony "fired my soul with the flame that burned so steadily in her own" and called her "the torch that illumined my life." She insisted that initially she saw her own role in their travels as "bonnet holder" to the famous Susan B. Anthony. But the audience's enthusiasm for her speeches soon made Shaw feel that she had come out from behind the beloved shadow and could truly hold her own. In fact, though Anthony was the major symbol and representative of the suffrage movement in the 1890s by virtue of her close to half-a-century leadership in the cause, she was an indifferent speaker. While audiences venerated her as a pioneer and a valiant spirit, it was Shaw who carried them away with what they received as oratorical brilliance. The two thus made an excellent podium team from the beginning, Anthony with her stature and Shaw with her skill.

Sharing platforms all over America with the famous Susan B. Anthony brought Shaw much quicker fame than she might have attained on her own. Anthony made it clear that Shaw was her heir apparent, as NAWSA members seemed to think in 1894, when Anthony was seventy-four years old and Shaw was forty-seven. Their birthdays were two days apart, so the organization staged a birthday banquet for them both, decorating the main table with floral 4's and 7's. During the first half of the banquet, the centerpiece represented 74, and during the second half the numbers were reversed to 47.

Shaw did eventually assume the presidency of NAWSA, but she surely would have said that the gift of the limelight was not the most important one she received from Susan B. Anthony. The greatest gift was Lucy, Susan's niece. The correspondence between

Anna Shaw and Lucy Anthony began soon after they met. Anna's April 27, 1888, response to a letter from Lucy (now lost) hints at Lucy's immediate infatuation and Anna's teasing, careful encouragement: "So you are very fond of me? You must be or you would not give me such unmerited praise for my sermon. Whatever there was of merit in it was due to the time and circumstances. . . . I just could not help doing my best, and you are all a part of it. . . . I shall always be glad to get a line from you."

By February 1889, when Anna was planning a lecture trip to California, Lucy had apparently "proposed" to her, offering to perform wifely duties if she could travel with her. "So you could not only write my letters, buy my railroad tickets, check baggage, etc., but look after my clothes," Anna teased her. "I wish you and your needle were here this minute." Their relationship escalated quickly after this point. The following July, Anna wrote to Lucy saying that she intended to make a new will since she traveled so much and railroad accidents were so frequent: "I believe you do love me and it would make a difference whether my name was on the list of killed someday to you." She assured Lucy, however, that "I am going to live as long as I can and make you [live long] too."

The two women soon began to plan the future, when they might share a home, and Lucy encouraged Anna to return to the ministry, which would enable her to stay in one place instead of traveling constantly. In a January 1890 letter, Anna promised that they would indeed someday have a home, "but that cannot be until we have suffrage for women. We have put our hand to the plow, and we cannot turn back to rest or enjoy ourselves in the quiet of a home nest." In the meantime, they would not only devote themselves to the cause but plan for the happier days to come, and as for the present, it would be "always . . . a happy rest time for us just to be together." Seven months later, however, they were making specific plans to live together *soon,* in Washington, D.C. Anna wrote to Lucy from South Dakota, "Just think of the blessed future we hope to have when we get into our little home life. . . . I long for it with all my heart, and I want you to feel the rest of it now."

Susan B. Anthony was puzzled in the beginning by the relationship between Anna Howard Shaw and her niece, not because she had not observed frequent romances between women in the movement or had not had her own movement romances, but because she thought the differences between them were huge, as Anna reported to Lucy. Susan had said, "I don't understand it. You are a strong, self-reliant, energetic woman," while Lucy, who was fourteen years younger than Anna, was "without experience" and a frail girl. It is possible too that Susan thought of the fleetingness of passion and worried for her niece. But Anna was reassuring about the steadiness of her commitment, as she wrote to Lucy: when she told Susan that "all I had was yours [Lucy's]," Susan responded, "That is if you keep on caring for each other," at which Anna insisted that her feeling would last a lifetime. Anna also defended her love by bringing Susan to agree with her assertion that "there is a good deal of a noble woman in Lucy."

It did not take Susan Anthony long to accept the connection between her niece and her favorite suffrage lecturer. In most of her letters to them, she addressed them together; she acknowledged that they slept together; and she spoke of their relationship as though it were a marriage, writing to Lucy, for example, "We [the Anthonys] are so settled with the feeling that dear Miss Shaw has you in hand that we almost surrender our right to any part or lot in you altogether." Ida Husted Harper, a fellow suffragist and friend of both Susan Anthony and Anna Shaw, claimed that Susan felt "the keenest pleasure" about the relationship between Anna and her niece.

Susan Anthony was right: there was a tremendous difference of personality and experience between Anna Shaw and Lucy Anthony. But Lucy was precisely the woman Anna believed she needed. As she put it in an early letter to Lucy, "I am thankful that out of all the world in my hour of need God brought you to me." Lucy was also a suffragist, and at one point she attempted to become a booking agent for suffrage speakers, using her assistance to Shaw as a credential. But primarily Lucy was a housewife, to Anna's great joy, and a perfect complement to Anna, who delighted in mowing lawns and fixing roofs but never in washing dishes. "I will teach you to be a useful man about the house as I am," she once wrote to a friend, offering to instruct the woman in carpentry.

Once Anna and Lucy became a couple, Lucy contributed to the suffrage cause not only by acting as Anna's secretary but, more important, by making Anna's hectic life as a traveling lecturer and then as president of NAWSA easier by tendering support, stability, and the solace of the ever-burning home fires. Until she met Lucy, Anna felt that except for her two brief years with Persis Addy, she had never had a home. Many of the one thousand extant letters from Anna to Lucy dwell on their domesticity — especially on Anna's deep longing to live with Lucy. In 1891, for instance, she wrote to Lucy from a lecture trip in Tennessee, "I wish I could let you see the inside of my love for you, but, better still, that you could know the depths of my trust and . . . [sic] I have had so many happy thoughts of that little house we are planning. It shall be yours to furnish just as you want it." Once the home was procured, Anna's letters became filled with joyful anticipation of returning home, loneliness for their home, weariness that could be cured only by being at home with Lucy.

Anna reveled in her triumphs as a speaker in her letters, but she was almost always certain to remind Lucy of how crucial she was to that success. It was the knowledge of Lucy at home — in the home they created together — that enabled Anna to do her work with peace of mind. "My dear, dear Balance," she called Lucy. "If I am of any use under the sun," she reminded Lucy after a particularly gratifying lecture tour, "it is because you have given me courage and hope, and the triumph of last week was due as much to you as to myself."

Anna needed Lucy especially to rescue her from her dark nights of the soul. Just as the public's view of Anna as grandmotherly was wide of the mark, so was the image of her as good-humored and easygoing. She was given to despair, which was greatly exacerbated by the now unimaginable difficulties of her roaming life as a suffragist star, which obligated her to be constantly hopping on and off trains and carriages, sometimes in the most primitive and unwelcoming parts of the country, for three decades. Her itinerant existence in the service of suffrage created a sense of anomie and perpetual exhaustion that cast her into deep depressions, which she battled against assiduously but not always successfully. A poignant letter to Lucy in 1892, written while Anna was campaigning in Kansas, suggests both her anxieties and Lucy's crucial role as a dispenser of comfort:

> The wind whistles around the house and the rain patters on the glass and I am alone. It seems as if all the world has left me and I am sad and lonely. . . . It is hard to live this homeless life with no hope of its ending. Year after year of constant toiling like a galley slave and no chance of release, and for what? Just merely to work to help others who do not want to be helped. It would be so easy to close one's eyes, shut out the pain and sorrow of living, and sleep — such a long restful sleep that one would never grow tired again.

But she snapped out of her death wish by remembering that she was no longer alone in the world. "I wish we could just sit and not speak but rest and help each other to feel the peace of perfect trust," she wrote. "I am thinking of the Haven," the home she and Lucy were planning to build, which she anticipated as their marriage haven.

When a young woman whom Anna knew slightly committed suicide some years later, Anna identified with her, giving vent to those dark impulses that were always just beneath the surface, though kept in check by her stable lesbian relationship with Lucy. She wrote to Lucy that she understood well "what a lonely hopeless thing" life must have seemed to the dead woman. But once again, as she had throughout the years, she shrugged off her attraction to despair by remembering, "Well, we have each other, and a lot of good friends, and our beautiful home, and with all these things there is no limit to the good helpful work we may do. How glad I am that we both want to do it and that we are both able, in many ways, to do much."

Despite the comfort of this relationship, however, Anna was susceptible to the attractions of other women. The loneliness she suffered during her constant sojourns in strange towns, strange hotels, and strange people's homes may help to explain her infidelities with women such as Harriet Cooper, a Californian who was probably Anna's lover during her 1895–96 suffrage trips to the West. This affair was clearly not an isolated incident. In an uncharacteristically catty letter to a suffragist friend, Carrie Chapman Catt revealed what was very well known about Anna Shaw in top suffrage circles by 1912. Mary Peck (who had a crush on Catt, and whom Catt called "Pan") had apparently apprised her that Shaw had made unwelcome advances. Catt responded, "I was interested in the love story. Naughty Pan to kick up such a row! Smash hearts and I know not what. Yes I think A[nna] S[haw] is too old for that sort of thing now. It used to happen often — about every *two years*. *You* ought to understand how that goes."

Regardless of Anna's other romances, her relationship with Lucy continued for more than thirty years, until her death. The extant letters from Lucy to Anna are not as plentiful as Anna's letters to Lucy, but Lucy's assessment of their life together is poignantly preserved in what she wrote in Anna's journal almost six months after Anna's death. On the last page of the journal, which Anna had started at the beginning of the year, is this entry in Lucy's handwriting: "December 31, 1919: On this the last night of the last day of the year which took away my precious Love — Her friendship and to serve her was the joy of my life. She was the most unselfish — the best friend one could have — In as much as I helped in her labors & to make her life easier perhaps — that much am I glad I have lived."

As Anna Shaw believed, she could not have tolerated the tremendous pressure she endured decade after decade as lecturer and leader in the suffrage campaigns without the intimacy and nurturing of women. If she had been a traditional wife and mother, she could not have played the role she did in the suffrage movement. If she been heterosexual and unmarried, it would not have been easy to be intimate with men, since illicit heterosexual behavior was not widely tolerated in a movement that needed to appeal to a large conservative base in order to succeed. Susan B. Anthony, Elizabeth

Cady Stanton, and the National Woman Suffrage Association had been the focus of outrage when they defended the free-love advocate Victoria Woodhull in the 1870s. Woodhull was often dubbed a prostitute for her views. Anthony's and Stanton's brief acceptance of her deepened the split between NWSA and the American Woman Suffrage Association, and for a time between the NWSA camp and all conservative women's rights advocates. Shaw could push the suffrage cause to millions of people because her female lovers made a difficult situation tolerable to her, and her asexual, grandmotherly persona (as those outside the inner circles saw it) made her tolerable to the public.

To the Brink of the Nineteenth Amendment

Shaw's greatest talents and successes in the suffrage cause were as an orator rather than as the leader of an organization. Though she excelled in diplomatic argument, she was much too impulsive and impatient with nitty-gritty details to be able to organize well, and she was too fiery to be able to deal in the subtleties of personal diplomacy. But in 1904, Susan Anthony urged Shaw to run for the presidency of NAWSA: "I don't see anybody in the whole rank of our suffrage movement to [assume the position] but you. . . . We must not let the society down into *feeble* hands. . . . Don't say *no*, for the *life of you*. . . . We must *tide over* with the *best material* that we have, & *you are the best*." Shaw could not refuse such an appeal from her mentor and hero. She held the post from 1904 to 1915.

During that time NAWSA membership grew from 17,000 to almost 200,000, and after long years of stagnation, the suffragists chalked up victories in several states. In 1910 Washington voted for woman suffrage; in 1911, California; in 1912, Oregon, Arizona, and Kansas ("Oh, the joy of it! Day of days! Thank heaven, I had a little part in it! I can hardly keep still. I want to sing and praise God!" Shaw gloated in her journal after getting the election results on November 2, 1912). Before she left the presidency, two million American women in twelve states could vote, and the tide had shifted so that total victory seemed all but inevitable. Ida Harper observed that under Shaw's leadership, the tone of the press had become "distinctly favorable" to woman suffrage, and everywhere prosuffrage audiences were huge, overflowing even the largest halls.

As disorganized an administrator as Shaw might have been, her contributions to those achievements were undeniable. She was a ceaseless campaigner; she was very successful in getting wealthy women to contribute significant sums, and NAWSA's annual budget increased tenfold during her years in office; and she made numerous wise leadership decisions. She was truly skillful in manipulating public sentiment, and with that skill she unquestionably furthered the cause.

Her relationship with the militant suffragists' Congressional Union, which was born under the leadership of two young women, Alice Paul and Lucy Burns, after they had observed the militancy of British suffragists, is a case in point. Shaw was as impatient for woman suffrage as the most radical militant and was initially attracted to the youthful energy of Paul and Burns. But her deeper conviction, which had always been manifested in her speeches, was that the best approach was to allay the fears of the recalcitrant, who were already terrified by the uncontrolled potential of women that suffrage seemed to threaten. The militants' approach exacerbated those fears. But Shaw knew how to use the militants to make her own brand of suffragism look less frightening. She made NAWSA into the "good cop," whose sweet reasonableness became very appealing to politicians and the public, in contrast to the militants' "bad cop" image. She used what she depicted as the extremism of the Congressional Union to emphasize the rationality of her own organization. "Votes for women were never obtained by militant methods. . . . Every victory for suffrage has been secured, even in England itself, by the orderly and constitutional procedure which has marked the agitation during the whole history of the movement in America," she told magazine reporters in 1913, effectively reminding them that NAWSA had been "civilized" in its demands. These had better be taken seriously, because a "savage" group, the Congressional Union, was ready to resort to disruption and even violence and unpleasantness like that perpetrated by British militants — hunger strikes, burning of public buildings, and chaining themselves to monuments.

More justly, perhaps, the Congressional Union might be viewed as the grain of sand in the oyster that produced the pearl of great price, the treasured right to vote. Naturally Shaw could not acknowledge how essential the Congressional Union was to her strategy. Nevertheless, her tactical use of the radical group was brilliant: she succeeded in getting people who had once seen NAWSA as terrible in its demand for votes for women to understand how modest, patient, and thus meritorious the older organization was. In effect, she used the Congressional Union to redefine what was a moderate (though no less insistent) position on suffrage. The *New York Times*'s encomium to Shaw's leadership after the amendment giving women the vote was passed sums up her strategy's success: "[Anna Shaw's] wise guidance of the woman-suffrage cause, a guidance which emphatically impressed upon the public mind that neither she nor the cause was responsible for the antics of the madwing, so-called militants, probably had as much to do with its triumph as anything that contributed to bring it about."

Shaw and NAWSA were sometimes forced to engage in damage control because of the militants, but Shaw usually managed to gain a benefit from each potentially embarrassing situation the militants perpetrated. For example, in 1914 the Congressional Union announced that it would organize a campaign to defeat all Democratic candidates, because the Democrats were then in power and had failed to give women the vote. Shaw saw a major opportunity to play good cop on behalf of her organization. She widely denounced the union's tactic, assuring those Democratic politicians who had been friends to suffrage that most women in favor of suffrage appreciated them and that female voters in suffrage states intended to work for their reelection.

She also helped convince President Wilson, a Democrat, that the suffrage cause merited serious support. Wilson had long been ambivalent but had begun slowly to bend toward women's enfranchisement; however, he became hostile to suffragists when the Congressional Union obtained an audience with him by pretending to represent the Federation of Women's Clubs, a national organization that had begun by encouraging women to read great books but had then turned its attention to social causes, especially the moderate promotion of women's enfranchisement. Having thus achieved entry to the White House, the Congressional Union proceeded to trash the president. Shaw removed the sting of that shenanigan by denouncing it in the name of NAWSA, and thereby received Wilson's gratitude and his commitment to suffrage as represented by women such as Anna Howard Shaw and the NAWSA women whom she led.

The suffrage cause was further helped by the stance NAWSA took toward the Great War. Initially Shaw opposed American involvement and called for explorations of alternative means to settle international disputes. But when it became clear that war was inevitable and that American women would be pulled in whether they wished it or not, she came to see this "war to end wars" as the sure and final means to get women enfranchised. Despite her early opposition to the war, she now pointed out that women in the combatant countries were helping the war effort by taking the places of men on farms and in factories, working in munitions plants, and running the railways, post offices, and hospitals. She made sure that no legislator could remain ignorant of these facts. Through NAWSA she reminded congressmen that if American involvement was indeed inevitable, the help of women would be crucial in the United States too — and that women would help best if they had the rights of full citizens.

Shaw was a pragmatist, just as she had been throughout her suffrage career. If war was really inescapable, she reasoned, and if women had to make the inevitable sacrifices that war demanded, then at the least they must finally emerge from their terrible experience with the long-sought, ever-elusive franchise.

In 1915 Shaw left the presidency of NAWSA, exhausted by squabbles and the effort of tending to the details of the job. But even out of office she continued to be a leading suffragist spokesperson, and in her lectures she now tirelessly insisted that in both peace and war, a modern country needed the cooperation of all its citizens, women as well as men. She never failed to draw a dramatic connection between what American leaders had presented as a sacred battle to make the world safe for democracy and the suffragists' duty to continue their own sacred battle while they helped in the fight against the enemies overseas. Without resorting to unpatriotic rhetoric, she managed to suggest that America was as bad as the corrupt monarchies it fought if it denied half its citizens representation. She explained to the public that suffragists had to continue their agitation for the vote even during the war because "for years woman suffragists have been fighting for democracy, for those who submit to authority should have a voice in government. If we laid down this campaign we should be turning against democracy."

She did not change her tactic even when President Wilson asked her, as one of the most famous and respected women in America, to serve as chair of the Woman's Committee of the Council of National Defense in 1917. The Woman's Committee was supposedly established as a clearinghouse to coordinate the war efforts of women's organizations all over the country, but it was superseded or duplicated by various government agencies. When Shaw began to suspect that the Council of National Defense had intended her committee as a form of window-dressing, a sop to American women — as in "We take your war work so seriously that we've given you your own federal committee" — her first inclination was to resign. But she once again became pragmatic, believing that at least she had been given a government-sponsored podium from which she could make clear to all America that it was time women had the vote and that women's role in the country must be expanded.

Speaking as the head of a federal committee, Shaw told her numerous audiences (hyperbolically perhaps, but nevertheless cleverly):

> There are two million members of the suffrage associations of the United States. What would it not mean if by one just act of Congress two million women could be set free to serve the Government with singleness of purpose and undivided allegiance,

and fired by a spirit of gratitude and loyalty, they should turn all their splendidly organized force, their initiative and ability for propaganda, into service to maintain the army in the field and to preserve the existing moral and spiritual as well as industrial forces in the States?

With every opportunity conceivable, she connected women's efforts for America during World War I to their suffrage struggle, always reminding the United States of its indebtedness. "Our country needs the army of women at home just as much as the army of men in France," she said over and over, in speeches, articles, and conversations with politicians. And the corollary of that fact was that women, as valuable citizens, must have the vote.

At the end of the war, Shaw became the first living woman to receive the Distinguished Service Medal, a reward for her service as the chair of the Woman's Committee, in which she did not believe. But much more gratifying to her was the success of her ploy of constantly reminding America that women had earned the vote through patriotic service. After the seventy-year struggle for the vote, which had taken up more than thirty years of Shaw's own life, Congress passed a constitutional amendment that enfranchised American women.

Anna Shaw was seventy-two years old at the end of the war. She had promised Lucy that once suffrage seemed assured and the war was finished, they would enjoy "wild oats for both of us in our own way the rest of our lives. We will have earned freedom from worry and can rest and go about the earth [or] stay at home, raise chickens and potatoes and enjoy the glory of our grove and Forest of Arden and the glorious sunsets." When her work on the Woman's Committee came to an end in March 1919, the two women were going to go to Europe, and afterward, Anna wrote to Lucy, "if we come home in the Fall we can go right to Florence Villa [where they had stayed during several vacations in Florida]. What an easy time we might have of it next winter. We must get all there is in life for us the next few years. Don't get run over or anything. Be careful of pickpockets."

But Shaw had never been destined for an easy time. In May,

before they could leave for their European trip, she was asked to share the podium with former president William Howard Taft on a three-week tour of the Midwest and New England in order to raise support for Wilson's peace treaty and the League of Nations. "There is no other woman speaker before the public whose help [Taft] believes will be as valuable as yours," the invitation said. She had spent her life as a vassal for pioneering challenges that would claim a place for women in the public sphere. How could she stop now? Against her better judgment, the exhausted Shaw accepted one last job on behalf of American women.

Halfway through the trip, in Springfield, Illinois, she became ill with pneumonia. She returned home to the woman with whom she had spent the last thirty years of her life. Under Lucy's care, she rallied briefly but then sank again. The Nineteenth Amendment had gone to the states to be ratified by then, but ratification took until August 1920. With her death on July 2, 1919, Shaw missed knowing for certain that the cause to which she had devoted her best years had come to fruition; suffrage would finally be guaranteed to all American women through an amendment to the United States Constitution.

❧ 4 ❧

VICTORY:

CARRIE CHAPMAN CATT

Mollie do you know who loves you best in all the world?
Well, she's writing you this letter.

— Carrie Chapman Catt to Mary Garrett Hay

IN A 1923 ARTICLE for the *Woman Citizen*, written after she had
been involved with Mary Garrett Hay for more than a quarter of a
century, Carrie Chapman Catt claimed that in 1890, four years after
the death of her first husband, Leo Chapman, the wealthy George
Catt had proposed that he and she form a partnership. According to
Carrie, George Catt had said that he would allow her to give her
energies to the suffrage movement, a cause in which he too believed, while he made the money to support them. The agreement
was that she was to have two months in the spring and another two
months in the fall to devote exclusively to suffrage lecturing and
organizing.

She did not point out in this article, to which she gave the romantic title "A Suffrage Team," that her commitment to the cause
and related interests very soon swallowed up much more time than
four months a year, that her husband's business also demanded
that he constantly be gone from home, and that, as Mary Peck, her
friend and first biographer, exclaimed, "the two of them spent an
increasing portion of their existence traveling in different directions!" Carrie insisted on her heterosexuality so firmly to the public
that researchers who had not seen her letters to and from other
women were long blinded to the possibilities of her lesbianism or
even bisexuality, stating, for instance, that Carrie Chapman Catt

lived "almost without a private life since the death of her husband in 1905."

Since all correspondence between Carrie and George Catt and all her diaries of those years have been lost or destroyed, it is impossible to know precisely what the nature of the personal relationship between them may have been. However, a large extant correspondence with several women leaves little doubt about Carrie's lesbian involvements — most especially with Mollie Hay, who was her partner in life for many years longer than the duration of her marriages to Leo Chapman and George Catt.

"A Suffrage Team"

By 1895, Carrie Chapman Catt had made a national name for herself as an organizer, speaker, and leading strategist of the suffrage movement. Before she came along, the national suffrage associations were run out of the hip pockets of their leaders, but Carrie Catt impressed Susan Anthony by calling for the correlation of national, state, and local suffrage branches and the establishment of programs with concrete aims. She proposed a standing committee on organization for NAWSA, which would map out the national work and put organizers in the field. Such a committee was soon established, and of course Anthony made Catt its chairperson and put her in charge of directing fieldwork. Mary (Mollie) Garrett Hay, of Indiana, was appointed secretary of the committee, possibly at Carrie's suggestion.

The evidence indicates that Carrie met Mollie five years earlier, at her first national NAWSA convention. But there is no record that they were together for long periods until the summer of 1895. George was away on business, so Mollie moved in with Carrie, who was then living in New York, and the two women spent the hot months planning committee strategy. Peck explained in her biography of Carrie Catt that this was the "beginning . . . [of] the intimate collaboration which united them for many years."

While the nature of their "intimate collaboration" was no secret to many of the workers in the suffrage movement, it was masked for those outside the movement; as Carrie wrote to Mary Peck, she understood that she had to "walk . . . the chalk line to get the vote." Thus Carrie presented herself to the public as a very married woman and then as a very grieving widow, retaining the last names of her first and second husbands until her death — though the marriages together spanned only sixteen years of her life. After George Catt's death, she established a permanent home with Mollie Hay until Mollie's death, in 1928. At that time Carrie bought a double plot at Woodlawn Cemetery in New York, large enough to hold her own coffin next to Mollie's.

Biographers' usual assessment of Carrie Chapman Catt's two heterosexual marriages is that they were happy and successful. One biographer explains that Carrie began to live with Mollie in 1905 because she was so shattered by her husband's death that her health was impaired; she could not cope with being in an apartment that was filled with memories of him, and she detested being alone. Such an unquestioning presentation of Carrie's intense heterosexual attachment ignores her strong homosexual motivations, for which there is excellent evidence.

Whether or not Carrie and George Catt were truly a "suffrage team," as she stated, she and Mollie Hay were indeed such a team, as well as a romantic couple. After their summer together in 1895, Mollie left Indiana permanently and moved to New York, where she could work closely with Carrie on suffrage issues. She was soon acknowledged as Carrie's confidante and constant companion within the movement. Though Carrie officially shared a residence with George Catt until his death, the two women were constantly with each other, traveling together at every opportunity — to suffrage meetings, conventions, speaking engagements, fundraising events. In 1899 alone they covered thirteen thousand miles, visiting twenty states, attending fifteen conventions, making fifty-one set speeches, and spending sixty-four days and twenty-eight nights on trains and innumerable nights in hotels. Surely Carrie spent at least as much time with Mollie as she did with her husband.

When Carrie Catt became president of NAWSA for the first time, in 1900, she began to transform it. She organized the group along professional lines, as no suffrage association had been organized before. She believed that any major fighting force or nationwide concern had to be organized with a strong leader at its head, clear lines of authority, administrative procedures, a fundraising plan that warranted a treasury, and a propaganda program that would effectively spread the word of what the organization wished to accomplish.

Much of Carrie Catt's success was achieved in tandem with Mollie Hay. Their "marriage" was so well known in suffrage circles that when Carrie — still George Catt's wife — became president of NAWSA, something like a nepotism issue was raised by certain prominent members, who feared that Mollie would have too much influence on her. Mollie was too outspoken and prickly to be universally well liked, and to stem her power, the Executive Committee dissolved the Organization Committee (on which she had been serving for five years), certain that Carrie intended to make her its head. But as Mary Peck pointed out, "Any hope which may have been entertained by those who disliked Miss Hay that she would be eliminated from the scene . . . was speedily dissipated. She went right on in an unofficial capacity doing the same things she had been doing. She also went right along conveying the impression that Mrs. Catt was Mrs. Catt and she was her prophet, and in time suffragists became reconciled to it." Throughout the years, people understood that if they wanted Carrie Catt's ear or a favor from her, they could get to her if Mollie Hay interceded.

The suffragists' eventual reconciliation to Hay had a good deal to do with their being forced to acknowledge how valuable a suffrage leader she was in her own right. She was superlative at fundraising, putting together deals, and persuading. She was able to make committed suffragists even out of members of the Daughters of the American Revolution. It did not take her long, though against considerable odds, to succeed in swinging the staid Federation of Women's Clubs to the suffrage camp and enlisting that organization's energy and funds for the cause. As their fellow suffrage worker Maud Wood Park observed of the team of Hay and Catt, "Mrs. Catt was essentially a statesman; Miss Hay, a politician, and together they were, in most cases, invincible."

Indeed, in the war to bring suffrage to its final victory, Mollie Hay was the "bird colonel" and Carrie Catt was the general. But it was also Catt's tremendous female charisma that was essential to her ability to rouse not only her officers but the suffrage troops, who were happy to perform according to her wisdom. Mollie Hay was far from being the only woman who was in love with her. Despite Carrie Catt's talents as a general for the cause, her style could be womanly — much more so than Anna Shaw's. She was captivating to huge audiences, but especially to the many individual women who were enamored of her. She was seen by many suffragists as a seductive earth goddess or a powerful and beloved matriarch and mother. As one eyewitness at a suffrage victory celebration reported, "She was queenly. Wore an exquisite white lace gown — a most Frenchy creation which fitted her as a mould — a large bunch of pink rosebuds at her waist. . . . She spoke easily and pleasantly, no oratory, and in a heart-to-heart way as though we were all one family and she was taking everyone into her heart."

In her biography, Mary Peck could not avoid discussing Catt's great personal attractiveness to women and how it worked to the advantage of the suffrage movement. Writing from both observation and her own besotted feelings, Peck observed that "the enthusiasm felt by the young workers for [Catt] was often just this side of idolatry." For the most part, Catt understood how to convert those feelings to altruistic efforts. As Peck pointed out, Catt "sublimated the affection of her lieutenants into work for the cause." But she was not always interested in sublimating, as her relationships with Mollie Hay and others reveal.

Despite her successes in bringing order to NAWSA during her first term, Catt resigned in 1904, citing as her primary reason one that would promote the public image she wished to promulgate of herself as a family woman: the ill health of both her husband and her mother, she said, required more of her attention than the presidency would allow. It is more likely, however, that her resignation was connected to the frustratingly slow progress of the suffrage struggle at the start of the century (no new states had voted to enfranchise women during her term) as well as her annoying battles with various factions in NAWSA who resented what they may have seen as her excessively tight organization, or her military style.

Having left NAWSA, Catt turned her attention to the cause on both a larger and a more focused scale. In 1902 she had founded the International Woman Suffrage Alliance (IWSA), to which she knew she could give more time if she no longer headed NAWSA. She attended the 1904 meeting of IWSA in Berlin and accepted the presidency of that group — certainly throwing in doubt her stated reasons for resigning from the NAWSA presidency. In New York, she brought together various city groups that were working on suffrage by forming the Interurban Suffrage Council, which became the Woman Suffrage Party in 1910 and was headed by Mollie Hay (who never stopped being Carrie Catt's chief colonel) from 1912 to 1918. By 1913, 100,000 New York City women belonged to that group. It became a nucleus for and then a subsidiary of the Empire State Campaign, which Catt and Hay organized that year in order to push for a New York State referendum. Catt chaired the campaign, and Hay became head of its New York City branch.

In 1914, with the advent of the Great War in Europe, Catt's international suffrage work came to a temporary end. She turned her full attention to the Empire State Campaign, believing that if New York voted to enfranchise women in the next election, in 1915, many other states would quickly follow. An army of suffragists, which Mollie Hay helped to recruit, lined up behind Catt to serve in any capacity she required. Although Catt was in her late fifties by then, her personal appeal was still powerful, as the gushing of one of her lieutenants, Marie Howe, suggests. "When she looks at me," Howe said of Catt in 1915, "my heart comes up in my throat and I can see in her face all she has lived through, and I can refuse her nothing she might ask."

In the Empire State Campaign too, Catt excelled in strategy, dividing the state into 12 large districts with strong leaders, who supervised 150 assembly district leaders, who supervised 5524 election district captains. Her fingers were on the pulse of almost all of it, and if she missed anything crucial, Mollie Hay filled in for her. Catt made sure that suffrage sermons were preached in churches all over the state on Mother's Day, and if a minister refused, she managed to get suffragists from the congregation to stand at the church door and hand out suffrage leaflets. She was a master show-woman. On Independence Day she had suffragists position them-selves on the courthouse steps of every county seat in New York and read a Woman's Declaration of Independence. During the whole of the summer, daylight and torchlight parades were going continu-ally. As a sort of finale just days before the election, she had her workers organize a Fifth Avenue parade in which every city and county of the state was represented, including hundreds of women's groups, who carried their colors in flags and banners, and 5000 schoolteachers, who carried blackboards chalked with suf-frage messages.

Despite the admirably fought Empire State Campaign in 1915, only 42 percent of the voters supported the enfranchisement of women. Yet as the *New York World* pointed out, the failure was really deceptive. Catt had started the campaign with little sympathy among men in New York, who were the voters, but she had man-aged finally to create "a body of opinion that registered hundreds of thousands of voters at the first summons for a radical reform." The magnitude of the vote in favor of suffrage, the article rightly sug-gested, was "a revelation of the astonishing growth of the move-ment." No suffragist who knew the inside workings of the New York campaign could doubt that such growth was due to the suffrage team of Catt and Hay.

Catt was certainly not one to let the momentum of the 1915 campaign die. Immediately after the election she called a mass meeting at Cooper Union to organize for what she dubbed "the decisive battle," which would come in the next election. Mollie Hay, as chair of the New York Woman Suffrage Party, presided, an-nouncing to an audience who "hurrahed" her every sentence, "All day I have been getting letters from women who never worked before, saying 'Call me in! I'm ready to work now!' Let us count our blessings and go forward!" This appeal, according to the *New York Tribune*, was followed by "hurrahs ad infinitum." When Carrie Catt asked for $100,000 to start a new campaign, $115,000 was pledged by the audience within minutes.

Carrie Catt and Mollie Hay continued to be a true suffrage team to the very end of the battle. When Catt accepted the presidency of NAWSA for the second time, in 1915, she understood that she would not be able to pay as much attention to the next Empire State Campaign as she had to the original one, but she could keep apprised of matters through pillow talk. In the 1917 campaign, Mollie Hay applied her partner's techniques and finally won New York for woman suffrage. Though upstate voters trounced the suffragists in this second campaign, it did not matter. Hay was able to produce a sweeping victory in New York City; as head of the New York City Woman Suffrage Party, she directed that part of the campaign personally, with superb attention to all the details and propaganda techniques, including energetic street rallies, pamphleting, and huge parades worthy of Catt. Thanks to Hay, New York City's large plurality balanced the negative vote from other parts of the state.

When Catt stepped into the presidency of NAWSA for the second time, she knew precisely how to turn the public's good feelings toward NAWSA, which Anna Howard Shaw had created during her eleven-year term, into the law that would enable women to vote, and Hay continued to assist her. To her flawless organizing throughout the country, Catt soon added other tactics. For example, she scheduled intense lobbying in Washington. She sent Hay there to direct the suffragists in persuading Republican congressmen, who were more recalcitrant than the Democrats, to pass the suffrage bill. Adopting Shaw's ploy, she also made sure that the country was constantly reminded how necessary the labors of women were to the war effort. Like Shaw, Catt had been a pacifist before America entered the war, and she returned to pacifism after the war, founding an international organization to explore "the Cause and Cure of War." But she supported U.S. involvement, in the hope that if the war were really about making the world safe for democracy, an extension of democracy to women might be its logical outcome. Laying her pacifist principles aside for the duration, she even agreed to serve on the Women's Committee of the Council of National Defense.

Though Catt repeatedly tried to quench the pyrotechnics of the National Woman's Party, which had emerged in 1916 from Alice Paul and Lucy Burns's Congressional Union, she played the good cop–bad cop game even more deliberately than Anna Shaw did, in the interest of winning the franchise. Catt knew how to profit from the militancy of the National Woman's Party. Reputedly she kept spies in that group, so that she could let President Wilson know in advance whether they were planning any embarrassing tactics. If this rumor was true, her efforts were not wasted: Wilson apparently became her debtor as well as Shaw's. He even agreed to address the 1916 NAWSA convention, where he assured women of his good will toward their cause and the inevitability of their success. Eventually he convinced the Democratic Party to support a constitutional suffrage amendment, and as Catt and Shaw had asked him to do, he pleaded with Congress for the enfranchisement of women as a war measure. In May 1919 the House of Representatives voted to enfranchise women, and the Senate replicated that vote in June. After Shaw's death, Catt carried on, with the help of Mollie Hay. She spent fourteen months leading the campaign for ratification around the country, until, in August 1920, the necessary thirty-six states had agreed that American women should be able to vote. Thus the suffrage team of Catt and Hay brought to fruition the task that women such as Mary Grew, Susan Anthony, Frances Willard, Alice Blackwell, and Anna Shaw had been laboring for since the mid-nineteenth century.

Mrs. Carrie Chapman Catt

Though in public Carrie Chapman Catt remained a lone widow until her death, in private — perhaps as a kind of personal revisionism that would make her earlier life consistent with her present life — she came to view her heterosexual phase as nothing more than making do. With her fellow suffragists, she seldom concealed her disdain for marriage. For example, in a 1930 note to an unmarried suffragist who had written about her own felicity in the single state, Catt said that she had been regrettably naive when young about choices outside of wedlock.

> I was born and brought up in the West, where there were a great many more men than women, and I was 21 before I ever met a spinster. She incited great curiosity in our neighborhood when she arrived to visit her mother. In due time I did Suffrage work and when I took my first tour through New England, I was impressed by the number of spinsters there who had inherited homes, who had their freedom and were very happy. I thought I had at last found the most perfectly located human being in the world. I have never lost this opinion, so I congratulate you.

Whether her two heterosexual marriages were really foisted on her by the compulsory heterosexuality of her society, Catt clearly had no interest in remarrying after the death of her second husband, though she was still a young woman. Yet "spinsterism" (unless she meant this as a code word for "homosexual") was no more appealing to her than heterosexual wedlock. All her emotional and domestic relationships were ostensibly lesbian for the next forty-two years of her life. Apparently she had come to feel, like many who were leading the war for women's rights, that heterosexuality was tantamount to sleeping in the enemy's camp.

Yet she had married twice — and not because she had no economic option other than to be supported by a husband. Soon after graduating from college, in 1880, she had a brief but truly meteoric career in education, first as a high school principal in Mason City, Iowa, and then, in 1883, as a highly regarded superintendent of schools — a position that was virtually unprecedented for a woman in Iowa. Two years later, however, at the age of twenty-six, she met Leo Chapman, who was the owner of the local newspaper. Within three weeks they were married, and Carrie resigned from her job.

No concrete evidence remains to provide insight into her impulsive decision to give up her career or to explain the almost bizarre haste of her actions. Was she really mindlessly swept up by the heterosexual imperative of her society, as she implied in her 1930 letter? Did she panic at the age of twenty-six, when she thought that her father's disgusted predictions about her unmarriageability might be true? Or did she actually fall in love with Leo Chapman? Her motives are indecipherable, and perhaps they were indecipherable to her also.

In any case, almost immediately after her marriage, Carrie organized women in Mason City to canvas for a petition to introduce municipal woman suffrage in Iowa. Her persuasive talents were quickly obvious. Though there had been no local suffrage association, 85 percent of the women in her town signed the petition. Her growing involvement in the cause of women eventually radicalized her, though she kept that radicalization a secret. Her sedate demeanor in public was little more than a guise, she insisted to Mary Peck, who teased her for her moderation. "I'm for Pandemonium let loose!" Carrie declared. "You do not know me. . . . To you privately I will say that I can keep up with you in radicalism and if I should unleash myself I might outstrip you." Such correspondence hints that for Carrie (just as for radical lesbian feminists in later generations), feminism was the theory and lesbianism was the practice.

A Question of Terms

Carrie Chapman Catt's intimacy with Mollie Hay is not difficult to trace, since a large correspondence still exists, though the meaning of many statements is not always unambiguous. Sometimes the letters are provocative in their suggestion of an exuberant sexual relationship. For example, did it really mean what it seemed to mean when, on August 27, 1911, in anticipation of Mollie's birthday, which they would not be able to celebrate together that year, Carrie wrote from abroad, "I'm sorry I couldn't give you 69 kisses, one for each year"? In 1911, Mollie, who was born in 1857, would have been *fifty-four* years old.

In spite of such declarations, which seem to carry a sexual meaning, it is not easy to say definitively how Carrie conceptualized their relationship. Despite her clear attachment to Mollie and other women and what she described as her "chum" relationship with Edith Lees (the "sexually inverted" wife of Havelock Ellis, who came to the United States to present lectures in defense of the sexually "abnormal"), Carrie apparently did not *identify* herself as either bisexual or homosexual. The distinctions she made between her own relationships and those of women whom she considered sexual inverts are confused and/or confusing, to say the least.

A 1910 letter illustrates this point. During the middle period of her life with Mollie, it seems, Carrie was somewhat resentful of Mollie's possessiveness and insistent on her own independence. When Mary Peck began declaring her attraction to Carrie, not long after they met in 1909, Carrie flirted with her, which presented a threat to Mollie. In Carrie's letters to Mary, she warned of Mollie's jealousy, calling Mollie "Step," as in "wicked stepmother." When Mary suggested that she and Carrie might have some private time if they went to a European conference together, Carrie replied:

> I received that double enveloped mysterious communication from you and lest I be caught red handed, I tore it into bits as soon as read. Now, how can I reply? Step has been made a fraternal delegate from the Federation of Clubs. I do not know whether she will be able to go, but if she did not and you did, her imagination would make her very unhappy. Her affection, altho never the A.[nna] S.[haw] kind, is masculine as far as ownership goes. She thinks she owns me and she apparently never doubted the perpetuity of her title until you appeared. I have now poked so much fun at her about it that she no longer shows signs of the monster but he's there. . . . The above will make no difference about your going I'm sure altho' you did say that you would go if Step did not. Did you mean that?

This letter reveals, first of all, Carrie's conviction that her relationship with Mary required stealth so it wouldn't further fuel Mollie's jealousy. It also reveals that Carrie did not quite know what she wished to risk with Mary. Initially she appears to discourage Mary about the possibility of the trip that would permit their intimacy, but her final question suggests that she hoped that Mary would go with her.

What is even more puzzling is the meaning of the sexual categories Carrie seemed to be conceptualizing. In this letter, she characterizes Mollie's affection toward her as masculine in its possessiveness. Yet she distinguishes it from the way Anna Shaw was with women. Was she saying that Shaw was an invert and Mollie Hay was not? Since she called Mollie's behavior toward her masculine, how was it distinguished from that of the inverted Shaw? Was Carrie suggesting that Shaw was sexual in her feelings and Mollie was not? If that was so, why did Carrie think that Mollie's imagination would make her unhappy if Carrie went off with Mary Peck? What was it that Mollie would be imagining? And if there was nothing to imagine, why did Carrie feel she needed to be furtive about her relationship with Mary? If there was indeed some reason to imagine — that is, if the potential for an erotic relationship between Carrie and Mary existed — what distinction was Carrie making between the way she herself was with women and the way Anna Shaw was with women?

Or was Carrie simply being disingenuous? Was she purposely hiding her conscious lesbianism from Mary Peck because in her ambivalence, she was afraid to arouse Mary further, as Mary would be if she thought that a sexual relationship between them might be conceivable? Or was she being disingenuous because she did not trust Mary with the knowledge that she and Mollie were having a sexual relationship, just as she assumed Anna Shaw had with the women with whom she was involved?

Such questions cannot be answered with certainty. The categories we have been so sure of in recent decades, which we have made into identities, may not have been understood in the same ways in Carrie Catt's era. People in the early twentieth century may even have invented categories (or refined the older ones of "romantic friendship" and "Boston marriage") that have been lost to us in the pat classifications of homosexual, bisexual, and heterosexual, which have been current in more recent generations. But Carrie's primary relationships by the end of her thirties, which were exclusively with women, would not have passed under the rubric of "friendship" as we commonly use the term today.

Women-Lovers

There can be no question that Carrie Catt and Mollie Hay loved each other and that their love benefited the suffrage movement. But their relationship was emotionally complex, as rich, long-term relationships are likely to be. Though Carrie and Mollie spent long periods of time together from 1895 to 1905, they did not live together officially until George Catt's death. From that point to Mollie's death twenty-three years later, the two women were united not only in their private lives but in much of their working lives as well. Twice, however, Carrie made long trips around the world to promote international suffrage while Mollie stayed in New York and pursued her duties first as a suffrage leader and then as a political figure. Those separations occasioned an important cache of letters that illuminate various aspects of their relationship as it had evolved to those periods.

Their first long separation began in July 1911, when Carrie was growing restless in her domestic partnership. She and Mollie had attended an international conference in Stockholm in the spring and spent about three months together in Europe. Then Carrie, as the leader of the international woman suffrage movement, went off on a world tour on July 24, and Mollie, as president of both the New York Federation of Women's Clubs and the New York Equal Suffrage League, returned to the United States. Despite Carrie's earlier resentment of Mollie's possessiveness, her first letter, written on her first morning aboard ship, reveals the tender feelings of the past months and her anxieties about the separation. Mollie had left the pier in Madeira and taken a train back to the hotel, where she stayed for a day before her boat sailed for New York. Carrie wrote: "Mollie Dear, I was glad to see you running off to your train, for my heart ached to see you standing there. . . . I sat quietly, too tired to want to move and with the memory of my Mollie tugging at my heart strings. [The next morning] I awoke thinking of you getting off and I knew no peace until I was eating lunch, when I knew that whatever had happened to you, you were eating yours."

As is clear from Carrie's December 1910 letter to Mary Peck, the affection Carrie and Mollie had for each other was not without complication at this midpoint of their lives together, but in Carrie's letters during her world tour, she was always certain to assure Mollie that her devotion was unchanged. "I love you still, now and always," she wrote from Capetown. "Mollie Brown Eyes," she called her a few weeks later. From Calcutta, Carrie addressed Mollie as "My Beloved," though she teasingly told her, "I have a new Sweetheart. Her eyes are big, shining brown ones, her lips like a cupid's bow, her hair black as a raven." Carrie hoped to get this young Indian woman to attend an international suffrage conference in Budapest, she wrote, but she confessed also (somewhat disingenuously, in light of her correspondence with Mary Peck, yet pointedly intending to flatter), "It is a long time since I have had a Sweetheart. As usual she doesn't know about it. What worlds of Sweethearts I've had, all brown eyed, and only one ever knew it." Of course "Mollie Brown Eyes" would have taken herself for that "only one." And Carrie assured her further, "Well precious Mollie I love you very much and send you telepathic dispatches every day."

A spark of eros often comes through in Carrie's teasing of Mollie in these missives from several continents. From North Africa, she wrote, "So you have a blue dress cut low fore and aft! I suppose your gown is *blue* — baby blue décolleté. . . . Do not wear it before I return." Despite the fact that Carrie was being received by a variety of dignitaries as the leading representative of the international suffrage movement, she often expressed her longing to be with Mollie again. "I don't suppose you are any nicer than those other folks," she teased, "but I like you a lot better."

Though Mollie was no housewife in the style of Lucy Anthony, nevertheless she nurtured Carrie, protecting her from those who demanded too much of her time, sending her to bed when she was ill but tried to work anyway, devotedly waiting on her whenever

Carrie needed to be waited on, and nursing her through a difficult hysterectomy in 1910 and a variety of other illnesses and exhaustion. Carrie was something of a queen bee and often seemed to take such service as her due. But the extent of her gratitude to Mollie is suggested by her anxiety to reciprocate. Though the nurturing role apparently did not come naturally to her, she attempted to foster it for Mollie's sake. For example, when she learned while she was in Egypt that Mollie had had a gallbladder problem, her worry was palpable: "I do not like that gall bladder affair of yours. I want to know what Dr. Mayne says of it. Are you supposed to have passed any stones? Do they seriously think you may sometime need an operation? You have to give me due notice so I can get there." In the next letter Carrie implored, "Dear, precious Mollie take best care of yourself for I cannot get on without you," and she promised that soon "I shall come home and look after you."

Because they were both in the forefront of the movement and under tremendous pressure to perform, they understood each other's anxieties and torments about their public roles and were sensitive to the need for assurance. Again, the role of comforter did not come naturally to Carrie, but she pushed herself to perform it, perhaps because Mollie unfailingly performed that role for her. Carrie, who was so idolized by so many in the suffrage movement, could understand Mollie's pleasure when (much less frequently) she was appreciated for her work, and Carrie encouraged that pleasure. Her loving attempts to affirm Mollie and foster her assurance of her worth are touching.

For instance, Mollie was worried about the success of a conference she was to chair in December 1911. When she received fan letters after the conference complimenting her on her efforts, she sent one of them to Carrie. "You are excusable if your head is swelled five inches," Carrie responded. "I am sure you made a fair just intelligent prudent wise chairman and as I always think you are adorable except when I'm mad at you, I can believe you were that also." Despite Carrie's occasional flirtations with others and the faithlessness of her mockery of Mollie to Mary Peck, the letters leave no doubt that she and Mollie were the most significant beings in each other's world.

It was always Mollie that Carrie came home to. From 1905 to 1919, the two women lived together in an apartment in New York City. In 1919 they acquired Juniper Ledge, a seventeen-acre estate with a twenty-one-room house in Westchester County, one and a half hours' drive from the city. When Carrie took her second extended international suffrage tour, in 1922, Mollie moved back to an apartment in New York, which she much preferred to the country — though her real preference was to make a home with Carrie, anywhere. Sensing that Mollie was feeling at loose ends, Carrie wrote from Rome, "It is a great comfort to get letters from *home*. To be sure, *you* have no home, but you are *home* to me." Their anxious anticipation of Carrie's homecomings is revealed by a letter Carrie sent several months later, instructing Mollie, "Now don't be the first on the pier this time, be the last and we shall then not have to look at each other over a rail for three or four hours."

Once the vote was won for American women, Carrie and Mollie worked together on other political matters as well as on their relationship. Mollie helped Carrie organize the League of Women Voters, which was intended to educate the newly enfranchised women, and she became its New York City chair, a position she held until 1923. In 1926 and 1927 she also helped Catt organize the annual conferences on the cause and cure of war. During those years they succeeded in working out a compromise with regard to their abode. Carrie loved gardening and the farm life of Juniper Ledge, but Mollie did not, so Carrie agreed to sell the property, and the two women visited Arizona and California to explore the possibility of relocating together in the West. They soon realized that they had become dyed-in-the-wool easterners, and they returned to New York to buy a house in New Rochelle. Mollie died only a short while after they settled into their new home, in August 1928.

In her biography of Carrie Catt, Mary Peck could not underplay the meaning of Mollie, her rival, in Carrie's life. Mollie's sudden death of a cerebral hemorrhage at the age of seventy-one was a "bereavement" that "shook [Carrie] to the soul," Peck observed. As a result of the shock of her loss, Carrie suffered from shingles immediately afterward and a heart attack several months later. She also betrayed a depth of emotion and even sentimentality that was entirely uncharacteristic of the superbly controlled "general." As Peck wrote, Mollie had always been terrified of lightning, and throughout their years together Carrie had comforted her during storms by lighting a candle and being close to her. The night before Mollie's funeral there was a thunderstorm. Carrie told Peck that she lit a candle, as she always had for Mollie's sake, and sat at the spot in their house where Mollie had died. "I felt that if she could know, she would be glad I was there," Carrie confessed.

The women in the suffrage movement who knew of their relationship understood how devastated Carrie was by her partner's death. Lucy Anthony, who had suffered a similar loss nine years earlier, sent Carrie words of condolence that were reiterated throughout the community: "It is impossible to realize that this vibrant and vivid personality has passed. My first thought is of you and your great loss of her sympathetic companionship."

After Mollie Hay's death, Carrie eventually lived with a younger woman, Alda Wilson, a professional architect who was also one of the first women in America to receive an engineering degree. But neither Alda Wilson nor either of Carrie's two husbands was her most important love. Through her tomb, Carrie said unequivocally, if not in complete detail, who had been the major person in her life: when she died, nineteen years after Mollie Hay, she was buried in their double plot in Woodlawn Cemetery, under the marker she had ordered to cover them both, which she had had inscribed, "Here lie two friends, for thirty-eight years united in service to a great cause."

❧ 5 ❧

TWO STEPS FORWARD...

There is a gay woman named Polly
Who has a firm pal yclept Molly;
They both crack their bones,
Yet say without moans,
"This staying in bed is *so* jolly."

— Virginia Bellamy, ca. 1962

The Long Sleep of the Postsuffrage Years

AFTER ALL THE WORK that culminated in the vote, most women in America seemed to have no more appetite for a continued struggle, and those few who did were discouraged at almost every turn. It was as though a conspiracy triggered by panic emerged in the 1920s: pundits, the media, and especially the medical profession, in which mental health workers were proliferating, seemed to be acting in concert to convince women that they should not be tricked into thinking that now they were full citizens, they also wanted full freedom and independence. Women who demanded such things in the nineteenth century had been called unsexed. Now a more virulent connection was made between those who wanted still more and normal women.

Psychologists and psychoanalysts, the post–World War I high priests of America, suddenly worried that suffrage and other changes induced by women's rights, such as the possibility of college study and careers, had created women with dangerously strong, "masculine" personalities. As Dr. Phyllis Blanchard observed in a popular 1929 book, "masculinized" women often found

satisfaction in guiding and protecting weaker women, which resulted in both the stronger and the weaker becoming "unable to
adjust to the more natural relationship" of heterosexuality. (As
Blanchard's title, Dr., indicates, she herself, of course, enjoyed
the hard-won privileges of higher education and a profession that
an army of "masculinized" women had procured for American females.)

Sexologists' theories on inversion, which had earlier been con-
fined to the medical journals, were now everywhere, promulgated
especially by the high priests, who spread the word of their god,
Sigmund Freud. Popular writers too became Freudians. Floyd Dell,
for example, a prolific author of the 1920s and 1930s, paid direct
homage to Freudian theory when he opined that an important
indicator of a child's approach to maturity was "becoming more
fully heterosexual" and that society would only emerge from its
"welter of neuroticism" by accepting "the full and passionate love
of the other sex as the normal goal of youth." Active heterosexuality
became a sine qua non of "mental hygiene," which meant that
women such as Susan B. Anthony, Frances Willard, Anna Howard
Shaw — in fact, most heroes of the suffrage cause — had been
neither mature nor hygienic. Beginning in the 1920s, such women
plummeted from being heroes to being negative role models.

Thus the old suffrage leaders were thrown into disrepute as
lesbians, in effect. The women's rights movement became virtually
rudderless and was stalled for decades; the hard-won vote made
almost no difference in the progress of women, either individually
or as a class. Politicians, who initially feared the potential of a
"woman's vote," soon understood that there would be no such
thing. Even by the 1940s, more than two decades after they were
enfranchised, women were not an autonomous voting force, as a
survey of married female voters indicated: only one in twenty-two
voted differently from her husband. Politicians were therefore no
more constrained to be concerned with women's rights than they
had been before women were able to vote. Like many other suffrage
women who had given years of their lives to the cause, Alice Stone
Blackwell came to feel by 1929 that her efforts had been in vain.
Her bitterness toward the heterosexual women whom nonhetero-

sexuals like herself had worked to enfranchise spilled out in a letter to Carrie Catt, in which she wrote that women were "fools because God made them to match the men."

The fight for women's rights and independence — "feminism," as it was now called — became passé for almost a half-century after women got the vote. In 1920, after the passage of the Nineteenth Amendment, Catt organized the League of Women Voters in order to equip women "for intelligent participation in politics and government." At the National American Woman Suffrage Association victory convention, which became an organizing meeting for the League of Women Voters, she exhorted her audience not to appeal to the two political parties for what they wanted but rather "to get on the inside and help yourself to the things you want." Ironically, by the 1940s the league's leadership explicitly denied any particular concern with women and was avowedly opposed to "feminism" (which was what had brought Catt into the suffrage movement in the first place).

Two prevalent caricatures of feminism were now current: first, that feminism tried to make women into men, and second, that feminism pitted women against men in a vicious sex antagonism. Both caricatures referred to lesbians in thinly veiled terms. Therefore, how could a woman who did not want to be considered morbid, masculine, a perpetrator of antagonism — that is, a lesbian — identify herself with a struggle for women's rights? With the exception of the brief respite of World War II, when, as in the previous war, womanpower was sorely needed and women were thus encouraged to be strong and independent (as only "masculine" lesbians supposedly were in other eras), feminism continued on its downhill slide through the 1950s. By 1956, a writer for *Life* magazine could describe feminism as only a dim memory in American history, "as quaint as linen dusters and high-button shoes."

A Few "Escaped Nuns"

It was in good part a socially inculcated fear of gender-inappropriate behavior that kept women from significant participation in the political arena, just as that same fear had long prevented many women from demanding the vote in the nineteenth century. In 1920, Carrie Catt advised women "to get on the inside" of politics. After the herculean efforts of the battles she led, with millions of female troops behind her, perhaps she could not have envisioned that most of the troops would retreat to the safety of more traditional gender behavior. Nor could she have envisioned that traditional gender behavior would be given fresh and powerful meaning as a sign of mental health.

With only masculine models of how to "do" politics, heterosexual women, who had reason to be concerned about losing their femininity, had little desire to take Catt's advice. It is not surprising that the few women who served in the House of Representatives in the 1920s for the most part were not career politicians but were merely completing the terms of their deceased husbands, as were the few who served as governors in the 1920s and 1930s. After more than a decade of universal woman suffrage in America, there were barely 150 women in state legislatures throughout the country.

Those women who did attempt to get on the inside of politics through their own merits were often unmarried and living with female partners. Like their counterparts in the nineteenth century, they felt less personally threatened by the idea that their pursuits might masculinize them than heterosexual women did. Also, without the duties of wives and mothers, they could afford the vast expenditure of time and energy that political careers required. They frequently tried to bring to politics their deep feminist convictions about the importance of the advancement of women. They also continued to promote essentialist notions about how women's "superior" moral values would improve politics and the society over which politicians had jurisdiction — much as their nineteenth-century predecessors, such as Frances Willard and Anna Shaw, had. But clearly most female voters were not interested in supporting their candidacy.

For example, Anne Martin, a firebrand who was president of the Nevada Equal Franchise Society and who led Nevada to woman suffrage in 1914, ran for the U.S. Senate on an independent ticket

Susan B. Anthony *(left)* and Emily Gross: "I shall go to Chicago to visit my new lover . . . so with my new hope and new life."
(Sophia Smith Collection, Smith College)

Anna Howard Shaw *(right)* and Lucy Anthony at home: "My dear, dear Balance."
(Schlesinger Library, Radcliffe College)

Carrie Chapman Catt, president of the National American Woman Suffrage Association, celebrating the passage of the Nineteenth Amendment.
(Mary Peck, *Carrie Chapman Catt*)

Catt (*left*) and Mollie Hay casting ballots in their first election, in 1918: "Do you know who loves you best in all the world . . . Mollie Brown Eyes[?]"
(Mary Peck, *Carrie Chapman Catt*)

Jane Addams, social activist and winner of the Nobel Prize for Peace.

(Jane Addams Collection, Swarthmore College Peace Collection)

Addams and Mary Rozet Smith in their later years. At Smith's death, Addams wrote, "I suppose I could have willed my heart to stop beating, but the thought of what she had been to me for so long kept me from being cowardly."

(Jane Addams Collection, Swarthmore College Peace Collection)

Molly Dewson (*right*), of the "Ladies' Brain Trust," and her life partner, Polly Porter. (Virginia Bourne)

Social activists Frances Kellor and Mary Dreier: "I'd give most anything to just see and feel you for a little while." (Schlesinger Library, Radcliffe College)

Frances Witherspoon and Tracy Mygatt, social activists: "We are a model for our married friends." (Mygatt and Witherspoon Papers, Swarthmore College Peace Collection)

Two views of Mildred Scott Olmsted, peace and freedom activist. "You should have been a man, Scottie, and we should have married and how happy our lives together would have been," Ruth Mellor wrote. (Olmsted Papers, Swarthmore College Peace Collection)

Prison reformer Miriam Van Waters and her lover, socialite Geraldine Thompson: "One can have no personal 'life' in this battle, so I have destroyed many letters of our 22 years." (Boston Public Library)

The Resolutes —
the 1876 Vassar
College baseball
club.
(Special Collections,
Vassar College
Libraries)

M. Carey Thomas
(*left*) and Mamie
Gwinn: "Shimmer
love. Pink — sweet
Shimmer — my
Shimmer."
(Bryn Mawr College)

(*Top left*): Mary Woolley, president of Mount Holyoke College, 1901–1937.
(Mount Holyoke College Archives)

(*Top right*): Jeannette Marks, Mount Holyoke professor of English literature and theater arts.
(Mount Holyoke College Archives)

(*Left*): Woolley and Marks: "I love you so, I love you so, sings itself over and over again in my heart."
(Mount Holyoke College Archives)

in both 1918 and 1920. She hoped that her candidacy would provide women with ways to be political in their own right, both as voters and as party workers. She promoted causes that were meant to improve the lot of women and children — which she had thought was a primary justification for women's enfranchisement — as well as causes that would protect farmers and natural resources in Nevada. Her lover, Dr. Margaret Long, helped manage her election bid and accompanied her as she sought votes across the state. They ran an efficient campaign, but Nevada women did not have much more interest in a female senator than Nevada men did; in the state where she was largely responsible for the enfranchisement of women, Martin received only about 20 percent of the vote. Similarly, Ohio Supreme Court judge Florence Allen ran for the U.S. Senate in 1926, assisted in her tireless campaigning by her life partner, Susan Rebhan. But though Allen had been elected to the state supreme court in 1922 by a wide margin, she too lost her Senate bid. Voters simply could not envision a woman in such a nationally powerful body.

Yet a few women continued to run for public office in the years just after women got the vote. Marion Dickerman, for example, made a bid for the New York State Assembly in 1919, in the election just after New York women were enfranchised. Dickerman ran against a reactionary assembly speaker, Thaddeus Sweet, who had opposed all the social justice legislation supported by early women's political groups such as the Women's Joint Legislative Committee (founded by an unmarried bisexual, Mary Dreier). Dickerman, whose life partner was Nancy Cook, was ridiculed by Sweet supporters as an "escaped nun" — an obvious mockery of her lack of heterosexual credentials. She lost the election, receiving a little over 30 percent of the vote.

Even though women had little luck in elected office, some did manage to achieve a modicum of political power in the early years. After the suffrage victory in New York, Carrie Catt's life partner, Mollie Hay, committed her remaining years to trying to make a place for women in politics. She first became active in the New York Republican Party. As a result of her prominent role in the successful 1917 Empire State Campaign, it was thought that she had influence over large numbers of female voters in New York (and politicians at that time still feared the potential of women voting as a block), so she was able to rise to some prominence within the party. The *New York World* was glowing in its portrayal of Hay at the New York Republican Convention of 1918, at which she was the first woman chair of the platform committee:

> The reading of the platform [which included the suffrage amendment] by Miss Hay was worth the experiment of bowing to a woman boss. Five-feet-four tall, of substantial proportions, white hair and wearing a flannel skirt and a white silk waist, the first woman chairman of a party Resolutions Committee in this state conducted herself like a veteran. In the first place, she read the long instrument of the party faith so that it was not an instrument of torture, which in itself was a novelty.

Despite — or rather, precisely because of — her butchness, Hay slipped easily into leadership positions. Her situation illustrates a troubling contradiction: while unsexed women often continued to be feared and mocked, as in Thaddeus Sweet's sour caricature of the "escaped nun," nevertheless a woman of conventional femininity could not and would not strive in the political arena. Indeed, the more a woman could approximate the masculine style of "the politician," the less jarring her presence in politics would seem. Hay, with her "substantial proportions" — a "boss," a "veteran" — was credible, as a more feminine woman would not be.

Predictably, considering Mollie Hay's long history in the suffrage movement, one of her primary interests within the Republican Party was women's causes. It was largely as a result of her efforts that the New York Republican Party endorsed the constitutional amendment for woman suffrage. In 1918 she took a seat on the Republican Women's National Executive Committee, and she became its chair the following year. From that position of power, at the 1920 Republican Convention she urged that the size of the Republican National Committee be doubled so that women could be given full recognition in all party councils. Her feminism did not hurt her advancement at this early date. She even rose to vice chairperson of the state party. Until her death, in 1928, she maintained an active role in politics, always serving women's interests. For instance, she chaired a group that was responsible for defeating James Wadsworth, a senator who had been an unregenerate foe to woman suffrage.

In the postsuffrage decades, lesbians such as Mollie Hay were much freer than heterosexual women to forge ahead and better able to explore the political and professional provinces that had belonged exclusively to men. And yet . . . if being a lesbian meant that one was, according to the current wisdom, immature and neurotic, how many women would want to be one? Women who suspected that tendency in themselves in the years after the suffrage victory often ran to psychiatrists (if they could afford to) rather than running for public office.

The Ladies' Brain Trust

Though not many women were winning elections in the decades after the passage of the Nineteenth Amendment, women did somewhat better in receiving appointments to various high political offices. Much of their success was due to Eleanor Roosevelt and/or the lesbian circle around her. The evidence of Roosevelt's lesbian friendships and relationships is abundant and has already been well documented by biographers, who have supported their conclusions with Roosevelt's letters, such as those she wrote to the journalist Lorena Hickok: "Funny, everything I do my thoughts fly to you. Never are you out of my heart & just one week from now I'll be holding you," and "Oh! dear one, it is all the little things, tones in your voice, the feel of your hair, gestures, these are the things I think about & long for."

Blanche Wiesen Cook's major study of Eleanor Roosevelt depicts the various influences on her of lesbians, beginning with Marie Souvestre, Eleanor's beloved teacher when she was a young girl. At a crucial period in Eleanor's life, Mlle. Souvestre "introduced an alternative [read "lesbian"] way of being — assertive, independent, and bold." Later in her life, Eleanor recalled, "Whatever I have become since [my school years] had its seeds in those three years of contact" with Souvestre.

The lesbians with whom Eleanor Roosevelt had relationships as an adult were generally successful professional women concerned with social reform, for which they had long worked through lesbian-dominated settlement houses and groups such as the Women's Trade Union League. Eleanor met many of these women in 1920 in a Greenwich Village community of postsuffrage feminist activists. They included Elizabeth Read, a lawyer, and her life partner, the journalist Esther Lape, as well as Nancy Cook, an officer in the Democratic Party's Women's Division, and her life partner, the would-be assemblywoman Marion Dickerman. These women helped restore Eleanor's sense of ambition, which she had lost early in her marriage to FDR. Through a newfound confidence and the political interests that the women stimulated in her, she eventually became America's first activist first lady. Perhaps her admiration for the women in this circle also made it possible for her to be receptive to a lesbian relationship with Lorena Hickok when they met a few years later.

Elizabeth Read helped Eleanor in her earliest political involvement. Just before meeting Read, Eleanor was persuaded to direct the national legislation committee of the League of Women Voters, but she felt that she was not sufficiently informed to do the job. Therefore, she asked for and was given assistance by Read, who, with her skills as a lawyer, coached the future first lady about congressional matters of interest to the league. Their lifelong friendship began. According to Hickok, who must have gotten the word from Eleanor Roosevelt herself, Read and Lape were "the first independent professional women [Eleanor] had ever known, and she was as awed as she was fascinated by them."

Through Elizabeth Read, Eleanor became involved with a large, exciting, and politically committed lesbian circle of friends. The home of Read and Lape was for many years, even after FDR became president, Eleanor's "sanctuary, a hiding house from the press and the rituals of First Ladyhood." It was through Read and Lape that Eleanor met Marion Dickerman and Nancy Cook. Clarke Chambers observes in *Seedtime of Reform* that the involvement of Dickerman and Cook in reform and liberal politics had an especially "profound influence on the political education of Eleanor Roosevelt," because these women brought her into the Women's Trade Union League, which molded her sympathies with the working class. Through the WTUL, Eleanor also became lifelong friends with Mary Dreier, who was a WTUL leader and who introduced her to still other politically aware lesbians.

According to Lorena Hickok, Eleanor frequently suggested to FDR the appointment of women to political offices and thus "should receive a large share of credit for the number of women given important positions in her husband's administration." Eleanor Roosevelt was directly and indirectly responsible for numerous political firsts for women. Because of her, for example, Mary McLeod Bethune became a top official representing African-American youth in the National Youth Administration, a federal department established during the Depression to help young people find employment. As Bethune's biographer, Elaine Smith, observes, Bethune occupied the first federal position created for an African-American woman in the history of the country. Eleanor Roosevelt also helped Bethune become effective in that post by inviting her to social functions at the White House, contacting government officials on her behalf, and arranging for her to see FDR whenever Bethune felt that such a meeting would help her endeavors.

Eleanor Roosevelt was also responsible for bringing to Washington what the columnist Drew Pearson dubbed in 1938 a powerful "Ladies' Brain Trust." This trust was made up of dynamic women (many of them members of her lesbian circle of friends) who brought unprecedented female political leadership to the Democratic Party. Like Bethune, they were given direct access to FDR by Eleanor Roosevelt. As Molly Dewson, the director of the Women's Division of the Democratic National Committee, later recalled, when she needed FDR's help on a matter, Eleanor "gave me the opportunity to sit by the President at dinner and the *matter* was settled before we finished our soup."

Molly Dewson was the virtual head of the Ladies' Brain Trust. She had gained her position through the intercessions of Eleanor Roosevelt, who had become acquainted with her when Dewson and Polly Porter resided across the hall from Nancy Cook and Marion Dickerman in a Greenwich Village cooperative made up of social feminists who lived mostly in lesbian couples. In her role as director of the Women's Division, Dewson eventually controlled 109,000 female workers for the party throughout America. During the Depression, collaborating with Nancy Cook and Caroline O'Day (who lived with Frances Perkins, the first American woman to hold a cabinet-level position), Dewson managed to build the Women's Division into "one of the most effective components of the newly revitalized Democratic Party, winning places for women in politics and government on an unprecedented scale . . . breakthroughs [which] gave women their own New Deal." Though her rough-hewn style was nothing like that of the elegant Carrie Catt, their organizational brilliance was similar. She too was superb at cultivating personal contacts and leading a devoted army of women, who spread the crucial message of the New Deal all over the country.

The Ladies' Brain Trust was responsible for some of the most innovative aspects of FDR's New Deal. Its members brought the values they had developed earlier in the century through social action organizations such as the settlement house movement, the National Consumers' League, and the Women's Trade Union League into the federal arena. Dewson's progressive politics had been influenced especially by the ideals of groups to which she had belonged twenty years earlier; through her work in those organizations, she came to believe that women had a particular sensitivity to vitally needed reform and that it was therefore essential to bring them into the administration.

Dewson had been involved with issues that were to become of central importance in New Deal philosophy. For example, while representing the National Consumers' League, an organization that encouraged consumers to put pressure on manufacturers to treat workers fairly, she had helped win the first minimum wage law for female workers, in 1912. She had also become interested in the concept of "social insurance," that is, social security. When FDR was still governor of New York, Dewson presented her blueprints on social security to her friends Eleanor Roosevelt and Frances Perkins. In 1935, FDR, as president, appointed Dewson to his Commission on Economic Security, where she helped devise the Social Security Act, which looked very much like the National Consumers' League's early ideas on social insurance. In 1937 the president invited her to serve on the Social Security Board, where she was instrumental in getting the federal government involved in unemployment insurance programs as well as old age insurance.

With Eleanor's help, Dewson also conducted in the Democratic Party a battle similar to the one that Mollie Hay had waged in the Republican Party fifteen years earlier — and she succeeded. She had been disgusted with the various ladies' auxiliaries she had encountered in party politics, and was convinced that women could be competent leaders if they were given the opportunity to take significant responsibility in the party organization. She thus pushed for state party rulings that would give women equal representation with men on party committees and in leadership positions at all levels, from precinct to national. She achieved a major victory at the 1936 Democratic Convention through a stunningly creative resolution which mandated that alternates to the Platform Committee must be of the opposite sex to the regular delegates. Since delegates often missed committee meetings, women were finally given a chance at significant representation, albeit by the back door. The *New York Times* understood the import of Dewson's ploy, reporting that "the biggest coup in years so far as women in politics are concerned materialized at the Democratic Convention this afternoon as softly and smoothly as a Summer Zephyr."

From the perspective of our day, after decades of virulent homophobia, it is perhaps difficult to imagine such successful lesbian leadership in an earlier generation. Did FDR really understand that Dewson and many of the other women with whom Eleanor surrounded herself were lesbians? Whether he did or not, he seemed fond of most of them, admired many of them for their intellectual strength, and was delighted with their work for the party. Did they actively hide their lesbian identity, or did they assume that as long as it was not articulated — as long as no one used the "l" word — heterosexuals would not suspect? Dewson had a foghorn voice and wore tweedy tailored suits, sensible shoes, and no makeup. Yet much like Frances Perkins, who once said that "the way [for women] to get things done" in political circles was to "so behave, so dress and comport yourself that you remind [male politicians] subconsciously of their mothers," Dewson may have prided herself on a certain ability to deceive. She may have been convinced that the men with whom she worked saw her as motherly (that is, *not* sexual) and were blind to her butch demeanor. She and Polly called themselves the Porter-Dewsons and described themselves as partners. Did she assume that only lesbians would understand that her relationship with Polly Porter, with whom she lived for fifty-two years, was a marriage?

Porter, a wealthy woman who was ten years younger than Dewson, was far more feminine than she was. As Dewson's recent biographer, Susan Ware, points out, in many ways their relationship "mirrored a conventional heterosexual marriage." Molly handled the money and made the financial decisions, did the heavy work around the house, and puttered with the automobiles. Polly managed the daily affairs of the household and added "'feminine' touches to their lives." But role divisions did not obviate their both being active suffragists and both being chosen as Massachusetts delegates to the NAWSA convention in 1915. During the Great War they went together to France to serve as social workers for the Red Cross. The letters they wrote to each other during their brief separations indicate their mutual reliance and devotion, as in a 1917 letter in which Polly addresses Molly by her pet name, "Puisye," from the French *puissante,* powerful (and "pussy"?): "Little danger that the Puisye will become unnecessary to me — I should be like a ship without sails and a pilot without a north star were she not a part of my life."

The leading women in New Deal politics were generally part of

Dewson and Porter's circle of friends. Most of them had met earlier in their work for Progressive-era causes and the suffrage movement and remained close through the years. They helped one another to power. Perhaps Dewson's greatest coup in promoting women's prominence in politics was her victory in having her old friend Frances Perkins appointed to Roosevelt's cabinet as secretary of labor. Dewson and Perkins met in 1922, when Perkins served on the Industrial Commission of New York and Dewson represented the National Consumers' League on a labor issue. Dewson had no wish for a cabinet position herself, because it would have taken too much time away from her domestic life with Polly, but she did hope to see a woman in FDR's cabinet. Frances Perkins was her first choice, because she knew that Perkins would bring to her office all the "woman's" values of reform that Dewson thought important. As Susan Ware states, "The two women understood each other."

As secretary of labor, Perkins in her turn brought talented women to Washington to work with her in the Labor Department, and she was deeply committed to expanding women's political representation. She had wanted the cabinet post so that she could carry out her progressive ideals, but also, as she claimed, so that she could help other women to high office: "The overwhelming argument . . . which made me do it in the end . . . was the realization that the door might not be opened to a woman again for a long, long time, and that I had a kind of duty to other women to walk in and sit down on the chair that was offered and so establish the right of others long hence and far-distant in geography to sit in the high seats."

Perkins was apparently "family." She married in 1913 but seldom lived with her husband (who suffered from chronic depression and was hospitalized during many years of their marriage). She was a private person throughout her life, and she carefully expurgated a great deal of evidence of her personal relationships from the papers she left behind. Nevertheless, she is known to have had long-term intimacies with two women, first with Mary Harriman Rumsey, an official in the National Recovery Administration, and after Rumsey's death in 1934 with Caroline O'Day.

Perkins, like Dewson, brought her progressive values into the

Roosevelt administration. She too had had a formative background in the National Consumers' League, and again like Dewson and Eleanor Roosevelt, she had done settlement house work early in her career. These women all spoke the same language of reform. Together with Dewson, Perkins played a major role in forging the Social Security Act. She drafted legislation for the Civilian Conservation Corps Act and the Fair Labor Standards Act. She encouraged unionization and collective bargaining. Through her, the goals of women-led social reform groups of the early century were incorporated into Labor Department policy. Molly Dewson had hoped that if she could get FDR to appoint a woman to his cabinet, it would set a precedent that would be followed in the future and would provide a role model that would make a permanent difference in how American women viewed themselves with regard to political participation. But there was no rush by subsequent presidents to appoint women to cabinet-level positions, despite Perkins's very creditable service as secretary of labor for twelve years, from 1933 to 1945.

That disappointment notwithstanding, Dewson was responsible for many high-level appointments of women: Nellie Tayloe Ross as director of the mint, Florence Allen as a judge on the circuit court of appeals (the highest position a woman had ever attained in the federal judiciary), Marion Glass Banister as assistant treasurer of the United States, Ruth Bryan Owen as minister to Denmark (the first woman to represent the United States abroad). Because of Dewson, women were afforded greater respect in the Democratic Party through two elections. Indeed, she had unprecedented successes in bringing women into the political arena at *all* levels, from the cabinet to a record-breaking number of delegates and platform committee members to the 1936 Democratic Convention. However, when she retired from the Roosevelt administration in 1938, at the age of sixty-four — she left Washington and went to live on a farm that she and Polly had purchased — no other powerful woman emerged who could or would push as hard for high-level political appointments for other women.

In 1941, when the United States entered World War II, gender issues seemed less vital, as both men and women had to contribute to the war effort. After the war, with Dewson no longer in a position to coerce politicians to be sensitive to women's issues, the subject of women's concerns became passé, as both Democrats and Republicans encouraged women to return to the pre-Dewson status quo.

A Lone Flickering Flame: The National Woman's Party

The militants of the suffrage movement who had been such a source of contention to Anna Shaw and Carrie Catt continued to congregate around Alice Paul and Lucy Burns when the Congressional Union became the National Woman's Party (NWP) in 1916. The NWP never placed confidence in major party politics, but the group's chief goal during the post-enfranchisement years was the passage of an Equal Rights Amendment, which it first managed to get introduced into Congress in 1923: "Men and women shall have equal rights throughout the United States and every place subject to its jurisdiction." For decades the NWP was a lone voice struggling for absolute equality for women, as it attempted every year to reintroduce the amendment into Congress.

The NWP was almost the only game in town for committed feminists until the reemergence of the feminist movement in the 1960s. Most members of the NWP were leftovers from the years of the suffrage campaigns. Their number was tiny and their cause was out of fashion. They themselves were out of fashion. When American women were supposed to be happy housewives, 76 percent of NWP members were professionally employed. Forty-one percent of them had never been married, and of those who had been married, approximately 25 percent were widowed or divorced. About one third of the never-married women lived with other women.

As it had been from the start, in the nineteenth-century women's rights movement, there continued to be good reason for the fact that even when the flame of feminism was barely flickering, the leadership came from unmarried women, many of whom lived together. Rather than distracting from their feminism, their personal lives enabled and encouraged it. Even NWP women who did not have lesbian relationships, such as Rose Powell, recognized how detrimental heterosexual marriage could be to the pursuit of women's rights in the first half of the twentieth century. Powell devoted much of her life to getting national recognition for the contributions of Susan B. Anthony. It was she, for example, who first proposed that Anthony's birthday be celebrated as a national holiday. Having been separated from her husband after a brief marriage, Powell confided to her diary thirty years later, "If my marriage had been a happy one, I might today have a home and security, but I am convinced that I never could have been able to make the contributions I have to the woman movement, to which so much of my life has been dedicated."

Many of the NWP leaders lived with other women who were also active in feminist politics, including Mabel Vernon and Consuelo Reyes, Jeannette Marks and Mary Woolley, and Alma Lutz (the mid-century biographer of Susan B. Anthony and Elizabeth Cady Stanton) and Lutz's partner of forty-one years, the librarian Marguerite Smith. Alice Paul's personal correspondence has been well culled by some hand, so that little about her private life is known directly from her, but rumors of her lesbianism abounded (and continue to abound). Doris Stevens, a militant feminist who became a fanatical red-baiter during the homophobic McCarthy era and quit the National Woman's Party, confided to her diary that she had heard tales of the "weird goings-on" at party headquarters, which suggested that Alice Paul was "a devotee of Lesbos." Stevens, who knew well that feminism was associated with lesbianism by the 1940s, was defensive in the reactionary company she kept at that time. She even wrote to Westbrook Pegler, the right-wing columnist, whom she had befriended, thanking him "for knowing I'm not a queerie," despite her feminist history.

The importance of the National Woman's Party lies not in its concrete successes but rather in its having kept the feminist flame burning, however feebly, even at the height of the feminine mystique. Although the NWP could not expand its base of support during the dry years, it created an environment where the survivors of the early battles could pursue their feminist goals, often in couples. The social theorist Doug McAdam has pointed out that movements take their trajectory from existing networks rather than starting from scratch with individuals who just happen to run into each other and then begin to build a movement. The National Woman's Party was just such an existing network and can be credited with preserving many of the ideas of the first women's rights movement. Its members handed down the base on which the second movement could begin to build in the 1960s, and that led eventually, in the 1980s, to significant efforts by women to claim a voice in American politics.

PART II

HOW AMERICA GOT A
SOCIAL CONSCIENCE

❧ 6 ❧

MOTHER-HEARTS /
LESBIAN-HEARTS

We can hardly think of Mary Grew at all without thinking of her friends Sarah Pugh and Margaret Burleigh,
especially the latter, devoted to her with that affection
passing the love of men which many of the anti-slavery
women manifested toward each other; in the affection of
Caroline Putnam for Sallie Holley finding one of its love-
liest illustrations.

— John White Chadwick, 1899

NINETEENTH-CENTURY LEADERS such as Frances Willard and
Anna Howard Shaw who hoped to wangle a place for women outside the home developed a compelling discourse in support of their
position. Women's distinctly feminine talents, they insisted, were
vital to cure the ills of a troubled society. In a speech entitled "The
Great Defect in Our Government," for example, Shaw proclaimed
that America desperately needed what men had been unable to
achieve: to figure out "how shall we make our streets clean; how
shall we banish contagious and preventable diseases . . . how shall
little children's lives be spared from avaricious business which con-
taminates food and drink." The answers, she said, lay in women's
participation in government.

Women had the best ability to minister to public needs because,
Shaw argued in another speech, the "mother-heart" was instinctive
to them. The mother-heart had nothing to do with biological motherhood, she said, since all true women, whether spinsters or wives
and mothers, possessed it. Because of her mother-heart, a woman
"finding any wrong, any weakness, any pain, any sorrow, anywhere

in the world, reaches out her hand to right the wrong, to heal the pain, to comfort the suffering." That being so, Shaw handily concluded, government needed women to vote and to work where their mother-heart would benefit society.

In the nineteenth century, volunteer work in which women could supposedly express their mother-heart became for many the one guilt-free method of self-development in which they could indulge. By the early twentieth century, such work actually gave a new generation of women paying jobs as social workers and public policy experts in the government agencies that were set up — in good part in response to their agitation — to address the problems of municipal housekeeping. In effect, a variety of new professions for women were established from the concept that women, because of their mother-hearts, were suited much more than men to "housekeeping on a large scale."

Such housekeeping endeavors not only provided useful occupations for women; they were also instrumental in the development of America's social conscience. In the latter part of the nineteenth century, they consisted, for example, of teaching former slaves to read and write, organizing working women to demand better conditions, and establishing settlements to tend to the various needs of the urban poor. These early efforts were often led and fueled by unmarried women, many of whom lived as lesbian couples. Although large numbers of heterosexual women also participated in such work, what was true of the suffrage battle was true here: a woman without conventional domestic responsibilities had more time and energy to devote to causes — and if she lived with another woman who shared her interests and inclinations (or who would take care of their shared home while she pursued social housekeeping), the time and energy available for such work were expanded.

Cleaning Up the Slavery Mess: Sallie Holley, Caroline Putnam, and Rebecca Primus

Abolition was one of the earliest nineteenth-century mother-heart pursuits in which female couples worked together, trying to right

the wrong of slavery. Once slavery was abolished, large-scale social housekeeping was required in a new area: the freedmen and
women had to learn to read and write (which they had often been
forbidden to do under slavery) and claim their citizenship. Female
couples often undertook such jobs together. Sallie Holley and
Caroline Putnam, who met as students at Oberlin College in 1848,
first became an antislavery team, much like Mary Grew and Margaret Burleigh, and then, after the Civil War, turned their efforts to
educating the former slaves.

There is no question that Holley and Putnam were sincerely
committed to their work. As Holley wrote, their "conscience and
heart would not be satisfied with doing nothing for the noble
cause." However, that work also provided them with an exciting,
legitimate means of grasping the personal freedom that was otherwise denied women in their day. It allowed them to travel in each
other's company rather than settling down with a husband, and it
provided an escape from the drudgery and confines of mere domesticity. Both Holley and Putnam had observed the limited lives their
mothers and other female relatives led, and they had both decided
they wanted no part of it. Holley claimed that when she was a
young woman, she received a number of marriage proposals but
turned them all down. Instead of having a conventional marriage,
she and Caroline Putnam created a virtual marriage, managing also
to forge careers as reformers at a time when there was almost no
such thing as a career for a woman. As Katherine Herbig, their
modern biographer, has observed, in the mid- and late nineteenth
century they "fashioned a full, satisfying life for themselves as a
working couple."

Holley and Putnam usually traveled together on the abolitionist
lecture circuit, often in company with other leading speakers, such
as the former slave Sojourner Truth. But when work separated
them, in their letters they lamented their agony over being away
from each other. An 1861 note, for example, was weighted with
Sallie Holley's separation anxieties. "Oh, my heart yearns toward
you this morning," she wrote to Caroline Putnam, "and the heavi-
est disappointment of my life would fall if *you* should die. Again and
again I thank you for all your love to me. . . . How I should love to

put my arms around your neck and kiss you." Sallie's letters constantly declared that whether or not Caroline was with her, she felt sustained by their relationship. Caroline cheered her on during these separations, addressing her as "Dear Loving Heart" and "My Best Angel" and assuring her that she too longed for "the old delight of working, sleeping, and talking by your side."

Though Holley was more famous as an abolitionist, in the years after the Civil War it was Putnam who took the reins. While Holley was still on the lecture circuit, trying to raise money in the North to help the freed people in the South, Putnam filled her carpetbag with dozens of used slates, primers, alphabet cards, and penmanship cards and headed to Lottsburg, Virginia, in order to teach the new citizens to read and write. Though the Freedmen's Bureau had made some effort to help establish black schools in the South, it had begun disassociating itself from the work by the time Putnam arrived, and it pulled out entirely in 1871. Many of the schools were discontinued, but Putnam felt encouraged to hold fast when she succeeded in convincing Holley in 1869 to join her in her efforts to educate the former slaves. Their school — which Putnam insisted on calling the Holley School in honor of her life partner — flourished. It soon became not just a school but in effect the first settlement house in America.

Putnam and Holley built a compound near the school and settled in, ignoring recurrent threats from their white neighbors. Like Jane Addams, the founder of the most famous settlement house a generation later, they believed that they must try not only to give to the black community but to become a part of it. Thus they were present at births, baked cakes for weddings, mourned misfortunes, served as scribes, and acted as personal friends.

Though ladies of the middle class, they consistently belied a gentility that was more apparent than real by a daring that was indispensable to their successes. For example, though as women they could not vote, they were determined to protect the new voting rights of black men, which were being challenged by unreasonable literacy tests, poll taxes, and intimidation. Defying their white neighbors, Holley and Putnam organized the freedmen to exercise their franchise, accompanying them to the polls when necessary, acting as witnesses, and encouraging them to ignore the former masters' warnings against voting for the hated Republican Party, which had been responsible for emancipation. While the Holley School's impact may have remained local for the forty-nine years of its existence, its concept was much larger, anticipating the work of northern civil rights activists who went south in the 1960s.

Idealistic young women who had just been to college and unmarried middle-aged women who had spent years teaching in northern schools were attracted to Holley and Putnam's work. They went to join them, to teach in the Holley School, and to learn what they could from the experience. As in most of the American settlement houses later in the century, the volunteers at the Holley School were primarily female. Their work at the school allowed them to explore a world beyond the limitations of private domesticity at a time when women were not supposed to have daring adventures on their own. Yet as bold as their adventures were, such work, because it could be seen as social housekeeping, was somehow within the realm of what was permissible for nineteenth-century women to undertake. Many who went to teach for a few months stayed for years, and they formed a women's community with Caroline Putnam and Sallie Holley.

African-American women from the North also went south during the years after the Civil War to help the newly freed slaves. For instance, under the auspices of the Freedman's Relief Association, Sojourner Truth counseled ex-slaves on how to maneuver in liberty. African-American women, like white women, were more likely to be able to undertake such work, which required them to uproot themselves from their homes, if they had no marital encumbrances. Rebecca Primus, for example, an African-American woman from Connecticut, went to Royal Oak, Maryland, right after the Civil War in order to establish a school for former slaves. She eventually married, but not until 1872, two years after the death of her female lover, Addie Brown.

Approximately 150 letters that Addie wrote to Rebecca between 1859 and 1868 have survived. Karen Hansen, who recently discovered the letters, characterizes the intimate contacts between the two women as "bosom sex," a reference to a letter in which Addie, working as a cook in a boarding school, admitted that she slept in a bed with a white girl but assured Rebecca, "My night dress *was* butten up so she could not get to my bosom." During their separations, each imagined that "I am near the[e], breathing the same air with your arm gently drawn around me, my head reclining on your noble breast in confidence and love." In several letters Addie complained of their separation and expressed her longing: "How I did miss you last night. I did not have anyone to hug me up and to kiss. . . . I don't want anyone to kiss me now. I turn Mr. Games [a suitor] away this morning. No *kisses* is like youres." Though the relationship was clearly intense for both women, it did not prevent Primus from serving the former slaves, a task she could not have undertaken if she had had a conventional marriage and a family rather than a female lover.

Northern-Style Social Housekeeping: Helen Marot

The challenges in the North were very different from those in the South, as European immigrants and the rural poor began flocking to large American cities, where they became a cheap labor force for burgeoning American industries. Simultaneously, an emerging middle- and upper-class female population wished to lighten their load. Young women from affluent families, many of whom had just gone through the heady experience of pioneering in higher education, were distressed to find that they were expected to return home to perform a daughter's duties, at least until suitable husbands manifested themselves. Of course, some female college graduates did not mind returning to the comforts of domestic life and eventually settling into a household of their own; they could adjust with grace to the contrast of the years that followed. But others had little or no interest in becoming wives and mothers. They were devastated to realize that they would never again have such exciting challenges as those they had experienced during their four years in college. Few professions were as yet open to them that would make use of the talents they had developed through higher education.

The great puzzle was what to do with their lives after college that would be absorbing, useful, and — a consideration for many — not so shocking a departure from women's roles that they would have to face resistance from family and community. Volunteer work had been popular earlier in the century, when women had undertaken such tasks as the establishment of orphan asylums and the reform of prostitutes. It is not surprising that many educated young women now thought to turn their abundant energies to reform, helping thereby to set off the Progressive era in America.

These women volunteered their labor in a variety of settlement houses and organizations that were being formed to aid the needy. Paradoxically, it was often expensively educated women who established the most effective organizations to help the exploited working class. They were determined to break away from the romance of acquisition, which had been responsible for making their capitalist fathers (and therefore *them*) middle and upper class. They were set on developing not only their own social conscience but also that of their complacent families and their class.

Many of the organizations that they helped establish were concerned specifically with working-class women. These activist middle- and upper-class women saw their role as "big sisters" to laboring women, who were virtually friendless. The men's unions, such as the American Federation of Labor — which should have been acting as "big brothers" to working women — feared that women would glut the labor market and thus endanger the men's hard-won and still meager benefits. According to the AFL's newspaper, *American Federationist,* organized labor had a duty to "keep women out of the trades, and if not, out of the unions." By helping exploited female workers achieve economic justice, the college-educated and affluent women felt they were performing a very vital kind of social housekeeping on which male workers had turned their backs.

The problems of female workers were exacerbated by the large numbers of poor southern and eastern European immigrants who began coming into America in the 1880s. Since salaries for uneducated workers were a pittance — less than a pittance for women — if a family was to survive, most of its able-bodied members had to go out to work, resistance on the part of male unionists notwithstanding. In response to the terrible exploitation of female laborers, especially in the garment industry, the Women's Trade Union League was organized in 1903. The league's first goal was to help female wage-earners secure better conditions by forming trade unions. Though the WTUL was founded by a man, the radical William Walling, women quickly became its most active workers. By 1905, Walling had lost interest in the organization and gone off to Russia to learn about socialism. When he returned, in 1908, his energy was directed toward founding the NAACP. But middle- and upper-class women, many of them lesbians, had already taken charge of the WTUL before Walling left.

The WTUL played a prominent role in the establishment of unions among garment workers, retail clerks, paper box makers, waitresses, laundresses, and many other female occupational groups. Its members helped lead strikes, such as the 1909 women shirtmakers' "Uprising of the Twenty Thousand," which eventually involved about 40,000 strikers and was the largest strike of female workers in history. The WTUL comprised feminist middle- and upper-class "allies" on the one hand and working-class laborers on the other. Several wealthy lesbians devoted their lives and fortunes to the Women's Trade Union League, and they proselytized for the WTUL among their class, bringing its concerns to suffrage organizations, settlement houses, and other women of wealth.

Helen Marot, one of the most effective allies, served as executive secretary of the New York WTUL from 1906 to 1913. Marot, the daughter of a wealthy publisher, and her life partner, Caroline Pratt, both had long histories of social housekeeping before becoming involved in the WTUL. In the late nineteenth century the two women owned a radical socialist library and coffeehouse in Philadelphia. They compiled the *Handbook of Labor Literature* in 1899, and they investigated the working conditions of Philadelphia tailors for the U.S. Industrial Commission. They were especially concerned about the exploitation of women and children. When they moved to New York at the start of the 1900s, Marot investigated child labor problems. The attention her work received led to the establishment of the New York Child Labor Committee in 1902, and the following year to passage by the New York state legislature of the Compulsory Education Act, which protected children by keeping them in school and out of the labor force until the age of fourteen.

Helen Marot, who always dressed in what her contemporaries considered mannish clothing, lived with Caroline Pratt in what was already the bohemian and heavily lesbian world of Greenwich Village that Eleanor Roosevelt was to discover a few years later. Pratt became a progressive educator and later the founder of the New York City and Country School, the most famous and successful of the American progressive schools in the 1920s. Marot became a major mover and shaker in the WTUL. She was instrumental in organizing into unions female bookkeepers, stenographers, and accountants. Her greatest role was in directing the Uprising of the Twenty Thousand, which helped garment workers go out on strike to protest their seventy-five-hour work week, for which they earned between four and five dollars.

Marot got the WTUL allies not only to give the workers financial support but also to join them in picketing the noncooperating shops. She also raised sympathy for the strikers in women's groups such as the Colony Club, to which "only women of the highest social eminence were eligible" for membership. Her own family fortune and American roots, which went back to 1730, certainly made her eligible for membership, and she succeeded in convincing the Colony Club to pledge both money and influence on behalf of the strikers. Marot was supported in this endeavor by several other lesbian Colony Club members who were affluent descendants of American colonists, including the theatrical entrepreneur Elisabeth Marbury and the woman who was her lover from 1884 to 1914, the actress Elsie DeWolfe, as well as the woman with whom Frances Perkins later lived, the social welfare leader Mary Harrison Rumsey.

Perhaps most important, the WTUL allies whom Marot organized in support of the uprising could serve the striking workers as witnesses, because their money and social position allowed them to be blasé toward the bosses, the police, and the law courts, which intimidated the mostly immigrant workers. Though the Shirtwaist Employers Association called the WTUL and the Colony Club strike supporters "uptown scum," they nevertheless bent quickly to the pressure these well-born women exerted: after two months of the strike, four hundred of the five hundred shirtwaist factory owners had agreed to reduce the maximum work week to fifty-two hours.

Under Marot's guidance, the WTUL enrolled many of the striking workers in what became the International Ladies Garment Workers Union. In cooperation with the National Consumers' League, she also spearheaded a campaign to "whitelist" manufacturers who accepted the strikers' terms, which meant that strike sympathizers would do business only with those companies. As the WTUL ally Rheta Dorr observed in a 1910 book, *What Eight Million Women Want,* the possibility that working women's "progress towards industrial emancipation would ever be helped along by the wives and daughters of the employing classes was unthinkable" — but that was precisely what happened through the efforts of women such as Helen Marot.

Marot resigned from her position as secretary of the WTUL to protest the fact that too many of the officeholders in the organization were allies instead of workers. After leaving the WTUL, she became an editor of the radical journal *The Masses* and then of *The Dial* and a writer on left-wing issues, especially as they affected working women. Like a number of women of their class who chose to make their lives with other women, Helen Marot and Caroline Pratt used their inherited wealth for social causes and spent their days promoting the reforms in which they believed. Perhaps their mother-heart pursuits helped justify their decisions not to marry and to choose each other instead. They detested the notion of housekeeping for the nuclear family, but they happily devoted their lives to (in Anna Shaw's words) righting wrongs, healing pain, and comforting the suffering. They encouraged each other in pursuits they regarded as much more meaningful than the leisured, trivial lives to which economic privilege such as theirs directed more traditional women.

An Interclass "Marriage" in the WTUL: Pauline Newman and Frieda Miller

The allies of the WTUL, like many radical feminists of the 1970s (who were also often middle- and upper-class lesbians), desperately wanted to reach across class lines and forge an egalitarian alliance with working women. But they were disappointed to find that working women were frequently hard to organize because they did not see their jobs as a permanent factor in their lives. Regardless of how fair and pleasant their working conditions might become through the efforts of the WTUL, their occupations would, after all, never be anything other than menial and dull. To the allies' frequent chagrin, most working women seemed to dream that they would not have to work for more than a few years and that they would be rescued from the shop by a man who would marry them. The workers could not understand the allies' admonishment that marriage would not liberate them from drudgery but merely substitute one form of exploitation for another. It was difficult for an ally to sympathize with the heterosexual aspirations of the workers if she had no interest in heterosexual marriage herself because of her fulfilling relationship with another woman, and the concept of a long-term domestic relationship with another woman, which many of the WTUL allies enjoyed, was unimaginable to most female workers. They would not have seen such a "marriage" as something likely to relieve them from toil in the shop, as they believed a heterosexual marriage would.

Yet while most intimate relationships among WTUL members were between allies, there were several instances of both romantic friendships and lesbian partnerships between a WTUL ally and a worker. These relationships had the potential of transcending the tremendous differences fostered by privilege and poverty, and even promoted the women's work for the cause. The lifelong partnership between Pauline Newman and Frieda Miller, for example, had its start in the WTUL. Newman, a Lithuanian Jewish immigrant, had risen in the labor movement through her innate talent as a speaker and organizer. She had come to America at the age of eleven, lived in a Lower East Side tenement, and worked in sweatshops, including the infamous Triangle Shirtwaist Company, which she left just months before a fire killed 146 young women. As a result of the miserable living and working conditions that she experienced firsthand, Newman joined the New York Women's Trade Union League at the age of fifteen and soon became prominent as a "fiery soapbox orator." Hers was just the kind of talent that the allies dearly hoped to help foster among the workers.

Her fame soon spread to the International Ladies Garment Workers Union, which retained her to represent "girl strikers." She was sent by the WTUL and also by the ILGWU to various organizations of the wealthy, where, as she later wrote, she "aroused the conscience of the rich" by presenting to them the story of the difficult plight of the working girl, "mov[ing them] to tears" and getting them to donate needed money so that striking workers could eat while they struggled for better factory conditions.

As a young woman, Newman had several relationships with men, including a socialist comrade named Frank Bohn, but she shunned heterosexual marriage. As her biographer, Ann Schofield, observes, "Her need for an independent life outweighed her desire for security." However, in 1917 Newman was sent to Philadelphia to serve as head of a WTUL chapter, and there she became acquainted with Frieda Miller, who was an economics professor at Bryn Mawr College. Not long after they met, Newman nursed Miller back to health from a long bout with the flu; Miller quit her teaching job, and she and Newman were soon working together full-time for labor reform in the WTUL. The lesbian partnership between them, which dramatically transcended both class and ethnicity, was a personal illustration of the WTUL's passionate philosophy, which insisted that such differences were insignificant in comparison to the deep emotional connections that were possible between women, whatever their background.

In contrast to Newman's early circumstances, Miller had grown up with a grandfather who owned a large manufacturing firm. She was sent to college and then attended graduate school at the University of Chicago, where she studied economics, sociology, political science, and law from 1911 to 1915. Frieda Miller represented the ideal for Newman, according to the daughter they raised together: "She was blonde, well-educated, comfortable in society." She was everything that Newman was not. Yet their living and working relationship endured for more than fifty years.

Though Frieda Miller's education and background opened more doors to her professionally than were open to Pauline Newman, both women had exceptional careers as labor reformers. Miller, who became a friend of Frances Perkins when Perkins was the industrial commissioner of New York, was appointed by her to head the state labor department's Division of Women in Industry in 1929. Miller played an important role in helping to transform the concerns of the WTUL into public policy. For example, she was instrumental in the passage of New York's minimum wage law for women and minors in 1933. In 1936, again through Perkins's help, she was appointed as one of the first American delegates to a permanent world body, the International Labor Organization (then under the jurisdiction of the League of Nations), whose task was to improve labor standards. Two years later, Governor Lehman made her industrial commissioner of New York, where she was in charge of implementing the state's new unemployment insurance act. She remained in that position until 1943, when she became special assistant for labor to the American Embassy in Great Britain.

In 1944, with the support of Frances Perkins, Miller was made director of the Women's Bureau in the U.S. Department of Labor, a position she kept until 1953 (when she was asked by the Republican Eisenhower administration to resign). She was especially concerned about reintegrating women into the economy when they were displaced by homecoming male veterans who reclaimed prewar jobs. Miller fought valiantly, but against overwhelmingly powerful opposition, to guarantee women continued equal opportunity and equal pay.

Like Miller, Pauline Newman also worked to turn WTUL concerns into public policy. Newman served on the New York State Minimum Wage Board and on a state committee that advised on issues regarding equal pay legislation. She was sent by the Public Health Service to investigate working conditions for women in the U.S. Army in Germany. She was on the Trade Union Advisory Committee of the U.S. Women's Bureau.

Although neither woman had an interest in heterosexual family life, they created a lesbian family together, never pausing in their reform and public policy work. In 1923, Pauline Newman and Frieda Miller went to Europe for the Third International Congress of Working Women. In Germany, Frieda adopted (or, by some accounts, gave birth to) a baby girl, Elisabeth, who became the daughter of both women. When Elisabeth later married and had two sons, both Newman and Miller were considered the boys' grandmothers.

Pauline's letters to Frieda reveal something of how their relationship combined shared commitment to social and political issues with emotional intimacy and a commitment to raising a child. On occasion the two women were separated, as in August 1927, when Sacco and Vanzetti were executed. Typically, in the letter Pauline wrote to Frieda after the executions, her political engagement merged with their relationship. "Dear Girl," she began, and then spoke of her sadness "not so much for Sacco and Vanzetti as for America and for justice. . . . I am sorry you were not with me last evening [when the news of the execution was received]. . . . I wanted, tho it be only sorrow — to share it with you. . . . It is still raining, and the heart is heavy while the spirit wanders toward you — where it might find some peace!" Frieda's letters to Pauline, whom she sometimes addressed as "Darling Paul," also combined political observations with revelations of their intimacy.

While Frieda often traveled abroad on business, Pauline finished raising Elisabeth. Pauline's letters during this time are filled with concern about the AFL, the Equal Rights Amendment (which she opposed, fearing it would wipe out protective labor laws), and especially her domesticity. "I spent my weekend getting the meals. (How do you like that? And we are still alive too!)," Pauline wrote to

Frieda, who was on her first international assignment, in Santiago, Chile, attending an inter-American labor conference.

Through much of Frieda's travels, Pauline kept the home fires burning, though occasionally she protested Frieda's long absences, which sometimes took her to dangerous places. In 1944, for example, when Frieda was at the American embassy in London during the German bombings of England, Pauline begged her to return home to safety: "The sun is out today and there is spring in the air — and hope in my heart that you will come soon to Elisabeth and to your P — ." She reminded Frieda of her responsibility to take care of herself for the sake of the family, recognizing that although she and Elisabeth were very close, the girl (who was now a student at Vassar) needed Frieda in her life because "I am no substitute for you. I have no wish to be. I love both of you too much to mind that."

Despite Pauline's occasional gripes over Frieda's travels and a period in the 1960s in which she was seriously alienated from Frieda, she clearly helped to make it possible for both of them to enjoy careers while they also enjoyed the satisfactions of family life. For her part, Frieda helped Pauline to gain national-level appointments to the World War II Women's Committee on Defense Manpower, advisory committees of the Women's Bureau, and a 1950 White House conference on children and youth. Few heterosexual couples in the early and mid-twentieth century could have achieved so much in public life while tending to a family life.

In a letter of condolence to Pauline when Frieda died, in 1973, a doctor friend characterized their full personal and professional lives and the unfortunate amnesia during the second wave of feminism about women like them. "You and Frieda had so much together and shared so many fine and wonderful things in life that you will have memories to comfort you," she wrote. "You know how tremendously I admire you and Frieda — and the women of your time — who went out and moved mountains — Your accomplishments are for all times — and I wish some of our women's libbers would do some homework and read history!"

In 1912, the newly formed Progressive Party held its first national convention. The delegates were addressed by their presidential candidate, Theodore Roosevelt, who praised them for having spent their lives "in the endless crusade against wrong." Many of those "endless crusaders," including Jane Addams, who made the speech that seconded Roosevelt's nomination for the presidency, were what later generations would describe as lesbian or bisexual. Though few of these women had biological offspring, they epitomized the mother-heart as Anna Shaw meant that term.

Linda Gordon, in her study of the history of welfare from 1890 to 1935, observes that 28 percent of the leading women reformers she examined were partnered in romantic, long-term Boston marriages with other women. As she also points out, that figure is conservative, since it refers only to women known to have had one long-term partner, not to women such as Eleanor Roosevelt, who was married to a man but had romantic involvements with other women. A scrutiny of the history of social reform from the mid-nineteenth to the mid-twentieth century leaves one with the distinct impression that women who were in love with one another played dominant and absolutely indispensable roles in the development of America's social conscience.

7

SOCIAL HOUSEKEEPING:

THE INSPIRATION OF

JANE ADDAMS

My Ever Dear. . . . When you get back we will talk over a
plan that is in my mind. I didn't say what I wanted to in
the confessional the other night because I didn't feel sure
enough of myself — but if you ever doubt my desire to be
with you — I wish you could be at the bottom of my
mind.

— Jane Addams to Mary Rozet Smith, February 21, 1897

IN HER ACCOUNT of how she founded one of the first settlement
houses in the United States, Jane Addams described her terrible
depression after she received her degree from Rockford College in
1882, when she had no idea what to do with the rest of her life. The
depression was exacerbated the following year when she went to
Europe for "finishing," as young women of her social class often
did. There, in places such as East London, she saw up close the
wretched poverty and misery in which much of humanity lived and
from which she had always been sheltered in her upper-middle-
class world. Addams claimed that her European experience made
her understand that her modern education, which stuffed a young
woman with culture and nothing more, was useless. It cloyed with
its self-absorption, its insulation from the problems of the world. As
she wrote in her essay "Filial Relations," what a college woman
needed after graduation was not "finishing" or a return to the
bosom of her family until she married but some activity that, "in-

volving the use of all her faculties, shall be a response to all the claims which she so keenly feels" — the claims to contribute more largely to the betterment of her society.

Jane Addams as a Radical

The historian Jill Conway has suggested that reformers such as Jane Addams and Lillian Wald (the founder of the second most famous settlement house in America, Henry Street) did little to change the weak position of women in their day. They never publicly challenged the conventional view of femininity (that is, the mother-heart cliché) or demanded nontraditional roles for women. Thus, Conway complains, the impact of their usefulness for females in the twentieth century was short-lived.

Indeed, it is true that in her public statements, Jane Addams seldom seemed to question gender stereotypes. For instance, as vice president of the National American Woman Suffrage Association under Anna Shaw, she argued that suffrage was not an "educated woman's issue." All women needed the vote for the sake of their families and neighborhoods, she said, in order to influence legislation regarding pure food, schools, rent control, and fire protection in tenements. In establishing Hull House, Addams claimed to be looking *backward* to the "less selfish time" of her great-grandmother's day, when women reacted to others' suffering or helplessness through works of charity and betterment.

However, Addams had conceived a brilliantly creative antidote to the pressures that called a young woman home to a passive life after college. By founding a settlement house, where educated women could operate independently of their families and where they could help people in need, she was actually looking *forward*. She was establishing one of the few professions that has been consistently dominated by women — even in the terrible mid-twentieth century, when women were being excluded once again from all the other professions that they had entered after the great struggles of the previous century. As the virtual mother of social work and related occupations, Addams had a tremendous impact on the lives of generations of educated women who attained professional status thanks to her. She must be credited, much more than Conway and others have been willing to do, for understanding what was necessary in her own day to effect the ends she believed to be important. While seeming to reify the category "woman" by expanding it to a larger scale, she actually found a way to help great numbers of women leave the prison of the domestic sphere and enter the public sphere.

Indeed, what a later era considered excessively cautious behavior, as Conway characterizes Jane Addams's public stance, was in Addams's day still considered by some as a wildly radical threat to the status quo. Though Addams obfuscated the revolutionary meaning of her work, she was viciously attacked, as her hate mail shows, simply because she suggested that women should have a role outside the home and a public voice. One anonymous letter she received, written in response to her campaign against government corruption, asserted that

> I love your sex . . . but no man can love a woman who takes her place among men as you do. . . . Of course I can speak very plain to you, as your highest ambition is to be recognized as capable of doing a man's work. When your maker created you, it was evidently a rush job as the most important part of the work was overlooked. Here then is your only resource. Did it ever occur to you that while on a tour of inspection, through alleyways, old barns and such places where low depraved men with criminal records may be found (such a place a virtuous woman would be afraid to go) you might for a small sum induce one of such men to sell you his pecker and balls? It would not be much loss to him and will be your only chance to prove yourself a man.

If merely leading a social housekeeping campaign elicited such violent personal attacks on a woman's gender, it is hard to imagine that a more obviously rebellious persona, of the kind that Addams has been criticized for avoiding, would have had any power at all to effect the changes she desired.

Jane Addams as a Lesbian, Part I

Addams had no interest in heterosexual marriage and spent her adult years, almost until her death, with other women, in long-term relationships that we would describe as lesbian today. In a homophobic society in which lesbianism has been considered tantamount to degeneracy and outlawry, to suggest that Jane Addams, one of the truly outstanding women in American history — the quintessential American heroine, one biographer dubbed her — was thus tainted has been wildly controversial. "No other single institution . . . did as much [as Addams's Hull House] to counteract the dogma of individualism and restore the social principle to thought about civilization," Charles and Mary Beard observed in their classic 1942 study of "the idea of civilization in the United States." Addams has been credited as absolutely instrumental in ushering in a new era in secular society that encouraged people of wealth to see the poor not as ignorant hordes to be exploited but as their responsibility. Even recent biographers have shown how Addams was "a central figure" in progressivism and a vital "moving force in [America's] transition" from the laissez-faire society of her youth to the welfare state it became in the years before her death. More than any other individual of her day, scholars have said, Addams was responsible for awakening America's social conscience. That being so, how could she have been a lesbian?

As an examination of Jane Addams's correspondence unarguably reveals, women were often enamored of her. Yet her numerous biographers have agreed that while she was a good friend to many, she generally kept an emotional distance. That assessment is largely true, except with regard to two women who were Jane Addams's domestic partners: first, Ellen Starr, the woman with whom she established Hull House, and later Mary Rozet Smith, a benefactor of Hull House with whom Addams had a relationship that became a primary one in the early 1890s and lasted until Smith's death, in 1934.

Jane Addams's relationship with Ellen Starr began in 1877, when they were both students in Illinois at Rockford Female Seminary (which became Rockford Female College before Addams graduated). Though Ellen left Rockford at the end of that year in order to support herself as a teacher, she and Jane continued to correspond. Their letters reveal in compelling detail the slow growth and increasing intensity of what they surely came to regard as a romantic friendship and then a Boston marriage.

The earliest letters are far from intense, and even portray something of the studied distance that generally characterized Jane's personal relationships. In an 1879 letter, the nineteen-year-old Jane, with cool objectivity, wrote to Ellen that their "social intercourse is probably over for all time. It is queer though, but a fact, that I am glad when I know some people just so much and then stop . . . [because] you remember them and retain the impressions they leave, go steadily on your own way, and meet someone else, who will sort of finish out what they began." This unemotional attitude is an ironic contrast to her later correspondence with Ellen, which mocked this notion of the interchangeability of their relationship.

Their growing closeness is first suggested by a letter from Ellen to Jane after a prolonged visit. "I suppose it is better that I can't see you very often," Ellen wrote. "I should get to depending on you, bodily, in a little while, and that would be quite sure to make me trouble in the end." But, she confessed, despite her fear of bodily dependence, "I can't help wishing that we could sometimes be in the same place long enough to do some work together. I believe we should work well." Embarrassed by her forwardness, she hastened to add, "So much for expressing my 'feelins.'" The next day, however, continuing the letter, she picked up where she had left off, though now humorously placing her sentiments in the mouth of a friend who had recently met Jane: "She said today, 'It would be so easy to love Miss Addams. I think her face is beautiful.' She said something about the way Miss Addams talked, too, but — I will not repeat the expressions of so deluded a person. I'm afraid I didn't do anything to scatter the delusions. I shall always like her better because she has seen you."

The fluster in some of Ellen's letters written during these years suggests an excitement that is generally associated with eros. "My Dear," she addressed Jane in December 1885, "it has occurred to me that it might just be possible that you would spend a night with me if you should be going east at the right time. If you decide to go the week before Christmas — I mean — what do I mean? I think it is this. *Couldn't* you decide to spend the Sunday before Christmas with me? Get here on Saturday and go on Monday? . . . Please forgive me for writing three letters in a week. It is virtuous in me to stop now."

Jane was by temperament more reserved than the spontaneous Ellen. But as her own letters reveal, she kindled to Ellen's spark. After becoming acquainted with a young woman who was interested in art (as Ellen was), Jane wrote in 1883, "It has set me to thinking very constantly of you. Not that I need any reminder." Over the next couple of years, Jane was confused by her feelings, as she wrote to Ellen in 1885: "I am very impatient to see you, and am haunted by a fear that I do not know you." A closer acquaintance must have proved happy. In 1888, Jane and Ellen traveled to Europe together, and in London they visited Toynbee Hall, a settlement house that brought (male) Oxford students to live and work among the poor. From that visit the idea of Hull House was born.

By 1889, with their settlement house project under way, they were both ecstatic that they were making reality out of Ellen's dream that they might someday join their energies. "Let's love each other through thick and thin and work out a salvation," Jane implored Ellen in January. Their salvation was to be their love for each other as well as their love of good works. During their brief separations at this time, Jane wrote often to Ellen and awaited her answering letters impatiently. "I need you, dear one, more than you can realize," Jane confessed, and (somewhat peremptorily), "My Dear One — a day without a letter is *blanc* as the French say of sleepless nights. I don't like such a day at all — and I have just had one."

The Significance of Hull House

In February 1889, Jane Addams and Ellen Starr decided to get a large, comfortable house in a Chicago neighborhood that was inhabited mostly by immigrants from eastern and southern Europe. They would invite other college-educated young women to join them there, and they would all exchange visits with their neighbors and be useful in whatever way they could. They would be different from the Lady Bountiful types of other eras, who had established orphan asylums or paid charity visits and then returned to the comforts of affluent homes. Addams and Starr and the young women who chose to work with them would become personally involved in the lives of the people they hoped to help. They would learn from the poor at least as much as the poor would learn from them.

Hull House, as they called the settlement, was to be not only a place to do good works but also a home in which Jane and Ellen were romantic partners. In the large house the two women "had our own bedroom," as Ellen recorded, and they set up "several others with little single beds" for the residents they hoped would join them. Hull House soon became a community of women. It was revolutionary because, as the historian Kathryn Kish Sklar has noted, while it was not a religious order, it provided Jane and Ellen and myriad other women with a lifelong substitute for marriage, "supplying in a radical degree an independence from the claims of family life and inviting them to commit their energies elsewhere."

Hull House was the beginning of one of the most effective social reform movements in America. It addressed itself eventually to correcting urban ills in all forms. Jane Addams and Ellen Starr's settlement very quickly included a separate little house fitted up as a kitchen, where meals were prepared for the sick and immigrant women were taught about American foods. A day nursery was established for working mothers. The saloon next door was transformed into a little gymnasium. In front of the main house another little building was erected, and its first floor was given rent-free to the public library to set up a reading room; the second floor was a studio for art classes and exhibits. College extension classes were offered at Hull House by University of Chicago graduates and faculty members, and Hull House sent 90 percent of the students to Rockford College for summer school. The settlement also became a meeting place for labor groups such as garment workers, and on its premises a trade union was established. At a time when kindergartens were virtually unknown, one was established at Hull House. Vocational training classes were instituted at Hull House long before the concept spread to schools. A cooperative lodging house was established there for young working women.

Though Hull House had been conceived as a fairly modest neighborhood project, its scope grew rapidly along with the interests of its founders. Addams and Starr were soon working with groups who lived far from the Hull House neighborhood. They reached out to include people of all ethnic groups and races in the battle for social justice. For example, Addams joined forces with female African-American leaders such as Ida B. Wells in the successful campaign against a move to segregate Chicago schools. She eventually also organized research and investigation teams of female social scientists who had been trained in the graduate programs at the newly established University of Chicago. (She was probably the first to take the work of female social scientists seriously.) She used their findings in a variety of ways that bore fruit for the poor and disadvantaged. The facts and figures they produced became indispensable in helping Hull House agitate for legislative changes not only in its district but also throughout the city and the state.

For example, under Addams's auspices, the social scientists conducted housing investigations, which provided information that enabled Hull House staff to organize a successful campaign for tenement ordinances. Addams also encouraged the social scientists to investigate sweatshops, and on the basis of their research, the Hull House staff pushed successfully for the first factory law in Illinois to address the problems of child labor and the exploitation of working women. As a result of the social scientists' investigation of the Chicago court system, settlement staff was able to exert pressure that resulted in the establishment of the first juvenile court in the country. As a 1915 observer stated, "With the exception of religion, there was no human interest that [Hull House] failed to touch."

But even more significant for America, Hull House was a replicable experiment. It may have been an idea whose time had come, but Addams's charisma and quickly growing national reputation helped to guarantee that there would be no delay. By 1900, almost one hundred settlement houses like Hull House were spread across the country, most of them founded by women. Addams's example also inspired the transformation of various groups into organizations whose main focus became working for social betterment. In the 1890s, the ubiquitous Women's Clubs, banded together in a General Federation of Women's Clubs, exchanged their original goal of "intellectual uplift" for goals such as the eradication of child labor, the establishment of public libraries, tenement reform — all causes that Jane Addams had brought to widespread public attention.

The relationship between Ellen Starr and Jane Addams fulfilled them both on various levels for a time. Because they were enchanted with each other, they became a team, which aided the realization of their ambition to devote their lives to bettering the world. Their romance with each other and with their task occurred at a time in their lives when young women of their era were supposed to be thinking hard about marriage and scheming for its advent. But the obligations inherent in nineteenth-century heterosexual marriage would have been counterproductive to Jane and Ellen's shared passion to do good works on a large scale. Unlike most marriages in their day, their "marriage" not only permitted their ambition, it made it possible.

In her autobiography, Jane Addams credits Ellen Starr as her partner in the establishment of Hull House. "The comfort of Miss Starr's companionship, the vigor and enthusiasm which she brought to bear upon it, told both in the growth of the plan and upon the sense of its validity," she wrote. At the start of their project, they seemed to shine equally, as the newspaper reporters who interviewed them proclaimed (as in the headline "College Girls Who Will Found a Colony in the Slums"). The *Woman's Journal* of 1889 wrote glowingly about their partnership, in which the passionate Starr supplied the zing of vivacity that balanced the businesslike Addams's more serious and stolid approach: "More perfect counterparts could scarcely be imagined. Miss Starr supplements Miss Addams completely." In the early days of Hull House, Jane needed Ellen emotionally. As Allen Davis observes, "More important [than the skills she brought to the Hull House project], Ellen was completely devoted to her friend."

Ellen Starr contributed to Hull House in concrete ways too. She opened culture to the working-class European immigrants of the neighborhood, who had before assumed that culture was only for the wealthy. She taught art history classes; she conducted literary clubs for working girls and young mothers, introducing them to Shakespeare, George Eliot, Robert Browning; she set up a program to lend reproductions of master paintings to families and schools in the neighborhood. She was also interested in the labor problems of these immigrants. When the workers who congregated at Hull House organized strikes, she not only collected money for them, she also walked the picket lines with them. She was a charter member of the Illinois branch of the Women's Trade Union League and battled against injustices such as child labor. She was even arrested in a 1914 waitress strike when she tried to protect workers from police brutality.

Jane Addams as a Lesbian, Part II

Though Ellen Starr continued to live and work at Hull House until 1920, her intimate relationship with Jane Addams had long been over by then. Perhaps the end was built in from the beginning. Even as a young woman, Ellen, who had been raised as a Unitarian, was thirsty for a more intense spirituality. She had converted to high-church Episcopalianism when she was twenty-five years old. Jane, who was emotionally at loose ends during that period, envied her friend's religious certainty and let herself be advised by Ellen in spiritual matters. The following year, with Ellen's encouragement, Jane joined a church and had herself baptized. But the act brought her no lasting sense of fulfillment, and she felt confirmed in her suspicion that she had no capacity for doctrine or veneration.

When the press and the public tried to find a religious motive in the establishment of Hull House, Jane was disgusted, as she wrote to Ellen: "I positively feel my callers peering into my face to detect 'spirituality.'" As her nephew James Linn later observed in his biography, "Her humanitarianism was too pervasive . . . to permit the entrance of any large interest in dogma." She was a secular humanist par excellence. Ellen, in contrast, became increasingly absorbed by religious dogma. Her own spiritual quest was intensified when she went to London in the early 1890s and became part of an aesthetic and spiritually inclined British circle. Like other Victorian and Edwardian aesthetes — Oscar Wilde, the lesbian couple who published poetry under the name Michael Field, and Radclyffe Hall are salient examples — Ellen Starr finally converted to Catholicism, in 1920. She joined the Convent of the Holy Child in 1930. In 1935, the year Jane Addams died, she became an oblate of the Third Order of Saint Benedict.

It is impossible to know for certain whether Ellen's recommitment to religion at the start of the 1890s was a cause or an effect of the alienation between her and Jane. But its apparent beginning coincided with the entrance into their lives of the daughter of a wealthy Chicago industrialist, Mary Rozet Smith. Linn says that Smith "drifted to the House in the course of its first year, to see whether there was anything she could do there." During the spring of 1890, Jane's letters to Mary invariably employed the plural pronoun; for example, "It would give us great pleasure to have you come on Monday." But by the following winter, Jane was often exclusive and quite personal in her correspondence with Mary, which is especially remarkable in the context of her very reserved letters to almost all her other correspondents. For instance, in December 1890, when Mary was contemplating spending the rest of the winter in California because of a cough, Jane wrote to her, "I have a great fear of your being whisked off. . . . It would make a great difference to me whether you were in the city or out of it." Mary and Jane soon began to see each other often. For a time, Ellen continued to make up their party, and some of Jane's letters to Mary in early 1891 sent "love from Ellen." But it was not much longer before mention of Ellen ceased.

The break between Jane and Ellen could not have been easy. They had been close for fifteen years, yet only a year after the opening of Hull House, as Allen Davis has observed, "Jane and Ellen drifted apart." Though on the surface Ellen remained a loyal friend to Jane, the loss of intimacy was for a time traumatic to her. She attempted to deal with it at one point by going off to Europe for fifteen months. Yet she complained to Jane once there, "I feel uncommon blue and homesick tonight. . . . I suppose you are working yourself to death. I don't get many letters." Several of Ellen's letters reveal her depression. In one, she began, "My dear, I'm tired. I make you that confidence." Self-pityingly, she wrote of being in a streetcar and letting "my eyes and mind wander over the most unmitigated barrenness and hideousness extant." Almost as if she were saying "So there!" she confessed that the crisis she was experiencing had turned her to "a fresh love of ecclesiasticism" (which she must have known by then would be annoying to Jane). "Perhaps I will get great spiritual gain out of my infirmity," she observed, adding, "It's good for me to go upon my knees." She apparently realized how bathetic the letter was and concluded, "I probably shouldn't have written."

An 1892 letter from Jane, written in response to another doleful missive from Ellen, demonstrates both Jane's attempt to be sympathetic and a surprising insensitivity. "My Dear One," Jane wrote soothingly, assuring Ellen of both her affection and her belief that Ellen continued to be important to their Hull House project: "Your letter was a little homesick. Of course I miss you all the time and have never wanted you more than the last few days when everything seemed to be moving at once." But she would not lie about Mary's presence in her life, though she must have understood that her admissions would not be easy for Ellen to bear. "We have put a single iron bed in the blue room (it has never looked so well). Mary and I may take it together," she wrote, and "Last night Miss Scammon was here for the night, Miss Babcock and Miss McLane, so of course Mary and I slept together."

To the end, Ellen and Jane tried to be gracious to each other. Jane attempted to provide for Ellen financially in her old age. And Ellen, at the age of seventy-six (only months before Jane's death, in 1935), perhaps in preparation for taking religious vows, reread their old correspondence, contemplated their young years, and wrote Jane a truly remarkable note that more than hints at her early emotional struggle over being replaced by Mary yet seems sincerely to proclaim her final placid reconciliation:

> I can see by the way you overrate me in these letters that it was inevitable that I should disappoint you. I think that I have always, at any rate for a great many years, been thankful that Mary came to supply what you needed. At all events, I thank God that I never was envious of her in any vulgar or ignoble way. One couldn't be of any one so noble and generous and in every way fair-minded as she.

Despite the termination of their intimacy not long after they founded Hull House, the relationship between Ellen and Jane had been vital to them both. Besides fulfilling their emotional needs for a time, it permitted them to begin the grand scheme of Hull House, which neither woman could have managed on her own. But Addams's extraordinary talents, especially her writing and speaking abilities, soon drew the limelight to her alone, garnering her a national and then an international reputation. As she recognized, however, she could not have taken the first step without Ellen. Their mutual romantic devotion for about fifteen years was what made the crucial beginning possible.

Almost every biographer of Jane Addams has recognized the importance of her relationship with Mary Rozet Smith, yet it has been difficult for most of them to discuss it as lesbian, since, as Blanche Cook has pointed out, a "conventional lady with pearls" (as both Jane and Mary were) has generally not been thought of in terms that the twentieth century has associated with perversion. Yet a perusal of their correspondence leaves little doubt of the romance and commitment of their relationship and the fact that they considered themselves a married couple. Even biographers who do not wish to deal with Jane Addams as a lesbian are constrained to observe that while her letters to almost everyone during the 1890s and later are emotionally remote, those to Mary, which address her as "My Ever Dear," "Darling," and "Dearest One," are unique in their fervor. Jane, who kept her emotions in check with regard to practically everything, could not and would not hide her feelings for Mary. By February 1893, she was even writing to her sister Alice Haldeman that Mary was "so good to me that I would find life a different thing without her."

Her sister may have construed this confession to refer to Mary's financial support of Jane's projects, but Mary's generosity to Hull House was not unique. By 1893 the settlement was serving approximately two thousand people weekly, and Jane's own funds had long since been depleted. However, she was successful in soliciting from a host of affluent people the sum of $100,000 a year, a huge amount of money in those days. Mary's support was important, but it could not explain Jane's devotion to her, since many were generous.

Though Mary's money may have helped somewhat to overcome the great imbalance of power between them, her biggest contribution to Jane Addams's life and work was not financial. Rather, it was the very personal love Mary brought. The ordinarily stolid Jane revealed as much in an 1895 poem she wrote, remembering her state when they met and how Mary altered her:

> One day I came into Hull House
>   (No spirit whispered who was there)
> And in the kindergarten room
>   There sat upon a childish chair
> A girl, both tall and fair to see
>   (To look at her gives one a thrill).
> But all I thought was, would she be
>   Best fitted to lead club or drill?
> You see, I had forgotten Love,
>   And only thought of Hull House then.
>
> That is the way with women folks
>   When they attempt the things of men;

They grow intense and love the thing
Which they so tenderly do rear,
And think that nothing lies beyond
Which claims from them a smile or tear. . . .
So was I blind and deaf those years
To all save one absorbing care,
And did not guess what now I know
Delivering love was sitting there!

As was true in her relationship with Ellen, Jane could achieve great things, but she needed a personal love that would not only nurture her but also put her in touch with her human side. The potential risk of such vulnerability was that it might interfere with her tremendous goals. But unlike heterosexual relationships, which could have hindered her ability to "attempt the things of men" — that is, to run a huge institution almost single-mindedly — her relationships first with Ellen and then with Mary were enabling.

What Mary Smith brought Jane Addams was as ineffable as deep emotional connections between two people frequently are. Several biographers have observed that there was "no affinity of mind" between Jane, a mature woman, and Mary, who was less than twenty years old when she first went to Hull House, in 1890. By all objective standards, they were never a match intellectually or in terms of personality. Mary became a trustee in 1895, financed a children's building for Hull House, and regularly wrote sizable checks to contribute to the running of the institution. Dr. Alice Hamilton, a Hull House resident, described her as "one supremely lovely figure . . . the most universally beloved person." But generosity and sweetness aside, she was not in Jane's league. In their letters they seldom exchanged ideas, though Jane's correspondence with other women is replete with intellectual content. But as Allen Davis observes, Jane "did not need someone to test her ideas against. . . . She needed someone who accepted her and wanted her the way she was."

Indeed, she needed someone with whom she could be human rather than Saint Jane, as she increasingly became in the public view. For instance, only with Mary could she let down the necessary guise of humility. She could brag during a 1902 lecture trip, "I will confide to you alone that I have never spoken so well and so many times as during this trip. It has altogether been successful socially and financially and in ideas." To whom else could she admit such personal feelings, such very human ego gratification in a cause that had to appear entirely altruistic in order to succeed?

Rather than exchanging ideas, Jane and Mary's letters expressed longing to be together, mutual dependence, joy about their domestic arrangements, and an affinity that transcended intellectualism. "I bless you, dear, every time I think of you, which is all the time at present," Jane wrote at the end of 1894. At the beginning of 1895 they took a trip together, after which Jane sent Mary a letter proclaiming, "I feel soberer and calmer than I have felt for a year. It is one more thing to thank you for." Less than two weeks later, she wrote, "I quite long for you to come" to spend time near her again. And a few days after that, having gotten a confirmation from Mary that she was planning an extended visit to Hull House, Jane expressed her joyful anticipation, saying that whenever she "need[ed] cheering," she would find it by repeating to herself Mary's promise to be with her.

Mary clearly reciprocated Jane's feelings. After a visit with Jane before she was scheduled to go south with her family, Mary wrote, "I came home with quite a glow at my heart. . . . You can never know what it is to me to have had you and to have you now." Mary spoke in this same letter of being overcome by a "rush of emotion . . . when I think of you." In 1896, she invited Jane to be a guest of the Smith family on a trip to Europe, promising that they would have time alone. "Mother and Father are going to abide quietly in one or two spots and I am prepared to go anywhere, from the North Cape to Greece. . . . This is a very fine plan," she quipped, "and you'd better consider it. I will offer you bribes to the extent of my fortune." When Jane accepted, Mary wrote, "When I think of your going away with us I am quite overcome. It seems too good to be true and I really can't take it in."

The two women traveled frequently together in subsequent

years. Often work was combined with pleasure, and Jane involved Mary in various pursuits. On the 1896 trip, for example, she and Mary visited settlement houses in Europe, met labor leaders and writers such as Tolstoy, and, as she wrote to Ellen, together bought "a good deal of literature [in order to] 'cram up' before we meet the folks who have written the books." Jane may truly have felt that the attractive Mary was something of an asset on professional trips; at any rate, she wished to suggest that idea to Mary. In 1897, for example, she implored Mary to accept with her "a very pressing invitation" from a Mrs. Ward to visit her in the West. Jane's relationship with Mary was such by then that she could joke about Mrs. Ward, "She was enchanted at the prospect of your going. . . . You know she has a grande passion for you." But Jane's own grande passion can be heard in the exigent lines that followed: "Please, please don't change your mind now after filling me with such joy."

As Mary approached thirty, however, Jane began to feel the awkwardness of their situation. At the end of the nineteenth century, when women of the middle and upper classes seldom claimed a conscious lesbian identity, regardless of their feelings or behavior, those who had no particular talent and no great ambition were supposed to marry. Mary Smith had neither, yet she had no apparent interest in finding a husband. Her emotions were focused entirely on Jane. At one point, in 1899, when Mary was visiting Germany with her parents, Jane wrote to encourage her not to turn away the attentions of a Mr. Robert Wood, a Hull House volunteer who was enamored of her and who went to see her in Germany. Was it in ingenuousness or guilt that Jane declared, "Bro Wood's letters have been so ardent with regard to you that I had perhaps cherished a dream which your letter of this morning doesn't exactly encourage"?

Yet how could Jane have been anything other than relieved when Mary did not heed her advice regarding Robert Wood? What would have happened to their exclusive relationship if Mary had accepted Mr. Wood? Fortunately for Jane, she had no serious reason to worry about Mary's defection to heterosexuality, and their bond continued to deepen. Only a few months later, she wrote to Mary, who had spent several days with her on a lecture trip in Wisconsin, "Dearest, It made me quite homesick [for you] to go by the hotel [in Milwaukee, where they had stayed] this morning. We did have a good time in it, didn't we?" By 1902, Jane permitted herself to express her belief that they were wed to each other. She wrote to Mary, who was off in Europe again with relatives, "You must know, dear, how I long for you all the time. . . . There is reason in the habit of married folk keeping together." Subsequent letters, particularly those written after the death of Mary's mother, in 1904 (which freed Mary to spend more time with Jane), depict the couple emphatically as "married folk" who enjoy, in Jane's terms, a "healing domesticity."

Shortly after Mary's mother died, Mary purchased a vacation home in Bar Harbor in both her name and Jane's (Jane put a small amount of money into it, to make it officially "ours"). Jane's enthusiasm over their shared abode was unique in its girlishness: "Our house — it quite gives me thrill to write the word," she told Mary, exalting over the "really truly ownership" of their very own home. By then, on the rare occasions when they were separated by Jane's business travels, they sent letters or telegrams to each other almost daily. Typically, Jane would tell Mary, as she did in a 1914 letter from Denver, "Dearest, I had a wave of real homesickness for you. . . . I wanted you very much."

Jane Addams's "marriage" to Mary Rozet Smith did not end until March 1934, when Mary died of pneumonia, after more than forty years of life with Jane. Jane, who was herself ill at the time, was devastated, as she wrote to her nephew, James Linn: "I suppose I could have willed my heart to stop beating, but the thought of what she had been to me for so long kept me from being cowardly." She survived Mary by only fourteen months.

Beyond Hull House

During her years with Mary Rozet Smith, Jane Addams became first a national and then an international figure. In 1904, as a result of her work against flagrant abuses of child labor, she was appointed to the board of trustees of the National Child Labor Committee. She led the committee in drawing up a model child labor bill that prohibited night work for children and contained provisions to enforce minimum age and maximum hours laws. In 1909 she became the first female president of the National Conference of Social Work (then called the National Conference of Charities and Corrections). That year she also played a major role in the fledgling National Association for the Advancement of Colored People. The following year she was the first woman to receive an honorary degree from Yale. She also became one of the founders of the American Civil Liberties Union. In 1931, after more than forty years of promoting humanitarian concerns, she received the Nobel Peace Prize. It is no exaggeration to say, as magazine polls often did, that for many years of her life Jane Addams was considered "America's greatest woman."

Throughout all these years, Mary Smith was usually by Jane's side, whether Jane was traveling to the capitals of Europe for her work in the international peace movement or traveling around America to promote the franchise or a variety of social causes. Although the two women lived together only after both of Mary's parents died, even early in their relationship Jane often took respite from Hull House to spend time with Mary and Mr. and Mrs. Smith (who greatly admired her) in their Chicago mansion. In later years, Jane lived at this mansion on Walton Place most of the time, though she remained the spiritual head of Hull House.

During her years with Mary Rozet Smith, Jane Addams also became a prominent pacifist. Her residence in an immigrant neighborhood led her to feel deeply about the folly of war between nations. She was sanguine in her belief that the forced integration of immigrants in American cities had worked to tame the ferocity of their nationalism and that a similar forced internationalism, on a worldwide scale, could be made "an effective instrument in the cause of world-peace." She lectured on the idea of a "united nations" as early as the start of the twentieth century, and in her 1907 book, *Newer Ideals of Peace,* she presented a blueprint for such an international remedy. She was opposed to World War I; through the Women's Peace Party, which she founded in 1915, and the International Congress of Women at the Hague, over which she presided, she made great efforts to bring the war to a mediated end. Unlike Anna Shaw and Carrie Catt, she refused to compromise her pacifism even for the sake of winning the franchise. Because of her inveterate pacifism, she was cast out of the Daughters of the American Revolution, decried as being a Bolshevik by the right wing, and given a prominent position in their "Spiderweb" chart, which connected her to fifty other American "radicals" who were attempting "to destroy civilization and Christianity . . . [and] the government of the United States."

When America entered the war, in 1917, the one federal post Addams was willing to accept was in the Department of Food Administration, for which she traveled around the country to encourage greater food production in order to aid starving war victims in Europe. She helped found the Women's International League for Peace and Freedom and was its president for twenty years. When she received the Nobel Prize for Peace, she donated half of her prize money to this group. Shortly before Addams's death, Eleanor Roosevelt, honoring the twentieth anniversary of WILPF and Addams's leadership, proclaimed from the White House, "When the day comes when difficulties are faced and settled without resorting to [war] . . . we shall look back in this country upon the leadership you have given us, Miss Addams, and be grateful for having had you live with us."

Addams's peace work bore little substantive fruit, Eleanor Roosevelt's optimistic projection notwithstanding. Nevertheless, her settlement house concepts helped direct the government's rethinking of its responsibilities to the weaker members of society. As early as 1897, Jane Addams was serving as a national conscience, pointing out that so much of what Hull House was doing — including child care and subsidized food programs for the poor — should be done all over the country and would be much better done by the federal government. She argued that private beneficence was good and necessary but not sufficient to deal with the disinherited of the urban world. New jobs in social work and reformist public policy were eventually created from the spirit she helped awaken in America, and many of those jobs were filled by women. Addams virtually paved the way not only for the Progressive movement but also for the liberalism that was a prominent political ideal in America for much of the twentieth century.

Daniel Levine has rightly observed in his book *Jane Addams and the Liberal Tradition*, "People listened to her — not only because her words seemed right, but also because she had put her words into action at Hull House. She knew what she was talking about." But more important, she knew how to maneuver within the limitations of her day: how to inspire other women so that collective female power might be created in what were virtually separatist institutions such as settlement houses, and how to bring that power to fruition on a large scale. She understood precisely how nineteenth-century female reformers could coerce those who inhabited the male spheres of power to take them seriously, to learn from the women how to "be better," and to support their efforts by necessary legislation.

Before Jane Addams was chosen to second Theodore Roosevelt's nomination as the Progressive Party's presidential candidate in 1912, Roosevelt had written to her: "Will you let me say a word of very sincere thanks to you for the eminent sanity, good-humor and judgement you always display in pushing matters you have at heart? I have such awful times with reformers of the hysterical and sensational stamp, and yet I so thoroughly believe in reform, that I revel in dealing with anyone like you." Roosevelt had perceived Addams as she wished to be perceived. Regardless of how radical her position was in awakening America's social conscience, she understood how to make her argument with such calm rationality that it appeared self-evident.

✵ 8 ✵

SOCIAL HOUSEKEEPING
BECOMES A PROFESSION:
FRANCES KELLOR

My own dear beautiful Sweetheart. . . . I find I have been
thinking many things to you out the window which do
not appear here or anywhere perhaps unless it be [in] the
Silences of the night where you nestle close to me to be
comforted and assured that you are not alone. This is a
poor substitute for what I would give you tonight.

— Frances Kellor to Mary Dreier, ca. 1905

New Professions for New Women

IN AN 1897 SPEECH, "The Idea of a Settlement Movement," Jane
Addams observed that the mother-heart by itself could not right the
wrongs of America. In order for the settlement house phenomenon
to make a significant difference outside the neighborhood, "scientific skills and patience in the accumulation of facts" were required
— professionally generated data and informed polemic that would
give reformers the ammunition to push legislation through the
various channels. The skills Addams called for were soon provided
by university-trained social scientists, many of them women, who
were entering graduate schools in increasing numbers. The settlement house was often a welcome field placement for them because
it permitted them to combine what had long been an accepted
female endeavor, betterment, with a new professionalism.

By the early twentieth century, Hull House and the settlements
modeled after it were no longer staffed primarily by volunteers

looking for an outlet from stifling lives as unmarried females of the middle and upper classes. A new generation of professional women — social workers and public policymakers — had emerged. They were well trained and had excellent credentials. Their settlement house experiences often led them to paid work that not only permitted them to expand reform in the public sector but also gave them the financial wherewithal to support themselves. They could be New Women in a new century that seemed open both to social reform and to women's professional role in it.

In 1910, Jane Addams was able to report that the majority of Hull House residents were working in professions that grew out of or complemented their settlement interests: they were salaried as sanitary inspectors, lecturers in the Chicago School of Civics and Philanthropy, administrators and social workers in the Juvenile Protective Association and the League for the Protection of Immigrants. The settlement movement not only called into being a variety of professional-level jobs for the New Women, but also helped make them ready for such careers and deeply influenced their approach. Frances Perkins, for instance, cut her teeth on public policy work at Hull House, where she came to appreciate labor unions and to defend workers who were taken advantage of by their bosses. What she learned at Hull House from 1904 to 1907 had great effects on her policies as secretary of labor from 1933 to 1945.

Educated women whose life partners were other women were especially likely to pursue the professional occupations to which the settlement house phenomenon led. These early twentieth-century lesbians (or sexual inverts, as such women were now often called even outside of medical literature) could see unprecedented opportunities opening for females in professional reform work, and they were able to seize them. Their ambitions were often marked by a clarity of purpose that might have been elusive to women torn between careers and domesticity.

However, while it was likely that in the early twentieth century a college-educated woman who saw herself as a congenital sexual invert would want to become a professional person, it was also likely that a woman desiring a profession would choose to make her life with other women. If a professional woman wanted love and companionship, she could find it more easily with another woman who shared her struggles than with a man who wanted a wife. Many of the early professional women were thus undoubtedly living challenges to the simplistic ideas of the sexologists about the congenital sexual inversion of females who made their lives with other females. Which came first, so-called sexual inversion or the desire for the kind of life that was inimical to heterosexual marriage, was far from evident regarding individual lesbians.

The Making of a "Sexual Invert" and a Professional Reformer

Frances Kellor, an early twentieth-century lesbian who took the torch from Jane Addams and made an exemplary career in social reform, is an apt illustration of these points. Kellor, who in 1898 became one of the first female graduate students in the sociology program at the University of Chicago, conducted fieldwork at Hull House and also resided there and at the Rivington Street College Settlement in New York as often as her other duties would permit. Her career as one of the leading Progressive professional reformers was thus forged in the settlement house milieu and the University of Chicago's department of sociology, which emphasized the study of problems such as those that Jane Addams had brought to Chicago's attention.

Kellor was among the most successful of those in the municipal housekeeping movement who took the next step, for which Addams had called in 1898. As a social scientist, Kellor knew how to conduct investigations, collect the facts, and use them as persuasive evidence in convincing city, state, and national legislatures of the need for reform. As a professional, she also brought the kind of continuity to reform that was generally impossible through the voluntarism that had characterized reform work in the nineteenth century. She helped establish what became a woman-dominated, and often lesbian-dominated, occupation that combined social science with social activism.

Unlike most nineteenth- and early twentieth-century lesbian pioneers, whose families were solidly middle or upper class,

Frances Kellor came from a working-class background. Her mother took in laundry and cleaned other people's houses, and while Frances was growing up, she too worked in these jobs. Her early life was formative both emotionally and in terms of her professional interests. Despite her phenomenal successes as an adult and the many years she shared with Mary Dreier, an heiress whose father had been a wealthy industrialist, Kellor never fully recovered from her childhood bitterness and frustrations because of poverty and the knowledge of her mother's powerlessness. She sought remedies for the social problems connected with such conditions throughout her career.

Havelock Ellis and Richard von Krafft-Ebing would have considered Kellor an excellent case to illustrate their theories of congenital sexual inversion. Even in childhood, she passionately eschewed femininity. However, that may have been because she saw that her mother's femininity got her nothing but a life of hard work. There is no credible trace of a father in Kellor's history, and it is very possible that she was what was then called illegitimate. A purposely assumed masculinity would surely have seemed useful to her as a girl; boyishness, she may have believed, would protect her from the victimization that her mother suffered.

Like so many female pioneers — Frances Willard, Anna Shaw, and Mollie Hay among them — as a child Kellor was a "fearless tomboy" who could use both a shotgun and a revolver to hunt, which she did in order to augment her mother's meager earnings. Ellen Fitzpatrick, who includes Kellor in her study of four pioneering social scientists at the University of Chicago (none of them married), interviewed a girlhood acquaintance of Kellor's from Coldwater, Michigan, who "disapproved of her because she 'wore her hair shingled and walked and talked like a boy.'" The woman's brother recalled in another interview that Kellor as a girl "could whittle out a slingshot and hit anything [at which] she aimed." On the school playground she could "outdo any of the boys."

Fitzpatrick characterizes Kellor as "never really [having] lost the tough persona she exhibited as a child." But Kellor put to good use that toughness, which the sexologists of her day assumed to be characteristic of gender inversion. Surely her hard-skinned demeanor, her bluntness and directness, helped her to achieve in a man's world far more than most women ever achieved.

Kellor left school at the age of seventeen to become a typesetter at the local newspaper, a far more lucrative position than the domestic jobs that had supported her mother. Her verbal skills soon landed her an even better job as a reporter. When she was twenty-one, she left her mother's home to live with two librarians, Frances and Mary Eddy. Biographers usually suggest that the Eddy sisters, who encouraged her to study and to apply to Cornell Law School, which had recently opened to women, wished only to help the bright young Kellor set out on the right road in life. However, that theory does not explain why Frances Eddy followed Kellor to Cornell in 1895 and lived with her there.

Kellor received her law degree within two years. But by then she had decided that she was more interested in the new field of experimental sociology than in the dry applications of the law, and she enrolled in the University of Chicago. Gertrude Dudley, the head professor of women's physical education at the university, helped Kellor finance her studies by hiring her to teach gymnastics. At this time, perhaps under Dudley's influence, Kellor published her first academic article, which foreshadowed the philosophy of Title IX by the better part of a century: she argued that physical education for college women should be expanded to equal the men's physical education programs. "If women are to accomplish the same quality and quantity of intellectual work as men," she insisted, "one of the essentials is a more active, variable physical life." Kellor, to whom appropriate gender behavior had never meant anything, appears to have been blessedly oblivious of the fact that in 1898 most people believed that women never could accomplish intellectual work equal to men's under any circumstances, and that on no account should they engage in serious physical education. Yet such ostensible oblivion may have been one of her bold strategies, in embryo form, for charging ahead and pulling other women in her wake, as she often did later in her professional life.

No letters that give insight into the relationship between Kellor and Gertrude Dudley exist, but Mary Dreier, who was Kellor's life partner from 1904 until Kellor's death, in 1952, has written that while Kellor was a graduate student, Dudley was her "close and intimate friend" (a common description in that era of a relationship that our era would dub lesbian). It appears likely that the two women were lovers while Kellor was at the University of Chicago. Their friendship, though probably not their intimacy, continued long after Kellor left Chicago. In 1909, they wrote on women's athletics together, publishing the book *Athletic Games in the Education of Women.*

Kellor left Chicago in 1902 and went to New York, where she did research on fraud and corruption in employment bureaus. She had suspected that many of these businesses swindled and led astray innocent immigrants and young women from rural areas who came to the city to find work. She visited employment agencies disguised as a prospective employer or employee, and once actually worked for some time as a servant in order to carry out an investigation thoroughly. The research resulted in her 1904 book, *Out of Work: A Study of Employment Agencies,* in which she was the first to call for government regulation of such agencies. The social philosophy her book propounded, which had been developed in the crucible of her firsthand experiences of deprivation and her later settlement house work, prefigured crucial ideas of the New Deal of the 1930s and 1940s and the Great Society of the 1960s. For example, Kellor was one of the first to articulate the point that unemployment is not a problem for the individual alone; it is also a problem for the government, because it must necessarily affect the welfare of the nation.

The same year *Out of Work* was published, Kellor met Mary Dreier, a socialite with a social conscience, who was awed by the energy and intelligence Kellor applied to the causes that both of them held dear. A few months later the two women were living together in the Dreier family mansion in Brooklyn, New York.

"A World Dear That Love Makes So Beautiful"

The early correspondence between Frances and Mary consists of surreptitious, indisputably passionate letters. The first extant letter, dated May 5, 1904, established a code intended to deceive Mary's sister, Margaret, with whom Mary then lived. (Frances and Mary probably met through Margaret, when Frances worked with her in the Women's Municipal League, which helped lobby the New York legislature to pass a bill regulating women's employment agencies.) In this letter, Frances intimated that her relationship with Mary had been in progress for a while. Hoping that Margaret "will be unable, as usual, to guess about our numbers," she suggested that from then on in their correspondence, Mary was to sign her name "Six" or "Sixy" and Frances would be "Seven" or "7."

The erotic nature of the letters reveals why Frances and Mary felt a code was necessary. "The colors and sunlight make me hungry for you, you dear small six," Frances wrote during a brief separation in their first year. "It was so hard to go and leave you. There can be no goodnight here dear." She had gone to investigate a tenement housing problem, but she would be returning to Mary soon, and "even tho it will be late I know I shall gather you up to give you . . . the tenderness and sweetness." A few months later, on the first anniversary of what had apparently been their first sexual encounter, Frances wrote to Mary from a train to Philadelphia, where she was going to investigate a labor problem:

> My own dear beautiful Sweetheart. I am wondering a little if you know what I am thinking about on this Phila trip. I am afraid dear it's not about the problems, the day, or what I hope to do. It's back a year ago this week. Was it not a year ago this week dear that I had you in C— and really took you for my own dear heart? Seems to me it was dear and my heart is full of love and longing to gather you up and to try and tell you how wonderfully beautiful you have been in all these months.

These love letters were written usually on trains or in unfamiliar hotels, in the course of lonely travel to various cities where Kellor, and Mary Dreier too, were trying to improve the lot of the poor and the disenfranchised. They are filled with playfulness and longing and the crying need for intimacy that even the most devoted of social reformers must feel to the bone. They reveal too the erotic tension between the two women and their sexual dynamic. "I have this whole car [on a train] to myself," Frances wrote during the winter of 1905, "and if you were here I could put my arm around you and hunt out one of those tiny curls — and embarrass you shy little girl. . . . Thursday isn't far away. There love burns through beautiful nights you dear sweetheart." Six months later Frances was still teasing: "Sixy dear, That was a naughty note last night and I guess it made you lonely and I am sorry."

Understanding the rather devout Mary's need for a spiritual confirmation of the physical, Frances was also careful to assure her, "There is such a sweet consciousness of the beauty of our love tonight and tho I want you I feel so strongly its beauty and strength and my soul goes out to you in a way the body cannot limit. We know dear the greatness and loneliness of the separation and when we are together it will be the holier for that." Yet the physical remained overwhelming for a time. On still another train, during the summer of 1905, Frances lamented to Mary, "I'd give most anything to just see and feel you for a little while."

Their relationship was probably complicated by Mary's bisexuality, though there is no record of Frances's response to it. As the papers Mary left behind reveal, by 1907, while she was deep in a relationship with Frances, she was also in love with her brother-in-law, Raymond Robins, a social activist, who married Margaret Dreier in 1905. Mary's love poems to Robins, written over a period of more than thirty years (during her relationship with Frances), employ elaborate metaphors of knights and ladies and honorable renunciations, suggesting that she and Robins agreed to sublimate their passion in good works. However, as the correspondence with Frances illustrates, Mary felt no restraint in her passionate lesbian relationship.

Despite the apparent complications, Mary and Frances's life together appears to have been fulfilling, even exciting, and conducive to both women's grand work. When they met, in 1904, Mary considered herself, as she wrote, "something of a wreck, without energy." Frances saw her weakness and encouraged her to strength, as she did throughout the next forty-eight years. "Along with your love — the depth and beauty of which I am just coming to know," Frances wrote in an early letter, "I want there to be dear a strength equal to the beauty, and individuality along with the duality."

To encourage that strength and individuality, Frances — after remarking on "that beautiful mind of yours which so depreciates itself and which so few have ever tried to help grow" — insisted that Mary go to school. Mary had always believed that her mind was lax and untrained but had accepted without argument her father's edict that college was unnecessary. However, now she followed Frances's urgings and enrolled at the New York School of Civics and Philanthropy, where Frances herself had studied when she first went to New York, in 1902. "Then it will be easier to express yourself," Frances wrote to Mary in 1905, arguing for the importance of higher education yet sensitively assuring her, "You dear heart I'm not thinking to change the real you a bit only the training."

Frances's hope for Mary was realized. Though Mary had been shy and self-effacing by all accounts, under Frances's influence she forced herself to assume the presidency of the New York Women's Trade Union League in 1906. She was especially terrified of the public speaking that a leadership position involved, but with Frances's help and with her new formal training, she became an increasingly confident speaker and organizer. Along with Helen Marot, she was a leading figure in the 1909 Uprising of the Twenty Thousand, bringing many workers into the strike and arousing the sympathy of the public through what was by then her superlative oratorical skill. In 1911, after the Triangle Shirtwaist Factory fire, she was appointed to a nine-member New York State Factory Investigating Commission. She was its only female member and, according to various accounts, its moving force and its soul. The commission drafted legislation that revolutionized New York labor laws regarding wages and safety.

In 1914, Mary Dreier became the chair of the Industrial Section of the Woman Suffrage Party, and she began lecturing widely on the importance of the vote to the concerns of working women. In 1916 she became an officer in the New York Women's City Club, where she started lifelong friendships with Frances Perkins, Eleanor Roosevelt, and other lesbian and bisexual women who shared her

Progressive ideals. They aided her in building important coalitions to agitate for legislation that she regarded as vital, such as the eight-hour day and health insurance for workers. Dreier played a prominent role in helping make social causes into public policy virtually until her death, in 1963, when she was in her eighties.

But the powerful Mary Dreier of those years was very different from the diffident young woman who came into Frances Kellor's life in 1904. Though Frances was only two years older than Mary, she was by far the more accomplished of the two when they met. She was living proof of what the liberal and radical daughters of the captains of industry had been insisting for more than a generation: if the poor were given adequate opportunities — which America could afford and the rich had the responsibility to help provide — their potential would be limitless. Mary Dreier was awed by Frances's brilliance, but surely she was also excited by this working-class daughter who had achieved success with her tough-girl drive and realism. Frances was only thirty-one years old when they met, but she had already completed a law degree and several years of graduate study, written two books, and published several articles. In the dynamic between them, Mary was happy to let herself be taught by Frances, who in turn was thrilled to assume toward Mary the role of parent and teacher as well as lover.

Yet Mary had qualities that Frances believed she herself lacked and that she could not help admiring. Mary was classy, attractive, feminine. Frances saw her as "always so dear and bright and fresh and lovely and never seem[ing] too tired to be thoughtful and loving," while she saw in herself an almost overly focused energy that she had had to develop in order to move beyond her early circumstances. Frances feared that her keen focus had made her "uninteresting and tiresome," quite without the discursive charm that she believed was possessed by the wealthy young women with whom she worked in reform organizations such as the Women's Municipal League. To Frances's pleasure, though, Mary did not seem to notice her deficiencies. What Frances loved especially about their relationship, as she wrote in the summer of 1905, was that they did not need to "know all about the past and talk it over" and dwell on issues that might divide them, such as class differences (and perhaps Mary's bisexuality?). Together they could be "so silently contented" and so happy in the moment — undoubtedly a luxury that the hard-striving, perpetually cogitating Frances seldom allowed herself outside of her connection with Mary Dreier.

Through the years, Frances Kellor and Mary Dreier worked side by side, whether in a formal capacity — as in 1912, when through the New York Women's Trade Union League the two women fought for a legislative bill that would mandate a maximum forty-eight-hour work week — or in an informal capacity, when Mary used her social position to open doors to philanthropists, which Frances was able to keep open through her brilliant skills. But perhaps Mary's most important function in Frances's life was to heal the wounds inflicted by her painful childhood. As Frances wrote to Mary during a pre-Christmas depression early in their relationship, "I don't do Christmas thoughts as you do, because there are always such sad and sometimes bitter memories of these days. They are going away with you in my life, but the memories do crowd in and make one feel a little cynical as to the whys and wherefores of being in the world at all." But most often, she assured Mary, she understood the whys and wherefores through her: "It is so beautiful to be in a world dear that love makes so beautiful, tho I am sure dearie I don't discern anything as beautiful as you are."

The Profession of Defending the Underdog

As bitter as she continued to be about her early deprivation, Kellor was nevertheless able to ameliorate the deprivation of others significantly in the course of her long career. Almost all of her professional life was concerned with social betterment in some form. In her early work, she conducted research using the muckraking techniques she had learned at the University of Chicago and practiced at Hull House. Her aim was not only to discover social ills and bring them to public awareness, but also to mobilize support for reform legislation. Kellor proposed and lobbied for laws that affected women particularly, but she often went beyond that major concern to issues such as tenement housing conditions and child labor practices. For example, after providing the shocking facts and figures of the continuing abuse of child workers, she drafted and successfully lobbied for the Prentice-Tully Bill, which put teeth into existing laws regarding compulsory education and the minimum age of workers.

As general director of the Inter-Municipal Committee on Household Research — a group Kellor founded with Margaret Dreier, in which Mary was also active — she once again focused on the problems of female domestic workers. Perhaps she kept returning to the subject because she had learned about such problems up close as a child, and even living with the very wealthy Mary Dreier could not make her forget that knowledge. Through the Inter-Municipal Committee, Kellor planned and supervised investigations into conditions for domestic workers and set up models for similar investigations throughout the country.

Realizing that many of the labor problems she was dealing with piecemeal could be handled more effectively on a national level, Kellor was among the first to lobby the federal government for a Department of Labor. When government was not forthcoming in its solutions to various ills, she also worked to establish efficient private organizations. For example, in her book *Out of Work* she was especially concerned with the exploitation of African-American women who had come north. Her research led her to the conclusion that often they had been promised decent jobs by northern employment agencies, but once they arrived, they were forced to take work — usually as domestic servants — that exploited them mercilessly and left them without recourse. Kellor dubbed this "a new system of slavery." In response to the situation, she and Mary Dreier worked in 1906 to instigate the formation of the National League for the Protection of Colored Women, a society that helped new migrants find better jobs and provided them with social services and housing. The National League for the Protection of Colored Women was a forerunner of the National Urban League, with which it merged in 1911.

Kellor's preoccupation in her work was always with the disadvantaged, the exploited, the underdog. Her own experiences as the child of a poor, unmarried woman and a "masculine" girl (an "invert") in a small midwestern town where girls were supposed to be traditionally feminine may have formed her as a champion for the alienated, but her undistracted focus as well as her forceful rhetorical and administrative skills permitted her to succeed so well in that role. While the feminine woman remained the social and erotic ideal in the early twentieth century, there was, thanks to Kellor's predecessors, such as Shaw, Willard, and Hay, enough space for the "unfeminine" woman of extraordinary talents to maneuver — and Kellor did just that, managing to win the professional admiration of influential politicians, who took her seriously and placed her in positions where she could effect important social changes.

In 1906, Kellor organized a major research project exposing the myriad ways in which new immigrants were exploited in America. She discovered that private bankers would "invest" the money of immigrant clients and never return it; employment agencies would send them to labor camps or sweatshops, where they were worked to death; agents would sell them bogus ship tickets for their families, who would then be left stranded in the old country; notaries public would fleece them with invalid leases or deeds of sale. Indeed, they were taken advantage of from the moment they set foot in America. Sleazy types would meet immigrants at the boat and sell them five-cent subway tickets for a dollar or five dollars apiece, or exchange the immigrants' foreign money for counterfeit or Confederate bills.

Kellor shared her research findings with Theodore Roosevelt, who had become her friend and admirer since reading *Out of Work*, and he was soon extolling her as an expert on the problems of immigrants. The immigration historian John Higham observes that Kellor "did more than anyone else" to direct Roosevelt's reformist zeal to the plight of urban immigrants. Roosevelt encouraged the governor of New York, Charles Hughes, to take Kellor as seriously as he himself did. In 1908, Hughes appointed her to a state commission looking into the living and working conditions of immigrants. When a bill was passed, through her maneuvering, creating a new Bureau of Industries and Immigration under the New York State Department of Labor, she was appointed its chief. She was thirty-six years old at the time, and women in most places in the United States still could not even vote. Yet Kellor became not only the first woman to head an executive department in New York, but also the state's youngest division head.

In 1910, the year Kellor was named chief, over 580,000 immigrants landed on Ellis Island, a good many of them poor, gullible, and friendless. Her job was monumental, since her bureau was the coordinating agency for all problems concerning immigrants in the state: enforcing and/or creating laws dealing with wages and working conditions, preventing fraud, prosecuting those who played on the ignorance of the newcomers. But under her, the bureau's interests went beyond legislative matters to practical services. For example, newly arrived immigrants were now rescued from the clutches of swindlers by welfare workers who spoke their language; the workers would meet the immigrants as they disembarked and direct them to special transfer facilities that would get them where they wanted to go in America. Kellor's earlier research and (perhaps especially) her emotional connection to the alien and the powerless permitted her to anticipate their needs by such personal touches.

Kellor generally promoted welfare programs for the immigrants that were financed and administered by the state. But, again following the model of Jane Addams, she also believed it was important to get wealthy private citizens and philanthropic organizations to pitch in and help the underclass. In her work with immigrants, as in her earlier work, Kellor understood how to appeal to the rich for these ends. It did not hurt that she was able to get Mary Dreier involved. Dreier's family connections and Kellor's persuasive intelligence enabled them to interest men such as the head of the Chesapeake and Ohio Railroad and the president of the National City Bank to throw their weight — financial and otherwise — behind Kellor's various projects: bringing sports, music, and dancing into immigrant neighborhoods; training young immigrants in sanitation and as teachers of English to other immigrants; promoting the hiring of public welfare workers who spoke foreign languages and could communicate with the populations they were trying to serve.

Kellor truly believed that the newest Americans could be assimilated, and that education (which had rescued her from poverty and permitted her to assimilate with other classes) was as vital for them as it had been for her. She thus led campaigns to establish public schools in the immigrant neighborhoods and in labor camps where immigrant workers lived with their families. Because she thought it was important to educate the older generation as well as the young, she set up permanent evening classes in English and civics for immigrant adults. Her efforts were far-reaching: the establishment of night schools for the education of adult immigrants paved the way for the public night school movement in America, which has for generations benefited working-class adults in particular.

As she did in all her work, Kellor brought a liberal, humanistic approach to her job as chief of the Bureau of Industries and Immigration. Her work was not easy, because she had to battle rampant ethnic hatred, particularly from nativist groups such as the Immigration Restriction League, the American Protective Association, and, of course, the Ku Klux Klan, all of which shared the conviction that the only true Americans were of Teutonic origin. But through her settlement house work, Kellor had come to believe that southern and eastern European immigrants, no less than immigrants from the British Isles, Germany, Scandinavia, and the Netherlands, were capable of learning to value traditional American conceptions of freedom, individual liberty, and self-government. That many of the new immigrants were illiterate or unused to self-government was only a temporary phenomenon, she argued; soon they would become not Polish-American, say, but simply American. Just as the country had absorbed immigrants into its melting pot in the past, it would again — to everyone's benefit, she believed. Her optimistic conviction about the simple and inevitable Americanization of even first-generation immigrants was perhaps somewhat naive, but there is no doubt that through her policies and the laws that her bureau helped get passed, she lightened the burdens of millions of immigrants.

Theodore Roosevelt's continued admiration ushered in the third phase of Kellor's career: she worked on a national level in Roosevelt's Progressive Party, which supported federal intervention on social welfare issues. During the 1912 presidential campaign, Kellor, as one of the first American women to penetrate the inner circle of a national political party, wielded power that was virtually unprecedented for a female. Roosevelt claimed in his autobiography that until his association with Frances Kellor and Jane Addams he had favored woman suffrage "only tepidly," but knowing them, he gladly included a suffrage plank on his platform. Both Kellor and Mary Dreier were delegates to the Progressive Party's national convention, and through Roosevelt's influence, Kellor and Jane Addams became national committeewomen to the Progressive Party. In that capacity Kellor drafted the platform planks in the areas of her vital interests: woman suffrage, federal protection of immigrants, workmen's compensation, and a minimum wage.

Though Roosevelt lost his 1912 bid for the presidency to Woodrow Wilson, the fervor of the Progressive Party continued past the election and into the congressional elections of 1914. Frances Kellor and Jane Addams had written a proposal to establish through the party organization an Office of National Progressive Services. In 1913, Roosevelt named Kellor to direct that major new office, and she resigned as head of the Bureau of Industries and Immigration in order to take the job. Serving on the subcommittees under her jurisdiction were such luminaries as John Dewey, who worked with her on public education issues, and Jacob Riis, who worked with her on immigration issues. With the help of Progressive congressmen, Kellor produced a number of legislative proposals that were passed either in part or in whole by the national government. Her most impassioned interests as head of the National Progressive Services centered on workers, including issues such as a national minimum wage, unemployment and sickness insurance, and old age insurance — that is, social security. But she also promoted such forward-looking programs as school lunches for children.

By World War I, it was apparent that even though reformers were enthusiastic about the National Progressive Services, most Americans were not. Yet during Kellor's tenure, she managed to do some lasting good, and the Progressive Party's demise during World War I meant only that she went on to other work along similar lines. She was in the forefront of those who maintained a liberal commitment even when it was no longer in fashion. For example, she took a leadership role on interracial councils during the 1920s, wishing to foster and promulgate the concept that Americans came in various colors as well as ethnic backgrounds.

Frances Kellor was probably more intimately familiar with the sexologists' pronouncements on female sexual inversion than any of the women discussed thus far. She was the first woman in the United States to write about female criminality, which sexologists and criminologists often associated with lesbianism. Her early studies, published while she was still a student at the University of Chicago — "Psychological and Environmental Study of Women Criminals" (1900) and *Experimental Sociology* (1901), which also deals with women criminals — were written in response to the work of Cesare Lombroso, an Italian criminologist and the author of the widely translated book *The Female Offender* (1895). Lombroso's book remarked repeatedly on the congenital sexual inversion of the female criminals he had studied, suggesting that the "bad genes" that led to criminality frequently also led to lesbianism. American criminologists of the day seemed to confirm this theory by revealing that homosexuality was rampant in women's penal institutions, where Kellor did her early research. Therefore, it is remarkable that Kellor never once mentioned lesbianism among her subjects. Clearly, she could not bring herself to articulate the topic publicly.

In both of her early works on female criminality, however, she did challenge Lombroso's general theory, widely shared by nineteenth-century sexologists, that human anomalies are congenital. She argued in social constructionist terms — a revolutionary position for the early twentieth century — saying that the individual is formed largely by "the tremendous forces of social and economic environment." Kellor must have felt that her lesbianism was a logical response to the personal and impersonal facts of her life — to the emotions she had developed through the particulars of her family romance and to the options her society gave her. She refused what she must have seen as the victimization her mother endured at least partly because of her femininity and heterosexuality. She chose to have intimate relationships with women rather than to marry a man — which would have made her peripatetic, pressured work life virtually impossible in the early twentieth century. She was thus able to become a force for social good, far exceeding what most feminine heterosexual women of her day could possibly accomplish.

Therefore, Kellor must have been horrified by the knowledge that the sexologists considered women like her to be products of a hereditary taint. The kinds of relationships that soothed her "bitter memories" (as she wrote to Mary), and her "masculine" spirit of self-confidence and drive (which made her professional successes possible), were seen by "experts" as inextricably bound up with congenital criminality and degeneracy. How could she not have been shaken by their pronouncements?

The lesbians she knew intimately and socially were, of course, not in penal institutions or insane asylums (another favorite place in which the sexologists gathered their earliest "knowledge" about lesbianism); rather, like her, they were in settlement houses, reform organizations, and Progressive politics, trying to save the world. Yet the connection being made between homosexuality and congenital defect was so insistent that Kellor must have believed that she and many of her reformer friends would have been discredited if they acknowledged that they had anything in common with sexual inverts. It is sadly ironic that despite her strong voice, which corrected hateful stereotypes about minorities and defended those who had been made defenseless, she could not feel free to correct the sexologists' pronouncements about "masculine," women-loving women like herself.

❧ 9 ❧

POISONING THE SOURCE

All, all of me that you want — and more, I suppose, because I go to you — flow into you with deep, strong tides
that an age less skeptical than ours might understand
and even welcome.

— Tracy Mygatt to Frances Witherspoon, April 12, 1933

THOUGH SOCIAL CONSCIENCE fell out of fashion between the
Great War and the Depression, lesbian reformers continued to
cheer each other on in their endeavors, often working through their
networks. For example, in 1921, the lesbian president of Bryn Mawr
College, M. Carey Thomas, cooperated with her friends in the
Women's Trade Union League to establish the Bryn Mawr Summer
School for female workers. With its ethnically and religiously diverse students (unlike those who were matriculating at most colleges in that era), the summer school dramatically democratized
higher education, divorcing it from its elite connections and tailor-
ing it to be useful to working-class women. Bryn Mawr Summer
School students were offered classes in economics, history of the
labor movement, causes and cures of unemployment, trade union
politics, composition, and public speaking — everything that was
directed toward (in the words of Eleanor Roosevelt, who honored
Thomas at a banquet in 1933) giving "people the tools so that they
[could] work out their own salvation wisely and well."

Convinced that now that women were full citizens, they must
influence government not to repeat the folly of the Great War,
activist women also took a prominent role in newly established
peace groups, such as Carrie Catt's annual conferences on the

cause and cure of war and Jane Addams's Women's International League for Peace and Freedom (WILPF). WILPF, founded in 1919, was the largest of the peace organizations that operated under the ostensibly essentialist assumption that women, with their mother-hearts, were more gifted in peacemaking than men. WILPF's leadership from the start largely comprised women who would be described in contemporary terms as lesbian or bisexual. Jane Addams was its first head. She was succeeded by Hannah Clothier Hull, whose correspondence with Caroline Biddle around the turn of the century reveals their romantic friendship. The dynamic president of Mount Holyoke College, Mary Woolley, who chaired a major WILPF committee, the People's Mandate to Governments to End War, lived for half a century with the activist Jeannette Marks. Mabel Vernon, the director of the People's Mandate committee, lived for twenty-six years, until her death, with Consuelo Reyes, a Latin American peace activist.

Whether or not the general membership of WILPF was aware of the lesbian domestic arrangements of its leaders, many of the leaders certainly acknowledged these arrangements among themselves. The leaders of the People's Mandate to Governments to End War were largely lesbian: in addition to Vernon, its director, and Woolley, its chair, Carrie Catt served as honorary chair, Lillian Wald was a vice chair, and the governing board included Anne Martin, Vida Milholland, and her partner Peg Hamilton. As their surviving correspondence reveals, Milholland and Hamilton, who were prominent speakers for the People's Mandate, often invited other lesbian couples from the committee, such as Vernon and Reyes and Woolley and Marks, to their upstate New York home.

These women referred to their dyads as "family" and used various other code words to signify to one another that they knew who they were. When Vernon accompanied some peace activists back to Latin America after a 1939 WILPF conference, Milholland wrote to a mutual friend who had just seen the women, "How is Mabel getting on with her South American bevy of gay Senoritas? . . . [Peg and I] found them delightful." To other lesbian couples in the peace movement, these women could openly acknowledge the importance of their domestic arrangements and mourn when their partnership ended. When Milholland died, in 1952, for example, it was to Vernon and Reyes that Peg Hamilton could confess, "I pray for courage and strength for it is a shattering blow."

While these lesbian reformers continued to fight the good fight, as the century wore on they were confronted with obstacles that were personally more difficult than post–World War I recalcitrance to social conscience had been. With the spread of what passed for sophistication about matters of sexuality, they found that the love relationships that often animated or made possible their best work were now widely seen as sick. Sometimes they merely ignored the fact that their own partnerships had anything in common with those that were being popularly described and denigrated as "homosexual" or "queer." Implicitly or explicitly, they claimed the protective coloration of earlier romantic friendships, as Mary Arnold and Mabel Reed did, and as Tracy Mygatt and Frances Witherspoon did. However, particularly when they played a controversial role in a position of power, they were attacked by their enemies on precisely the grounds of their sexuality. Then they could not avoid the realization that their intimate relationships, which contributed to their personal happiness and encouraged their professional successes, made them vulnerable to accusations of perversity. Their response was panic and categorical denial; this was true of Miriam Van Waters, for instance. In other cases the women were convinced, often by well-meaning relatives or the medical profession, that their love for each other was pathological; this held true for Mildred Olmsted and Ruth Mellor. Then they responded with self-loathing and confusion.

Protective Coloration: Mary Arnold and Mabel Reed, Tracy Mygatt and Frances Witherspoon

Mary Arnold and Mabel Reed spent much of their long lives together trying to make life better for their fellow citizens. They had been girlhood sweethearts. In 1892, at the age of sixteen, they had "decided to share all our respective belongings to the dismay of both [of our] families." As Mary Arnold described it, in 1892 she "made three important decisions: Would not marry. . . . A lifelong association with Mabel Reed. A business career." To facilitate the latter, Arnold and Reed went to Cornell University together to study agriculture and then ran a fifty-five-acre farm. Arnold blithely reported in a personal narrative written about sixty years later, "We have lived together ever since and continued, without a ripple, to hold all things in common."

Farming did not satisfy them long, however. They wanted adventure, and they wanted even more to reform the world according to their lights. In 1908 the two New Jersey women became field matrons for the U.S. Indian Service in California. They had always hated gender restrictions, including the prison of the Victorian female's corset and gown. Thus they were delighted that in their new jobs they could wear Stetson hats, high boots, and "divided skirts" (that is, pants). They could escape from the usual role foisted on women of their class as *"ladies* — the kind who have Sunday schools, and never say a bad word, and rustle around in a lot of silk petticoats," Mary Arnold scoffed. Though their values were "maternal," they were decidedly not ladies.

The Indian Service told them in the most nebulous terms that their assignment was to "civilize the Indians [and] as much as possible to elevate them and introduce white standards." They were on their own. At a loss as to what that paternalistic order was supposed to mean, they settled on opening a much-needed and very popular school for Native American children and adults, just as Caroline Putnam and Sallie Holley had done for freed slaves in the previous century.

Like the settlement house workers of the intervening years, Arnold and Reed understood that whites had no monopoly on "civilization" and that it was important to learn the ways of the people they hoped to serve — to learn from them as well as to teach them. They determined to emulate what was worth emulating, such as Native American "reserve and dignity," which came to replace their inconsequential East Coast small talk and made friendships within the community possible.

Their 1957 book, *In the Land of the Grasshopper Song,* recollects their work as Indian matrons, but as they tell the story, Arnold and Reed also reveal the life they led together during those early years. With no evident self-consciousness about how readers might construe their words, they make it clear that while they loved mankind, they did not love men. As young women they acknowledged that the high adventures they craved would have been made easier by male muscle, but they generally found creative solutions that were more palatable to them than intimacy with a man would have been. For example, at one point they befriended a Klamath River Native American woman, Essie, who had liaisons with three men. Mary and Mabel recognized that in the East, it was relatively easy for women to be self-sufficient, but in the Wild West, "masculine qualifications certainly do sing out, and there is no doubt about it, men are valuable. Essie, with the brains that distinguish her, perceives this and attaches three — Mart, Les, and Eddy. We, with the brains that distinguish us, attach Essie, and so enjoy the blessings of all three with no embarrassment and none of the problems."

Arnold's and Reed's experiences with California Native Americans were formative. For the rest of their lives, well into their old age, they were involved in struggles on behalf of those without economic and social power. They were enamored of the possibilities of spreading the advantages of democracy and empowering workers, as Arnold often wrote, very much in the Jane Addams spirit. Unlike the settlement house women, however, who focused on urban problems, they usually worked in small towns and villages, where they organized and helped build consumer cooperatives, including cooperative housing and cafeterias; they encouraged land settlement movements among the poor; they established credit unions for workers; and they fought for the rights of coal miners and lobster fishermen.

The spirit that Arnold and Reed brought to their tasks was characterized by a former coworker in the cooperative movement who had gone on to less inspiring occupations. He wrote to them in 1941, when both women were in their mid-sixties, "I'd give all I possess . . . to be with you today, just be there to be enthused again about how damned wonderful everything is. I understand very clearly the thing Coady [another cooperative worker] said to me on several occasions. He said, 'Those two women make me feel strong and powerful.'"

Mary Arnold and Mabel Reed made others feel strong and powerful by their ability to help the needy help themselves, in the best mother-heart tradition, and never, of course, by feminine wiles. They continued to make no pretense of gender-appropriate behavior or heterosexuality. Nor did they hide their relationship from others, though they never gave a name to it. *In the Land of the Grasshopper Song* was published at the height of the feminine mystique and American homophobia, yet in that book Arnold and Reed claimed the privileges of an earlier generation and evinced no awareness of how unpopular their attitude toward gender and their affectional preferences had become. They wrote, for example, of a female acquaintance who was dependent on her husband for transportation, observing that though they themselves had no money and few possessions, "at least we were not sitting waiting for a husband to bring us [anywhere]." Mary quoted Mabel as saying, "If I lived the life of some married women, I'd commit hari-kari on our nice new hatchet."

The pacifist and civil rights leaders Tracy Mygatt and Frances Witherspoon present yet another example of a female couple that was formed in a time when same-sex love relationships might still be considered romantic friendships and two women who set up a household were thought to have an innocent Boston marriage. Because the psychosexual possibilities of such relationships were not often considered by prepsychoanalytical generations, lesbophobia was not common. When Tracy Mygatt, writing to Frances Witherspoon, referred to "an age less skeptical than ours" that "might understand and even welcome" their love, she revealed her awareness of the ways in which attitudes toward love between women had changed in the past decades. Yet Mygatt and Witherspoon never internalized those attitudes that had become dominant in the external world, and they refused to change how they conducted their partnership.

They met as students at Bryn Mawr College, where they began their political activity as suffragists under the influence of M. Carey Thomas. Together Mygatt and Witherspoon became the first organizers of the Woman's Suffrage Party in eastern Pennsylvania. But like Jane Addams, and unlike other suffragists, they were not willing to sacrifice their pacifist convictions with the advent of the Great War, even for the sake of the vote. In 1915, in the midst of American war fever and a preparedness movement, Tracy Mygatt helped organize the Anti-Enlistment League, which encouraged men to resist conscription. Two years later, when the United States entered the war, Frances Witherspoon founded the Bureau of Legal Advice, the first organization in America whose goal was not only to support the rights of conscientious objectors but also "to protect free speech victims." The Bureau of Legal Advice was the forerunner of the American Civil Liberties Union, which was founded five months later. The BLA and the ACLU (first called the National Civil Liberties Bureau) worked closely together on numerous occasions, including a defense of aliens who were being deported in 1918 under the accusation of abetting the "Red Menace."

Tracy and Frances remained virtually inseparable in both their private and public lives for sixty-five years. They even managed to die within three weeks of each other, at the ages of eighty-seven and eighty-eight, in 1973. Since they were almost always together, their correspondence is not voluminous, but what exists indicates their passionate commitment to each other. "It's a wonderful thing to love as we do. Let's thank God for it!" Tracy wrote to Frances in 1923, at a time when lesbianism was getting a bad press everywhere in America. After they had been together for more than a quarter of a century, they were still sending each other love letters, ignoring the fact that much of the rest of the world considered their love perverse. "My own dear Darling," Tracy responded to a note Frances mailed when she had gone to Mississippi on a family matter in 1933, "Oh, if you knew the meat and drink your words are to me — not the *many-ness* of them — for indeed I know how tired you are . . . but the things they make me know and *re-know*."

So far from agreeing with Dr. Phyllis Blanchard's 1929 pro-

nouncements about the dangers of love between women, they believed that their relationship brought them strengths and joys. In
this 1933 letter, Tracy is solicitous of Frances and encourages her to
attend to writing fiction and drama, which was a happy distraction
as well as serious business for both women. "And I'll work on my
book, too," she bravely promises, before giving vent to her poignant
loneliness for Frances: "And I'll try so hard to be that Nexcy [sic]
Kitty of whom you see so fair a portrait in your mind's eye! And
some day, please God, I'll be again the little kitty in your dear, dear
arms." Years later, they still continued to write in the same desiring
vein, during even brief separations: "Darling dear — I don't see
how I can stay away til Friday. . . . Your own, own Little Thing."
They never stopped being proud of the love and stability they provided for each other throughout the years, as they admitted in an
oral history interview they gave in 1966, seven years before their
deaths, in which they described their domestic life as "a model for
[our] married friends."

Shoving Same-Sex Love into the Closet: Elizabeth Gurley Flynn, Miriam Van Waters

In the half-century between 1920 and 1970, female same-sex love
was widely vilified in America. Perhaps it had come to be seen in
a new light because of the successes earlier generations of feminists had had in opening professions to women and making them
full citizens. Women's changed status might mean that those who
wished to could now more easily be totally independent of heterosexual arrangements. If women were able to choose a life partner
without concerns about economic security or social and political
status, might not the institution of marriage be under siege? Other
than Mygatt's provocative comment about being "a model for [our]
married friends," there is no record of how her sixty-five-year
Boston marriage with Frances Witherspoon was received in their
radical circles. But in general, heterosexual radicals had no more
sympathy with homosexuality than heterosexual conservatives did.
Those who had power on either end of the political spectrum ada-

mantly refused to acknowledge that one of their number might be lesbian, and they exercised censorship if they considered that an individual who represented them was indiscreet about such matters.

Elizabeth Gurley Flynn, a feminist and labor organizer who was elected chair of the American Communist Party at mid-century, provides one example of such censorship. The party made no attempt to hide her heterosexual "irregularities"; it was not shocking to mid-century leftists that in 1913 she left her husband of five years in order to live for the next dozen years with a married man, the Italian anarchist Carlo Tresca. But in 1926, a year after leaving Tresca, Elizabeth began a relationship with a physician and political radical, Marie Equi. For the ten years that followed, Elizabeth lived with Marie, an acknowledged lesbian, in Portland, Oregon. That information the Communist Party leadership found very disturbing, as did most historians, who until recently omitted discussing the nature of Flynn's relationship with Marie Equi from accounts of Flynn's life. Purportedly, Flynn revealed her lesbianism in a draft of her 1955 memoir, *Alderson Story*, but according to one source, the party not only censored the chapter but even insisted on "substitut[ing] an anti-gay chapter" in its place.

Other women leaders of the mid-twentieth century were themselves assiduous in hiding their lesbian relationships, often after "outside help" had convinced them that revelation would be perilous to their positions of influence. Miriam Van Waters is a case in point. As a penologist, she maintained Progressive goals in a post-Progressive era, revolutionizing the field of corrections. In 1932 she became the superintendent of the Massachusetts Women's Reformatory, a position she held for the next twenty-five years. Emulating the values of Jane Addams, whom she admired, she called the inmates students, permitted prisoners who were mothers to keep their children in the prison nursery, allowed inmates to take day jobs for wages outside the prison walls, and instituted many other humane policies in the treatment of delinquent women. But her career almost came to an abrupt end in the late 1940s, when she was accused first by the conservative Hearst papers and then by a commissioner of corrections not only of being lenient on lesbianism in the prison but also of being a lesbian herself.

Van Waters, who was loved by inmates, reformers, and liberal penologists alike, managed to hold on to her position until 1957. Her supporters, who included Frances Perkins and Eleanor Roosevelt, succeeded in convincing an investigative body to overturn the commissioner's edict to terminate her. However, she felt forced to alter her management of the inmates drastically and to become more circumspect in her own life.

Van Waters's romantic relationships with other women included one that began while she was still an undergraduate, in 1908, and another with a fellow judicial referee for the Los Angeles court in the 1920s. By 1930, four years after she met Geraldine Thompson, a wealthy woman who was known as the "first lady of New Jersey" because of her strong influence on philanthropy and politics in that state, Miriam was involved in a "deeply romantic" intimacy with her. Miriam, as superintendent, lived on prison grounds most of the time, and Geraldine lived with her husband, with whom she had an arrangement that was apparently similar to that between her good friend Eleanor Roosevelt and Franklin Roosevelt. The intimacy between Miriam and Geraldine continued for three decades, almost until Geraldine's death, in 1967. Only a few love letters from Geraldine to Miriam survived a panicked orgy of immolation when Miriam was under scrutiny, but they are passionate enough to reveal something of what the two women meant to each other. For example, Geraldine declared her desire "to kneel down and worship your loveliness" and to "catch your soul's breath [in kisses]," and she addressed Miriam as "My own dear, blessed precious sweet, my dearest love."

Unlike earlier romantic friends, who may not have been cognizant of the categories that the sexologists had devised in the nineteenth century, Van Waters was well read in psychological and sexological literature, and in her journals she even discussed books such as Radclyffe Hall's *Well of Loneliness*. As a student of social science, she could not escape the reigning notions of her day that "homosexual" signified "pathology" and "maladjustment," and consequently she refused to define herself by the word. The attacks on her in the 1940s, however, made her understand that whether or not she accepted that term for herself, her enemies tarred her with it. As Van Waters despairingly wrote to a friend, "The evil Hearst newspapers began this attack and have hinted that I was 'run out of California' because of personal immorality. They call it the 'doll racket.' They mean homosexuality." She was especially upset when a former prisoner informed her that a man who "was going around to all us girls that did time years ago" asked the ex-inmate, who had been employed doing day work at Van Waters's residence, if she had "seen anything queer going on."

Van Waters vehemently denied the charges against her. As Estelle Freedman suggests in her excellent biography of Van Waters, *Maternal Justice,* she may not have been entirely disingenuous in her denials, since she really did not see herself as suffering from the pathology that she believed was inextricably associated with "the homosexual." If all homosexuals were sick, how could she be a homosexual, despite her lifelong intimacies with other women? Realizing, however, that others saw her as one, she felt forced to be careful of "evidence" that could mark her. In June 1948 she set about burning love letters that she had received from Geraldine, sadly confiding to her journal, "The Burning of the Letters continues. One can have no personal 'life' in this battle, so I have destroyed many letters of our 22 years."

By the 1950s, Van Waters appears to have internalized the homophobia that was used against her. In her last years as prison superintendent, she altered her enlightened policies regarding the inmates and their consensual activities, permitting authorities to label as "hardcore" any woman who had sex in her prison and transferring "aggressive homosexuals" to the county jail for punishment.

Confusions: Mildred Scott Olmsted

Van Waters was far from alone among twentieth-century lesbian leaders who came to internalize homophobia. Mildred Scott

("Scottie") Olmsted, a leader in the Women's International League for Peace and Freedom, had a lifelong lesbian relationship with Ruth Mellor. It began when they were students together at Smith College in 1910 and continued virtually until Ruth's death almost eighty years later (Mildred survived her by one year). It outlasted their intense jealousies during Ruth's affairs with at least two other women and several men, as well as Mildred's fifty-five-year marriage to Allen Olmsted, who died in 1977. In 1982, when Mildred was ninety-two and Ruth ninety-four, the two women were still taking Caribbean cruises together. But even to her death at the age of one hundred, Mildred vehemently denied to everyone, including Margaret Bacon, her biographer (*One Woman's Passion for Peace and Freedom*), that she was a lesbian. Her surviving correspondence with Ruth, however, leaves little room for denial, though it also hints at why she felt denial was necessary.

Some aspects of Mildred Olmsted's intimate life were surely unusual for her day. For example, Ruth actually lived with Mildred and her new husband in an emotional triangle for several years after Mildred's marriage. But Mildred's tortured ambivalence about lesbianism and her belief that it was absolutely necessary for her to marry — despite her fear that being a wife would prevent her from achieving important things in the world — were not at all unusual for many ambitious women who came to maturity during or following World War I. Her life provides rich material to illustrate her generation's dramatic departures in attitudes from those of many women who shared her ambitions but were born a generation or so earlier.

First of all, the earliest love letters between Ruth and Mildred, dated 1913 and 1914, indicate a significant difference from most of the extant love letters between women of earlier generations: they suggest, on Ruth's part in any case, a more insistent sexuality. She was clearly conscious, with a New Woman's aggressive awareness, of her sexual needs and the "healthfulness" of their fulfillment, and she was determined not to deny them. "My dear 'Little Lady,'" Ruth wrote at the end of the summer of 1913, "Those nights were precious. I am a better woman because of them and stronger too I think." She teasingly tried to goad Mildred to a more explicit discussion of eroticism in their letters. "You say as usual just too little, lady," she wrote a few months later. "Tell me now — How did you surprise yourself? Did you find too that platonic friendship is nice to *read* about, but not very practical?"

While Ruth's sexuality early in their relationship may have been decidedly modern, Mildred remained on the cusp, not quite ready to overcome the Victorian mores of her childhood and much less clear than Ruth about whether or not she could permit herself sexual pleasure. Yet she gave Ruth reason to believe she was really in love with her. "Jewels," Ruth called the emotional gifts from Mildred. "How many I have. So precious I scarce dare think they are mine." The letters also indicate that despite Mildred's trepidation, she did not always wish to avoid a sexual exchange with Ruth. "That you want me sometimes makes me know that you aren't sorry and makes me feel more surely that you aren't ever going to be," Ruth wrote several weeks later, explaining about her own erotic drive, "I want you so badly sometimes that I just rebel like a little child."

Years later, Mildred, looking back on their early sexual relationship, tried to analyze the nature and cause of her ambivalence. She admitted "the conflict within me between my sometimes almost uncontrollable impulse to take you and the love you offered me without question and the older fear of insecurity and the habit of self control." Referring to the "Puritan and religious demand that I should not do myself what I disapproved of in others," she acknowledged that rather than having a guilt-provoking sexual relationship with Ruth, she had longed for a "Damon and Pythias" romantic friendship, which she believed would have been possible in a more idealized era, and which would have been far easier for her to deal with than having to "face the possibility that physical attraction was a dominant rather than a subordinate part" of their relationship.

From the perspective of our era, when "abnormality" and "pathology" are signified by a *lack* of sexual appetite rather than by desire, it is not easy to understand Mildred's very Victorian anxieties about sexual pleasure, yet they were certainly real to her.

Though some women in her cohort escaped such anxieties (as Ruth did for a time), others, such as Mildred, could permit themselves passionate emotional relationships much more easily than genital relationships, which they regarded as illicit.

Despite Ruth's apparently genuine insistence that she continued to love Mildred, Mildred's sexual ambivalence eventually caused Ruth to become involved with another woman, "Maisie," in what was initially an exciting sexual fling. But Ruth's confessions to Mildred about the affair were couched in terms so tortured that they could have served as a model for the pulps of the mid-twentieth century. "Oh — Scottie," Ruth wrote about her lesbian peccadilloes in 1916 (in a letter that stands in startling contrast to the September 1913 letter quoted above), "may you never know the Hell of Shame — nights and days of it — it seems ever with me now — I wonder if it will always follow — I know now that no matter what other suffering may come there is none to equal this." The melodrama of her tone almost suggests she was mocking Mildred, but later events demonstrate that despite Ruth's flourishing libido, Mildred's guilt over lesbian sex and the growing expression of homophobia of their era may have been contagious.

Ruth had demanded the sexual satisfaction to which the modernist New Woman was coming to believe she had a right. But having been born and raised in a Victorian society, she, like many modernist women, could not yet feel entirely secure in her convictions. "Unorthodoxy" in sexual expression might have made her fledgling feelings about her right to sexual pleasure even more of a problem. Her still beloved Mildred would not let her forget the Victorian virtues of self-control and avoidance of "moral indecency." Ruth's solution to the dilemma was both to let her libido have free rein and to feel guilty about it.

In her own confusion, Mildred constantly chipped away at Ruth's initial confidence in the rightness of lesbian sexuality. Her lectures soon went beyond moralizing to make love between women seem pathological. "Passionate friendships spring from starved childhoods like pent-up oil from the ground. And if they do not right themselves and strike their balance they exhaust and retard and dissipate all that should go into work and the real business of life," Mildred lectured Ruth in a 1919 letter. She ignored the living evidence of people like Jane Addams, whom she greatly admired, and she believed instead the amateur psychologizing about "abnormal sexuality," which was becoming a fascination for American intellectuals in the years after World War I.

But Mildred was not alone in chipping away at Ruth. At this point in their lives, when both women were around thirty years old, they were also being incessantly urged to heterosexuality by their families. Ruth's mother was telling her that between two women, an intense "friendship wasn't natural and people thought it queer and strange." Mildred's older sister, Adele, to whom she was very close, was telling Mildred that she disapproved of her continuing friendship with Ruth. Adele encouraged the suit of Allen Olmsted, a young lawyer who wanted to marry Mildred, and Mildred feared that she would have to bear her loved sister's disapproval if she turned him away.

Perhaps Mildred and Ruth were finally simply worn down. Their attachment to each other never abated. But Mildred could not bring herself to discourage Allen Olmsted entirely, despite her great ambivalence toward him. There were myriad reasons to accept his suit: she enjoyed his friendship; love between women was becoming increasingly unacceptable in popular cultural views, and so it had become increasingly difficult for young women to contemplate living in a same-sex partnership; her sister was constantly pushing her toward heterosexuality; and lesbian sex (any sex, as it turned out) made her anxious and unhappy. In view of all that, how could she throw away a suitor as eligible as Olmsted, who appeared so loving and determined to win her? He was a bright professional man, and he shared her radical politics. He was even court-martialed because he protested American attitudes toward "the Hun."

In her occasional attempts to discourage him, Mildred admitted her intense feelings for Ruth, but Olmsted was not put off. He apparently felt he could help Mildred overcome what was now seen as an unfortunate matter of "arrested development." In 1920, with the spread of Freudianism in America, Olmsted, who liked to consider himself knowledgeable with regard to psychological matters, wrote to Mildred, in textbook language, that there was a "complete absence from your make up of the feelings and instincts which normally attract the sexes to each other"; he dubbed what he called her "sex abnormality" as being "in the nature of a sad perversion." Yet not even his feeling that her lesbianism was "as abhorrent to me as my animal side is to you" could convince him to drop his pursuit of her.

Perhaps truly believing that he loved her, he could not conceive that she would never love him. Perhaps her lesbianism added a piquancy to her allure for him and made the challenge irresistible. In any case, from the time they met in 1916 through the war and the years after the war, when Mildred was in Europe doing relief work and Ruth went to join her so they could reconstruct their "bonds on a firmer basis," he continued his pursuit, until in 1922 Mildred agreed to marry him.

She was in shock at the step she had let herself take. During the early years of their marriage, she even defended her lesbian feelings toward Ruth and complained bitterly in letters to her husband that she had been much more compatible with Ruth, in both important and trivial ways. But more difficult for her even than their incompatibility was a fear that Mildred found impossible to overcome. This was precisely the worry of many of the earlier women pioneers, who had avoided marriage and chosen instead a same-sex partnership that would foster the work they considered vital.

Mildred, who had done various types of settlement work before her marriage and had formed her attitudes in that milieu, took a job with WILPF in 1922. She rose through the ranks, eventually becoming national executive secretary. She often led the charge on vital social issues such as racial integration and civil liberties. Through WILPF she was in the forefront of the push to get America to open immigration to European refugees during World War II. However, regardless of her accomplishments, Mildred feared that Olmsted wanted in her only a wife and mother and did not take her ambitions seriously. "Do you, in your secret heart, feel cheated?" she challenged him, insisting that she would not be a traditional wife. "And do you cherish a deep unconscious wish to keep me in the home? Do you in the last analysis feel no pride and joy in my work and feel it is of no great value to the world and of no importance except as one of my foibles?"

Despite Olmsted's assurances to her, she continued to suspect that the answer to all those questions was yes, and that suspicion contributed to her disgruntlement in the marriage. She felt that if she had been able to marry Ruth instead of Allen, she would have had no cause for such doubts. Years later, Ruth revealed in a sad letter that she too believed they had both missed their lives. "You should have been a man, Scottie," Ruth wrote in 1936, "and we should have married and how happy our lives together would have been." With all the advances pioneering professional women — lesbians — had made in the generations before and handed down to young women who followed them, the right to a life together could not withstand the pressures for compulsory heterosexuality that had emerged in the new century.

The compromise that Ruth and Mildred made for a time was thus a very modern one. Ruth joined the Olmsted household in 1924 and remained until 1927. With Allen as camouflage, Mildred could live with Ruth, though she could not have permitted herself to live in a dyad with another woman in what the world by then saw as a lesbian relationship rather than a less socially disturbing romantic friendship between two old maids. Through all these various turmoils, Mildred and Ruth worked at their careers. Ruth, taking advantage of the place Jane Addams had carved for women, became a social work administrator. Mildred continued to fight some of WILPF's most important battles. Yet she never really stopped feeling that she was also battling Allen's low regard for her achievement, whether or not her perception was accurate. It is provocative to imagine what more she could have done in her professional life if her personal life had been less full of conflict.

In 1927, three years into the ménage à trois, Allen, Mildred, and Ruth, in the mode of intellectuals of that era, went to see psychiatrists about their complex relationship. At one point both Mildred and Ruth sought help from Otto Rank. Ruth was apparently really affected when Rank asked her, with reference to her lesbianism, why she needed two mothers (needless to say, he never asked Mildred why she needed two fathers). At this point Ruth decided that she would leave Pennsylvania, where the three lived, take a job in Connecticut, and try to get involved with men.

Otto Rank had effected a partial "cure," at any rate, since in the next few years Ruth had a series of brief affairs with men and then a long-term relationship with a married man. During this time she wrote to Mildred with obvious intentional cruelty as a payback for the pain she had felt over the years: "No woman could ever have loved a husband more intensely and completely than I loved you for years and years — the complete concentration of the libido on to you is not so complete now, because some of it has gone to men where I have always believed it was natural for it to be. Sorry to have you suffer but I won't be apologetic." However, Ruth was not completely cured. After her heterosexual phase, she returned to Mildred, and once again they were often together, traveling frequently both for work and pleasure, either alone with each other or in the company of Allen.

At one point Mildred decided that she would divide all her free time in thirds: among Allen, Ruth, and her three children (two of them adopted, one born to her after a very difficult and unwelcome pregnancy). At other times Ruth simply became one of the family. Eventually, according to Margaret Bacon, this "modern" triangle actually became workable: "Ruth was confidante and supporter to Allen. . . . Allen helped Ruth to continue to feel confidence in herself as a woman [sic]. . . . Mildred [remained as] the apex of the triangle, needing the admiration and love of the other two." The husband and wife even managed eventually to achieve a modicum of peace in their marriage.

Yet as Mildred wrote to Allen in 1975, two years before his death, "Marriage has been a long and difficult adjustment for us both — more difficult for me than for you because of many things." Her difficulties had certainly been exacerbated by her conviction that being a wife and mother was a distraction from what she needed to do in the world, as well as by her continued ambivalence about her love for another woman. Given her ambitions, which made her resent the responsibilities of wifehood and motherhood, and her undying attachment to Ruth, who she felt nurtured her far more than her husband could, it is hard not to believe she would have been better off in a premodern (or postmodern?) generation, when she would not have felt so intently the push of compulsory heterosexuality.

The homophobia that had been inculcated in her as a young woman never died. Despite her virtually lifelong love relationship with Ruth, even to the 1980s, Mildred felt that she had to deny in interviews with Margaret Bacon, whom she considered her official biographer, that she and Ruth had ever been lesbian together. Though she permitted herself to admit that Ruth "had several times been a passive partner in a lesbian love affair," she continued even to deny that Ruth was a lesbian. Despite the lesbian and gay revolution of the preceding years, she never felt comfortable with that maligned word, which triggered her conflicts about her deepest feelings.

The story of the relationship between Mildred Olmsted and Ruth Mellor stands as an unhappy contrast to those of their older counterparts, who were innocent of modern pseudo-psychologizing and of the homophobia that was universally articulated in the concepts that that psychologizing created. Compare, for instance, Mary Grew's contented description of her life with Margaret Burleigh in the nineteenth century as "a closer union than that of most marriages" with Mildred's tortured lament to Ruth in 1919, "Passionate friendships spring from starved childhoods like pent-up oil from the ground." The generations that preceded Mildred and Ruth had far less pressure from an expressly homophobic society to abandon what Ruth called the "jewels" that they held most dear.

PART III

HOW AMERICAN WOMEN
GOT EDUCATED

❧ 10 ❧

"MENTAL HERMAPHRODITES":
PIONEERS IN WOMEN'S
HIGHER EDUCATION

[At Smith College] they write each other the wildest
love-letters, & send presents, confectionery, all sorts of
things, like a real courting of the Shakespearean style. If
the "smash" is mutual, they monopolize each other &
"spoon" continually, & sleep together & lie awake all
night talking instead of going to sleep; & if it isn't mutual
the unrequited one cries herself sick & endures pangs
unspeakable.

— Alice Stone Blackwell to Kitty Blackwell, 1882

Education and the "Semi-Women": Mary Lyon and
Zilpah Grant, Sophia Packard and Harriet Giles

In EIGHTEENTH- and early nineteenth-century America, education of females from any class was minimal. In Boston from 1789 to
1822, for example, girls were allowed to attend the public schools
during the summer only, and for a time for two hours in the afternoon during the school year, after the boys had gone home. The
girls' curriculum consisted primarily of the "4 R's" (the fourth being
religion). Emma Willard's Troy Female Seminary, which opened in
1821, was revolutionary in its intention to provide serious study for
girls, including courses such as physiology and algebra, but it was
met with general disfavor. Though Mrs. Willard tried to be assuring
in her "Address to the Public" that her school would not "masculinize" girls, many were not convinced. As one clergyman com-

plained, study of higher mathematics and science would surely unfit young women for husbands and babies.

Catharine Beecher was even more direct than Emma Willard in her attempts to convince the public that more rigorous education would not unsex women. She vehemently claimed to oppose the proto-feminist moves that were afoot. She later became an avowed antisuffragist. Yet Beecher argued that female education must be taken seriously — as a preparation for women's "distinctive profession," which was "the nursing of infants and the sick, and all the handicrafts and management of the family state." At Hartford Female Seminary, which she founded in the 1820s, young women were given courses in subjects such as chemistry and mathematics, but Beecher insisted that the purpose of such studies was to teach future housewives what they needed to know about chemical or mathematical principles in the workings of the kitchen or the handling of the household accounts. In making "domestic scientists" of the women she educated, Beecher was looking for ways to expand women's stature. She wished to help them to a more exalted position, yet she was unable to move beyond the conventional construction of womanhood. Unlike Anna Shaw and Jane Addams, who cleverly used the gender constructions of their day to expand women's roles outside the home, Beecher never acknowledged a function for women apart from the domestic setting — though she herself did not marry.

In the decades before the Civil War, institutions similar to Beecher's were also founded for southern white women — for example, the Georgia Female College, in Macon (1836), and the Tennessee and Alabama Female Institute, in Winchester, Tennessee (1851). However, higher education for women could not become a serious business without leadership from women who had no interest in domesticity, who could think beyond the conventions of women's appropriate sphere, and who had no investment in femininity. Mary Lyon was just such a woman. Lyon designed an education for females that would be as rigorous as she could get away with in the mid-1830s. Like Catharine Beecher, she never married, but unlike Beecher, she had no wish to train young women for a domesticity that she herself never knew.

Lyon was "unfeminine" in appearance and manner, as her contemporaries repeatedly observed. When young she had a number of romantic friendships with other women, but "the outstanding personal relation [of her life]" — as even a homophobic 1937 biographer was constrained to admit after perusing the letters between them — was Zilpah Grant, who was her partner at the beginning of her pioneering pursuits. As Mary Lyon wrote to her sister, "I love Miss Grant's society more than ever, and I believe we may love our friends very ardently." That ardent personal love led Lyon and Grant to dream about a shared mission to expand the possibilities of women's education.

The two women met in 1821, when both were teaching at Byfield, a girl's school. Grant became the head of a female academy in New Hampshire a couple of years later, and Lyon soon followed her. Together they planned a course of study for girls that would be equal to what boys were given in the best academies, including natural philosophy, astronomy, and chemistry (without Catharine Beecher's excuse of its usefulness in the kitchen). In 1828, when Zilpah Grant established an academy for girls in Ipswich, Massachusetts, Lyon followed her again.

Four years later, Mary Lyon conceived of establishing a larger institution for the serious training of female teachers, but she postponed her pursuit of the plan, expressly so that she could remain longer with Zilpah Grant. She felt conflict over this decision, however. As she wrote in 1834, she believed she had a vital mission: "My heart has so yearned over the adult female youth in the common walks of life, that it has sometimes seemed as if there was a fire shut up in my bones." When she finally resolved to found her seminary for "adult female youth," she was equally pained by the anticipated separation from Zilpah. "I have to bid Miss Grant farewell," she wrote mournfully, "no more to live with her on earth," which, she lamented, shook her heart with "all emotions of affection." Zilpah too was pained at the separation. As an 1887 historian of Mount Holyoke College characterized it, her letters "show at what sacrifice of feeling to both the decision to separate was reached."

In 1835, with plans well under way for Mount Holyoke Female Seminary, Mary implored Zilpah to join her on the new campus, but

Zilpah elected to remain at Ipswich. What happened between the two women during these years of separation is not entirely clear; however, in 1841, at the age of forty-four, Zilpah married a man. Yet as Mary often acknowledged, it was with Zilpah Grant that she had been able to conceive of rigorous academic training for women, and like Hull House, which owed its founding to the relationship between Jane Addams and Ellen Starr, Mount Holyoke would not have been established without the women's joint conceptions.

Though Lyon perfunctorily agreed that God designated "a difference in the situation of the sexes," the course of study she established for Mount Holyoke students did not acknowledge that difference. She emphasized "high standards of mental discipline" and a "slow, thorough, and patient manner of study." Her focus was on classics and hard science. She was preparing women *not* to be housewives or social ornaments but rather to be serious scholars and independent beings through a career in education. As she wrote in a pamphlet outlining the focus of Mount Holyoke, through the seminary's stringent program young women would be prepared as "educators . . . of youth, rather than . . . [as] mere teachers," who had often been badly trained and were sometimes barely fifteen or sixteen years old. Thanks to Lyon, female *educators* might now be professionals.

Protests were predictable and were generally meant to dissuade and mortify. One critic, for example, claimed in *The Ladies' Companion* that the only women who would want a serious education were "mental hermaphrodites" and "semi-women." Another declared in *The Religious Magazine* that the "principles and design of Mount Holyoke Female Seminary" were deplorable because the institution would create "characters expressly formed for acting a *manly* [sic] part upon the theatre of life. . . . Under such influences the female character is fast becoming masculine." Gender inversion was consistently the great fear of those who abjured serious education for women.

Oberlin College authorities, who had declared in 1833 that their new college would admit women in order "to prepare them to become the useful wives of the male graduates," understood how to avert accusations that an institution was turning women into men. They made sure not to "neglect" female students' "domestic education" and assigned them tasks of cooking and cleaning for the male students. Womanly modesty was also carefully enforced by the administration: though any woman who had completed the regular college course was required to write an essay for the commencement exercises, a male student was appointed to read it for her. As Oberlin's president, James Fairchild, declared, "It is a thing positively disagreeable to both sexes to see a woman in a public character." At Mount Holyoke, however, there were no men to keep the women demure and womanly.

Though there was little enthusiasm for "educating women like men" during the first half of the nineteenth century, the Civil War caused some shifts in attitudes. First of all, it opened various employment opportunities to women, who were needed to take the places of men who had become soldiers. An author of the period, Lizzie Bates, observing the ways in which conditions were changing, voiced the question of presumably many females: "What can I do?" Her answer was, "Nothing but what God has given you the ability to perform; or, in other words, anything that you can do, and do well." For good numbers of women, a new day had dawned. At least a few of the 338 occupations that women filled during and soon after the war required advanced education. And many more women had to prepare themselves for work, since the Civil War had forced them to become self-supporting: more than 600,000 men had been killed, which meant that more than a half-million women over the usual number would never have husbands. After the 1860s, higher education was perceived as useful by some, not only because it would occupy the bereft spinster for four or more years of her life but because it might prepare her to make her own living.

Teaching was still the most likely career for a daughter of the middle class. Since Mary Lyon had helped create an interest in well-educated teachers, young women without apparent marriage prospects were now often sent to college in order to learn the profession. Work opportunities for teachers also increased. The need for them in the democracy had been further expanded by immigrants who were coming to America in a new wave, beginning in the 1870s, and by the freed slaves, who had been kept largely illiterate in slavery and now had to be educated. These new populations also provided a pool of inexpensive domestic labor, which meant that a middle-class daughter's hands were no longer needed in the parental home. Her domestic work would not be missed if she went off to get an education.

Therefore, in the years after the Civil War, colleges for women proliferated, as did colleges that had been exclusively male but were now opened to women. The war had reduced the number of young men who would be going to college, and coeducation helped underenrolled institutions survive. All over the country, numerous universities, both private and state-supported, began accepting women. By 1870, eight thousand women were attending seminaries and three thousand were attending degree-granting colleges. In the course of that decade, several women's colleges that came to play a crucial role in the history of women's education opened. Vassar had been founded in 1865, and in the 1870s, Smith, Wellesley, and Radcliffe were established. Mount Holyoke Female Seminary claimed to have upgraded itself to college status in the 1880s, and Bryn Mawr and Barnard opened their doors in that decade as well.

Although these colleges were generally interested in "elite" young women — that is, those of the middle and upper classes and of white Anglo-Saxon Protestant parentage — the move to educate women soon affected a broader spectrum. The most notable of the early efforts to educate African-American women was undertaken by a white female couple, Sophia Packard and Harriet Giles, who, like Mary Lyon and Zilpah Grant, felt a devotion to each other that fueled their devotion to the cause of women. In 1881, Packard and Giles founded Spelman College, in Atlanta, Georgia. They had met years earlier, when Harriet was a senior at a New England girls' academy where Sophia, who was ten years older, was a preceptress. In 1859 they had opened a short-lived school together in Fitchburg, Massachusetts, and in the years that followed they taught together in various other New England schools. Sophia's diary entries at this time suggest her two main desires: they refer to Harriet as "my darling Hattie," and they implore God to "lay me out for usefulness!"

In 1864, Sophia Packard became the head of the Oread Collegiate Institute in Worcester, Massachusetts. A nineteenth-century *History of the Oread Collegiate Institute* describes her as "a woman of powerful intellect and strong will, aggressive and energetic, with almost a masculine genius for business and capacity for leadership" (though the usually disconcerting gender reference was modified by the assurance that she was "a thoroughly conservative and devoted Christian"). The author does not draw the conclusions that became inevitable in the twentieth century when recalling that Packard was assisted in her various duties by "Miss Hattie E. Giles, her devoted friend, with whom she had been constantly associated in all she had done for ten years. . . . It would have been impossible for a school girl of those days to speak or think of one without the other. They dressed alike and in leisure hours were nearly always together. Miss Giles was in character quite unlike Miss Packard, being most gentle, mild, and self-effacing."

Their romance of opposites was enhanced by their similarities. Both women were interested in the welfare of the freed slaves, and on a trip to the South in 1880 they decided to start a school for African-American women. The Baptist church, to which they appealed, was slow in coming to their assistance, and in her impatience, Harriet Giles sold her piano for start-up money. Eventually they were helped by the church, as well as by John D. Rockefeller (the school was named after Rockefeller's wife, Laura Spelman). The statement of aims that Sophia Packard prepared emphasized the school's serious goals: "to train the intellect," "to store the mind with useful knowledge," "to inspire love for the true and the beautiful."

When Sophia Packard died, in 1891, the "feminine" Harriet Giles transcended her habits of demureness and became the head of Spelman. Though the school was not named a college until 1924, Giles established a "college department" in 1897, and in 1901, through classes taken jointly at Spelman and Atlanta Baptist College, a men's school, two African-American women became Spelman's first college graduates. Spelman was now called alternately "the Wellesley of the South" and "the Mount Holyoke of the South." Though Giles, like Packard, emphasized professional training in teaching and nursing, students were also encouraged to take liberal arts courses like those given in the elite colleges of the North — rhetoric, Latin, moral and natural philosophy, zoology, geology.

Harriet Giles made Spelman the foremost school in the country for African-American women. At her death, in 1909, she was buried with the woman with whom she had shared her life for almost forty years. The single tombstone that covers both their graves bears their names on one side, and on the other is the inscription "Founders of Spelman Seminary."

"But Who Will Bake the Pies and Have the Babies?"
Not Lucy Salmon and Adelaide Underhill

With the proliferation of educational possibilities for women came a proliferation of fears about what that education might lead to. Initially the concerns centered on the possibilities that females would become not-women. "Who will bake the pies?" one critic of educated womanhood blurted, reducing the panic to its most basic terms. That fear of "unsexing," as the prevalent term was, soon led to the fear that educated women would become not only economically but also emotionally independent of men. Indeed, both in college and after, many women were forming romantic ties and even quasi-marriages with other women that kept them from heterosexual arrangements. From the fears of unsexing and same-sex dyads developed the fear of "race suicide." Since women of the elite classes were being educated in the greatest numbers, the pundits claimed, waving statistics before the eyes of a troubled public, they were less likely to marry and thus to procreate. Meanwhile, immigrants from eastern and southern Europe were "invading" the country and reproducing in what those same pundits considered dizzying proportions. The imminent death of the elite classes was predicted, and female higher education was given a lion's share of the blame. Such fears became the stuff of popular books and magazine articles for more than fifty years, from the 1870s to the 1920s.

Those who wished to limit females to the conventions of femininity, who believed that all Anglo-Saxon women needed to give birth to four or more children, or who were opposed to love and companionship that was not heterosexual actually did have a realistic basis for their conviction that women's higher education posed a serious threat. The pioneers — the first generations of female college students — did often reject what had been considered "womanhood." M. Carey Thomas, the president of Bryn Mawr, bitterly wrote of childhood feelings that must have been shared by many pioneering college women of her generation. One summer day, she recalled, "when sitting in a hammock under the trees with a French dictionary, blinded by tears more burning than the July sun, I translated the most indecent book I have ever read [Michelet's *La Femme*]. I was beside myself with terror lest it might prove true that I myself was so vile and pathological a thing [as Michelet had described woman]."

Carey Thomas rebelled violently against *La Femme*'s hurtful stereotypes of inferiority and their inevitable corollary, that women were fit only for the prison house of compulsory domesticity. Many young women with mental energy, imagination, and intelligence must have felt as she did. Of course they envied the broader freedoms of young men of their class. To study what men studied and valued must have seemed to hold the promise of vaulting them from the despised category of "woman." Gender inversion in various forms — but for them, especially the inverted desire to lay claim to the role of scholar — surely represented escape.

The fear of race suicide voiced by those who opposed higher education for women was based on statistics that demonstrated a high rate of spinsterhood among educated women. Spinsterhood was especially common among those who graduated from college between 1885 and 1905, perhaps because those years saw an exciting proliferation of professions that enabled educated women to become self-supporting. A common prod to marriage for many nineteenth-century women — economic necessity — disappeared for some. Even those college-educated women who did marry, the race-suicide observers pointed out, generally did so late in life (sometimes after they had enjoyed a career for several years), and they had far fewer children than the average woman of their class. Thirty-two percent of married Bryn Mawr graduates had no children; 23 percent of married Wellesley graduates had no children.

And the majority of women who graduated from college by the early 1890s were likely not to marry at all. Of Bryn Mawr graduates, only 43 percent married. Other women's colleges produced similar marriage rates: among Wellesley graduates of that period, only 49 percent married; among Radcliffe graduates, only 41 percent married. Even female graduates of coeducational institutions were much less likely to marry than women without educations: among Oberlin graduates of that period, 61 percent married; among University of Michigan graduates, 52 percent married. Of their female cohorts in the general population, over 90 percent married!

Women who received Ph.D.'s and went on to become professors to future generations of women were especially unlikely to marry. Conventional domesticity would have been virtually impossible in academia. When Lucy Salmon went to Vassar in 1887 as its first history professor, she was expected to live on campus and be almost always on duty. In a letter to friends, she described her typical workday, which began at 6 A.M. and ended at 10 P.M., with barely a moment of privacy, even in her own rooms. "It is considered quite the proper thing for students to call on the teachers — all the members of your classes expect to call and bring their friends who are not, all the students rooming on your corridor expect to call, all who occupy your [pew] in chapel expect to call, all who bring letters of introduction call," she wrote. Not even meals at Vassar could be a time of privacy, because "as a rule one teacher sits at each table" in order to lead uplifting conversations.

Even if a female professor was not constrained to live on campus, a workload such as Salmon had, of 170 students, would make it impossible for her to conduct a conventional household — which demanded being a loving maternal guide to several children and being a companion to a husband who was likely to have socially reinforced expectations about his due. Not even the Sabbath could be a day of respite for an academic, as Salmon reported to her friends. One Sunday she attended "a beautiful chapel service at 9 o'clock," but, she added, "I'll not say anything of the notebooks and papers I examined after that."

Lucy Salmon did ultimately find domestic happiness in a relationship, the kind that was so commonplace at Wellesley College that it was dubbed a Wellesley marriage. It was commonplace at Vassar and most other women's colleges as well in the late nineteenth century. In her first history class at Vassar, Salmon met a senior student, Adelaide Underhill, who went off to study library science after graduation and then returned to Vassar as a librarian in 1892. Salmon and Underhill collaborated in building the Vassar library into one of the most impressive among liberal arts colleges. They also took up life together in their own off-campus home, where Salmon often held her history seminars and they jointly entertained students and faculty.

Years later, an alumna writing in the *Vassar Quarterly* reminisced romantically about the home of Lucy Salmon and Adelaide Underhill, with its "porch covered with wisteria, . . . the door wide open in welcome, . . . [an] ample desk, the walls lined to the ceiling with books," the dining table "with its centerpiece of brightly-hued flowers," and a manservant to cook and serve. The domestic arrangement the two women created together was what many of the female pioneers in education longed for and not infrequently achieved. It was a deep and permanent commitment that gave both women the delicious refuge Susan B. Anthony had described in her 1877 lecture "Homes of Single Women," but it also gave them each space and time to pursue work that was all the more exciting because it had been withheld from generations of women before them. They were the pathbreakers, they thought, for the generations of women after them. Having their work, each other, and the home they created together, they had what they needed. Heterosexual marriage would have deprived them of the forms of excitement and achievement they valued most.

Clearly Salmon and Underhill felt no need to hide their intimacy from others, since they saw it as neither unique nor pathological. A cousin of Lucy Salmon's, who visited them in their Poughkeepsie home and also when they were abroad, wrote to Adelaide after Lucy's death in 1927, reflecting how the relationship between the two women appeared to sympathetic outside observers:

> You . . . were her greatest love and care! For I realized that summer when we were in France, how greatly she loved and admired you, from her own words as well as in other ways, and two years ago I saw there was the same strong affection and regard for you on her part. Indeed the friendship between you had always seemed to me to be perfect. Each of you gave what the heart of each needed. It must surely be a joy to you now to think that you made her life so happy and complete as you did. She so greatly enjoyed her home, after the years during which she longed for one, but it was you who made it home for her.

Such relationships were not seen as "happy and complete" by those who cried "race suicide," of course.

College Inverts

Like the women who led the suffrage movement, such as Anna Shaw and Mollie Hay, or those who established professions for women in reform or politics, like Frances Kellor and Molly Dewson, many of the early female academics were virtually case studies of sexual inversion, seemingly right out of the pages of sexological tomes. The nineteenth-century Wellesley German professor Carla Wenckebach is an example. As a child, she rebelled violently against sewing and knitting and hated whatever seemed "sissy." She much preferred boys' games and boy companions, with whom she climbed trees, played marbles, went eel-catching, smoked, and whistled. She exchanged her dresses for a masculine "Russian blouse and bloomers" for as long as her parents permitted. In her youth she rejected her feminine Christian names and insisted on being called Cato, after the Roman poet and grammarian of the first century B.C. A school friend recalled that the name "suited her well," since her "carriage was commanding and the whole bearing repudiated everything suggestive of feminine weakness or dependence."

Wenckebach's gender inversion was accompanied by a rejection of men as romantic objects. As a student, she was "the center of an adoring crowd of enthusiastic girls." As a professor at Wellesley, her loves included Alice Freeman, who was Wellesley's president. When Freeman married, Wenckebach's biographer observes, "the blow was a bitter one. [Wenckebach] was irreconcilable and went to the wedding as if to a funeral," though in later years she formed a dyad with Margarethe Müller, a colleague in Wellesley's German department, which lasted until Wenckebach's death, in 1902.

Pioneering academic women knew that they were accused of gender inversion by those who opposed higher education for females. Yet since they deplored femininity, they saw its opposite quality, masculinity, not as undesirable but rather as consisting of attributes that permitted the freedoms they coveted. In "The True Womanly Woman," a one-act nineteenth-century satire that made fun of those who feared the educated woman, Rose Chamberlin presents a university student, Thomasina (or "tomboy"), who comes onstage wearing a "neat cut-away coat; her billy-cock hat set rakishly askew, smoking a short pipe, and cracking a whip." When Thomasina offers to help the silly, feminine Angelina adjust to university life, Angelina responds, "You surely cannot think Thomasina that I could condescend to receive information and instruction as to my conduct from an amphibious — at least — no — not amphibious, I mean carnivorous — no — I don't — dear me what is the word? [hermaphrodite?] — oh I know — from a *she male-ish* creature like yourself?" Thomasina responds, with only partial sarcasm, "Many thanks for the compliment my love."

There is no question about whose side Rose Chamberlin — who was a Bryn Mawr graduate student in the 1880s — is on. She concludes with a disgusted narrative explaining that the dainty Angelina manages to continue at school though "she maintains the character of a most womanly woman — throughout her college career — by carefully eschewing even a pretense of study — and by keeping up her reputation for slavish admiration of the male sex." "The True Womanly Woman" illustrates that for committed college women of Chamberlin's generation, not only was higher education an escape from the limitations of womanhood, but a rejection of attributes that were considered feminine — that is, an "unsexing" — was seen to be crucial to the success of their academic endeavors.

For several decades, women like Thomasina were generally not called lesbians or homosexuals, though their critics sometimes hinted at abnormality. In an article in the *American Journal of Heredity* in the 1890s, for instance, such women were accused of being "more or less lacking in normal sex instincts." The writer opined that colleges actually served a useful purpose in segregating these women from others!

Early in the twentieth century, such accusations became even more explicit. Merely a woman's desire to be seriously educated was enough to arouse suspicions about her sexuality. Such suspicions crossed race and class lines. As May Edward Chinn, an African-American woman who was in college around 1920, bluntly recollected, "My father objected to me going to college, number one. . . . His idea of a girl was that you got married and had children. A girl that went to college became a queer woman. And he did not want to be the father of a queer girl." As it happened, Chinn, who went on to medical school after college, was the only female doctor in Harlem for fifty years. She never married.

Smashes, Mashes, Pashes, and More

It is not known when the word "queer" was first used in America, whether in black or white communities, to describe women who loved other women, but pioneering college women would probably not have seen themselves in the term, since the dyads they formed were the norm in their milieu. Professor-student relationships like the one between Lucy Salmon and Adelaide Underhill led often to "marriages" such as theirs. With few female role models for serious achievement in nineteenth-century America, Underhill, whose girl-hood ambitions went beyond the usual domesticity, would naturally have been awed and fascinated by Salmon, an attractive young woman who had already accomplished a great deal by earning a graduate degree and becoming a college professor. And Salmon would have been touched by Underhill, who was bright and eager and anxious to take the torch of women's progress from her hand and run with it. Deeper and more personal feelings would have followed easily and with less worried reflection than in the twenti-eth century, when pathologizing terms were current and sexual harassment became an issue.

A poem written in the early years by a professor at Smith College about her student suggests how the spiritual conviction of mission was reified in sensual expression:

> I need no bells nor chanted hymn;
> Her silk-soft hand, so white, so slim,
> Shall bless for me my way.
> Her kiss upon my lips shall be
> An absolution full and free
> That hell cannot dismay.

Women who met as professor and student in a classroom and be-came a couple — often for the next forty or fifty years — included not only the founders of Spelman College but also the Wellesley professors Margaret Sherwood and Martha Hale Shackford (who was Sherwood's student in 1896); the Mount Holyoke president Mary Woolley and the professor Jeannette Marks (who was a twenty-one-year-old freshman in Woolley's first class at Wellesley, in 1895); and the writer Florence Converse (the author of *Diana Victrix*) and the professor Vida Scudder, who taught Converse shortly after she went to Wellesley in 1887, to name only a few.

Romances between female students were even more common than those between students and their professors. Numerous terms were coined to describe such passionate love between women on campus: "smash," "mash," "pash," "crush," "rave," "spoon," "flame," "twosing." In an era before "sexual identity," young women were sometimes humorously confused by their crushes, as a Smith freshman at the beginning of the twentieth century demonstrated in declaring her love for a junior who had invited her to tea: "Miss Shipp, I wish I were a man . . . a Harvard graduate. . . . I'd like to make love to you . . . Only if I were a man I couldn't be here to see you serve tea so charmingly." The impulse was ubiquitous and overt in both northern and southern women's colleges.

Love poems written by students to other students were frequently printed in college publications. Typically, such verses pledged eternal devotion to the beloved woman, enumerated her beauties, or lamented unrequited, jealous love for her. For example, students at Sophie Newcomb, a women's college in New Orleans, published poems such as "My Lady of Dreams" in the school's *Newcomb Arcade*:

> Like the blue of the sea are My Lady's eyes,
> Like a benediction, her face;
> And the sunbeams that touch her hair with light
> But reveal all her gentle grace.
>
> And the song that is on My Lady's lips,
> That she sings in her voice of gold,
> Doth pass to my soul with its message of hope,
> With its meaning manifold.

Sentimentality and excess were so rampant in these poems that one Wellesley wit saw fit to satirize them, writing in *Wellesley Lyrics* (1896), a collection of verse that included numerous love poems from female students to other female students, "Can I tell you how I love you / With your beautiful brown eyes, / And your pretty lips just parted / In a smile both sweet and wise?" The reader's assumption, of course, is that this is a love poem from one female student to another. But the object of admiration is revealed in the last lines, in which the speaker refers, smirking, to the "darling little furry sable, / That around my throat I wear!"

Smashes between female students were encouraged by the rituals of romance in which they engaged. For example, women's college dances in the late nineteenth century did not include men, but they did include dates. One student (usually an upperclassman) would call for her date with flowers or candy in hand; sometimes she would wear a tuxedo and her date would wear a gown, and always she would take the lead in dancing and would act the part of a gentleman. Letters and diaries of students of the era often suggest the practice between them of a kind of *amour courtois,* as Tiziana Rota describes it in her work on Mount Holyoke College. Much more significant than these romantic rituals, however, was the fact that these students shared the excitement of their pioneering endeavors in education. In the absence of male distractions, they could dare to see one another as heroes and objects of intense admiration rather than as rivals. At coeducational colleges also, female students in the nineteenth century were likely to fall in love with each other. They took each other seriously, while the male students were often hostile to them, as a popular Cornell song of the 1890s shows: "I'm glad all the girls are not like Cornell women; / They're ugly as sin and there's no good within 'em."

Those who observed the love relationships between college women from a distance often trivialized them, like a 1906 writer who assured his readers that crushes between young women were "a mere forerunner" to the real thing, just as "the ragdoll is to the infant"; those same-sex passions would end at the altar, "when one is the other's bridesmaid." But many of the women involved would have disagreed vehemently. They often envisioned continuing their passionate love relationships with other women for their entire lives. The Radcliffe College student commencement speaker in 1900 prophesied that of the sixty-three graduates, only six would end up at the altar. The others would live as what she called "New Women," engaged in a fulfilling profession and "unmarried but not lonesome." She was not hinting at heterosexual cohabitation, as she made clear by her suggestion that these New Women would be sharing "bachelor quarters" with "kindred female spirits."

The Wellesley Marriage vs. Straight Marriage

Large numbers of female professors of the era had just the kind of domestic arrangement that the Radcliffe commencement speaker described, often with another academic woman. As Maria Mitchell, Vassar's famous astronomy professor from 1865 to 1888, observed, "A woman needs a home and the love of other women, at least, if she lives without that of a man." In many cases such arrangements resembled marriages; hence the terms used to describe them, such as "Boston marriage" and "Wellesley marriage." As Lucy Salmon's account of her packed days as a professor demonstrates, academic women had no time for conventional marriage. It is not surprising that of fifty-three female faculty members at Wellesley in the late nineteenth century, only one, Ethel Puffer Howes, married. As Patricia Palmieri points out in her study of Wellesley, Howes's married life left her little time for scholarship; she never obtained a professorship, and she felt obliged to leave Wellesley.

But there are other, more emotional reasons than time constraints that explain why many academic women preferred "marriage" with one another to heterosexual marriage. One such reason is their intense lifelong resentment of what they considered men's assumption of superiority over women. The ambitious girl of the nineteenth century was galled by the injustice of her position vis-à-vis males, as the Wellesley professor (and the author of the song that almost became our national anthem, "America, the Beautiful") Katharine Lee Bates wrote in her diary when she was a child in the early 1870s: "Men think they are more important than women. . . . I am happy to say [women] have become impatient under the restraint men put upon them. So the great question of women's rights has arisen. I like women better than men. . . . Sewing is always expected of girls. Why not of boys? . . . It isn't fair."

Bates's prepubescent feminism never left her. Indeed, it became stronger as she grew older and realized that regardless of her talents and attainments, she still lacked privileges commonly accorded to men. Her deep-rooted anger made heterosexual marriage unthinkable. When, in 1889, as a thirty-year-old scholar at Oxford, she aroused the amorous interest of one or two male tutors, she wrote that she "sternly nip[ped] these frivolities in the bud." But, as she had told her diary years earlier, she "lik[ed] women." While it was impossible for her to trust men, she could trust and love other women. She could write to them, as she did to the woman with whom she shared her life for almost thirty years, Katharine Coman, "I want you so much my Dearest, and I want to love you so much better than I have ever loved."

Such anger over the injustices females suffered because of gender transcended racial lines. To Mary McLeod Bethune, for example, the African-American civil rights leader and founder of what became Bethune-Cookman College, heterosexuality was no less problematic than it was for Katharine Lee Bates. Bethune was as vehement over gender issues as she was over those of race. "The work of men is heralded and adored while that of women is given last place or entirely overlooked," she declared. "We [women] must go to the front and take our rightful place; fight our battle and claim our victories." Though Bethune married in 1898 and had a child the following year, she separated from her husband, because, as the scholar Elaine Smith explains, "marriage and family experiences were unsatisfactory for her." To Bethune, a more fulfilling kind of experience was her relationship with a young widow, Frances Reynolds Keyser, who matched her in ambition and devotion to their shared cause and with whom Bethune "stood shoulder to shoulder" in the running of her school.

But resentment over the generic male's complicity in woman's inferior position could not alone have kept these women from heterosexuality or made them prefer partnerships with other women. More important was academic women's conviction that no man they had ever met on a personal level would accept and nurture their professorial positions. A 1903 article, "Confessions of a Woman Professor," states the case as many female professors must have seen it: "The male attitude of mind I have found to vary from a mild objection about my ideas of professional life . . . as 'impracticable' to a fierce jealousy which refuses to tolerate the suggestion that a woman may possibly love at once her profession and her husband." The writer's conclusion was that marriage would bring her nothing she needed and would demand of her an "unspeakable sacrifice." She thus refused "to exchange the work to which my best efforts and dearest ambitions have been given" for "the considerably overestimated boon of being supported." The notion of being transported by love or passion for a man seems never to have occurred to her; heterosexual romantic susceptibilities would have been psychologically as well as practically devastating to the efforts and ambitions dearest to her.

Yet some academic women had been educated in heterosexual romance as well as Greek and Latin. They neither desired to nor could transcend heterosexuality and the very gendered roles that nineteenth-century heterosexuals usually adopted. Such longings sometimes brought them conflict. They came to see their pioneering positions as burdensome and a strong male hand extended to lift them out of their difficult duties as inviting and even compelling. When George Palmer, a Harvard philosophy professor, began courting the Wellesley president Alice Freeman, she was deeply moved by his understanding of how exhausted she was by her stressful role. Men too would have been exhausted in her position, but they would not have had the luxury of escape, as Freeman, a woman formed by the nineteenth century, did — nor would a woman in a committed relationship with another woman have the luxury of escape from difficult duties. Palmer wrote to Freeman in 1886 that he was "distressed to see you look so worn, and to find you were having little appetite and sleep." He offered her a refuge, which many pioneering academic women would have considered insulting but she found overwhelmingly seductive: "Will you not become a girl again and come like a child to our Class Day?" The invitation signaled to her his "power / As I had never known till now," as she later wrote in a poem. He was assuming the role of the beloved patriarch, calling her back gently but firmly to the Victorian gender agreements from which she had strayed.

As Freeman's response indicated, the temptation to abdicate the "masculine" responsibilities that she had assumed was irresistible. "Perhaps if this 'becoming a girl again' should succeed, it would be just as effective as a longer vacation," she replied with pathos. Palmer took his cue: "Then as a little girl you will read carefully the following directions," he wrote, outlining precisely how the day would go and permitting her what must have seemed like blissfully childlike, feminine mindlessness.

When Freeman and Palmer married, in 1887, Alice Freeman Palmer did not cut all her ties with Wellesley (she became an influential trustee); nevertheless she resigned from the presidency. She had been an effective leader of the college despite her exhaustion, but the role was incompatible with the nineteenth-century conceptions of womanhood that continued to sit deep in her psyche. Her verses describing her life with Palmer (published posthumously in 1915 as *A Marriage Cycle*) suggest the extent to which she had found her burden of "masculine power" reprehensible. The poem "Attainment," for example, sums up the heterosexual dynamic between her and her husband, which provided what she considered a necessary refuge and made her continuation as president of Wellesley College impossible.

> Great love has triumphed. At a crisis hour
> Of strength and struggle on the heights of life
> He came, and bidding me abandon power,
> Called me to take the quiet name of wife.

Of course, some men did not wish to be daddies to the women they loved, or to be like the tyrants whom the author of the 1903 article "Confessions of a Woman Professor" described. When Wesley Mitchell, an economics professor at the University of California at Berkeley, proposed marriage to Lucy Sprague (who in 1906 had become dean of women and one of the first females to be given a regular faculty appointment at Berkeley), she expressed a fear that was common among academic women: "If I marry you, your work and your standards will prevail." Mitchell had written to her in proto-Lawrentian terms that had aroused her suspicion:

> You have lived splendidly, proudly alone, as much as a man lives alone. You have been independent. You have cultivated a sense of privacy. A man may do as much and set store by all these things, yet marry without great reluctance at giving them up in a measure. But a girl? Don't these things, when she has them all, become more part of her fibre? Does not she become a bit of an Amazon in soul? . . . And while she longs to be captured, must she not flee? And can she even understand what *wild*, shy thing of *forest freedom* it is within her which holds out — which bids her struggle against her judgment and passion?

Though Lucy Sprague must have been annoyed by his conception of independent women, nevertheless she was fascinated by the romance of the heterosexual chase that he articulated. The wild thing within her (which had been carefully nurturing an academic career for years) continued to hold out for a time. However, Mitchell soon assured her that he would accept her terms. "You would not have to give up your plans," he wrote. "On the contrary, you would realize them more effectively by marrying me." Though Lucy Sprague Mitchell quit her Berkeley position after the marriage and moved with her husband to New York for a new professional venture of his, he did help her in the career for which she became best known: together they established the Bureau of Educational Experiments, and Lucy Mitchell became a pioneer in progressive education for children.

However, most academic women of the era who had achieved such hard-won professional success were not willing to renounce it or to alter their career in order to accommodate a husband's moves. Therefore, although Alice Freeman married a man, many of her faculty members found their happiness in Wellesley marriages. In the late nineteenth and early twentieth century, virtually the entire English department at Wellesley was paired off in lesbian arrangements: Katharine Lee Bates with the economics professor Katharine Coman, Martha Shackford and Margaret Sherwood with each other, Vida Scudder with Florence Converse, Sophie Jewett with Laura Hibbard. At Vassar too, couples such as Salmon and Underhill and Gertrude Buck and Laura Wylie abounded, as they did at Mount Holyoke, Bryn Mawr, the University of Chicago, Columbia University — everywhere that female academics were employed. In choosing each other rather than men, they constructed brilliant solutions that allowed them to fulfill their longings for love, affection, eroticism, companionship, and support of all kinds while holding on to the fruits of their efforts and ambitions. They were thus able to claim a foothold in higher education for themselves, and they paved the way for future generations of women as college students and as academics.

☙ 11 ☙

MAKING WOMEN'S HIGHER
EDUCATION EVEN HIGHER:
M. CAREY THOMAS

If it were only possible for women to select women as
well as men for a 'li[f]e's love'. . . all reason for an intellectual woman's marriage wd be gone. It *is* possible but if
families would only regard it in that light! Apriori [sic]
women understand women better, are more sympathetic,
more unselfish, etc. I believe that will be — indeed is
already becoming — one of the effects of advanced education for women.

— M. Carey Thomas to Mary Thomas, November 21, 1880

How M. Carey Thomas Became a College President

IN 1883, the twenty-six-year-old M. Carey Thomas wrote to Dr.
James Rhoads, a prominent trustee of the yet-to-be-established
Bryn Mawr College, offering herself as its first president. The ges-
ture would have been outrageously presumptuous if perpetrated by
any other woman of her age in that day. But Thomas had earned a
bachelor's degree from Cornell, done graduate-level work at Johns
Hopkins and the University of Leipzig, and in 1882 received a
Ph.D., summa cum laude, from the University of Zurich — the
first woman (and first foreigner) to achieve such an honor. Further-
more, she had precise and forceful ideas about how a women's
college should function. Foremost among them was the idea that it
was appropriate for a *woman* of intellectual attainment, not a man,

to be the head of a college whose goal was to encourage women in serious study. And, as she modestly pointed out in her letter to Rhoads, her background for the position, compared to that of any other woman in America at that time, was "unusually good."

Aside from her theory that women needed other women as role models in order to achieve, Carey Thomas gave no lip service whatsoever in her 1883 plans for Bryn Mawr to the notion that women were different from men and should be educated differently. She wished to bring the academic rigor she had experienced in Leipzig to Bryn Mawr and to place the new college in the first rank of American schools, whether for men or for women. She would aim at far higher standards than those at Wellesley, Vassar, and Smith. She would provide fellowships to attract the very best female minds and offer postgraduate education to women so that they would not need to go off to Europe to get a Ph.D., as she had been forced to do. She would encourage "solid and scientific instruction" (without Catharine Beecher's excuse of preparing women to be intelligent in the kitchen), and she would bestow professorships on the very best female scholars, thereby providing women not only with educations but also with careers. Hers would be a woman's college unlike any that existed.

Though his colleagues on the board of trustees chose to appoint James Rhoads, an elderly medical doctor, as the first president of Bryn Mawr College, Carey Thomas's bold proposals apparently piqued their interest (it did not hurt that her father and other relatives were among the trustees). Despite her age, she was given the powerful position of dean of the college. With the acquiescence of President Rhoads, who had few ideas himself about how to run a women's college, Carey Thomas set about fulfilling her plans to make Bryn Mawr as outstanding for women as Harvard was for men.

M. Carey Thomas had been in training for this challenge her whole life. Her adolescent diaries reveal a girl who was bright, ambitious, deeply bitter about the limitations arbitrarily imposed on females, and bent on transcending those limitations. A few days after her fourteenth birthday, she went to hear Anna Dickinson's lecture on Joan of Arc, during which Dickinson speculated that a young man of Joan's talents would have been blessed and encouraged by his parents to go forth, while Joan's parents locked her in a chamber, hid the key, and thought they had thus "done their duty." Anna Dickinson's comparison triggered in Minnie (as she was then called) a righteous anger and an incipient commitment to revolution. "Oh my how terribly how *fearfully* unjust that seems," she wrote in her diary in 1871. "A girl certainly [should] do what she chooses as well as a boy. When I grow up — we'll see what will happen," she concluded with restraint.

Thomas had early decided that the crucial difference between males and females was not in essence but rather in society's impositions of ladylike behavior on females. Even at the age of six she was a gender rebel, because she could see that boys had the better deal in life — they could get dirty and run free. Her maternal aunt Hannah, whom she visited in the summer of 1863, permitted her to dress in pants and play with the boys. She loathed the return to tame and boring girlhood. "Min says she wants to turn into a boy," Hannah wrote to her sister with amusement, "and wants to know why she can't."

What did it mean "to turn into a boy"? To Minnie it meant to be able to range widely through life and escape the overdetermined narrowness of a female's existence. If she had been a daughter of the lower classes, she might well have donned men's clothes when she grew up and gone through the world passing as a man, as did various of her working-class contemporaries, such as the women who called themselves Harry Gorman, Charles Warner, and Ralph Kerwinieo. She would thus have been able to travel freely without concerns about molestation and to do working-class men's jobs (and get paid double what she would have received if she had worn skirts). But she was a daughter of the upper middle class; her father was a medical doctor and a respected community leader. The flip side of domestic trammels in her milieu meant not adventuring on the roads in men's clothes or working in men's trades but engaging in serious and dignified pursuits — as she decided at the age of thirteen, when she and a friend did scientific experiments with a mouse they had caught. She confessed to her diary, "I greatly prefer cutting up mice to sewing worsted."

To prefer dissecting animals to hemming skirts meant not only that Thomas was refusing to act like a young woman, but also that she was *not* a woman in the era's conception of the term. Women would "naturally" prefer domestic occupations. Yet if she was not a woman, what was she? A new answer to that question, based precisely on a female's refusal to accept her society's construction of womanhood, was being devised by the sexologists at just that time; but for now, Minnie did not have to be locked into any identity. She could thus exuberantly advise herself in her 1872 journal, "Go ahead! Have fun! Stop short of nothing but what [is] wrong (and not always that)! Never mind if people call you 'wild,' 'tomboyish,' 'unladylike,' 'masculine.' They like you all the better for it in the end." More important, she had discovered what men of her class valued among themselves — what brought the kind of respect she too deemed worth having. Her "one *aim* & concentrated purpose," she decided with excited determination, would be to show that a woman "*can learn, can reason, can compete* with men in the grand fields of literature & science & conjecture that open before the nineteenth century."

Thomas vehemently rejected the role of woman, yet she felt that she must achieve success at least partly for the sake of womankind. Only through professional success could she change the meaning of "womankind" to something grander than what it seemed to her it was. When she thought her studies were not going well, in 1878, her first despair was not for herself. "I shall *fail*," she wrote in her diary. "I who care so much for women and their cause — will *fail* & do them more harm than if I never tried."

M. Carey Thomas refused to be distracted from her goals by men, though she was attracted to several of them. Her intimate history illustrates how a human being can be capable of any manner of sexual and affectional object choice, and that contrary to the theories of the nineteenth-century sexologists and modern essentialists, genes or hormones alone do not determine whether an individual will select a man or a woman to love. At the age of twenty, Thomas found herself romantically fixated on a young scholar named Frank Gummere. As she confessed to her diary, thoughts of him overtook her whatever she was doing, even as she turned the pages of her Greek dictionary, "and when I go to bed at night . . . I cannot help thinking about him." Yet, she concluded, though he seemed to return her interest, she must not give in to her romantic inclinations toward him, because such surrender would mean that "I would have to give up, I am afraid, my dearest work that has lain next to my heart from my childhood." As his wife, she would be his helpmeet rather than his equal, she feared, and after all her brave dreams, such a position would signify for her a mortifying failure.

But in addition to her heterosexual feelings, Thomas was romantically attracted to women. Her longest and most significant attachments were with Mamie Gwinn and Mary Garrett, who were both part of a Baltimore circle of five young women from wealthy and prominent families to which Carey belonged when she did graduate work at Johns Hopkins. Her diaries of 1877 and 1878 indicate that she fell in love with Mamie and Mary simultaneously. But since Mary was already involved in an intimate relationship with Julia Rogers, another member of the circle, it was Mamie with whom Carey was first coupled, in a mutually nonmonogamous partnership that lasted for almost a quarter of a century.

Mamie, an aesthete, was brilliantly literary, though she lacked a clear focus for herself and was attracted to the looseness of bohemian life. She was also beautiful and sensual, and her letters to Carey in the early years of their relationship leave no doubt about her intensely erotic nature. "To think I was with you yesterday evening . . . & what wld I not give to be with you now — I am hungry and sick for it. . . . Goodnight, Shimmer love [one of her pet names for Carey]. Pink — sweet Shimmer — my Shimmer," she wrote in March 1882; and then again, only days later, "My love, my little big love! — 'tis 11:30 but I am awake and longing for you. . . . My darling, I am so forlorn in my rising up & my lying down, my going out & my coming in! I lie on the sofa & don't undress because

I am a coward & am miserable undressing without you. . . . I am starved, frozen up, numb for lack of Cecil Schimmerle [another of her pet names for Carey]." While Carey could not permit herself to express her own passionate nature with a man — since she so feared it would mean a permanent "giving up" — erotic love with another woman did not pose the same threat.

Mamie was also a practical help to Carey. After receiving a degree from Cornell, Carey spent a frustrating year at Johns Hopkins, which barely accepted women for advanced study. But in 1879 she convinced her parents to let her go to Europe to work for a Ph.D., because she was able to say that she would not be unaccompanied (her unaccompanied travel would have been unacceptable to them). Dreaming of the ways in which their love and work would come together in Europe, Carey wrote to Mamie, "Yes, dear love, our love shall be a help to everything we really care for &, being what it is, a greater power for good. No, I am nothing but glad & believe there is happiness & good work & completeness ahead & it will be inexpressibly sweet to have us go toward it together."

In Mamie's company, Carey studied in Germany and then received her Ph.D. from the University of Zurich. When Mamie finally also received a Ph.D. (from the graduate program that Carey eventually established at Bryn Mawr), Carey was able to hire her as a professor in the English department. The two women lived together as a couple in the Deanery until 1904, when Mamie, as inherently bisexual as Carey, ran off to marry Alfred Hodder, a former Bryn Mawr professor with whom she had been having an affair for the preceding ten years.

Mamie's defection was painful to Carey. She blamed herself for various reasons, including the conviction that if she had not become president of Bryn Mawr in 1894, when Rhoads retired (at about the time that Mamie took up with Hodder), she could have pursued a writing career — which she knew that Mamie, an aesthete to the end, would have preferred.

But Carey could not be swerved by a woman, even one she loved, any more than she could once have been swerved by a man. At Bryn Mawr her sacred work had finally been crystallized. As she declared in an 1894 letter, she could not allow herself to give up "the *Cause,* that troublesome *Woman,* with a capital *C* and a *W,* too near my heart . . . for me to crawl out." She had absolutely no doubt that she needed to serve Bryn Mawr as its president — not merely for her own gratification but because as president she could best nurture the educated Woman. Her duty was to forge that Woman into the brave image that had "lain next to [her] heart from [her] child-hood."

Mary Garrett spoke to an entirely different side of Carey than Mamie Gwinn did. What Mary found exciting and encouraged in Carey Thomas was not her aesthetic or bohemian potential, which appealed to Mamie, but rather her potential as a powerful and effective leader. Carey was the person Mary would have liked to have been — indeed, might have been, if she had not been man-acled by the restrictions of an overbearing father and his tremen-dous wealth, accumulated as the head of the Baltimore and Ohio Railroad. At her father's death, in 1884, Mary Garrett became one of the richest women in America, and she summoned all her re-sources, financial and social, to the promotion of Carey Thomas's causes, which had become her causes as well.

In 1878, when Carey had fallen in love with Mamie and Mary simultaneously, she had written sonnets to Mary and recorded in her diary their "elegant times" together, her attraction to Mary's "sweet strength," and her jealousy of Mary's beloved at the time, Julia Rogers, whom Carey deemed shallow. But Mamie, who was not encumbered with another romantic friend, overwhelmed Carey when they went together to the Adirondacks that summer. On her return, Carey confessed to her diary about Mamie, "I am devoted to her." Yet the mutual attraction between Carey and Mary Garrett never ceased. As letters indicate, it grew more intense through the years, apparently becoming physical after the permanent rift be-tween Mary and Julia Rogers in 1890. Carey's letters to Mary often mentioned her longing for the days to pass quickly so she could again "take you in my arms and kiss you" or recalled wistfully the time a few days before when "my lips were on yours."

Their passion was somehow tied to their politics. Mary Garrett was entirely committed to helping the cause of women's education, perhaps because her father had frustrated her own profound desires for an education by demanding in 1879 that she permanently drop her plans to attend Harvard Annex (Radcliffe) in order to accompany him on pleasure travels. Such frustrations may account also for the frequent militancy of her tone. When Carey became discouraged over her various battles with the board of trustees, Mary admonished her to persist, if not for her own sake, then for womankind. "That chained woman [that is, females of their day] does so sorely need the helping hand — the very strongest — & needs it now at once, and you can do so much where you are," Mary wrote emphatically in 1892.

In 1894, Mary Garrett succeeded in procuring the presidency of Bryn Mawr for the woman she loved. She made the trustees an offer they could not refuse. "Whenever Miss M. Carey Thomas should become President of your College," she informed them, "[I will] pay into her hands the sum of ten thousand dollars yearly so long as I live, and she remains President," which Carey Thomas could then use to enrich the academic programs at Bryn Mawr. Having dangled what was in that day a tremendous sum before them, she also made sure that the trustees understood that her "interest in the College depended" solely on M. Carey Thomas's "connection with it." She was determined to see Carey in the most effective position possible, because with "the power and opportunities of such a position," Mary wrote to her, "you will be much more able to help things as we want them helped." She was undoubtedly referring to their shared convictions, in opposition to those of many of the men who ran the board of trustees, that the most important mission of Bryn Mawr should be to prepare women to take their place in the world, not as better wives and mothers but as scholars and professionals. With Mary Garrett's help, Carey Thomas thus became the most prominent spokeswoman for women's *equal* higher education in the United States, and Bryn Mawr became the leading women's college — where women could be certain of receiving an education unadulterated by the influence of those who wished them to remain domestic.

M. Carey Thomas and Sexual Identity

Like many women of her era, before the concept of sexual identity demanded that a person block out the possibility of conflicting romantic or erotic choices, M. Carey Thomas was susceptible to both men and women. But she recognized early that unlike her susceptibility to men, her susceptibility to women, far from threatening the "dearest work" that lay next to her heart, would encourage it. Its corollary would be that she must make something of herself so that she would not have to rely on a man to support her. From adolescence on, she fell in love with girls as well as boys. As she described one such relationship when she was sixteen years old, she and Libbie Conkey had "'smashed' on each other or 'made love,' I don't know. I only know it was elegant." The following year she and Carrie Ladd shared a passion. At Cornell, Margaret Hicks fell in love with Carey, as she now called herself, and she reciprocated.

How did she distinguish between these relationships and mere friendships in the 1870s, when friendships could be very romantic and there was not yet a widely known category of identity called lesbian? A philosophical-personal essay she wrote at the age of twenty-one is revealing in the ways it blurs the lines between the emotions that a later era attributed to lesbianism and those that her era could still call friendship. In the idealized rhetoric of the nineteenth century, she began her essay, "Friendship," with a paean to same-sex relationships, whether between men or between women. Through such friendship, she wrote, "we are carried out of self & we see through another's eyes. We understand another's nature as we never can unless love [shows?] the way." She sharply distinguished (in ways she was later forced to modify) between what she considered "romantic friendships" and "love between a man and woman." Always in the latter, "there must be a more or less of coming down. There is an element of selfishness, or self-gratification in it," she insisted, continuing to build her case against heterosexuality: it was of course the woman who would be forced to "come down" in a relationship with a man. Society had given men the right to what Carey Thomas considered selfishness and self-gratification.

However, her political reading of male-female relationships aside, there was in fact not much to distinguish between the emotions of same-sex love and opposite-sex love in this essay. The friendships Thomas described were not merely spiritual; she wrote of their physical manifestations in "clasped hands & loving eyes & close kisses." And she was also forced to acknowledge that despite her high sentiments, in truth passionate friendship often involved the same capriciousness of feeling that she more easily attributed to male-female passions. Neither could it escape the human failing of fickleness, for example. With chagrin she admitted that her attachments to Libbie Conkey and Margaret Hicks had once been deep, but now "the feeling has gone. How perfectly unaccountable! I can give no reason for it!" But since as far as she yet knew the only categories were friendship between those of the same sex (which was by definition ideal) and love between those of opposite sexes (which was by definition erotic), she had no explanation for her confusing realization that sometimes the friendships she experienced contained the disquieting and un-ideal elements of love.

An individual as probing and introspective as Carey Thomas was sure to try to fashion a satisfying explanation for this puzzle. But she would have had little external help. If she had known of the formulation of the female sexual invert that was being developed in the 1870s and '80s, she would have considered the category foreign to her. True, like many of the female inverts of Krafft-Ebing's *Psychopathia Sexualis* (1882), she despised the situation of women in the nineteenth century, preferred the pursuits that were considered appropriate to boys and men, and could fall in love with other women. However, Krafft-Ebing had formulated sexual inversion as inherently pathological and aberrant, while Thomas believed that it was the role into which the nineteenth-century female was pushed that was pathological and that *all* females should rebel against it. Therefore, though she inverted her gender role, she would not have acknowledged herself as one of the sexologists' inverts.

In a provocative article, "*Nous Autres:* Reading, Passion, and the

Creation of M. Carey Thomas," Helen Horowitz has pointed to another lesbian image that was current in Thomas's day and that Horowitz believes she identified with. Through poetry and fiction about same-sex passion by nineteenth-century European aesthete and decadent writers such as Gautier and Swinburne, Horowitz suggests, Thomas was able to obtain "the materials with which to fabric a new self." She was able to formulate who she was by identifying herself with the "passionate sensibility" of *"nous autres,"* a phrase she adopted to signify the bohemian, the artist, the woman who, like Mademoiselle de Maupin, the entrancing eponymous transvestite of Gautier's 1835 novel, lived outside the restraints placed on women and could even lay claim to her desire to make love to another woman.

Horowitz's point is persuasive with regard to the *young* Carey Thomas — off in Europe with Mamie, away from the world of her Quaker family, not yet the leader of Bryn Mawr College, experimenting with bohemian life with Mamie's encouragement. Indeed, as early as 1879, Thomas declared that she was enthralled with Baudelaire's "bizarre and heavily perfumed" poems in *Les Fleurs du Mal,* which she deemed "glorious" and "inspiring." She scoffed at common judgment, which "cried [the book] down as immoral and disgusting." *Les Fleurs du Mal* provided fanciful, outrageous images of rebellion against the limitations posed by dull, constricting convention. Such rebellion had tremendous appeal to her as a young woman.

But upon her return to the United States with her doctorate in hand, the feasibility of that form of rebellion became much less clear to her. She had, after all, proposed herself as head of Bryn Mawr, which was to be an orthodox Quaker college. Though she did not believe in the religion of her parents, she did not dare to resign her membership in the Society of Friends until after she retired as Bryn Mawr's president, in 1922! Her position at Bryn Mawr thus challenged her brief bohemianism, which came to seem much less seductive to her than institutional power. That being so, would she have been able to continue to acknowledge herself in the fevered, decadent images of Swinburne's women or of Baudelaire's *femmes damnées,* whose lesbian loving is described as "frenzied mirth combined with dark despair," who are "wretched victims" on a "steep descent to torment without end!"?

Thomas's friends through most of her adult life were women such as Anna Howard Shaw, Frances Willard, Sarah Orne Jewett, and Mary Woolley, who were not bohemian, though like herself, they were partnered with other women. While they acknowledged one another's relationships, they could find no acceptable words to suggest a sexual identity around those relationships. In relating various incidents of passionate love between women in her letters, Carey Thomas often used the word "devotion," but she did not acknowledge that such devotion was seen in some circles as unorthodox, unconventional, or abnormal. Though the twentieth century must have forced on her and her friends the recognition that their relationships had something in common with those that were called lesbian, they could not be comfortable with the term or the image of the lesbian that was being promulgated. In stark contrast to her enchantment with Baudelairean images a half-century earlier, when Thomas saw an American production in 1927 of Edouard Bourdet's play *The Captive,* about a married woman who cannot escape her passionate lesbian feelings, she called it "vile," disassociated from it completely, and told her niece that she was "grieved that this was the sort of thing that would make it difficult for women to develop the warm and close relationship some of them needed so very much."

Yet her voluminous letters and diaries leave no doubt that Carey Thomas, having realized that she could love either women or men but that heterosexuality would be incompatible with what she wished to accomplish, committed herself to domestic, emotional, and (as an 1895 letter to Mary Garrett makes quite clear) sexual relations with other women. Though she may have had no lesbian identity, the preponderance of her intimate experiences were nevertheless what we would describe as lesbian. As she confessed to her diary in 1878, "It is difficult to conceive a woman who really feels her separate life work to give it all up when she marries a man, and yet I think . . . that it is and must be a giving up." Through her lesbian relationships she found the solution to the ambitious nineteenth-century woman's dilemma. In fact, it was those relationships that ultimately made possible the professional and political achievements that she believed heterosexuality forbade.

What M. Carey Thomas Accomplished for the Cause of Women

As the head of Bryn Mawr College in the late nineteenth century, still under the spell of the values of her youth, M. Carey Thomas wished the women in her charge to become what she had always considered the highest type of human beings — scholars. As scholars, they would be female equivalents of Cardinal Newman's nineteenth-century gentleman; they would be "as well known and universally admired a type as the Oxford and Cambridge man," she dreamed in an 1899 presidential address. But she realized that these women, whom she wanted to create in her own hard-won image, must be economically self-sufficient, and she encouraged them to that end. As the ruling spirit behind Bryn Mawr College, Thomas succeeded for many years in providing young women with an education that prepared them for professional life better than the education that women could receive anywhere else in the world. Sixty-one percent of Bryn Mawr graduates from 1889 to 1908 went on to graduate study, compared, for example, to only 36 percent of Wellesley students. Ninety percent reported having a career, compared to only 35 percent of Wellesley students.

The professional achievements of Bryn Mawr students were due to Thomas's great ambitions for them, which were reflected in the policies she put into place in spite of the conservative Quaker board of trustees. The board often tried to pressure her to emphasize the Christian commitment of Bryn Mawr over all else and not to stray far from the ideals of other women's colleges of the day. However, as she justly recalled in the years after her retirement, the original trustees "had set out to produce a well behaved fowl resembling those already living in the neighborhood barnyards, but found that they had hatched a soaring eagle instead."

To Thomas, the most ethereal heights were of course those of the intellect, and they could be attained only by devoted, concentrated study, which women had seldom been encouraged to pursue. The Ph.D. program she instituted at Bryn Mawr — the only women's college with such a program — was meant not only to produce female Ph.D.'s but also to provide role models for the undergraduates. In this way, Thomas believed, a female tradition of scholarship would begin to be perpetuated. "Women scholars can assist women students, as men cannot, to tide over the first discouragements of a life [devoted to the intellect]," she unabashedly declared in a 1908 essay. She was directly answering poisonous books and articles such as G. Stanley Hall's *Adolescence* (1904), which described the "Amazonian" female scholar as being out of touch with "the deepest law of the cosmos," which determined a true woman's true goal — to be an object of beauty and a comfort to her family. Bryn Mawr's scholars, Carey Thomas hoped, would defy such an essentialist and offensive view of women.

She tended to every detail that might contribute to making Bryn Mawr College a community of women devoted to scholarship. While in other women's colleges students were expected to spend several hours a week in domestic work on campus, Thomas decided from the start that just as male students never had to do domestic work, Bryn Mawr students should not engage in such duties, because they took precious time away from study. (An apocryphal story said that when the maids went on strike one semester, Thomas actually begged the students not to waste time making their own beds.) To assure that Bryn Mawr College would accept only the very best applicants, she required students to pass the Harvard entrance exam or its equivalent, which was administered by Bryn Mawr. She scotched a move to establish a Phi Beta Kappa chapter on campus because, she said, *all* Bryn Mawr students were Phi Beta Kappa quality.

Thomas was outraged when Charles Eliot, the president of Harvard, expressed the opinion that woman's education must be different from men's, that the traditions of past learning and scholarship could be of no use to them, and that women's colleges ought to be essentially "schools of *manners.*" In her essay "Should the Higher Education of Women Differ from That of Men?" she responded with a resounding "no!" to the question triggered by Eliot. "What is the best attainable training for the physician or lawyer [or bridge builder], man or woman?" she asked, revealing the lofty ambitions she held for Bryn Mawr students. "It is simply inconceivable that the preliminary instruction given to two bridge builders should differ in quality, quantity, or method of presentation because while the bridge is building one will wear knickerbockers and the other a . . . skirt." The mind was ungendered, she insisted — just as abilities were (or could be, with equal training), and just as opportunity should be.

Carey Thomas has been unfairly accused of bringing into the twentieth-century academy "aims" with which she was impressed in her youth but that were "abandoned nearly everywhere else by 1890." In fact she was dynamic in her leadership, making numerous shifts in the course of her long presidency (1894–1922) in response to the changing times. For instance, realizing that the Germanic lecture system that had so awed her was thought to be old-fashioned and ineffective in the twentieth century, she had her faculty institute a tutorial system in its stead. When she learned of exciting experiments in early childhood education, she established a program in progressive education and a grade school where Bryn Mawr students could observe experimental techniques firsthand. Though it did not come easily to her, since she had been used to controlling all aspects of the college for almost thirty years, in 1915 she approved self-governance by the faculty, in keeping with the recommendations of the American Association of University Professors.

Even Thomas's unfortunate, unthinking, nineteenth-century racism, anti-Semitism, and class prejudice underwent modifications with the changing times. For example, in the 1880s she fought against the establishment of a scholarship fund for poor students, arguing that the college had been intended for "young women of the upper classes." But in 1921 she established the Bryn Mawr Summer School for Women Workers, because, as she said in an address at the opening of the summer school, she now envisioned that "the coming of equal opportunities for the manual workers of the world might be hastened by utilizing . . . the deep sex sympathy that women now feel for one another." At the Summer School for Women Workers, which became a model for such schools over many years, women of academic privilege (who had until then been largely of white Anglo-Saxon Protestant background) opened "the opportunity to study liberal subjects" to working-class women of diverse ethnic backgrounds (about 25 percent were Jewish). Though it is impossible to excuse Thomas's earlier narrowness, she must be credited with the ability to change.

Thomas did move with the times when she considered such transformations valid, but she fought changes that seriously threatened the important goals to which she had devoted her life. She was horrified when domestic science programs — that is, home economics — became the rage in colleges such as Vassar, as well as in coeducational universities. To offer such programs, she said in 1908, would be "to barter for a mess of pottage the inheritance" that her generation had procured with great pain for women of the present generation — that is, the right to mind-expanding study, which had once belonged only to gentlemen. She firmly resisted the establishment of home economics courses at Bryn Mawr. Perhaps 50 percent of college women will marry, she wrote determinedly, and of that 50 percent, half will probably have husbands who are not able to support them in comfort. They will have to work, as will the unmarried college graduates. Therefore, she said, continuing her ingenious (but by then lonely) argument, if only 25 percent of female college graduates will end up being housewives, it is as unreasonable to compel all women students to study domestic science (as influential pundits such as Charles Eliot and G. Stanley Hall had recommended) as it is to compel all college men to study dentistry or medicine.

Thomas was ultimately forced to recognize that most women would not be like herself and her dearest women friends, that tribe of bold pioneers who had arranged their lives and loves with female partners, which gave them freedom to fulfill heady dreams that had been denied to women in the past. Most women would chose marriage to a man, if they could get it, above all else. Once the pioneering fervor of her own generation became history, there would probably never again be enough women in America made in their image to fill a college like Bryn Mawr. Statistics were already pointing the way to new developments. Between 1909 and 1918, 67 percent of Bryn Mawr graduates were marrying — up a full 20 percent from the previous decade. But would her mission not be even more valuable if it could reach out to the more common run of women and help them lead productive and interesting lives?

Thus, by the second decade of the new century, Carey Thomas was attempting to modify her tack and her message. She had been quoted as saying "Only our failures marry" (though she claimed that what she really had said was "Our failures only marry"). She continued to insist that women, like men, would always "find their greatest happiness in congenial work." Nevertheless, she now felt compelled by the times to admit that many women who trained for professional work might want to marry. Though in the past professional women had generally been expected to give up their jobs when they married, Thomas now challenged the wisdom of that expectation. In her address "The Future of Women's Higher Education" (1913), for example, she led the fight in insisting that female scholars had every right to marry if they wished, just as male scholars had, and that they should not have to sacrifice their work if they married. There was nothing disingenuous in her new position — only a practical realization that what she and other (unmarried) female pioneers had started by expanding educational possibilities for women like themselves had evolved. Now a broad spectrum of women wished to go to college, even women who did not want to fashion themselves after the image of the pioneers. She responded by altering her mission to serve them as well as the minority of women who were like herself.

Together with Mary Garrett, M. Carey Thomas ministered to the cause of women in other ways too. In the name of equal education and professional opportunities for women, Garrett used her fortune and Thomas her considerable persuasive powers to coerce

Johns Hopkins University to admit women into the medical school it wanted to establish in 1889. The university was having difficulty raising the money, so Carey, Mary, and two of their friends decided to head a national fundraising campaign and then fund the medical school, with the proviso that women would be admitted. Their campaign raised more than $160,000, but that sum was far short of the half-million dollars needed. With Carey acting as the main negotiator, Mary Garrett offered to donate the rest of the money if her group's proviso was honored.

The trustees of Johns Hopkins were not happy with this condition; some even preferred to drop the idea of a medical school rather than admit women to it. But like the Bryn Mawr College trustees, finally they could not bring themselves to refuse the offer. Therefore — thanks primarily to Carey Thomas and Mary Garrett — Johns Hopkins Medical School, which opened in 1893, was one of the first university medical schools in the country to admit female students on the same basis as male students. Never before in American history had such a vast fortune in the hands of a woman (or rather, a female couple) been used so lavishly, in so many ways, to promote women's equality.

Carey and Mary worked together on behalf of women in nonacademic causes also, each directing the other's attention to what was needed. For example, Mary was the one who turned Carey into an active suffragist. Carey had always had suffrage sentiments, of course. In 1881, for instance, though she expressed sadness at the news of the assassination of President Garfield, she added with pique, "Until women have the ballot he is not pres. of mine." Yet the vote was not in the forefront of her concerns until the 1890s, when Mary convinced her that their neglect of the women's suffrage cause had been unwise, because suffrage "is so absolutely essential to the accomplishment of everything we have most at heart." In 1902 they became friends with Susan B. Anthony and Anna Howard Shaw. Working as a team, Carey Thomas and Mary Garrett assumed dynamic roles in the suffrage movement, culminating in 1906, when they established a $60,000 fund (well over $1 million in today's money) in honor of Susan B. Anthony, to be used for the salaries of full-time workers at the National American Woman Suffrage Association. In 1908, along with Mary Woolley, the president of Mount Holyoke College, Carey Thomas and Mary Garrett organized the National College Equal Suffrage League. Carey was its president, and Mary Garrett was head of its finance committee.

Though in her later years as chief of Bryn Mawr College, Carey Thomas tried to help other women be heterosexual and have a profession too, she was consistent in her conviction that a heterosexual lifestyle was incompatible with the goals she most cherished for herself. She believed that for many, the "yearning" that is intrinsic to "the multiple and complicated needs of a complex human being" can be satisfied "with equal success through man or woman." Thus she chose woman — or rather women.

With Mamie's departure from the Deanery, Mary had moved in. Her partnership with Carey — domestic, amorous, and political in the service of women — flourished, from all appearances, over the next years, though their later relationship is much less graphically documented in letters, because the two women were virtually inseparable from 1904 until Mary's death, in 1915. In 1912, Mary was diagnosed with leukemia. During the three years of her illness, Carey cared for her tenderly. Carey's numerous extant letters to her brother-in-law, Simon Flexner — a medical man who headed the Rockefeller Institute, and whom she consulted regularly about Mary — are a moving testimony to her love and daily solicitude.

For example, when it became clear after a hospital stay in July 1914 that "there was no hope," as Carey wrote to Flexner, she determined, despite her terrible despair, that she and Mary would return to the Deanery, where "we shall turn the big sitting room into Mary's bedroom for the summer & move her bed on the terrace whenever possible & sleep out & try to get a little happiness out of cruel fate." Yet she could not help breaking down to lament, "It is a very grim thing to face — death of the person one cares for most in the world — I find myself unprepared." She was deeply devastated for long after. In 1925, at the age of sixty-eight, ten years after Mary's death, Carey began a relationship with Edith Lowber. But to the end of her life she felt that (as she said in a haiku-like note to herself that speaks volumes) "after Mary's death, Poetry — forgotten."

It is impossible to deny that her female loves played a monumental role in Carey Thomas's achievements for herself and for other women. Not only did they keep her happily from heterosexual marriage, which she was convinced would interfere with her ability to "do something," but they also gave her emotional and practical support in the doing, as well as in concrete accomplishments. Her primary goal had been, as she said in a 1917 speech to the Association of Collegiate Alumnae, to mold young females, through "strenuous intellectual discipline, into glorious thinking, reasoning women fit to govern themselves and others." As old-fashioned as her rhetoric was by 1917, her efforts had been valiant. She had fought against all the experts, powers, and social forces that had opposed women's higher education and that had urged — when they lost the battle, thanks to the determination of women like her — a modified education for women, one that would not make females resentful about performing "the functions peculiar to their sex."

Whatever M. Carey Thomas's various faults (on which her biographers have generally loved to dwell) — overzealousness, overweening ambition, nonmonogamous behavior, unreflecting prejudices — she wrested for women the right to choose an education that was in no way inferior to what men were given. Though she originally intended such a choice for a narrow group of women, it has become available now to any young woman who can handle the challenge. Perhaps her most useful contribution to women of her day (and to other eras that have been alive to feminist sentiments) was summed up in a letter by a former Bryn Mawr College student. "I have forgotten everything I learned at Bryn Mawr," the alumna admitted, "but I still see you standing in chapel and telling us to believe in women."

❧ 12 ❧

THE STRUGGLE TO
MAINTAIN WOMEN'S LEADERSHIP:
MARY EMMA WOOLLEY

Oh! My dear little girl, do you not know, can you not
understand, that you do just as much for me as I can
possibly do for you? I want to be what you think I am,
Jeannette — The fact that I love you makes me wish to
be more in the world.

— Mary Woolley to Jeannette Marks, April 1900

The Bryn Mawr Ideal at Mount Holyoke

MARY LYON's Mount Holyoke Female Seminary, which had been a
bold experiment in higher education for women in the 1830s, no
longer seemed revolutionary fifty years later, after the establishment of Vassar, Wellesley, Smith, and Bryn Mawr as genuine
women's colleges. But in 1888, enthusiastic alumnae who wished
their venerable old "female seminary" to become more like the
recently established but far more impressive colleges finally over-
came the resistance of Mount Holyoke's timid trustees. The curriculum was revamped, and bachelor of arts and bachelor of science degrees were now offered. The new president, Elizabeth
Mead, even attempted to professionalize the faculty by instituting
professorial ranks and raising salaries. The name of the school was
changed to Mount Holyoke College.

Yet these endeavors to create a college from a seminary fell far
short of the mark. The inbred professoriate continued throughout

the 1890s to be made up chiefly of Mount Holyoke graduates who had no training beyond their four seminary years, which had emphasized "moral education." Of the thirty-seven faculty members, only seven had Ph.D.'s (as compared to Bryn Mawr's thirty-eight-member faculty, of whom thirty had Ph.D.'s). Mead's hope to encourage academic rigor fizzled, and the name change notwithstanding, Mount Holyoke College could not be taken seriously as a major player in higher education.

Mary Woolley, who became the president of Mount Holyoke College in 1901, succeeded in transforming an indifferent institution into one that equaled the very best of the early twentieth-century colleges. She is a crucial figure in the history of women's higher education, because of her superlative successes in combining M. Carey Thomas's hard-driving, "masculine" emphasis on scholarship with what was still perceived as the "feminine" emphasis on social service (though she was instrumental in helping to give such service professional status). As she announced in her inaugural speech, she believed that a college education should create a woman who, like an educated man, understood how to accumulate facts and apply logic, but such skills alone were not sufficient. She wished the Mount Holyoke graduate to become (as she herself was) a professional "grounded in reality but well versed in ideals" — most particularly, the ideal of public service.

Woolley proclaimed that she hoped to disperse the graduates "among all sorts and conditions of people, into the desolate places of the earth, into the slums of our cities and to the far-off districts of the East . . . into the obscure corners of service." Throughout the years of her presidency, women's higher education continued to be under attack by vociferous critics who said that college made females unfit for domesticity, but she consistently refused to pretend that Mount Holyoke aimed at creating better wives and mothers. "It is not often asked whether college fits a man for home or not," she began her tenure by pointing out. "It is taken for granted that his education equips him better for all aspects of life," and it should be merely taken for granted with regard to the educated woman as well.

When domestic science became a fad course of study for women in American colleges, Woolley, like her counterpart and friend at Bryn Mawr College, refused to institute such a program at Mount Holyoke. She argued that the purpose of college was not to teach cooking and cleaning but to enlarge minds and prepare them to contribute to society through the public sphere. Indeed, she even rid Mount Holyoke of the requirement — instituted by Mary Lyon and maintained for more than seventy years — that each student must engage in several hours of domestic work around the campus every week. Woolley was thus a powerful force in carrying on the ideals that continued to revolutionize women's higher education in the first decades of the twentieth century, and in holding out against those who wished to vitiate it by driving it again in the direction of the domestic sphere. Yet her personal history also demonstrates how and why power such as hers, vested in a woman, was squelched by the 1930s.

Woolley immediately set about transforming Mount Holyoke into a true college once she took office. In her 1901 inaugural address, she had lamented that in the past "ability in leadership and organization has been more peculiarly the heritage of men," but she declared her intention to ensure that Mount Holyoke women would get the kind of education that would permit them too to "develop the power of controlling circumstances rather than being controlled by them." She was as good as her word. Because she was a remarkably successful fundraiser — she eventually increased the endowment tenfold — she could offer very attractive salaries, which enabled her to hire women with the most prestigious graduate degrees from institutions such as Yale, Cornell, Bryn Mawr, and the University of Chicago. She gave sabbaticals to faculty members without advanced degrees so they could attend graduate school, and she gently persuaded older, entrenched professors who had no interest in going back to school to retire. Believing that student scholarship could be nurtured only by faculty members who were serious about their own scholarly work, she convinced the trustees to support faculty development and gave the professors time to do their research. By promoting academic freedom, a relatively new concept in American higher education, she also guaranteed her faculty members liberty in their research interests. Through her efforts, Mount Holyoke was transformed into a community of female scholars.

Woolley also raised admission standards and greatly expanded the academic programs in the hard sciences as well as in the humanities and the social sciences. The unit requirement for a bachelor's degree was raised to 120, 10 units more than Vassar required and equal to Bryn Mawr's requirement. The number of Mount Holyoke graduates who went on to have serious careers reached an apex under her presidency and was surpassed only by graduates of M. Carey Thomas's college.

Like Thomas, Woolley wanted desperately to subvert the rigidities of nineteenth-century gender notions, though she was not entirely clear as to how much they should be subverted for all women. She insisted in speeches that "woman" must signify *only* "a member of a sex having the power and rights of a human being." Yet she seemed to recognize another category of woman — those who not only had claim to "the power and rights of a human being" but also transcended what was almost everywhere deemed to be inherent in gender. Indeed, that category had much in common with the one the nineteenth-century sexologists called the third sex. In a 1909 article for *Harper's Bazaar,* for instance, Woolley observed that of course "a man would more *naturally* [italics are mine] be a carpenter or a machinist or a merchant than a cook or a dressmaker or a milliner," yet there were occasional men who chose the latter professions, "and we are not greatly shocked thereby!" By implication, most women too would choose occupations "more naturally" suited to their gender. However, in the name of justice, Woolley suggested, just as a man had a right to determine the "manner of life for which he is best fitted," so must a woman be granted that right. "If John Jones has a right to become a dressmaker because he prefers it, why should not Jane Jones become a doctor because she prefers that?" Obviously there were few Jane Joneses, Woolley implied, but a just society is obliged to honor the *rara avis* regardless of its gender.

Her argument, while apparently modest, forged an escape from the limitations of femininity for those young women who dared to proclaim themselves "best fitted" for a different kind of life. Yet it also rested on dangerous ground in suggesting that some females were inherently different from others. Was a Mount Holyoke education intended only for such "different" women? Was Mount Holyoke responsible for turning the "natural" woman into something else — the third sex? In the 1930s, the reactionary trustees' suspicion that Woolley herself modeled values that would lead to such a metamorphosis — that she was a member of that dangerously different category and would encourage young women to become like her — may have led them to take actions that unravelled for a time all the revolutionary work that Woolley had done in the interests of women's higher education.

Mary Woolley's resistance to the imposition of gender conformity on all females was rooted in her personal experiences. She recognized early that she herself was best fitted for a life outside of conventional nineteenth-century womanhood. She worked for a few years as a teacher at Wheaton Seminary before deciding that she wanted a serious college education. The option of getting married seems never to have occurred to her, since she apparently never had significant heterosexual interests. Like her principal at Wheaton Seminary, Ellen Stanton, whose lifelong companion was Clara Pike, a science teacher and Stanton's administrative assistant, Mary Woolley had intimate relationships only with other women.

Did Wooley enroll as the first female student at Brown University in 1891 because she realized that she had no desire to marry and thus needed a career so that she would not *have* to marry? As a pioneering coed at Brown, she had to endure the disdain of the male students for "those coldly intellectual females — those prospective old maid doctors and lawyers," as one male student described them in an 1895 editorial for the student newspaper. "I don't admire a manly woman or a womanly man," the annoyed young man concluded. Woolley took such hostility in stride. She coached the five women who eventually became her classmates "not to 'seem to notice'" the male students, to look straight ahead when they had to walk across the campus, to attend to the business of scholarship only. She and another woman were the first females to graduate from Brown, where Woolley, the daughter of a minister, majored in theology.

In the autumn of 1895, having received a master's degree, Woolley accepted an appointment in biblical history and literature at Wellesley College. Her rise was meteoric. The following year she was promoted to associate professor, and in 1899 she became the head of the department of biblical history and literature at Wellesley. Before that year was over, Woolley was offered the presidency of Mount Holyoke College. By all accounts, her rapid advancement was inevitable in the pioneering days of women's leadership in higher education. As the *Springfield Republican* described her on the eve of her election to the presidency, she was tall, with "a good figure, a[n] . . . intelligent face, a bright manner, and a firm but sympathetic mouth," and seemingly she was "an earnest Christian woman" to boot.

Unlike M. Carey Thomas, who could be abrasive and brash, Mary Woolley was generally seen to be wise, fair, and judicious. She had a melodious voice that captivated her listeners. She had also the knack of seeming utterly interested in the person before her, whether it was a freshman to whom she spoke at a tea, a prospective donor to the college, or a visiting clergyman droning through the Sunday sermon in the Mount Holyoke chapel. Her ability to learn the name of every student at Mount Holyoke — and remember it years later during a chance encounter — was legendary. Though her thirty-six-year career at Mount Holyoke did not end happily, during the greater part of her presidency she was loved and venerated by students and faculty alike.

"Oh, love, love, lassie"

In her first class of biblical history at Wellesley, Woolley met a twenty-one-year-old freshman, Jeannette Marks, who became the woman with whom Mary (or May, as she was called by her intimates) was to live the rest of her life. In her 1955 biography, *Life and Letters of Mary Emma Woolley,* Marks recorded her first impression of the professor who was eventually to become her life partner. Woolley was a "young and vigorous" thirty-two-year-old, a "tailored woman . . . par excellence" who wore beautiful tweed suits and neat ascots and immediately entranced her freshman class with her Hebrew, Greek, and Latin as well as her "friendly eyes" and "strong mouth." Professor Woolley was the object of many a Wellesley freshman smash.

From the beginning of her college career, Jeannette Marks sought friendships outside the classroom with all the most interesting (and, perhaps not coincidentally, women-identified) professors at Wellesley: Katharine Lee Bates, Katharine Coman, Margaret Sherwood, Martha Shackford, Sophie Jewett, Vida Scudder. They generally responded, because she seemed singularly bright and a sure heir to their enthusiastic commitments to learning and independence. Jeannette was determined to devote herself to writing and scholarship, in their image. (She dedicated her first book, *English Pastoral Drama,* to Bates, Jewett, Scudder, and Sherwood.) She also shared their passion for social causes. She worked in a settlement house with Vida Scudder and was an active suffragist and women's rights militant. She was tall, slim, golden-haired, ethereal; as one of her students later described her, she looked "like a poet."

May could not help but notice her. Not only was Jeannette in her first class at Wellesley, but she was also assigned to the table in the dining hall over which May gracefully presided for the next five years. It was in that out-of-class setting that the friendship gradually deepened. When Jeannette had a bout with typhoid fever during what was to have been her senior year and left campus for an extended period, May came to understand that her concern and loneliness for the younger woman signified something more than ordinary friendship. Letters from May to Jeannette written about this time suggest that May was surprised and bemused by her own response. "Dearest, I thought never to love as I love you!" she declared. "My life is just bound up in you and my heart is oh! so lonely and sore without you." She found herself disturbingly distracted by her feelings, as a wry poem that she sent to Jeannette in this same letter confessed:

> Oh, love, love, lassie,
> Love is like a dizziness;
> It winna let a puir body
> Gang aboot his (her!) business!

Yet as the relationship developed into a mutual commitment, her love for Jeannette and their life together became precisely what made her believe she could "gang aboot her business" with the energy for which she became renowned.

Literally thousands of love letters from May to Jeannette, filling numerous cartons in the Mount Holyoke College Archives, have been preserved. They reveal in minute and sometimes painful detail a powerful intimacy that was occasionally stormy and fraught with emotional complexity but was always for May the sine qua non of her contentment, her productivity, her very life. They are punctuated repeatedly with references to Jeannette as "my heart's great happiness," and are filled with declarations of May's desire "to hold you close without a word and to know that every heart beat which I feel is just as much mine as if it were my own heart throbbing. . . . I love you so, I love you so, sings itself over and over again in my heart." May longed "to lavish my love upon you, to let eyes and lips and hands tell you that I love you." Though fewer letters from Jeannette to May have been preserved, those that are extant demonstrate that May's feelings were reciprocated. In a 1905 letter, for instance, Jeannette lamented their (brief) separation and begged for assurances: "May, I want you so. Write me that you *do* love me for *I* love you, love you, love you with all there is of me." She ends by vowing that in her thoughts, "over all these miles tonight," she will take May in her arms and kiss her "dear" eyes and mouth.

The overwhelming erotic element in this relationship was tempered, even at the beginning, by May's fire for her work as a leader of women and by a genuine commitment to a life of public service, which she and Jeannette could share. Though Jeannette's sentiments about social causes, especially about the cause of women, were identical to May's, early in their relationship she had not yet found an ongoing focus for her concerns. May, out of true conviction as well as a fervent desire to bind Jeannette more closely to her in their Wellesley marriage, was intent on helping her find that focus. In the early months of their intimacy, she wrote to Jeannette with overflowing enthusiasm for the work she hoped would unite them: "Just think of the opportunity you are going to have — the greatest which is possible in influencing [by educating them] the women of the land whose influence, in turn, will be without limit. Dearest, I think that that is where God calls you and me to work. I like to think that we are to be one in our life work as in all else." Jeannette may have been unsure of her commitment to such service, but May felt a desperate need to pull her along. For May, their personal passion had to be somehow linked to the passion for doing good in the world — most particularly, doing good for women.

Though May was offered the presidency of Mount Holyoke at the start of 1900, she delayed assuming office until 1901, claiming that she wished to begin her tenure on the first day of the first year of the new century. But she may have postponed assuming office so that she could remain at Wellesley until Jeannette graduated, in the spring of 1900, and could be persuaded to join her at Mount Holyoke. Clearly, May's plan from the beginning was that she and Jeannette would import a Wellesley marriage to Mount Holyoke. It was only in the hope of such emotional solace that she dared to envision herself taking on the tremendous responsibility of a college presidency. "As I look down the years," she wrote to Jeannette during the summer of 1900, anticipating her assumption of her new job, "I can see us working together, trusting each other implicitly, having no secrets, the one from the other — helping to bear each other's burdens, loving more deeply year by year as we have learned to love day by day during these happy [last?] months."

Their relationship suffered from various strains throughout the years, yet in many ways it was extremely successful. Mary Woolley was so imbued with the conviction of its success that she virtually presented it (or relationships like it) as a model when she spoke to women's groups. For example, in a lecture she wrote for the Chicago Club in 1908, "The College Woman's Place in the World," she observed that women cannot easily combine wifehood, motherhood, and a profession: "The demands of the home, especially where there are children, are necessarily so exacting" and require "the best" of a woman's physical, mental, and spiritual energy. And yet, she observed, speaking of herself as well as of her friends, "my own experience among professional women convinces me that the home feeling is a very strong one." How does a career woman reconcile her desire for a home with the impossibility of married domesticity? Woolley offered her personal solution: "In the college and university towns, as well as in the city," professional and business women were establishing homes together — "and very cheery, charming homes they are too," she exclaimed, extolling the ways in which such homes satisfied "the need of the refuge, . . . strength and cheer, which are bound up in the very thought of home."

To make possible her own home and refuge, May procured, almost as her first act after she took office, an appointment for Jeannette as an instructor in English literature at Mount Holyoke. She also encouraged Jeannette to write a master's thesis so that she could get a graduate degree from Wellesley. Once Jeannette received the degree, May promoted her to head the English literature department.

It was a promotion that Jeannette came to merit, through energetic innovations that increased the prestige of the college and the scope of the education young women received there. For example, she introduced her students to a literary world beyond the printed page by inviting poets such as Robert Frost, Edgar Lee Masters, Amy Lowell, Vachel Lindsay, and Carl Sandburg to talk about their work in her classes. She instituted a very popular experimental theater in which the work of the best of her playwriting students was produced. She helped bring a social conscience to Mount Holyoke, not only through her suffragism but also through her work with groups such as the College Settlement Association, which she led.

Though May was delighted at the ways in which her beloved took hold as a member of the faculty, she also encouraged Jeannette's primary ambition, to be a writer. She assured her, "Your success means as much to me as my own, Dearest, and I will do everything in my power to make it possible." Jeannette taught for almost forty years, but she also managed to publish approximately twenty books, with the support of May, who often handled the business end of publication. "No stone in the path of your interest shall be unturned," May wrote to Jeannette in 1910, reiterating her conviction of Jeannette's genius: "You are the stuff of which heroes are made. Your nobility, your greatness of mind and heart and soul make me feel like falling down before you."

In the context of May's worship of her female lover, it is interesting to compare Alice Freeman Palmer's worship of George Palmer, which led her to give up what she considered the excesses of her own power in her admiration of his. Alice Palmer believed that she could relax into "femininity" in the assurance that George Palmer would take the responsibilities of power; his superb power permitted her to be less powerful. In contrast, May's faith in Jeannette's superiority, whether merited or not, sharpened her commitment to develop her own power, as she declared in the letter that prefaces this chapter. Though Jeannette was her hero, May could not be the heroine. She too had to be a hero in order to be worthy of her beloved. "Femininity," with its luxury of passivity, was by their *choice* not an option for either of them in their relationship. Consequently, Mary Woolley held herself to a standard of performance that rendered her, as *Good Housekeeping* announced in 1931, "one of the twelve greatest living women in America" (along with other protolesbians such as Jane Addams, Carrie Chapman Catt, and Willa Cather).

To become "one of the twelve greatest living women in America" required constant attention to duty, unremitting devotion to her work, frequent travel away from her home and her bed. Wherever May's professional commitments took her, however, Jeannette was always fixed in her mind's eye. In the midst of a business trip to Rhode Island, where she conferred with academic dignitaries and benefactors, for example, she wrote to Jeannette,

I can picture you now in my room and I so hope that you are not a lonely little girl. My love is with you, my precious. Every minute and every step of the way. . . . It seems weeks since I saw you. Now it will be only two days and then I will kiss you and kiss you until you are *smothered* with kisses! I love you so and miss you beyond all words. If only you were with me so that I could . . . look into your dear eyes and kiss your sweet mouth and love and love you in a thousand ways. I will, when we are together, my Dearest, and make up for lost time.

Two days later, only hours away from the end of her business trip, she could not refrain from writing again to Jeannette: "The week has been brilliant beyond words, but my heart has been with my little Girl, lonely and alone." Yet having placed her heart where she believed it belonged, her intellect and energy were freed for business.

The Struggle Begins

As admired as Woolley was by students and faculty, her overweening devotion to a young instructor was at first puzzling and then disturbing to a number of people on campus. In their early years at Mount Holyoke, before the president's house was built in 1909, Woolley and Marks lived in separate quarters, though they spent a great deal of time together. The students often observed "with some amusement and a little criticism" (according to the recollections of a 1907 graduate), "Miss Woolley's late evening climb of three flights of stairs to say goodnight to dear Jeannette." A campus humorist had a doll whom she named Jamew, combining the initials of Marks and Woolley. While the students treated the relationship lightly, some faculty members were upset, because they resented the president's favoritism. As one professor observed, Woolley never obliged Marks to attend faculty meetings or be on committees, "as everyone else had to do." As the same professor pointed out in the early decades of the twentieth century "the whole place was divided up by [female] couples," but when such "twosing," as it was called at

Mount Holyoke, privileged a faculty member above her colleagues, naturally it was resented, even by other "twosers."

Perhaps also an unmarried female president was expected to be somehow above a personal life. That Mary Woolley was *not* eventually made her vulnerable to grave criticism that, though veiled, was probably exacerbated by growing homophobia. It led not only to her downfall as president but also — temporarily, at least — to the tragic dissolution of her hopes and goals for women in higher education.

Her downfall as president would not have been intolerable to Mary Woolley. By 1910, though she loved her job, she knew that she was not willing to compromise her intimate life for its sake. In any case, she believed that she had already done much of what she had set out to do at Mount Holyoke College, and though she had the skill and energy to do more, another woman could assume the presidency if necessary. In that year Jeannette Marks took a leave of absence and went to Wales, ostensibly to write full-time, but also because she felt that gossip over their relationship had begun to make life awkward and uncomfortable for both of them. By October, May implored her to come back, declaring in a remarkable letter that she would give up her position for the sake of her love if she had to, yet she was confident that she was much too valuable to the college to be forced into that sacrifice.

> My anxiety about you and the loneliness I cannot stand much longer. I do not see why I should. If my work depends upon your being away from me, it is not worth the keeping. If I have made no place for myself, if I have to ask a group of alumnae or anyone else to approve my choice of a friend, if my hold upon the college depends upon pleasing them in a personal matter — I would better give up! But that is absurd, Dearest. There has never been a more general recognition of my work than there is this autumn — and I have never felt that I could do it more firmly than I feel it this year.

She vowed her intention to "be wise and not antagonize people unnecessarily." Yet (either disingenuously or out of tenacious naiveté about how same-sex love had come to be stigmatized by now) she insisted that "there is *nothing* in our friendship for which to apologize," affirming, as she often did, that "it has been the greatest power in my life, you know that, Darling."

She was correct in her conviction of her abilities and her value to the college. Her tenure was to continue for over a quarter of a century more, but not without hostility from certain trustees. They grew less and less charmed with Woolley's concept of female education — which refused to acknowledge that women's primary jobs were those of wives and mothers — and with the presence of Jeannette Marks in her life. The most powerful of the trustees came to see Woolley and women like her as bad examples for Mount Holyoke students.

During the many years when those trustees were assiduously building a case against Mary Woolley in particular and female college presidents in general, Woolley ventured further and further out of the closet as a feminist. Her writings from her university days indicate that she had long been a women's rights advocate, but her active involvement increased dramatically in the twentieth century (though she never permitted herself to be as blatant as Jeannette Marks, who was a banner-waving, Alice Paul–style suffragette). Like M. Carey Thomas, Woolley became a strong spokeswoman for suffrage. She was a leading organizer and officer in the National College Women's Equal Suffrage League. Fully half the students at Mount Holyoke became active in the league under her influence.

Moving in the opposite direction from her increasingly conservative trustees, who wanted to hold the lid on education for women by instituting domestic science programs at Mount Holyoke, Woolley came to see higher education for women as "a feministic movement," as she phrased it in one speech. She argued that women's education should confirm that even before women are feminine, they are human beings who share in "the inalienable right . . . to self-development." Her public pronouncements frequently included uncompromising statements of women's equality — even in the 1920s and '30s, when such ideas were far less fashionable than they had been during the last years of the suffrage movement.

While the trustees' disenchantment with her was growing to a dangerous degree during these years, Woolley's reputation as a leading American woman, as *Good Housekeeping* described her, was also growing. Woolley took leadership roles on a national and an international level, not only in higher education but also in social causes, hoping to set an example to Mount Holyoke students to think beyond parochial and domestic concerns. She became the first woman to be elected as a senator in Phi Beta Kappa. She was the national chair of the College Entrance Examination Board. She served as president of the American Association of University Women for several terms, and under her leadership the AAUW had the largest membership increase in its history. Among her many achievements as its president was the establishment of a well-endowed fund to support women of talent to work in science, which by the 1920s was again an area that seemed to intimidate women greatly. As M. Carey Thomas wrote to Mary Woolley when she proposed to nominate her to preside over that organization, "You are the one person, I think, who could be unanimously elected. . . . I am anxious that those of us who have been presidents of women's colleges in these days should unite to help the young college women of the country to direct their energies where they are most needed. Under you as president we can do this with harmony and enthusiasm."

Woolley's support of freedom and equality extended to other economic and social issues. She became prominent in groups such as the American Association for Labor Legislation, which, like the Women's Trade Union League and the National Consumers' League, raised awareness of sweatshop conditions and discouraged consumers from purchasing goods made under such conditions. She became the vice chair of the American Civil Liberties Union, where she was prominent in the fight against requiring teachers to sign an oath of loyalty to the U.S. government. She worked closely with Thomas and a lesbian couple, the Barnard College professor Caroline Spurgeon and the dean of Barnard, Virginia Gildersleeve, to organize the International Federation of University Women, many of whose members around the world were, like Woolley, pacifists and supporters of the League of Nations. Right-wing groups were not happy with her prominence or her message. The once progressive Daughters of the American Revolution (which became increasingly reactionary after World War I) saw fit to blacklist Woolley, who, like her friend Eleanor Roosevelt, had once been an active member. The American Legion attacked Woolley for being "pink."

Despite these criticisms, Woolley's greatest national and international recognition came in 1932, when, at the request of President Herbert Hoover — who had been pressured to appoint a woman by many women's groups — she became the only female member of the American delegation to the Reduction and Limitation of Armaments Conference in Geneva. Hoover's appointment of Woolley was perhaps an indication less of his sympathies with her pacifism than of his understanding that she was one of the most respected women in the United States. Whatever his motives, Woolley was the first American woman to represent her country at a major convention of international diplomacy. She continued her activities as a pacifist throughout the 1930s, chairing the international People's Mandate to Governments to End War, which worked valiantly (though fruitlessly) to find means other than bloody battles to settle disputes.

The Tragedy of the Lost Presidency

Though Mary Woolley was loved and admired throughout feminist and liberal America, her problems with many of her trustees were ongoing. Not infrequently, those problems centered on principles that somehow involved Jeannette Marks. For example, during World War I, Marks, who was more militant in action than Woolley but identical to her in political ideology, spoke out at public meetings in defense of political prisoners. Joseph Skinner, who chaired the trustees, stormed over to the president's house, where Marks was now living, to tell her that she was harming the college and should cease her public declarations. Marks refused to be silenced and offered to resign instead — at which point Woolley, tired of the trustees' attempts to control faculty speech and of their meddling in what affected her personal life, informed Skinner, "If Jeannette Marks leaves Mount Holyoke, I shall leave with her." Needless to say, incidents such as these did not endear her to the trustees.

Sensing the trustees' growing displeasure and disgusted by the continuing conflict with them, Woolley vaguely hinted toward the end of the 1920s that she would retire in 1931, after she had completed thirty years as president of Mount Holyoke. But when 1931 rolled around, she felt, perhaps, that she could better promote a suitable successor if she outlasted some of the more hostile trustees. (A minimum requirement was that her successor be a woman.) In any case, she then announced that she would retire at the age of seventy, in 1933. When the situation of the trustees did not change, she declared that she would not retire until the centenary of the founding of Mount Holyoke, in 1937. She was encouraged in this delay by many alumnae, who petitioned her to remain in office in order to preside over the college's centennial celebration.

Mount Holyoke had been led by women since Mary Lyon founded the institution in 1837. But Mary Woolley had reason to fear that the chain might be broken by the trustees. Not only had she had personal problems with some of them, but by the 1930s it was impossible not to realize that the world had changed and women's progress was being reversed. Throughout the 1920s and into the '30s, women's colleges were virtually the only significant institution over which a few women still exercised power as chief executive officers. But Woolley's generation of powerful women was dying off and was not being replaced. An unmarried female head of a college could now be deemed old-fashioned with impunity; she was considered a throwback to an earlier era which many, including a majority of the Mount Holyoke trustees, thankfully saw as being over. In 1935, the trustees worried Woolley greatly when they declared their intention to appoint as her successor "the best person possible, regardless of sex."

Indeed, she saw the succession as the most important issue of her last years in the presidency. It seemed to her that if the recalcitrant trustees could be made to understand that another woman must be appointed as head of Mount Holyoke, then the national trend that ran counter to her dreams for women might be reversed. But if a woman was not appointed as the next president of Mount Holyoke, it would be taken as a sure sign that women no longer had to be considered as heads of women's colleges.

Worse yet, if Woolley failed to get a woman appointed as her successor, despite her accomplishments at Mount Holyoke (which even the trustees would be hard put to deny), the failure would go down in history. It would resound as a patent statement that she, the last female president of the college, had not been up to the job. It would signify that her life's work, all that she had done in her career to educate women for positions of great service and power, her earnest desire to prove and foster women's "ability in leadership," as she had said in her 1901 inaugural address, when she had come to the college as a hopeful thirty-seven-year-old president — all had come to naught.

Mary Woolley waged a pitched battle in favor of a female successor. She presented an impassioned and poignant statement to the trustees:

> If the college were a college for men, would the possibility of appointing a woman as president be given a moment's consideration? . . . I can imagine no greater blow to the advancement of women than the announcement that Mount Holyoke celebrates its centennial by departing from the ideal of leadership by women for women, which inspired the founding of the institution and which has been responsible in large measure for its progress.

But her plea fell on deaf ears. Frances Perkins, who was an alumna of Mount Holyoke and a trustee at this time, waged a lonely, futile battle on the board as the sole supportor of Woolley's position.

Mary Woolley did appeal effectively to her faculty, which still loved her, and they voted eighty-seven to eleven to demand a female successor. She also received strong support in the struggle from the older alumnae. (Many of the younger alumnae had no problems with a male successor — one more sign of the changed times!) She was able too to enlist the help of the American Association of

University Women, which protested the possibility of a male president at Mount Holyoke.

Yet public opinion was largely against Woolley and her supporters. The glorious experiment of women's leadership in higher education had virtually come to an end. When Roswell Ham, an undistinguished professor who was unable to get promoted at Yale, was appointed the new president of Mount Holyoke, the press portrayed Woolley as a poor sport for protesting. *Newsweek* claimed that a man was desperately needed at Mount Holyoke in order to "get [the college] out of its feminine rut." The *Boston Globe* was even more to the point, proclaiming in its front-page story that "Mr. Ham's big durable he-man personality and solid scholarship [sic] would be a fine tonic for the spinster management of Mount Holyoke." The press played up the fact that Ham was a family man, with young children and a wife to act as a gracious hostess. The new occupants of the president's house would serve to model nuclear-family life for the students of Mount Holyoke.

After going before the board of trustees with great agitation twice in one day to object to Ham's appointment, Mary Woolley suffered a heart attack, which was almost fatal. She rallied to preside with grace over the centennial celebrations of the college, and then she left Mount Holyoke. Though she lived for ten more years, she refused to meet Ham, would not accept any of the honors the college wished to bestow on her, and never returned to Mount Holyoke. As it happened, she was not wrong to be worried about Roswell Ham's appointment. He did undo a considerable amount of the good she had done. Not only did Mount Holyoke students no longer have the model of a woman at the helm, but Ham often squelched the appointments of women to the faculty, preferring men as professors for female students. Since women were seldom hired to teach at coeducational or men's colleges, Ham's lack of interest in female professors thus stole from any woman who had prepared herself to teach in a college one of her few possible options.

Mary Woolley never fully recovered from the pain of the lost succession battle, but she continued to be active for several years, lending her illustrious name to feminist and pacifist causes. For example, she joined Alice Paul's National Woman's Party, through which she promoted the Equal Rights Amendment, and she was a chief organizer for the Committee on the Participation of Women in Post-War Policy. When she could not travel, she led causes from her living room, with Jeannette Mark's assistance. During her last years, she and Jeannette lived together at Fleur de Lys, a large house that Jeannette had inherited in Westport, New York, two hundred miles and a world away from the campus where May had done her life's work.

In 1944, May suffered a cerebral hemorrhage, and for the next three years, until she died, Jeannette cared for her devotedly. After May's death, Jeannette wrote the biography of the woman who had been her partner for almost five decades. *Life and Letters of Mary Emma Woolley*, which was published in 1955, is undeniably hagiographic, presenting May as the noble hero she wished to be for Jeannette and as a feminist martyr to the woman-hating trustees of Mount Holyoke. Yet it reveals accurately how she built a glorified female seminary into one of the best liberal arts colleges in the country, how she inspired Mount Holyoke students to social service, and how she tirelessly promoted the advancement of women. Though it avoids any reference to Mary Woolley's Wellesley marriage to Jeannette Marks, it is nevertheless implicitly a moving final tribute to their relationship, as Margaret Sherwood, May's Wellesley colleague and Jeannette's old professor, recognized. On reading *Life and Letters of Mary Emma Woolley*, Sherwood remarked to her own partner, Martha Shackford, "Jeannette writes as if she had kissed each sentence as she wrote it down."

❧ 13 ❧

THE TRIUMPH OF ANGELINA:
EDUCATION IN FEMININITY

Nine [professors] lost their jobs [because they were suspected of lesbianism] and it really put the fear of god
in me. . . . Being a lesbian is not an easy choice . . . so
graduate school was my year to really try the straight life.

— A lesbian who was a college student
in the mid-twentieth century

Educating Women for "a Woman's Life" — Again

EDUCATIONAL LEADERS such as Charles Eliot of Harvard, who
had opposed higher education for women from the beginning, were
happy to observe in the 1920s that the factions that had pushed
women into scholarship and careers at the start of the century
were losing ground. They had been doomed to failure, Eliot wrote
with some glee. "Women as a whole" — normal women (the opposite to whom must be "abnormal" women such as Carey Thomas
and Mary Woolley) — had demonstrated that they were content in
woman's sphere. "Wiser ways and methods" had prevailed, he said,
because "it is not the chief happiness or the chief end of women,
as a whole, to enter these new occupations, or to pursue them
through life. They enter many which they soon abandon, and that
is well — particularly the abandonment!"

Though women went to college in increasingly high numbers
as the twentieth century progressed and more and more colleges
opened to them, the ideas of leaders such as Carey Thomas and
Mary Woolley about educating women for scholarship and careers

slipped out of fashion. Even most women's colleges did not follow the lead of Bryn Mawr and Mount Holyoke in resisting the pressure to offer a domestic science program. Some institutions, such as Vassar, dressed up such programs with titles such as "euthenics," meaning "the scientific study of the home," and offered courses such as "Chemistry of Food and Nutrition." But as Debra Herman observes in her study of Vassar, these developments were virtually an acquiescence to the belief that "equal education for women . . . was folly in a society committed to divergent roles for men and women." Instead of educating women for careers, Vassar — which by 1920 had moved far from the ideals of early faculty members such as Lucy Salmon and Maria Mitchell — had decided to educate women "for a woman's life."

That trend reached far beyond Vassar, becoming for many years the reigning view on female education. Not only were the female leaders in education who had bucked that trend considered obsolete, but they were castigated for having harmed young women. They gave "little thought to the unique kind of education that [women] should have" and foisted on women an "education designed for men," as a 1942 book, *Women After College*, phrased it. The old leaders were accused of pretending that there were no important differences between the sexes. They had tried to invert gender by making men out of women.

By mid-century they were long forgotten. In 1920, women made up 30.1 percent of all college professors in America. By 1959, their proportion had dropped to 19.4 percent. Though some women were hired at coeducational institutions during these years, it was generally to teach in *women's* areas, such as home economics, women's physical education, nursing, and social work. In women's colleges, the one kind of academic institution in which women had once been taken seriously and hired to teach in all disciplines, they were disappearing as faculty. For example, at Smith in 1910 women made up 75 percent of the faculty. By 1966, they made up less than 35 percent. Departments often made no attempt to hide their preferences for men in hiring. And if both men and women were hired, women were likely to receive appointment as instructors, while men received professorial appointments, even at women's colleges.

The decrease in female college administrators was similarly dramatic, as Cynthia Brown has pointed out in her historical work on female leadership in higher education. However, interestingly, African-American women were being appointed to head black colleges at just about the time that white women were being replaced in predominantly white colleges by white men. Perhaps this was because black women fell outside the gender dictates that were applied to white women. Indeed, the institution of racism may have been threatened more by the ascendancy of black males than by that of black females, and African-American women were thus allowed to attain token power in black colleges that were dependent on white philanthropy. Mary McLeod Bethune held the presidency of Bethune-Cookman College until 1942, when her work with the New Deal's National Youth Administration began to require most of her time. Other African-American women assumed college presidencies in the 1920s and '30s. For example, Artemesia Bowden became president of St. Philip's College in 1926, and thus the first woman, black or white, to head a college in Texas. Mary Elizabeth Branch assumed the presidency of Tillotson College, also in Texas, in 1930.

That countertrend aside, the mid-century saw a spate of books and articles written by new college presidents (almost invariably white men) with titles such as *On the Education of Women* and "How to Educate a Woman," which insisted that young women were best served by an education that differed from that of young men. These male college presidents were sometimes joined in their views by a new breed of female professor who saw herself as a woman first and foremost and believed that college women should be trained in her image. As Professor Dorothy Lee observed in a 1947 *Mademoiselle* article, more valuable to a female student than learning about Plato was learning how to make the home peaceful and comfortable — for instance, learning what a wife ought to say when her husband comes home upset because he has been stuck in a traffic jam or fired from his job. Views such as hers held sway even in the women's colleges of the era. As members of the Radcliffe class of 1952 bitterly recalled in their twenty-five-year alumnae report, the "prevailing view" foisted on them at Radcliffe had been that they must and would "seek a successful husband on whom to piggy-back for the rest of [their] lives." The Mrs. degree had become the only really desirable one for a woman, even in institutions that had once led the way in serious higher education for females.

College administrators and educators sometimes did recognize, however, that what was true of "most women" was not true of all women. Some space was therefore reserved for the exceptional few. It continued to be possible for highly motivated, stubborn, "odd" women to pursue stringent study, to get into decent graduate programs, and even to earn Ph.D.'s. But by the 1920s, those exceptional few who wanted to pursue such a course were generally stigmatized. As the psychiatrist John Meagher wrote in "Homosexuality: Its Psychobiological and Psychopathological Significance," a 1929 article that reflected prevalent ideas of the era, it was *not* the normal woman "who yearns only for higher education and neglects [heterosexual] love." A woman's passion for education, Meagher believed, was connected to her immaturity; female homosexuals, he observed, were often "intellectual and cultured, though sexually infantile."

Through equations such as these, a woman's desire for an education "like a man's" signified that she was inverted — not just in terms of gender, but also with regard to her sexuality; that is, she was a homosexual. Intrinsic to such a theory was the notion that homosexuality signified an arrested development. Thus, in one neat sweep, women were warned against desiring both a serious education and the love of another woman. Those two desires were seen as often intertwined, and both were characterized as pathological.

Ideas such as Meagher's were not new, of course. Havelock Ellis and other nineteenth-century sexologists had long ago observed that inverted women were attracted to such "male pursuits" as education, and the early twentieth-century theories of Freud are also evident in Meagher's language. But what had changed was that such views, promulgated by "experts," were now no longer relegated only to medical journals. They were also fed regularly to the public. For example, Carl Jung's 1928 essay "The Love Problem in the Student," published in a Modern Library edition, observed that "homosexuality among women" was prevalent in those who have notions about women's rights and advancement. In such ways, higher education for women, and especially for those unmarried women who had been instrumental in leading the pursuit, came under hostile public scrutiny.

Obviously, the mental health profession was not single-handedly responsible for convincing large numbers of young women that they did not want a man's education or the love of other women, which only men should want. As Christina Simmons pointed out in her classic article on companionate marriage in the 1920s and '30s, the popular print media were inundated with books and articles that reminded young women that real happiness could be achieved only in heterosexual marriage, that study for careers and independence interfered with the pursuit of such happiness, and that only "mannish" females would put their energies into goals outside domestic fulfillment. Serious higher education for women, which had been promoted most effectively by women who wished to make lives for themselves outside heterosexual marriage and conventional womanhood, was tarred by its connection with those pioneers.

Perhaps young women were somewhat complicit in the push to guarantee that college would not prepare them for independence. After all, what were the ramifications of study for a lifelong career? Marriage and motherhood were full-time jobs — or at least they were still constructed as such, even with all the labor-saving devices that were becoming available to the ordinary household by the 1920s. (The invention of vacuum cleaners and the availability of packaged bread did not come to mean that a woman had more time for her own pursuits but rather that she should find new, different, and more time-consuming ways to care for the home.) If, as common wisdom had it once again, marriage and motherhood alone could fulfill one as a woman, what was the purpose in studying for a career that would inevitably interfere with domestic bliss? And after arduous study, was there even any guarantee of happiness in professional life? Would it be worth the sacrifice of married love and children? Who but abnormal, mannish women could be content to substitute twosing for heterosexual domesticity? A 1923 survey of women at Vassar, where same-sex twosing had once been a norm, found that 90 percent wanted marriage, which they regarded as "the biggest of all careers."

The Effects of the Heterosexual Imperative on Women's Higher Education

As the sociologist Jessie Bernard observed in her study of academic women, the excitement the pioneers had experienced when higher education was first opened to women had quite worn off by the 1920s and '30s, when college-educated women "turned their backs" on scholarly life and career preparations "and ran to rock the cradle." Clearly a heterosexual imperative had developed to counter the efforts of women such as Carey Thomas and Mary Woolley. The imperative of the 1920s and '30s often sounded different from the Victorian imperative, which had relied on tradition to keep women in the home. The new feminine mystique was given voice by women such as the author of "Autobiography of an Ex-Feminist," who could argue "been there, done that" with regard to women's higher education and the false values it fostered. The "Ex-Feminist" claimed in her 1933–34 *Atlantic Monthly* articles that at the age of twenty she had naively "thought with the founders of our best known women's colleges that young women should have 'opportunities for education equivalent to those provided for young men.' There was no sex to the mind. There should be no sex in education." But life had taught her differently, she wrote. Her education had been a failure; it had not prepared her for "a woman's work," the tasks that inevitably lie in wait for the "normal" woman. Her education had sent her to seek after the false gods of professionalism, which were totally incompatible with motherhood and domestic peace.

It may also be that by the 1920s, the college experience was attracting different kinds of women from those it had attracted earlier — women who, unlike their predecessors, did not see themselves as rebels against the accepted constructions of womanhood,

Professors Carla Wenckebach and Margarethe Müller.
(Wellesley College Archives)

Professors Martha Shackford and Margaret Sherwood.
(Wellesley College Archives)

Professors Katharine Coman and Katharine Lee Bates.
(Wellesley College Archives)

Rebecca Perot, nineteenth-century Shaker leader. After the death of her life partner, Minister Rebecca Jackson, she renamed herself Rebecca Jackson, Jr.
(Western Reserve Historical Society)

Phebe Hanaford. Ordained as one of the first women ministers in the Universalist Church, she left her Baptist fundamentalist husband and lived for thirty years with Ellen Miles.
(Nantucket Historical Association)

Dr. Emily Blackwell, cofounder and head of the New York Infirmary for Women and Children and the Women's Medical College: "A something sprawling in my character and way of doing things." (*Woman's Journal*)

Dr. Elizabeth Cushier, gynecological surgeon and professor of medicine at the Women's Medical College of the New York Infirmary, and life partner of Dr. Emily Blackwell. (*Woman's Journal*)

Edith Cadwallader, M.D., at the Women's Medical College of Pennsylvania, 1900.
She captioned this picture "the Manly Medic."
(Archives and Special Collections, Allegheny University of the Health Sciences)

Dr. Ethel C. Potter. "Don't be a Vegetable Wife; Husbands Don't Like Them," she advised readers in a 1919 newspaper column. (Archives and Special Collections, Allegheny University of the Health Sciences)

Dr. Martha Tracy, dean of the Women's Medical College of Pennsylvania and Dr. Potter's life partner. (Kate Campbell Hurd-Mead, *Medical Women of America*)

Lilian Welsh (*left*) and Mary Sherwood, medical doctors and life partners: "We . . . had looked forward from early childhood to the possibility of self-support." (Dr. Lilian Welsh, *Reminiscences of Thirty Years in Baltimore*)

Martha May Eliot
(*left*) and Ethel
Dunham at Johns
Hopkins Medical
School, 1915.
(Schlesinger Library,
Radcliffe College)

Dr. Eliot, chief of
the United States
Children's Bureau —
what an "unnatural
female celibate"
might do.
(Schlesinger Library,
Radcliffe College)

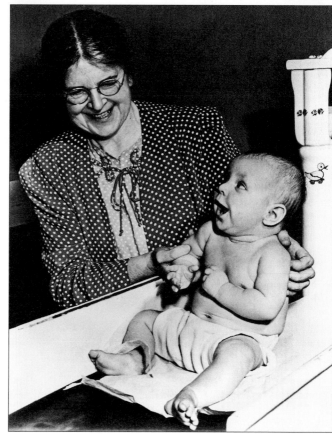

Pauli Murray, lawyer, priest, and civil rights activist. She captioned this picture "A creature of many moods and facets — my 'id.'"
(Schlesinger Library, Radcliffe College)

U.S. Congresswoman Barbara Jordan, 1987.
(Larry Murphy/University of Texas, Austin)

or even as fired by the intellect. As increasing numbers of females went to college, higher education for women came to be seen not as a bold statement of feminism or intellectual hunger but rather as a credential to show that one was a reasonably cultivated, non-working-class female. William Neilson, the president of Smith in the 1920s, astutely compared Smith students fifty years earlier with those of his day. The pioneering students had been that "handful of eager souls, brought into this place because of their appetite for intellectual things." Their present counterparts had come to college, "we must confess, largely in obedience to social convention." On the backs of the rebellious pioneers, college for women had become not only commonplace but even conventional. In fact, by 1920, as a result of little more than half a century's efforts by those with a feminist bent, the number of women in college had almost reached parity with men: 47.3 percent of American college students were female.

However, the growth of the number of women in higher education proved to be unstable whenever the going got rough. If a college education really had no grander purpose than to create a cultivated housewife, was it worth the time, effort, and money? Young women and their parents rethought the college fad from time to time, such as during the Depression years, when money was scarce and what was dispensable had to be dispensed with. College educations that did not end in material advantage had to be sacrificed. By the end of the 1930s, the proportion of women among college students had dropped to 40.2 percent. By 1950, when a new, post–World War II feminine mystique was recreating the happy housewife, it had dropped an additional 10 percent, to 30.2 percent.

There were undoubtedly diverse reasons for this dramatic drop, but one important influence must surely have been the fact that the goal of many pioneers in female education — to help women achieve interests outside traditional domesticity — had become suspect. Such a goal was associated (often rightly, as I have illustrated) with a willingness to forgo heterosexual marriage, frequently in favor of setting up a household with a like-minded female. By mid-century, the motives for such twosing were widely thought to be not convenience or even romantic friendship but lesbianism — which signified abnormality and morbidity.

Predictably, the percentage of women getting graduate degrees also decreased during these decades. Women who had been under-graduates during the 1920s or earlier had attended graduate school in record proportions in order to earn Ph.D.'s. In the nineteenth century, Carey Thomas had had to go to the University of Zurich (which opened to women in 1867) to get her degree. But by 1930, 18 percent of all Ph.D.'s awarded in America went to women. The proportion (though, in a generally expanding university popula-tion, not the number) dropped precipitously in the decades that followed. By 1940, only 13 percent of American Ph.D.'s went to women. In 1950 and 1960, women claimed only 10 percent of Ameri-can Ph.D.'s.

Perhaps the major clue in explaining the proportional drop in female doctorates can be found once again in marriage statistics. As the detractors of higher education for women had been scream-ing from the start, serious study and the careers to which it led were inimical to married life. Of 1025 women who received Ph.D.'s be-tween 1877 and 1924, 80 percent were not married. By the mid-twentieth century, the pursuit of the Ph.D. apparently continued to conflict with married life — but proportionally fewer women were willing to give up married life than had been the case in the pio-neering generations.

As Helen Astin has shown in her study of women who received doctorates during the 1950s, an unmarried woman continued to have a far better chance of completing a Ph.D. than a woman with a husband in tow. Fifty-five percent of the women Ph.D.'s whom Astin studied were single, as opposed to 6 percent of women in their age group in the general population. The married women in Astin's study complained often of the difficulties that marriages in the 1950s imposed: problems in getting help at home while they pursued their work, husbands' negative attitudes toward the wives' professional goals, husbands' job mobility, which meant wives had to move too and often sacrifice career development, and so on.

If marriage interfered with the pursuit of a highly desired degree and a subsequent career, why marry — particularly if one felt that the alternatives, such as a domestic life with another woman, were attractive? In fact, only 11 percent of female professors were married in the 1920s; many of them continued to live together in long-term relationships. But such a life had become much less comfortable than it was in earlier eras. Academic women who did not marry were suspect. They were besieged in all directions, even by those they might have assumed would be protective. For instance, in 1922, the journal of the American Association of University Women published a critical, even snide article about unmarried female faculty members, who were accused of presenting "an air of single superiority toward the commonplace of being married and bearing children, which Herr Freud might define as a defense reaction." In the same vein, a speech given later in that decade by Clarence Little to the National Association of Deans of Women criticized unmarried female college administrators who "threw off the normal biological inhibitions of gender" and were "pseudo-masculine." He called them "amazon" types (using the nineteenth-century euphemism for those who were suspected of sexual inversion), and he more than hinted that they were dangerous to students and should be eliminated from college administration.

These various shifts in attitudes and concomitant decreases in female representation on faculties and in college administrations had far-reaching effects. A critical mass of women in academia — who would fight for women's right to be educated, funded, hired, and promoted just as men were — was lost. The academic woman who could happily have made her life with other women was actively discouraged, as the student whose recollection prefaces this chapter observed.

Not only was it difficult for the woman who actually believed herself to be a lesbian to acknowledge an identity that was so widely stigmatized, but it was also difficult for her to prepare herself for the economic independence that would permit her to live without the help of a man. Even she felt pushed into marriage, as Lorraine Hansberry, the African-American playwright, who was married to a man though she was a self-identified lesbian, observed with agony in a 1950s lesbian magazine: "The estate of woman being what it is, how could we ever begin to guess the numbers of women who are not prepared to risk a life alien to what they have been taught all their lives to believe was their 'natural' destiny — AND — their only expectation for ECONOMIC security." Despite her lesbian desires and her talents (which she did not know in 1957 would bring financial rewards), Hansberry felt constrained to marry.

Attacks on unmarried women in the academy became absolutely virulent in the 1950s. For example, in 1951 the Mellon Foundation provided a grant to study academic and personal advising of students at Vassar. The study was headed by a psychiatrist, Dr. Carl Binger, whose subsequent resignation from the project made the front page of the *New York Times* because he revealed that he was leaving in disgust at what he saw as Vassar's woman-centered policies. "I don't believe that matriarchy provides a wholesome atmosphere in which students are likely to develop satisfactorily," he was quoted as saying. He was especially concerned about "sexual developments of undergraduates in an atmosphere of supervision by matriarchy." There were "too many unmarried women at Vassar in supervisory capacities," he concluded. It is not surprising in the context of such patent homophobia that when President Blanding, an unmarried woman, retired a few years later, a man was chosen by the trustees to replace her.

Unmarried female college administrators who managed to keep their jobs were on the defensive, both for themselves and for their female faculty members. For instance, Dean Virginia Gildersleeve, who was the top administrative officer at Barnard from 1911 to 1947, never married. She lived with an English scholar, Caroline Spurgeon, until Spurgeon's death, in 1942, and then with another Barnard professor, Elizabeth Reynard, until Reynard's death, in 1962. (During World War II, Reynard was instrumental in organizing the WAVES, the American women's naval force, whose advisory council Gildersleeve chaired.) Though Gildersleeve fought fiercely to encourage female scholars, she understood by the 1930s that she had better make some heterosexual noises if she wished to maintain credibility in her position as dean. She instigated a revolutionary year-long paid leave of absence for pregnant (married) faculty members, but the justification that she made for this excellent policy in her 1932 annual report seemed pointedly to emphasize her encouragement of her faculty's heterosexuality and to ignore the possibility that there were roads to "full and rich lives" outside heterosexuality (as she had herself discovered). "It is of great importance that our teachers should be normal and interesting human beings, with as full and rich lives as may be," she wrote. "Neither the men nor women on our staff should be forced into celibacy and cut off from that great source of experience, of joy, sorrow and wisdom, which marriage and parenthood offer."

That even M. Carey Thomas, the once bold standard-bearer for women like herself, should have felt the pressures of the heterosexual imperative indicates how powerful that imperative had become. As a Bryn Mawr student during the later Thomas days remembered years later, at senior receptions Thomas seemed "almost always" to encourage discussions of "how we could best combine a career with marriage and children. She was more realistic than the feminists of today [1950s]." According to this same alumna, Thomas even presented herself as a frustrated heterosexual, quite erasing her lifelong romantic involvements with other women; she "used to say regretfully that she had given up both marriage and close friendship with men because she feared it would damage her effectiveness in running a women's college." Such defensiveness and erasure of their personal histories on the part of Gildersleeve and Thomas attest to their perceptions of the venomous homophobia directed at female academics as the twentieth century wore on.

"The Attraction of Colleges . . . for Overt, Hardened Homosexuals"

Female students, for their part, were wind harps on whom the contending forces of their immediate milieu and the larger society played. As early as 1920, veneration of the learned female professor, the female students' crushes on her, which had been common in earlier generations, and the desire to take her as a role model and follow in her footsteps seem to have been disappearing. The learned spinster was becoming laughable instead of admirable to a generation that was discouraged from sharing her lust for knowledge and power. As a limerick by a female student in 1920 put it,

There was an old maid of Peru
Who thirty-one languages knew;
With one pair of lungs
She worked thirty-two tongues;
I don't wonder she's single; do you?

The growing "sophistication" in the population about what was perceived as sexual pathology scared young women away from what, as Alfred Kinsey phrased it, comes naturally to all mammalians — attraction to members of the species *regardless of gender*. College women thus chose heterosexual marriage in increasingly greater numbers throughout the twentieth century, so that by the end of the 1950s, 90 percent of all female college graduates married. The female college graduate's tendency to spinsterhood, established in the nineteenth century, was quite reversed (though again, as with college presidents, the reversal was not true for African-American women: only 42 percent of African-American female college graduates married in the 1950s, attesting perhaps to the paucity of African-American men with college degrees).

Students who did not follow the heterosexual imperative also suffered from the slings of homophobia. Books such as Dorothy Bromley and Florence Britten's *Youth and Sex* (1938) demonstrate how closely and with how much disapproval same-sex intimacies among students were scrutinized, "whether or not [they] were accompanied by physical manifestations of affection." Love between persons of the same sex had become so pathologized, first by the "experts" and then within the popular culture, that even a hint of it now met with opprobrium.

In their study of 1300 college students, Bromley and Britten insisted that only 4 percent of their female sample had had same-sex love experiences. Their figure, when contrasted with that which Katharine Bement Davis produced in a comparable 1920s study, provides an eloquent statement regarding ostensible behavioral changes that accompanied the growth of homophobia. In Davis's study of college women of the previous generations, 50.4 percent said they had had "intense emotional relations" with other women, and half of those admitted that their experiences had been accompanied by sexual expression or "recognized as sexual in character." Indeed, of those born in the late nineteenth century in Davis's sample (they were between the ages of thirty and thirty-nine at the time of the study), 46.2 percent admitted to homosexual experiences! Of those born in the early twentieth century, only 21.4 percent admitted to having had such experiences. As a further illustration of the growth of homophobia by the time *Youth and Sex* was published, Bromley and Britten also insisted that of the 4 percent who admitted to homosexual experiences, all but one individual had "outgrown" it.

Of course, the researchers' own nervousness about same-sex love may lead one to suspect that their interviewees were not entirely forthcoming. Bromley and Britten warned, for example, that even when homosexual relationships were not accompanied by erotic exchanges, "they frequently tend to encourage tyrannical possessiveness, incessant demands in the name of love, recurring states of instability, and an exclusiveness that cuts off the partners from other interests and friendships." If they shared such opinions with their interviewees, how many would have lied rather than admit to homosexual interests?

Books such as theirs not only denigrated same-sex love and alerted others to the existence of that "morbid" phenomenon; they also created a self-consciousness — an awareness of "difference" — in those young women who continued to love other women. Yet such an awareness did not have to be wholly negative. Self-consciousness made possible a lesbian identity, which had barely existed in the United States during the previous century. Potentially, that identity could allow young women with a passion for education and careers to regroup and fight with renewed vigor the trend to lock all women into dependent heterosexual domesticity. However, in the milieu in which the concept of "the lesbian" had been formulated, it was difficult for "lesbians" to accept without conflict that potentially useful identity.

In fact, the recognition of those feelings that society now dubbed as sick could literally make a young woman sick. Lenore Thompson, who was a student from 1936 to 1940, recalled a half-century later that "I felt passionately toward one of my classmates, but I was petrified someone would find out, and [I] wound up in the infirmary every once in a while at the edge of some kind of breakdown." To counter her sick feelings, she married and had four children. (She returned to lesbianism, but not until the milieu had changed significantly, in 1985, when she was sixty-seven years old.) In her fear of what had come to be seen as lesbianism, she — and probably many thousands of other young women between 1920 and 1970 — became paralyzed by the very feelings that Mary Woolley had once been able to characterize as "the greatest power in my life."

It would be no exaggeration to say that during the 1950s, homosexual students in American colleges and universities were the victims of a witchhunt. They were threatened with expulsion, exposure, and worse. A 1955 article, "The Sexually Deviant Student," written by the dean of students and his assistant at UCLA and published in a journal for education administrators, actually warned other deans about the "attraction of colleges, both public and private, for overt, hardened homosexuals." The deans' recommendation was that homosexual students be identified and given the choice of expulsion or psychotherapy to change their orientation. Entering freshmen at UCLA had to undergo psychological tests that asked such absurdly blatant questions as "Have you ever wished to kiss someone of the same sex?" and "Do you have fantasies about being close to a person of the same sex?" All who were savvy about homosexuality surely answered no. But sometimes homosexual students were discovered through other means. A student at Vassar during the 1950s was called up before the president and told that "if I didn't relate the names of my [lesbian] friends to her (she had a legal pad handy) they would fix it so that I could not be accepted in any college or university in the United States ever."

Despite threats, or ridiculous claims such as Bromley and Britten's that only one out of 1300 students never "outgrew" her homosexuality, women's intimacies did not disappear entirely from academic life. Yet the female couple in academia became much less commonplace. The once ubiquitous crush among female students virtually disappeared or was unspoken when it occurred. Women in intimate relationships with other women, whether students or faculty members, knew they had to hide what was central to their lives if they wished to remain at their college.

Perhaps the most notable same-sex academic intimacy in the post–World War I decades was that between the anthropologist Ruth Benedict and a woman who had been her student at Barnard, Margaret Mead. Benedict, a Vassar graduate, had married in 1914, but when she decided four years later to get a Ph.D. at Columbia, her husband was not happy with her. They soon separated. In 1922, as a teaching assistant at Barnard, she met Margaret Mead. According to a recent biographer, the chronic depression from which Benedict had suffered apparently disappeared permanently in the course of their lesbian relationship. As their journals and letters reveal, they fostered each other's brilliant work. Ruth Benedict was the first woman in America to become preeminent in an academic field dominated by men — and her lover may be said to be the second.

Mead, who was bisexual, eventually married, but she and Benedict continued to use each other as sounding boards for their work, and they engaged in joint projects for the next twenty-five years. After Mead married, Benedict began a relationship with Ruth Valentine, a psychotherapist, with whom she lived until her death, in 1948. Central to Benedict's best work (for example, *Patterns of Culture*, 1934) was the idea that traits that are considered abnormal in one culture may be highly valued in another — a concept she may have come to understand by being involved in a same-sex intimacy at a time when such once-honored relationships were taboo.

The histories of the pioneers in women's education provide ample proof that an individual's affectional and sexual cathexis has reference not simply to biology or to the Freudian "family romance" but also to what will help her realize the internal image of who she is, and to what is possible and permissible in her immediate milieu and the larger society. M. Carey Thomas is a salient example of how and why one might *choose* whom to love. The late nineteenth- and early twentieth-century pioneers in women's education knew that to choose heterosexuality, as it was constructed in their day, would make it impossible for them to realize their internal images of who they might be. The choice of a female mate (especially one who engaged in similar pursuits, or at least valued them) offered a far greater potential for nurturing the realization of that image. And they had little difficulty in making that choice. The larger society was generally complicit with female twosing, considering it a romantic friendship or a convenient domestic arrangement between spinsters, and their immediate milieu — either the all-woman campus or a coeducational institution where they had to band together against hostile male students or professors, who might ridicule them for their desire to get an education — fostered such intimate relationships between women.

In the decades after World War I, heterosexual marriage may have become companionate, but it still interfered with a woman's intellectual ambitions. Yet the Wellesley marriage was no longer the easy alternative it had once been for academic women. The larger society, and even the college milieu, now frowned on those intimacies that had been greatly responsible for making women's earlier academic successes feasible. It is assuredly no coincidence that for the subsequent half-century, women's further advancement in academia was on hold.

However, in the 1970s, not only did the nature of heterosexual relationships begin to change, but also women could once again claim intimacy with each other with relative impunity — though now that claim was often called lesbian or lesbian feminist. The proliferation of these new styles of relationships (both heterosexual and homosexual) surely played a significant role in helping to break the feminine mystique that had reigned through much of the previous half-century. And when women were finally able to resume the academic quest in large numbers, they did not have to begin at the beginning. Pioneers such as Carey Thomas and Mary Woolley had already established their right to serious higher education and a position within the academy.

PART IV

HOW AMERICAN WOMEN GOT
INTO THE PROFESSIONS

❧ 14 ❧

"WHEN MORE WOMEN ENTER PROFESSIONS": LESBIAN PIONEERING IN THE LEARNED PROFESSIONS

Dr. Culbertson has a most devoted friendship with a Dr. Smith who studied here 5 years ago & then took the direction of the Boston hospital where Dr. Culbertson was under her. She & Dr. Culbertson are both surgeons & are going into partnership when she returns. Dr. Smith has just begun & the first week made enough to pay the year's rent of her office. This Dr. Culbertson is so homesick for Dr. Smith that I cannot help being amused & yet it is charming to think they are going to pass their lives together. It is the way it sd be & will be when more women enter professions — they will choose to live with each other & go off and make homes.

— M. Carey Thomas, November 14, 1882

Professional Women as Legatees of "Amazons" and "Mental Hermaphrodites"

DURING THE COLONIAL and Revolutionary eras in America, women engaged in a wide variety of revenue-earning jobs both inside and outside the home. But many of those activities were forgotten in the early nineteenth century. The brutalities of capitalism that the industrial revolution encouraged helped create the concept of "home" as a shelter from the cruelty of life outside. Such a haven seemed to necessitate a full-time housewife and mother for any household that could afford that luxury. What has been called "the cult of true womanhood" — the nineteenth century's version of the feminine mystique — worked to convince women that their families needed their total attention, and that to spend her life providing such undivided attention should render any true woman happy. Indeed, there were considerable benefits for women connected to nineteenth-century domestic life. As Peter Filene has phrased it, a wife and mother might enjoy "the privilege of being economically supported, the esteem of being a homemaker (in contrast to our own 'just a housewife'), and the nurture from a husband's and children's love."

Yet there were many women who, for one reason or another, had no husband and children. Such "benefits" had little appeal for some. With the opening of greater educational opportunities for women, there was also an increase in those who looked beyond the benefits of conventional domesticity. Female college graduates had expended vast amounts of energy on serious study, and now a good number of them believed that it should have been for something grand — for some manner of self-fulfillment or for the hope of bettering the lot of humanity rather than for serving only the few individuals that made up a woman's own family.

An 1888 contributor to *Alpha,* a journal edited by a medical doctor, Caroline Winslow, spoke for many educated women in saying that "a woman who has open before her the broad avenues of usefulness, who has ambition and energy to develop her powers, who will not be satisfied to tie herself down in the soul-cramping marriage . . . has learned [that] woman's highest duty to herself and humanity demands her full development as *Woman,* not as a *Wife* or a *Mother.*" What the writer meant by *"Woman"* was, of course, very different from the concept of "true woman." She meant something analogous to *"Man"* — which was diametrically opposed to what the "true woman" was supposed to be. There was no question that a female who wished to "develop her powers" outside marriage was not a "true woman." She was a New Woman — and the New Woman was much like the women who had been called amazons and mental hermaphrodites just decades earlier. A later era would have called many of them lesbians.

The New Woman's pioneering predecessors in the mid-nineteenth century were already deemed unnatural in their desires to tread paths that were considered masculine. Loving parents trembled for daughters who challenged gender by becoming doctors or lawyers as much as they would have trembled if those daughters had tried to go through life dressed in men's clothes. Marie Zakrzewska, a resident physician at Elizabeth and Emily Blackwell's New York Infirmary for Women and Children in the late 1850s, was told by her father, "You give me more grief than any other of my children. If you were a young man, I could not find words in which to express my satisfaction and pride in respect to your acts; for I know that all you accomplish you owe to yourself: but you are a woman, a weak woman; and all that I can do for you now is to grieve and to weep. O my daughter! return from this unhappy path."

In 1862, Marie Zakrzewska founded the New England Hospital for Women and Children, which served the poor and was staffed entirely by female doctors. The hospital, which continued into the late twentieth century, attracted from its beginnings the best female physicians in the country, who continued to have difficulty procuring positions at male-run hospitals. Marie Zakrzewska herself became one of the preeminent female hospital administrators and medical doctors of her century. If her father had wanted a conventional married life for his daughter, he had excellent reason to grieve, though his tears would have been in spite of her satisfaction with her choices.

Zakrzewska's history, like that of so many pioneering women, was the history of an invert. She never married a man. Her childhood, as she described it, should by now be predictable to readers of this book. At school she played only with the boys; "With them I was merry, frank, and self-possessed, while with the girls I was quiet, shy and awkward" (as a boy would be), she confessed. She struggled with her parents, who wanted to impose feminine pursuits on her: "I could not see why, at home, I should be forced to do housework. . . . When I complained of this last grievance I was told that I was a girl and never could learn much, but was only fit to become a housekeeper." As an adult, her close friends were women who were coupled with other women, such as Mary Louise Booth, the first editor of *Harper's Bazaar,* and her life partner, Anne Wright. Zakrzewska's most important intimate relationship, which began in the early 1870s, was with Julie Sprague, with whom she lived until her death, in 1902.

As was true of nineteenth-century women in academia, those who entered and remained in the learned professions — that is, medicine, theology, and the law — were usually unmarried. That was so in any salaried occupation. Even by 1900, only about 3 percent of white women (26 percent of African-American women) who were married were working for wages. By 1920, the number among white women had risen to 9 percent. By the 1930s, the percentage had risen again. But among professional women — despite the push heterosexual "normality" in the 1920s — the percentage who married remained small. For example, a 1932 survey of Vassar alumnae showed that of the fifty-one who were doctors, only fifteen were married; of the twenty-three who were lawyers, only six were married.

Perhaps throughout all these years, women who wanted to undertake the long-term commitment that was necessary for professional training felt forced to question whether they could fulfill their ambitions if they were set on heterosexuality. Those who saw marriage as the sine qua non of their happiness might have been less likely to undertake goals that would be incompatible with it in the first place. But those who desired relationships other than heterosexual marriage were freer to pursue a profession — and, like many of the academics and public policymakers examined in these pages, they would have been attracted to a serious career because they knew they had to make their own way economically.

It is no coincidence that the professional woman in America was first permitted to get a significant foothold in the Civil War years and shortly after, when it was clear that many women would not marry because war fatalities had created a large number of "superfluous women," as spinsters were sometimes called. The Civil War also created a particular need for women's labor in the medical area. Women were trained as nurses in unprecedented numbers, and although there were still few women doctors, their skills too were utilized during the Civil War, because they were considered particularly apt at training nurses.

Dr. Mary Walker, who worked as an army surgeon and was awarded a Congressional Medal of Honor, was even employed as a surgeon in tent hospitals. Walker, who later attempted to found an all-women's colony called Adamless Eden, was, like many of the pioneering professional women, a gender outlaw. Nineteenth- and early twentieth-century sexologists saw her as a representative invert. (A 1902 article in a San Francisco medical journal referred to her as "the most distinguished sexual invert in the United States.") She dressed as a man, though she let her curls show through her top hat so that no one would think she was trying to pass. She was an ardent suffragist and a flamboyant lecturer on women's rights. Though she was briefly married, her major relationships appear to have been with other women, including the lawyer Belva Lockwood (the first woman to argue before the Supreme Court), with whom Walker lived for several years. The New Women who followed pioneers like Walker in the professions were generally subtler than she in their dress and style, but like her, they were warriors against their era's conception of "true womanhood."

Though many working women returned home once their soldier husbands and fiancés donned civvies, the effects of the Civil War in providing work alternatives for women continued. By 1870, few women were employed in prestigious jobs such as the so-called learned professions, yet thanks to amazons and mental hermaphrodites, some had broken through even in those occupations: 525 women were medical doctors, 67 were ministers, and 5 were lawyers.

Throughout the rest of the nineteenth century and much of the twentieth, the number of women in the learned professions was never huge. However, an examination of the female presence in those professions over the past 150 years can reveal a great deal about women's changing status. The learned professions have represented the zenith of occupational prestige in America. Obviously, women have generally not been welcomed into them. They all require considerable formal education and a great expenditure of undistracted time and energy. They are not jobs in which one simply earns a wage but rather lifetime careers that bring personal fulfillment as well as honor. Many of those who were able to become pioneering leaders in the learned professions, or who maintained the female presence in them even while most women were being convinced to have no ambitions beyond their home, were the kinds of women whom I have been describing as lesbian.

"Strong-Minded Females" in the Ministry: Mrs. Hanaford and Mrs. Jackson

A second Great Awakening in the 1830s and '40s had given women the opportunity to organize together within churches, which spurred various reform movements in which they played crucial roles. But it had done little to push women into the pulpit as ordained ministers. Although women invariably constituted large numbers of church attendees and had been preaching in America since the colonial days of Anne Hutchinson, no woman was ordained in a mainstream church until 1851, when the United Brethren Church ordained Lydia Sexton. But her ordination did not assure women an easy acceptance into the ministry. Indeed, what could be more unfeminine than a woman's taking the pulpit? As one historian observed of Catharine Beecher, who had her younger brother deliver her addresses in the 1840s as she sat silently in the pulpit by his side, "Well did she know the public scorn and disapproval that was showered at that time upon those 'strong-minded females' who dared to address an audience from a public platform."

It took tremendous will and a sense of mission in the mid-nineteenth century for a woman to dare to assert herself as a "strong-minded female" (the term was *not* a compliment). Such women were rebuffed even in the era's liberal institutions. For example, although the Oberlin College charter declared that women must be permitted to take any course open to men, Antoinette Brown's enrollment as a theology student created horror and havoc among the male student body and the faculty. She was allowed to study, but she was not allowed to participate in her 1850 commencement exercises except as a listener. For many years her name did not appear in the alumni catalogue. When she was ordained in the First Congregational Church in 1853, it was amid terrible dissension among the pastorate. Only a few years earlier, a pastoral letter issued by the General Association of the Congregational Ministers of Massachusetts had rebuked "froward females" who wished to stand at the pulpit. The letter warned against such "dangers which at present seem to threaten the female character with widespread and permanent injury." Many of Antoinette Brown's fellow clergymen continued to share that view.

Antoinette Brown was able to pursue her harassed path as a theology student and then a minister with constant support and encouragement from Lucy Stone, who was a classmate at Oberlin and on whom, as correspondence reveals, Brown had "smashed." However, despite the difficulties Brown had in getting a theological education and in getting ordained, she gave up her pulpit. Months after Lucy Stone married Henry Blackwell in 1855, Antoinette married Henry's brother Samuel. Her marriage led to seven pregnancies. For the first eighteen years of her married life, she did almost no work outside the home and devoted herself to the tasks of the "true woman."

Before they were ordained, nineteenth-century women who were attracted to the ministry invariably faced a battle that was not for the faint of heart; but the battle was even more difficult for women who were married, not only because of their household responsibilities but also because of public opinion about a wife's role. When Anna Howard Shaw sought ordination in 1880, she was contested by the Methodist Protestant Conference, despite her degree in theology from Boston University and her four years of preaching in Cape Cod churches. As one minister told her, "Paul said, 'Wives, obey your husbands.' Suppose your husband should refuse to allow you to preach." She was happy to be able to counter that she was a spinster. (When another protested that the church had declared that a Methodist minister "shall be the husband of one wife. How is it possible for you to be the husband of a wife?" she retorted that her interrogator was a bachelor and therefore that "I am as much of a husband as he is." Her proto-lesbian wit seems to have disarmed them.) In any case, because she had no husband, they could find no further excuses to refuse her. If she had been married, it is doubtful that she would have succeeded in her bid for ordination.

Those women who fared best in the nineteenth-century ministry were generally unencumbered by the trappings of heterosexuality. Phebe Coffin Hanaford, for instance, had married Joseph Hanaford at the age of twenty and had two children, but her life and career trajectory were virtually the opposite of Antoinette Brown Blackwell's. After devoting herself to domestic life for a few years, she turned to writing to supplement her husband's income and then, at the age of thirty-five, to preaching. In 1868, with her children almost grown, she was ordained as a Universalist minister. For approximately twenty years, she had parishes in Massachusetts, New Jersey, and Connecticut and earned salaries equal to those of very well paid men (about $2000 a year, several times what female teachers were receiving). In the early 1870s she served as chaplain in the Connecticut Senate and House of Representatives, a position never before given to a woman. She also became active in the Equal Rights Association and was a leader in the American Woman Suffrage Association, which she represented as a popular speaker throughout the United States.

How did Hanaford move from housewife to renowned minister and lecturer? Her husband's letters to her make it clear that it was not with his approval — which may partly account for their permanent separation in the early 1870s. As a Baptist, he was upset that she was "preaching a doctrine as diverse from mine . . . as day and night, light and darkness! And then, the changed order of things — so different from Paul's doctrine" (which not only admonished women to be silent but also, as Anna Shaw's opponents pointed out, ordered that wives should obey their husbands). Joseph Hanaford was disgusted that Phebe had undertaken "such labors [which] must be crushing, such as no *real* woman can long bear, as too many are now showing." He was particularly annoyed at her activities in women's rights organizations. He accused women's rights leaders of being of scandalous repute and warned his wife, "Decent women will soon find it necessary to secede [from the women's movement] or remain in *bad company.*"

Though Phebe found no support from Joseph in her work as a minister and women's rights lecturer, she was encouraged by Ellen Miles, a teacher and writer, with whom she lived for more than thirty years after leaving her husband. Ellen Miles's letters to Phebe make a telling contrast to Joseph's. First of all, they constantly reiterate her loving passion: for instance, "My loved one, My first written word shall be to you, my darling, who comes first to my waking tho'ts, and last before my eyes close to sleep," and "It seemed to me that I left all the world behind me when I left you in that depot, and I could not keep the sobs down all the way out." But they are also significant in their express support of Phebe's professional work. "If there is anything in the world that I pray earnestly and hopefully for," Ellen wrote, "it is that your success in Jersey City may be complete in every respect. Eyes are on you in all directions. And I am so willing to work for you and with you." Phebe's husband, a fine and loving father, was not a villain. But he was all too typical of most nineteenth-century men in that he could not accept any of his wife's activities that signified, as his 1872 letter hinted, that she was not a "*real* woman."

Phebe and Ellen surrounded themselves with those who were certainly not "real women" in Joseph Hanaford's definition of the term. Their letters indicate close friendships with many whose intimate relations were with other women, such as Anna Dickinson, Frances Willard, and Alice Stone Blackwell. At Ellen's death, in 1914, Marietta Holley, the author of the feminist "Samantha" stories, consoled Phebe in a letter that suggests the extent to which those in the women's movement were aware of the nature of the relationship between the minister and Ellen Miles. Holley refers to "the golden links that bound you two together," and she assures Phebe, "I know how lonely and desolate life must be to you, if you should think of her as utterly gone from you — But I do not believe that — I believe she is with you — the one she loved best, all the time."

The nineteenth-century husband's discomfiture with a preaching wife transcended racial lines, which may explain why Rebecca Jackson, a free mid-nineteenth-century African American, experienced a personal and professional trajectory similar to Phebe Hanaford's. She too felt that being a wife was incompatible with her desire to become a preacher. Like Phebe Hanaford, she broke from her husband's African Methodist Episcopal Church and went in a direction entirely her own.

Rebecca Jackson's experiences not only with her husband but also with his church had been unhappy. Though a few women had been permitted to preach in the AME Church shortly after it was founded by a former slave in the late eighteenth century, opposition had become formalized by the mid-nineteenth century. Women petitioned the church's General Conference to be "licensed," but they were refused. As the official AME journal argued, women were weaker than men "both physically and mentally," and thus they must remain "in their sphere [of] easier toils." Such pronouncements were as offensive to Rebecca Jackson as the Paulist pronouncements of Joseph Hanaford were to Phebe.

After visiting a utopian woman-led Shaker community, Rebecca Jackson chose the Shaker religion. She became a minister herself, insisting that visionary revelations had shown her that the divine spirit was female. Her "mystical visions" (often fascinating revelations of her psyche) were markedly feminist, with homoerotic undertones. For example:

> She was going east, I was afollowing her. That way the way I was agoing the first time I ever saw her [sic]. As she stepped before me, and was about twelve feet ahead of me, I did not see her face. But the more faithfully I lived, I found the nearer I got to this woman. So I found that I was to catch up with this woman. So when I found that that was what I was supposed to do, I labored hard day and night to do so. I found that she was sent from God to teach me the way of truth and lead me into the way of holiness and in God's own appointed time I would overtake her.

Jackson's mystical visions helped to propel her out of her unhappy marriage. In 1836, just before leaving her husband, she renounced sexual relations with him. Through a vision, she wrote, she had come to understand that intercourse was "of all things the most filthy in the sight of God, both in the married and unmarried, it all seemed alike." It was about this time that she met Rebecca Perot, another African-American woman, who became her lifelong companion.

Jackson's recorded visions, which often deal with Rebecca Perot, depict that they went through a kind of marriage ceremony together, "unit[ing] in the covenant." In one of Perot's own visions she claimed to have seen Rebecca Jackson "crowned King and me crowned Queen of Africa." A powerful sensual element helped to seal their relationship, as indicated in Jackson's visions: "I saw Rebecca Perot coming in the river, her face to the east, and she aplunging in the water every few steps. . . . She only had on her undergarment. She was pure and clean, even as the water in which she was abathing. She came facing me out of the water. I wondered she was not afraid. Sometimes she would be hid, for a moment, and then she would rise again. She looked like an Angel, oh, how bright!" Their intimate relationship lasted for more than thirty-five years, until Jackson's death, in 1871.

Together the two women joined the primarily white Watervliet Shakers, but perceiving that blacks were discriminated against even there, they left. Jackson then founded and was minister to a predominantly female African-American Shaker group in Philadelphia, which survived her by forty years. After Rebecca Jackson's death, Rebecca Perot took over leadership of the sect and called herself Rebecca Jackson, Junior.

The editor of Jackson's writings, Jean Humez, after observing Jackson's "close relationship with a single cherished intimate friend," speculates, "Perhaps had she been born in the modern age she would have been a lesbian." We can come to no other conclusion when we look at her record. Her affinity for women was obviously more complicated than what the twentieth century has called a sexual drive, though it is impossible to ignore the emotional and sensual elements in it. It was also bound up with her ability to pursue her career as a minister, which her husband opposed.

"Assertiveness Is Not a Virtue in a Woman": The Law Profession

The law historian Karen Morello has found that in colonial America there was at least one female lawyer, Margaret Brent, attorney to the governor of Maryland in the 1630s and 1640s. (Brent never married but adopted a Native American girl.) This early instance notwithstanding, female lawyers were rare throughout the eighteenth and much of the nineteenth century. Women who wished to become lawyers had an even more difficult time than those who wished to join the clergy. It was possible to argue that women's spirituality — a characteristic that was thought to be inherent in the "true woman" — fitted them for ministering to others, but no analogous argument could be made in favor of women as litigators. As Eula Young, herself a lawyer, observed in a 1902 article, "The Law as a Profession for Women," even female medical doctors were thought to have more of a raison d'être than female lawyers. Female doctors were sometimes welcomed in specialties such as pediatrics and gynecology, and tending the sick could be seen as consistent with women's "natural" duties and talents. But as a survey that Young conducted showed, no one — not even female lawyers themselves — thought that any areas of the law were especially suited to women by virtue of their gender.

A woman who wished to challenge the universal prejudice against female lawyers must have felt obliged to hide whatever could be construed as feminine in her; yet the masculine woman was threatened with opprobrium. Who would want to assume such confusing contradictions and difficulties? In 1880, there were only two hundred female lawyers in the entire country — ten fewer than the number of female physicians in Boston alone — though several law schools were accepting women as students. Even thirty years later, in 1910, when more than 9000 female doctors were practicing, there were only 558 female lawyers. As Young cogently observed, while assertiveness was an important asset in a lawyer, it was considered "not a virtue in a woman." Much more than in any other profession, success as a lawyer required qualities that were diametrically opposed to those that a Victorian woman was supposed to have.

The development of such qualities obviously had little appeal for women who prized femininity. Predictably, the marriage rate was low among female lawyers, partly because a successful lawyer would not have been attractive to the typical nineteenth-century man, but also because marriage would probably not have been attractive to most successful female lawyers in the nineteenth century. As the 1889 *Annual* of the Equity Club, an organization for female lawyers, declared, "The majority of the practitioners who are sticking to their work and plodding on in the sure and safe way to win success are unmarried." Those who married apparently often were pushed or escaped from a profession that was hostile to them. They left the law to raise a family, or they did charity work or clerical work, or sometimes they followed a husband to a state where women were forbidden to practice.

But finding employment as a lawyer was problematic whether or not a woman was married. Since female lawyers were not in great demand, it was difficult to procure a job in a law firm. Some women gave up after discouraging attempts. If the woman was not white, the difficulties were multiplied. Charlotte Ray, for instance, the first African-American female lawyer in the United States, graduated from Howard University and passed the bar examination in 1872. (She was the first woman of any color to be admitted to the bar in Washington, D.C.) Though by all accounts her abilities were exceptional, she could not find a job in an established firm, and when she attempted to set up a practice of her own, she got little business. Because she had to support herself, she gave up her office after seven years and went to New York, where she became a schoolteacher.

One law historian has suggested that women who were married to male lawyers sometimes fared better, since they could join their husband's practice and ride on his coattails, as it were. But there are not many instances of such successes in the early years, when women began studying law. A lawyer wife would probably have been considered a liability to a practice rather than an asset. Sometimes there were even laws that prevented married women from practicing. For example, the Illinois Supreme Court rejected an 1869 application from a married woman for a license to practice, arguing that because of her marital status she would not be bound by express or implied contracts. That is, in the eyes of the law, she was a "femme couvert" rather than an "adult," and therefore she was not legally responsible. The U.S. Supreme Court upheld the decision.

Thus, while it was difficult for any nineteenth-century woman to establish herself as a lawyer, she might have been somewhat better off if she could not only dispense with femininity but also envision a domestic life with another woman rather than a husband. When Frances Kellor attended Cornell Law School in the 1890s, the only woman in a class of eighty-three, she was able to find encouragement by remembering Mary Perry, who had shown her that what she wished to achieve was possible, in ways that Kellor would have found especially appealing. Perry, who was from Kellor's hometown, Coldwater, Michigan, graduated from the University of Michigan in 1875 and with Ellen Martin, whom she met in law school, established a practice in Chicago — in the same state that had prevented a married woman from practicing only a few years earlier. Perry and Martin often represented poor women gratis, and it is said that Perry never lost a case. Theirs may have been the first female law partnership in American history. It was also a domestic partnership, which lasted until Perry's death, in 1883. Martin continued to practice, retaining her partner's name in the firm until she retired, a year before her own death, in 1915.

Women in Medicine: Partners in Practice and in Life

Women also met with discouraging opposition when they tried to enter medicine in the mid-nineteenth century, but like Jane Addams, who virtually created her own profession, they often cleverly carved out niches for themselves in areas where it was thought that women would naturally have certain advantages, such as pediatrics, obstetrics, and the developing fields of preventive medicine and public health. They established or practiced in the first dispensaries to treat the poor, such as the New York Infirmary for Women and Children, which Emily Blackwell ran; Marie Zakrzewska's New England Hospital for Women and Children; and the Evening Dispensary for Working Women and Girls in Baltimore, where Lilian Welsh and Mary Sherwood (a committed couple) practiced.

As in the areas of theology and law, a few women could be found in the medical field in the earliest eras of American history. They were generally midwives in the colonial years, though that position had no professional status. When obstetrics became a part of professional medicine in the eighteenth and early nineteenth centuries, such women were usually put out of business, though as Regina Morantz-Sanchez observes in her study of female physicians in America, *Sympathy and Science,* the low level of medical education "made a mockery of physicians' claims to superior skill in the lying-in chamber."

In 1846, the American Medical Association was founded in order to raise the level of medical training and practice for male physicians. When Elizabeth Blackwell attempted to gain admission to medical school the following year, she was turned down by almost every major school in the East because she was a woman — as might be expected, in view of the new attempt to raise the profession. One professor at a Philadelphia college told her that he did not disapprove of her desire to "gain complete medical knowledge," but he could not let her into his classes as long as she looked like a woman; he proposed (who knows whether with cruel facetiousness or melodramatic seriousness) that she should dress like a man. He promised to guarantee her safety by telling two or three of his students about her disguise and ordering them to act as spies, so that if anyone else suspected that she was masquerading, the spies would give her timely warning and she could escape before trouble started.

Blackwell was not forced to that adventure, however, because she was finally admitted to medical school at Geneva College, which later became part of Syracuse University. The college was in financial difficulty, and the attention-hungry dean believed that by admitting Blackwell, "[even] if no other advantage is to be gained, at least it will attract notice." Soon several medical schools began accepting women. Some were established in order to serve women exclusively, such as the Woman's Medical College of Pennsylvania, which opened in 1850, and the New England Female Medical College, which opened in 1856. A few medical schools that had been all male gradually and cautiously agreed to take female students, such as the one at Western Reserve University, which in 1853 accepted Elizabeth Blackwell's younger sister Emily. The medical profession thus became the target of dreams for women who had no interest in marriage and who wanted to do something for humanity. Anna Howard Shaw, Carey Thomas, and Jane Addams all wished to study medicine in the 1870s or '80s.

African-American women with professional ambitions, sufficient resources, and no desire to marry also came to see medicine as a likely field. For instance, in 1903, after graduating from Howard Medical School with three other women in her class, Ionia Whipper interned in the Freedmen's Hospital (where the other doctors were male), then became the "physician of girls" at Tuskegee Institute. She later established the Ionia Rollin Whipper Home for Unwed Mothers in Washington, D.C. Her romantic relationships were with other women, such as Dr. Hillyar, an African-American pharmacist.

For the most part, women who pioneered in medicine (like those who pioneered in the other learned professions) saw marriage as incompatible with their work — or they entered medicine because they knew they had no interest in marriage. As Lilian Welsh wrote of the choice of medical careers that she and her life partner, Mary Sherwood, had made, "We . . . had looked forward from early childhood to the possibility of self-support." In an 1894 article in the *Woman's Medical Journal* titled "Should Professional Women Marry?" the author, Dr. Gertrude Baillie, answered her own question in the negative. "No woman can serve two masters," she insisted. "Either her work or her family will feel the neglect." This was especially true of medical doctors, Baillie said, since their careers were so demanding. In any case, between the 1850s and 1930, close to 70 percent of female doctors who practiced for any length of time were not married. Though there were a few notable exceptions, such as Mary Putnam Jacobi, those who married generally gave up their practice or practiced only until they became pregnant.

It would be no exaggeration to say that a preponderance of women who made their mark in medicine during the early years lived in intimate relationships that we would consider lesbian. Many of them formed long-term domestic relationships with other female doctors. Examples include Dr. Lucy Sewall, who became director of the New England Hospital for Women and Children in 1869, and Dr. Elizabeth Keller, senior surgeon at the hospital; Dr. Emma Culbertson (the subject of Carey Thomas's 1882 letter that serves as the epigraph to this chapter) and Dr. Mary Smith, one of the first women to be admitted to the American College of Surgeons; the pioneering female physicians of Baltimore, Dr. Lilian Welsh and Dr. Mary Sherwood; Dr. Eliza Mosher, who was president of the American Medical Women's Association, and her partner in both medicine and life, Dr. Lucy Hall; Dr. Martha Tracy, the head of the Woman's Medical College of Pennsylvania, and Dr. Ellen Potter, who was the first woman in the country to be a member of a governor's cabinet (she was secretary of welfare for the state of Massachusetts); and Dr. Sara Josephine Baker, a public health pioneer, and Dr. Louise Pearce, who achieved fame for her research in cancer and sleeping sickness.

In many cases, the women met in school, encouraged each other through the rigors of medical education and the uncertainties of establishing practices in a world that was still suspicious of female physicians, and formed permanent relationships, as did Martha Tracy and Ellen Potter, who met at the Woman's Medical College of Pennsylvania, and Lilian Welsh and Mary Sherwood, who met at the University of Zurich.

In other cases, the older woman of the couple served as a role model or mentor, as Mary Smith did for Emma Culbertson, showing the way into the profession. Emma (Noel) Musson was a professor of laryngology and rhinology at the Woman's Medical College of Pennsylvania in the late nineteenth and early twentieth centuries. Elizabeth Clark, her life partner, received her medical degree from the WMCP in 1909, but it took her several years to establish herself as a physician. When Musson died, in 1913, not long after the tenth anniversary of their shared life, Clark was still trying to build a private practice but was meeting with great frustration. At Musson's death, Clark wrote to a confidante about the good years she and Musson had had together, and also about how Musson had fired her determination to succeed in the profession they both had chosen:

> The whole dreadful week when Noel was fighting it out . . . we fought it out together — and we both knew that the dice of God were loaded. . . . She just held my hand and told me how glorious our ten years together had been — and it was then that my old heart broke — after that she was unconscious, rousing occasionally to speak my name and to tell me that she loved me. Ten such years as I have had cannot but leave their mark and I am going back into things with a curious faltering step but back of it all a certain exaltation because I have been so blessed.
>
> My heart is utterly and entirely gone out of me but I have *got* to make good — it is the only chance I have.

To "make good" was to continue in the profession, in the footsteps of her beloved Noel. Despite her grief, Clark felt she did not have the luxury of surrender, not only because it would have destroyed her, she feared, but also because she and Noel had encouraged each other in the conviction that as female physicians they had a mission. Clark eventually became the chief gynecologist of the Woman's Hospital of Philadelphia.

Many pioneering professional women apparently believed that their (lesbian) domestic arrangements made their careers possible and was the backbone of their work. Florence Converse, the partner of the social reformer and academic Vida Scudder, captured the conviction as she felt it in an 1897 novel, *Diana Victrix*. Converse presents a persuasive argument of the kind that was surely made often by nineteenth- and early twentieth-century professional women, whether in dialogue or to themselves. *Diana Victrix*, which is based on Converse's and Scudder's lives, is about a rela-

tionship between two professional women, Enid and Sylvia. In the
novel, Enid forms a friendship with a young man, Jacques, who
falls in love with her and proposes. Enid is briefly tempted. But she
realizes finally that what she really wants and needs is to make a
home with her beloved Sylvia. Such a life would, among other
things, help her pursue her "real work," as she tells Jacques, rather
than distract her from it:

> "I do not need you. It is true I have no man friend whom I enjoy
> as much as I do you, but I have a woman friend who is dearer to
> me. . . . I share with her thoughts that I have no wish to share
> with you. I give to her a love surpassing any affection I could
> teach myself to have for you. She comes first. She is my friend as
> you can never be, and I could not marry you unless you were a
> nearer friend than she. You would have to come first. And you
> could not, for she is first."
>
> "And this is all that separates us," said Jacques, in a tone of
> amazement. "Only a woman?"
>
> "The reason the woman separates us," said Enid, "is because
> the woman and I understand each other, sympathize with each
> other, are necessary to each other. And you and I are not. It is not
> simply her womanliness, it is her friendship. There might be a
> man who could give me the inspiration, the equalness of sympa-
> thy, I find in her, — there might be, — some women find such
> men. But there are not yet enough for all of us. . . . For a moment,
> because I was tired, I thought I wanted you — your home. But
> I do not! . . . I am not domestic the way some women are. I
> shouldn't like to keep house and sew . . . It would bore me. I
> should hate it! Sylvia and I share the responsibility here, and the
> maid works faithfully. There are only a few rooms. We have time
> for our real work, but a wife wouldn't have. And, oh, I couldn't be
> just a wife! I don't want to! Please go away! I have chosen my life
> and I love it!

By necessity as well as choice, Diana, the symbol of flight from
heterosexuality, was often "Victrix" among pioneering women in the
learned professions.

❧ 15 ❧

MAKING PLACES FOR
WOMEN IN MEDICINE:
EMILY BLACKWELL

I have often thought that if I followed solely my inclinations I should assume a man's dress and wander freely
over the world throwing away the constant weary shack-
les that custom and poverty surround [women] with so
closely, but that would be but a selfish life. There would
be no great aim for the future such as has animated me in
all the long years of labour and privation I have spent. To
establish great principles, to found great institutions, to
be one of the foremost rank through whom the great
ideas of the age are developed, that is the true position
for those who can occupy it.

— Emily Blackwell, July 16, 1853

The Advantages of "Perverting Woman's Nature"

IT WAS the various qualities that later eras would associate with
lesbianism that permitted Emily Blackwell to develop her dreams
and ambitions from the start, as a 1911 memorial tribute written by
her life partner, Elizabeth Cushier, suggests. For example, Emily
earned a medical degree in 1854, when she was twenty-eight years
old and should have been in panicked pursuit of a husband. She
had heard accusations that "her [professional] desires were a simple perversion of a woman's nature, a stepping out from her place in
creation," Cushier recalled, but she was "not daunted" by them. If
such accusations had bothered Emily Blackwell, she would have

given up as soon as she began — when, for instance, she entered a medical classroom in 1852, the only woman, and saw scrawled on the board a cartoon of an outlandish female in bloomers with the words "strong-minded woman" (a nineteenth-century version of "dyke") written across it.

Emily Blackwell herself articulated the idea that her achievements would not have been possible if she had not escaped from the attributes that were called "woman's nature." She often expressed disdain for the qualities of "femininity" in women and compared them to her own qualities: "very persevering and very resolute — and very ambitious," with "a something sprawling in my character and way of doing things." Women, as they were conceptualized in her time, were not and could not become medical doctors, since the attributes required for such an achievement were seen as patently unwomanly. As the administrator of the New York Infirmary for Women and Children, Emily Blackwell worried about interns who had "little womanly airs," as she described them. Some of those women may have been intelligent, she granted, but intelligence alone was not sufficient. "Ladylike" women — her characterization of the types opposite to her own type — "had no more idea of taking hold of things and working like a man than of flying. . . . They are most utterly disqualified by their nature itself." Thus, when her detractors accused her of not having a womanly nature, it was to her an assurance of her fitness for the challenging work she had elected to do.

Indeed, for the sake of a medical degree, she had been prepared to pervert woman's nature even further. Despite the very creditable performance of her sister Elizabeth, Emily's application for admission was turned down by eleven medical schools. All of them continued to refuse to train women in medicine. Finally Emily was accepted by Rush Medical School. She simultaneously worked as an intern in a doctor's office, but that experience was short-lived, because a patient objected to being treated by someone of her gender. It was then, she wrote in her journal at the end of the semester, that her recurring "idea of studying in disguise [that is, in men's clothes] in Paris rose before me — the more I thought of it, the more it appeared to be the only resort." She was (as one of her students later described her) "tall, broad-shouldered and commanding in her presence." She had reason to believe she could carry it off. When she was told after her first year at Rush that the Medical Society of Illinois had censured the school for admitting a woman and that she would not be allowed to return, the plan occurred to her again. She would go to Europe, she reiterated, and "study in disguise [because] I certainly shall not otherwise obtain the opportunities I need."

As it happened, such heroic methods were not necessary, since she was accepted into the medical school of Western Reserve University a couple of months later. In 1854, still the only woman in her class, she received her medical degree with high honors. Because she despaired of being able to do further specialized study in the United States, she then went abroad — in skirts — and convinced doctors in London, Paris, Berlin, Dresden, and Edinburgh to allow her to study with them. Specializing in obstetrics, she was involved in some of the earliest experimental uses of chloroform in childbirth.

Gynecology interested her for various reasons. As she wrote to Elizabeth Blackwell from Edinburgh, practically no research had been done specifically on women. It was as yet a clear field in which the two sisters could make their mark. "If we could study the diseases of women which are so little understood . . . we could compel the profession to recognize us," Emily wrote, prodding Elizabeth. But Emily was also motivated to study women because she believed, long before Margaret Sanger, that one way "woman" might be changed was by bringing pregnancy "more under her control," which would permit her more individuality and freedom. To change the construction of "woman" (or as Emily Blackwell put it in a contradictory phrase that both accepted and refuted essentialism, to study "the *nature* of women and how they may be *improved*") was a primary goal throughout her career.

The reasons for her efforts in that direction were personal as well as principled: she was plagued by the notion that in their current form, women could never equal men in inventiveness and intellect.

Ostensibly (though superficially), she was herself a "woman," and therefore she suffered from prejudice against females, no matter how she disassociated herself from their feminine characteristics or prided herself on her "sprawling" character. Nor could she permanently escape from being a woman through disguise, because transvestism generally depended on anonymity, and her ambition was "to establish great principles, to found great institutions" — which one could not do anonymously.

Therefore, while Blackwell may not have been intimidated by the accusation of being unwomanly, she nevertheless felt that it was crucial to make "woman" something higher than what that category was at the time. "If I might but see that I was doing something to raise them not in position only but in nature — to inspire them with higher objects — loftier aspirations — to teach them that there is a strength of woman as well as of man," she fantasized in her journal when she was twenty-six years old. The New York Infirmary for Women and Children and the Women's Medical College of the New York Infirmary, which she opened with her sister Elizabeth but ran by herself for three decades, were intended to encompass all of her earlier goals.

"To Found Great Institutions . . ."

In 1856, Elizabeth Blackwell expanded her struggling practice to include Emily, who had just returned from Europe after two years of medical postgraduate study. The sisters met with numerous frustrations in their early attempts to conduct a private medical practice, since female doctors were suspect in both their morality and their competence. Emily lived with Elizabeth in a house Elizabeth had had to buy because no respectable boarding or lodging establishment in New York would take in female physicians. The sisters rented out most of the house for the revenue, slept in the garret, and received patients in the parlor. In a drawer, Emily kept bread, oranges, and dates, which she ate when she wasn't eating at a cheap basement restaurant in the neighborhood. Years later she quipped that that just about summed up the life of a female doctor at the time: "They slept in the garret and dined in the cellar, when they dined at all."

After a year of shared frustrations in private practice, Emily, a born administrator, helped raise funds for a novel enterprise of which Elizabeth had dreamed, a hospital to be called the New York Infirmary for Women and Children. The hospital would rely largely on charity, since it would serve the poor. It would give female doctors the opportunity to do postgraduate study (there was still almost no place in America where medical women could serve an internship), and it would provide employment opportunities, which were being denied them in other hospitals. It would have another, not inconsequential merit as well: it was not uncommon for Victorian women to let certain diseases go untreated, sometimes at the cost of horrendous suffering, rather than permit a male doctor to touch their breasts or vaginas, but at the New York Infirmary no patient's modesty would be compromised, because all of the doctors would be women.

The infirmary opened in May 1857. In 1858, Elizabeth Blackwell, restless after her trying years as the first female medical student and always better at beginnings than at sticking it out for the long haul, went off to England, where she entertained the idea of setting up a practice. She urged her sister to close the hospital, but Emily resisted, pointing out their obligation not only to patients but to the women who were already working there. On her own, Emily attempted to put the hospital on a firmer footing. She was remarkably successful, convincing the state of New York to help subsidize it and to give it official blessing. Within a year she was able to procure a larger house, which she converted into hospital and dispensary facilities, as well as a dormitory for the female interns. Elizabeth returned in 1859, and together they instituted many innovations, including a "sanitary visitor" program, under which a "tenement physician" visited indigent patients in their homes. The program was virtually the first organized attempt to deliver medical/social services to the needy, and it provided a model that other hospitals emulated. It was also unique because the first appointee was Rebecca Cole, an African-American doctor who was one of the first women of color to receive a medical degree in the United States.

On Elizabeth's return to America, the two sisters realized that if the infirmary were to continue as a women's institution, they needed to engage in the business of training female doctors. The increased services they wished to offer could not be staffed adequately by those who were being trained in the few medical schools open to women. The Blackwells therefore formulated plans to apply to the New York legislature for a charter that would confer college status on the infirmary.

They were interrupted for four years by the Civil War, in which both sisters participated by training wartime nurses — a strategic ploy that demonstrated to the public the usefulness of female doctors. After the war, they applied for a charter for a college that would offer three years of graded instruction to women who had had adequate premedical preparation, which they would also offer. By design, their standards were equivalent to those of Harvard and much more stringent than the requirements in most medical colleges of the day. Until enough good female physicians were available to teach, they would employ as instructors the very best male doctors available. The Blackwells also promoted credibility by establishing an external examining board composed of eminent (male) members of the medical profession. When they received their charter from the legislature, Emily and Elizabeth Blackwell opened the Women's Medical College of the New York Infirmary for Women and Children, on Stuyvesant Square, in 1868. But within a year of the college's opening, Elizabeth, once again growing restless, returned to England. She remained there for virtually the rest of her life, devoting much of her energy to "moral reform," by which she meant temperance, antivivisection, and antiprostitution.

Emily then ran both the college and the infirmary, which became a pioneering medical center. As Dr. Elise L'Esperance, president of the American Medical Women's Association and a graduate of the college, observed in a 1949 tribute, Emily Blackwell's efforts resulted in "the first practical demonstration of the importance of the close association of a medical college with a hospital" — a pairing that became common in America only after the example of the Women's Medical College of the New York Infirmary.

From 1869 to the closing of the college thirty years later, Emily Blackwell served as its chief administrative officer as well as a professor of obstetrics and diseases of women and a practicing surgeon. (She was the first female doctor in the modern world to engage extensively in major surgery.) As the head of the Women's Medical College, she created a truly remarkable institution, managing to attract to both the student body and the faculty many of the early leading women in medicine, including Mary Putnam Jacobi, who was one of the first medical doctors to be interested in the effects of environmental forces on illness; Martha Wollstein, who conducted pioneering work on congenital tumors in children; and Sara Josephine Baker, who established the New York Bureau of Child Hygiene, which provided a blueprint for such bureaus all over America. The woman who became Emily Blackwell's life partner, Elizabeth Cushier, was a student at the college from 1869 to 1872 and later a professor of obstetrics and a leading gynecological surgeon. Under Emily Blackwell's direction, the Women's Medical College was the first institution to establish a chair in hygiene and one of the first to establish a chair in pathology; it was the first to develop a full-fledged training school for nurses; and it was a pioneer in preventive medicine.

Leading a Full Life While Leading an Institution

A recurrent theme in Emily Blackwell's diaries when she was young was her desire to achieve on a grand scale: to be one of those through whom the great ideas of the age were developed. But as she often wrote, she despaired of being able to find personal happiness as she accomplished her elevated goal. Though she fervently wanted to have an intimate relationship in which two "friends," "by their intellect, character, lives[,] roused each other to noble action, thought, and feeling," she sadly concluded in 1850, "I have never had, I believe I never shall have a friend." She had to wait a long time for such a friend, but for the last twenty-eight years of her life, Elizabeth Cushier provided what she had feared she would never have as she struggled to make a place in medicine for herself and the women who followed her.

As female physicians at a time when the term was oxymoronic, Emily Blackwell and her sister Elizabeth had chosen a lonely path. But while its loneliness tormented Emily, Elizabeth actually claimed in her autobiography, *Pioneer Work in Opening the Medical Profession to Women,* that she had elected her career not despite its solitude but precisely because of it. "Whenever I became sufficiently intimate with any individual to be able to realise what a life association might mean," she confessed, "I shrank from the prospect, disappointed or repelled." After rejecting a potential romance with a young man, she wrote in her journal, "I felt more determined than ever to become a physician, and thus place a strong barrier between me and all ordinary marriage." Boston marriage with another woman had no more appeal for Elizabeth Blackwell than ordinary marriage. On a visit to England in 1851, she met the young Florence Nightingale, who "proposed" to her, telling Elizabeth that she would "be perfectly happy working with me, [and] she would want no other husband." But beyond superficial sentimentalities, Elizabeth could not share Nightingale's feelings.

Emily Blackwell was very different from her older sister. From the beginning, Emily's intent to pursue a medical career came not out of her distrust of personal relationships but out of yearning ambition — a tremendous desire for work that would allow her to be instrumental in bettering the human condition. She sometimes feared, though, that her pursuits had condemned her to "utter social deadness," as she wrote to her brother. By 1871, her isolation had become so painful that she was considering "pulling up stakes," she told him, and indulging a restlessness like her sister's. But unlike her sister, Emily did dream of quelling her restlessness through personal relationships. In that same year she adopted an infant, Nannie, and she felt a good deal of satisfaction in the maternal role. She wrote her relatives charmed letters about the baby's teething and crawling and babbling. "The house would seem very dull and empty without her baby prattle and jolly little laugh," Emily confessed. But a child could not satisfy her longing for a companionship of equals. "How much it would add to one's life to renew personal intercourse," she wrote to Elizabeth when Nannie was ten years old, admitting that she felt "wearisome" pressure in her loneliness and wondering whether she and Nannie ought to move to Europe and join her sister and other family members who had settled there.

Yet if she had indulged the impulse to "pull up stakes," that would have been the end of both the New York Infirmary and the Women's Medical College, which she had worked so hard to help establish and to maintain. A dilemma such as hers must have been experienced or anticipated with dread by all women who hoped to achieve something beyond conventional domesticity in the nineteenth century. How was it possible to lead a full life while one was leading an institution or leading a profession or a movement? Emily Blackwell felt that she desperately needed a satisfying adult intimacy, yet it had to be one that would not distract from her needful work but would give her the energy for it. For years she continued to be troubled by the longing that she had confided to her diary as a young woman:

> As I walked along the hillside and felt the full fresh life that seemed to pervade everything, my old loneliness came back. I thought how beautiful it would be to live in the constant companionship of truly noble loving natures, and I longed deeply and intensely for affection and sympathy, and yet even when that feeling rises strongest it is not for a man's affection, it is [for] a noble human being, neither man nor woman, for the old Ideal. Some time, in a higher life, when I shall be more worthy of them, I shall meet them, the kind beautiful companions of my dreams. Till then I will concentrate myself on my work for no lower alliance will I ever seek.

The difficulties of continuing all alone, year after year, often seemed overwhelming to Emily Blackwell, particularly in her role as the head of a medical school for women. Few women were up to the challenge — intellectually, emotionally, or socially — to study medicine in the nineteenth century. It took not only tremendous courage but also a very unwomanly self-confidence, and an unwomanly selfishness, to believe that one could get through the stringent program and then pursue an independent career, in which one was welcomed neither by most of the profession nor by the general public. Unsurprisingly, therefore, not many women flocked to Emily Blackwell's Women's Medical College, and Emily sometimes doubted whether she would be able to keep the institution solvent. For several years after leaving America, Elizabeth Blackwell was uncertain whether she would remain in England or eventually return, so Emily maintained her sister's name in prominent connection with both the infirmary and the college, but Elizabeth Blackwell contributed nothing more to their ongoing operations. The anxieties and burdens were all on Emily.

At the start of the fall 1869 semester, Emily wrote to her sister in England that since their opening year had gone fairly well, the trustees, the faculty, the students, and she herself had taken "it for granted we should do well this year." But only seven old students returned and seven new students enrolled. "Everyone came in in good spirits and with a good deal of zeal, but the smallness of the class has been a great damper, and a surprise," she lamented. She speculated that the rigor and length of the program "deters all but those who have some personal reason for coming," but she refused to modify its stringency.

The following year, 1870, brought new difficulties. Two of the best male faculty members resigned because their connection with the school had "brought them in contact with all the professional dislike & distrust & jealousy toward the movement [of medical education for women]." Unlike Emily Blackwell, who was willing to endure widespread hostility for the sake of inspiring women "with higher objects — loftier aspirations," the men who resigned did not feel that the fledgling and still tiny college was worth suffering the disdain they experienced from other male physicians.

In addition, Emily often had reason to complain in the early 1870s of the hurdles of attempting to run the infirmary and the school and conduct a practice while raising a child, all of it by herself — which "taxes my strength exceedingly." By 1873, the college was on a somewhat better footing, with thirty-six students, but she despaired of making it grow larger without help. Yet though it exhausted her, she could not give up the work in which she so passionately believed. By the 1870s, the Woman's Medical College of Pennsylvania, the New England Female Medical College in Boston, the Woman's Medical College of Chicago, and various nontraditional schools such as the Homeopathic New York Medical College for Women were all training female doctors. In fact, Emily could have bowed out at that time without bad conscience — if she had not been certain that the other medical colleges for women were "easy[,] indulgent and coddling" compared to hers. Though it would have simplified her life to close her college, she determined to hold on, in the conviction that only there could women get a medical education equal to the best that men were offered.

It may well have been Elizabeth Cushier's return to the Women's Medical College as a faculty member in 1876 that helped Emily's determination. They did not form a domestic relationship until 1882, yet there is no question that from the start Emily not only admired Cushier personally but also believed that the existence of the Women's Medical College was stunningly validated by the skill and success of such alumnae. Elizabeth Cushier had gone to the Women's Medical College as a student after having spent a disappointing year in 1868 at a homeopathic college for women. After graduating from Blackwell's school in 1872, she became an intern and then a resident physician at the infirmary. In addition to her work in obstetrics and gynecology, she developed an interest in histology. Because there was still nowhere in the country that a female doctor could do laboratory research in histology, she decided to go to Zurich, as did so many other lesbian Americans intent on pursuing professional study in the 1870s. After eighteen months of research, she returned to the infirmary and the college.

From that point, Emily Blackwell and Elizabeth Cushier worked together. In 1882, as Cushier reported in a later autobiographical sketch, she joined her life with Emily Blackwell's. The two doctors and Emily's adopted daughter, Nannie, became a family of three until Nannie married. Emily and Elizabeth then lived together until Emily's death, in 1910. "We had a delightful home," Cushier wrote, declaring that it brought her "constant interest and delight." Emily too felt that interest and delight, and did not hide it from her relatives. For example, Alice Stone Blackwell, Emily's niece, who was very attuned to suggestions of lesbianism, has charmingly described a visit from Emily while Alice and her family were on Cape Cod, when Elizabeth Cushier came to join them. Seeing Elizabeth at the gate, "Aunt Emily," who was by then in her late fifties, ran to meet her "with a hop skip and jump of exultation . . . actually capering, in spite of her avoirdupois."

Elizabeth Cushier gave Emily what she truly needed at a point when she was feeling drained and bankrupt: a shared life, love, and the intimacy for which she had always longed. Elizabeth was also vital to Emily in more practical ways. Never pausing in her own career, any more than Emily paused, she shared the burdensome work of making a home. It was Elizabeth who generally took charge of the house — supervising the help, hiring the workmen. At the end of their summer vacations, she would sometimes return home first to open the house, put up shutters, change the curtains. "Much as I want to see you dear," she wrote, "I am not sorry you will not be here until next week, for I do not wish you to come into an unsettled house." She shared with Emily decisions about Nannie's education and concerns about the girl's growing pains; she soothed Emily through "all the petty emergencies of college and practice." Emily happily wrote to her sister about the "family life" she had succeeded in building with Elizabeth, observing during the course of an illness-filled winter that "it might be a great deal worse, for I have every comfort at home."

In the autobiography Elizabeth Cushier wrote in 1930, her own pleasure in their years together is evident in her tone. For example, she remembered that

in 1887, Dr. Blackwell and I spent part of the summer in Holland, Belgium, and Normandy, and their attractions . . . added one more pleasure to our store of memories. In 1893 Dr. Blackwell and I decided to establish a summer home for ourselves, and selected the coast of Maine, where on a bit of rocky woodland we planted our cottage, "Seawold." It proved for years a source of joy for us. Dr. Blackwell found much pleasure in sketching, and I in digging and planting, for I had learned the art and love of gardening.

As a young woman Emily had refused an invitation to a wedding because, she had written, "marriages are so far from what they should be, they often fetter and narrow the parties, that I am not willingly present at one." But in her own Boston marriage, she felt expanded. Both the infirmary and the college flourished over the next years, along with their leader. Many thousands of patients, generally women and children who could not afford medical care elsewhere, were treated in the infirmary. The college's twentieth annual catalogue indicated that students in that year, 1888, came from ten states as well as from Canada, Germany, India, Sweden, and Russia. In 1889, Emily was able to purchase a site near the infirmary on which an additional six-story building was erected for the college. In 1893, the curriculum was expanded to a mandatory four years in order to equal Harvard Medical School's newly expanded curriculum. Emily attributed her staying power to Elizabeth Cushier, as she wrote to her sister in 1894, confessing, "What I should have done without her help in the work the last few years I do not know."

In 1896 the college met with a disaster, when the seven-year-old building was gutted by fire. But Emily immediately found the energy to rebuild, and by that winter a new fireproof building, with increased space for pathology and chemistry labs, was ready for students. Two years later, however, Emily was obliged to rethink the continued existence of the Women's Medical College, when Cornell University opened a medical college in New York City at which female students would be accepted.

Emily Blackwell was by then seventy-two years old and had been considering retirement for several years. The world had ostensibly changed since she and her sister had begun their struggles a half-century before. "What a difference is round me as compared with [the] time of our early New York work. When I recall those times they seem to belong to a bygone age," she sanguinely wrote to Elizabeth Blackwell. "It seems to me that progress is inevitable, it is in the order of things, and is being worked out even without the Conscious Cooperation of men." Much of that progress was due to the pioneering work of her sister and herself, and to her determination through the years to keep both her women's medical college and her hospital going. By then there were many other female doctors — more than seven thousand of them, in fact — who she had reason to believe would continue what she and her sister had started in that bygone age.

Nevertheless, Elizabeth Cushier urged Emily not to retire in the mid-1890s. First of all, no heir apparent to Emily's leadership had appeared. Also, Emily had sometimes expressed the desire to leave New York on retirement and to travel, and she did not want to do that without her companion. Cushier, who was eleven years younger, wished to continue the medical work in which Emily had inspired and helped her for a while longer. It was a potentially difficult time for them.

Together with that personal difficulty was Emily's ambivalence about the Cornell medical school. She realized that a medical degree from Cornell "would carry much more weight than [one from] a private institution like ours," and she wished female medical students to have every advantage. Yet she continued to believe that coeducation was risky for women, as she wrote to her sister: "It depends largely on how cordially and fairly they treat their women students . . . [but also] I do not like the women to have exclusively masculine teachers. They need the influence of elder and more experienced women — the lack is a real one at Johns Hopkins" (where, thanks to Carey Thomas and Mary Garrett, women were allowed to study medicine, though they were not yet accepted on the medical faculty).

The choice of whether to continue the Women's Medical College was taken out of Emily's hands in 1898. With the opening of Cornell's medical school in New York City, the entering class at her

Women's Medical College dropped to half of what it had been two years earlier. Emily realized that it would not be economically feasible for the Women's Medical College to continue as a separate entity, though for a time she hoped that Cornell might agree to maintain aspects of it by incorporating the facility that had been built just a couple of years before into its new medical college. She proposed that Cornell permit female students to do their first two years of anatomical and laboratory work in what would continue to be called the Women's Medical College. She further proposed that Cornell "keep a certain proportion of women teachers." However, while her students were automatically accepted into the Cornell medical school and credited with the work they had already done in the Women's Medical College, Cornell would not agree to her other proposals.

The class of 1899 — which included women such as the public health pioneer Sara Josephine Baker — was the last to receive M.D. degrees from the Women's Medical College before it closed its doors. In her autobiography, *Fighting for Life,* Baker recollected her alma mater and its chief: "[Emily Blackwell] inspired us all with the vital feeling that we were still on trial and that, for women who meant to be physicians, no educational standards could be too high. It was a real advantage to be trained under that tradition. . . . Not only were the highest standards maintained but the pioneering spirit persisted. I think not many of us realized that we were going out into the world as test cases, but Dr. Blackwell did. Later I realized the wisdom and extent of her vision."

After thirty years of directing the Women's Medical College, Emily Blackwell had good reason to believe that her students, who had gone out into the world imbued with her wisdom and vision, would spread the legacy to others. When her work at the college terminated, she also retired as the chief administrator of the infirmary, but not with a sense of defeat. She wrote to her sister with well-deserved pride in July 1899, "I feel that I have done my active medical work, have bequeathed the institution [the infirmary] with a good reputation, and a valuable property to my juniors, and I know the work itself will grow." The building that the college had occupied was converted into more space for the infirmary, which continued to serve the poor women and children of New York City into the 1970s. The infirmary also continued for many more years to provide a much-needed place where female doctors could serve their internship and residency and could even hope to become heads of departments, as they generally could not elsewhere.

When Emily irrevocably decided to retire, Elizabeth Cushier was in a quandary. She was sixty-two years old and felt that she still had energy for her work. Yet she wanted to please her older and much-loved partner, who was urging her to follow her into retirement so that they could travel the world. In her autobiography, Cushier does not dwell at length on her reluctance to give up her work, other than to say that "though I did not feel that I actually needed to make the break at this time, I could not resist the thought of travel with such a companion." Her focus is on their "eighteen delightful months" abroad, their shared tastes, and the "permanent joy" of their memories. On their return to America in 1901, they established a winter home in Montclair, New Jersey, and maintained their summer home at York Cliffs, Maine.

Nannie, who married in 1899, had four sons. As Alice Stone Blackwell wrote in an article for the *Woman's Journal* in celebration of her famous aunt's eightieth birthday, "Dr. Emily is surrounded in her old age by the pleasures and interests of a grandmother." Cushier shared that aspect of domestic life with her too. Writing to Elizabeth Blackwell from Maine in the summer of 1902, Emily described her old age with Cushier in euphoric terms: "We were fortunate in securing two very good women, one of them an excellent cook, so we are very comfortably established here. Both of us enjoy greatly the sense of home, of freedom and ease in our own cottage. It has been a very good season for growth." Clearly Cushier would have concurred. "Thus the years happily passed," she concluded in her autobiography, "until in September, 1910, a sad blow came in the death of Dr. Blackwell, making an irreparable break in my life." Emily was eighty-four years old. Cushier survived her for another twenty-two years.

In a final paean to her aunt, Alice Stone Blackwell recalled words that Emily had used shortly before her death to describe the struggle she had had to endure in order to become who she finally was.

> No woman whose memory does not run back sixty years can realize what an iron wall hedged in every young woman who wanted to do anything outside of the most absolutely conventional groove — any girl who wanted to support herself, to earn money, to be educated, to do any one of a hundred things which would now be an everyday matter, but then was considered altogether improper. A woman who attempted anything of that kind was simply crushed if she did not have a very strong character; and those whose characters were such that they could not be crushed without a struggle simply had to break a way through the iron wall for themselves and for those who followed.

Emily had managed to do it all: escape from the conventional groove, be educated, earn money, run a hospital and a college — break through the iron wall and show the path to any who cared to travel on it. And she had succeeded in snatching a modicum of personal joy for herself as well, of "happy . . . companionship," as Alice characterized her twenty-eight-year "marriage" to Elizabeth Cushier.

❧ 16 ❧

CARRYING ON:

MARTHA MAY ELIOT, M.D.

It is dangerous for an innocent girl to take long trips with
an active homosexual woman, who though cultured on
the surface may have a tendency to seduce girls. . . . Girls
should avoid older women who are fond of them, especially if they attempt any undue intimacies.

— John Meagher, 1929

You take with you the deep satisfactions that you have so
rightfully earned for the splendid leadership you have
given over the years to the cause of better health and
welfare for children, not only in your own Nation but
around the world. . . . Future generations of children will
be the beneficiaries, as past generations have been, of
the forward-looking and selfless service you have given
on their behalf for 30 years.

— President Eisenhower to Dr. Eliot on her
retirement from the Children's Bureau, 1957

Working as a Team

BY 1891, THE YEAR Martha May Eliot was born, Emily Blackwell,
Jane Addams, and Carey Thomas had already accomplished a great
deal to enlarge the prospects of American women. But in the half-
century between 1920 and 1970, it seemed that what those pioneers
had accomplished would go largely unheeded and unappreciated.
Nevertheless, Dr. Martha May Eliot and a few women like her were

their beneficiaries and by their own successes managed to keep the victories of the earlier generation flickering through the dim years. Eliot, who died in 1978, even lived long enough to witness that flicker turn to a flare again, in a new movement that encouraged unprecedented numbers of women to take up the rekindled torches, which lit their way into medicine and other professions.

Martha May Eliot — a distant relative of Charles Eliot, the president of Harvard and sworn enemy of M. Carey Thomas — was denied entrance to Harvard Medical School because she was a woman. Johns Hopkins University had to accept her under the terms of Mary Garrett's endowment, which had been negotiated by Carey Thomas, and she received her medical degree from Johns Hopkins in 1918. Her impressive successes, which followed soon after, certainly had no effect on her uncle Charles's opinions about the appropriateness of serious study for women; at just about the time she became the first resident doctor at Yale University's newly established department of pediatrics, he was writing that "the prime motive of the higher education of women" should be to develop "the capacities and powers which will fit them to make family life . . . happier." Martha carried on in spite of her venerable relative.

Though Martha Eliot devoted her career to the health of children, family life in a conventional sense never had interest for her. Her earliest memories were of wanting to escape from the usual parameters of little girlhood in the late nineteenth century — "to leave home. Go out and see things. Go out and see the world." Among her papers was a school essay written by a friend in 1907, which she saved for the next seventy-one years and passed on for archival preservation. The essay, "The Importance of Purpose in the Life of a Girl," declared that girls often have grand ambitions when they are young that get lost when they become fifteen or sixteen. "Boys as a matter of course have to pass their college examinations and while they are young they must work for this and arrange the rest of their lives to suit them best for this end." But girls, the author complained, are permitted by society to be directionless. The essay concluded with a plea that girls too be given something to strive for. Martha Eliot, who was sixteen in 1907, took the essay to heart, vowing that she would never be distracted from her own grand ambitions.

Marriage would have been the ultimate distraction. While in medical school, when Martha received word from her mother that a cousin had announced her engagement, she reiterated her determination in no uncertain terms: "When I announce my engagement, we can take the paint off the front of the house!! but to tell you the truth, if some other opportunity comes for getting it done, don't wait for me." By then her mother undoubtedly did not have to be admonished that her daughter would not be announcing her engagement. Martha had set her course against marriage years earlier and had refused to swerve from it. Yet while heterosexuality could not tempt her, relationships with other women, which would not threaten her ambitions as marriage would, did have power over her. In high school, for instance, she had a romantic friendship with a girl who later became a Bryn Mawr College student. Martha's parents sent her to Radcliffe, but after the first year she took a leave in order to spend her sophomore year at Bryn Mawr with her friend. As she recalled when she was eighty-three years old, the dean at Radcliffe, who had "thought I was pretty queer to want to do this," had tried to dissuade her from leaving Radcliffe by threatening to record her Bryn Mawr courses with no grade higher than C, but she went off to Bryn Mawr anyway.

The romantic friendship that took her to Bryn Mawr was short-lived. However, there she met a twenty-six-year-old freshman, Ethel Dunham, who had gone to college after eight years of a pointless social life as the unmarried daughter of the president of Hartford Electric Light Company. Ethel found her direction at Bryn Mawr — together with Martha. From 1910 to Ethel's death, in 1969, the two women were inseparable. They decided, very possibly under the influence of the redoubtable Carey Thomas, that they would go to medical school together, practice together, and live together for the rest of their lives. As Martha remembered sixty-four years later, "So that year in Bryn Mawr was productive for me in more than one way."

As a couple, Martha Eliot and Ethel Dunham provide an interesting illustration of how a few women were able to carry into the twentieth century the legacies of the pioneers. The heterosexual imperative of 1920–1970 seemed to pass them by, just as all the other social strictures that prevented most bright women from pursuing serious careers during those years did. Eliot and Dunham succeeded in times that were as unsympathetic to professional women as they were to lesbians. Yet they both seemed to be almost oblivious to the ethos that said that they were not supposed to have ambitions that were not domestic, they were not supposed to succeed, and they were certainly not supposed to want and be able to make their lives with each other. Their story can be seen as paradigmatic of how what was not supposed to be doable could be done if it was desired enough.

After Martha Eliot and Ethel Dunham met, their professional and personal lives invariably depended on each other. Martha, who had started college a year before Ethel, graduated from Radcliffe in 1913, but she did not go to medical school immediately, because she wanted to begin with Ethel. Waiting for Ethel to graduate, she took a job as a social worker at Massachusetts General Hospital. (How would she have supported herself that year if women such as Jane Addams had not opened a profession of social work for women?) When Ethel graduated, in 1914, they entered Johns Hopkins Medical School together, two of eleven women in a class with eighty-four men.

The open hostility visited on Emily Blackwell when she tried to get a medical education in the mid-nineteenth century had long passed. But it must nevertheless have been extremely difficult to be part of a small minority studying for a profession in which women were still far from accepted or prominent. "We [Ethel and herself] braved the dangers of the School office this morning and only encountered one male student," Martha wrote to her mother nervously, shortly after arriving at Johns Hopkins. The female students banded together. They were helped by Carey Thomas and Mary Garrett, who, as the medical historian Regina Morantz-Sanchez characterizes it, "continued a watchful scrutiny over the Hopkins women and obsessively monitored their success." Martha Eliot's letters show to what a great extent Carey Thomas remained a salient presence at Johns Hopkins, even after Garrett's death, in 1915. Martha reported that Thomas attended teas given by the Women's Committee of the Medical School, listened receptively to the students' problems and suggestions, and continued to provide money for their benefit, such as the $10,000 she donated in 1917 for the building of the Garrett Room, a gathering place for female medical students.

Martha and Ethel were also able to alleviate the alienation of being women at a medical school that was primarily male by making a home together from the start, in an off-campus apartment. Their domestic satisfaction crept constantly into Martha's letters home: "E. and I get our own breakfast now and so start out earlier and better for the day's work"; "E. keeps me out doors which is great. This P.M. we are going canoeing"; "Tonight we are having supper here — oyster omelet, a concoction of Ethel's — and apple sauce and toast and nutbread." They shared everything. They cheered each other on through the difficulties of dissection and bandaging and late-night studies. Ethel bought a car and taught Martha how to drive. Together they even kept the suffrage movement going at Johns Hopkins. At Bryn Mawr, under Carey Thomas, they had become committed to the cause; in Baltimore they worked at suffrage bazaars and distributed suffrage literature together.

Because Martha Eliot was among the top 10 percent of her class in 1918, she was nominated for an internship at Johns Hopkins Hospital before graduation. However, she turned it down. As she wrote to her mother, "Part of my reason for my lack of enthusiasm was because Ethel didn't get an appointment. I was frightfully disappointed." Because she hoped that Ethel might be accepted at Massachusetts General, Martha finally took an internship at Peter Brigham Hospital in Boston, where no female doctors had been accepted before. Ironically, Ethel was then informed that she would be accepted at Johns Hopkins Hospital after all. Many of the male students had gone into the Army Medical Corps when the United States entered World War I, so, as Martha wrote with some bitterness, "it didn't leave so very many to choose from for internships and hence the girls had a good show."

Although Martha knew she was lucky to have gotten the Peter Brigham internship, she was in despair at being separated from Ethel. Through much of that year, she schemed over ways for them to be together, but the next year was even more difficult. Ethel became one of the first female house officers at the New Haven Hospital in Connecticut, and Martha undertook a residency in pediatrics at St. Louis Children's Hospital in Missouri. That year too was spent in wishing they could be together and working at every opportunity to make that possible.

By 1920 Martha was feeling desperate, as she wrote to her mother in a remarkable letter, which may be read as the closest thing to coming out that a woman of her day and class would have been capable of.

> You will be interested to know that after much changing of mind and many mental gymnastics and more hours of thought I have come to the conclusion that I will come back to Boston next year and see what's to be done there and try to find out what the future will bring forth not only for me but for Ethel too. It has taken a great deal of arguing with myself to give up the place [in St. Louis], but I believe I am right. . . . My idea is that by another year [in Boston] I will know things well enough to find work that Ethel will like, and then she will come up, I hope, and we can have a little apartment together such as we have always planned.

Martha went on to make clear to her mother that "I am not as I was seven years ago [before she made the decision to delay her entrance into Johns Hopkins until Ethel could go with her]. The values of life have changed very much for me and I have got to live accordingly." The plans she outlined in the rest of this letter, both short-term and long-term, centered on Ethel. For example, she would visit her parents, she wrote, if Ethel would come with her, "but I must confess that unless she wants to do that I will want to stay with her in Keene Valley [where Ethel was spending her summer vacation]." Martha's letters home had been shared with the entire family in the past, as she knew. But this letter she ended with a statement that suggested she did not wish to come out to her other family members: "This letter is for your own benefit and not for general perusal or to be read out loud."

Her dependence on Ethel was perhaps not very different emotionally from what many women experienced toward men. She had difficulty envisioning her life without Ethel. She was willing to sacrifice almost everything for the sake of their "marriage." Nothing satisfied her as much as their connection to each other. However, as was true for the pioneering women of the generations before hers, the ways in which Martha's relationship with Ethel differed from heterosexual relationships of their day mandated that Martha try to become a professional success. Women who were interested in heterosexuality usually gave up medical careers, as they were generally expected to do, when they married. Even more likely, women in the early years of the twentieth century who believed that heterosexual marriage was essential to their happiness would surely not even have started medical study in the first place, despite their aptitude, because they knew that a career as a doctor would be incompatible with their eventual roles as wife and mother. They would have considered that among women who practiced medicine, only about 30 percent were married, and they would have decided that such a career was not for them.

In contrast to heterosexual women, the only way Martha could maintain her primary relationship during these crucial years was to go through medical school with Ethel, become self-supporting, and find a position near her. Martha's lesbianism was thus instrumental in helping her realize the other great passion of her life: to become a doctor. If she had not qualified for a profession, she would have had to return to the bosom of her family. Eventually, perhaps, she would have been coerced to bend to their wishes to "take the paint off the front of the house!!" despite her lack of interest in heterosexual life. Her emotional dependency on Ethel made her brilliant career not only possible but necessary.

Martha returned to Boston from St. Louis, as she told her mother she would, and set up a private family practice, hoping to find a way to bring Ethel to Boston. It was still a difficult time for her. She was uncertain about when she and Ethel would be able to be together again, and she was not happy in private practice. She felt especially uncomfortable because she was pressured by male doctors to charge higher fees — fees comparable to their own — when she was already thinking that her fees were too high and that "it was frustrating not to be able to accomplish all the things for the families . . . like laboratory work or x-ray which some could not afford." But at the height of her personal and professional discontent, a miracle happened — or her persistence paid off. Her former professor at Johns Hopkins was establishing a department of pediatrics at Yale, in New Haven, where Ethel was, and he invited Martha to be its first resident doctor.

The only drawback was that the position required Martha to live in the university hospital. Yet she managed to take many of her meals and to sleep often in Ethel's apartment. "I spent the night with Ethel and shall return there again tonight"; "[Ethel's] maid is very good and has no objection to my dining there very frequently so I shall continue to do so several times a week"; "I came over here tonight to have supper with Ethel after a busy day in the hospital and it is very refreshing," Martha wrote to her mother, usually on stationery stamped "Ethel C. Dunham, M.D." She desperately needed the comfort of Ethel in the midst of her demanding work.

Bringing the Jane Addams Influence into the Medical Profession

However, Martha and Ethel still did not have the home together that Martha craved. That longing continued to influence the trajectory of her career. "Whether I shall stay on at the hospital is not yet settled," she wrote in March 1923. "I am contemplating taking on some work with rickets which would let me live outside." She may have first planned to work on rickets, largely a disease of poor children, because that would give her the freedom to live with Ethel, but the move was entirely consistent with Martha Eliot's view of the social duties of a medical doctor. Even while in medical school, she had tried to arrange her packed schedule so she could do volunteer work at a children's clinic. "I sometimes get wild to have something to do that . . . isn't purely for my own satisfaction," she wrote in 1914, echoing Jane Addams. And again in 1915, "I have had a strong feeling right along that every chance I could get to do any social work would be more than worthwhile . . . If I should practice I want to keep attached to the social end of it, in other words, be some kind of a 'social doctor.'" Her research on the prevention of rickets among economically deprived children stemmed from that impulse.

This project was revolutionary for its day. As the *American Journal of Public Health* observed in 1971 of Martha Eliot's early rickets work, "Those of us who have grown up with scientific clinical investigation may find it difficult to appreciate the courage and imagination required in such studies [fifty years ago]." There was little tradition for this kind of investigation. Eliot had to develop her designs almost from scratch; her training at Johns Hopkins had included nothing about community health research. Work such as hers became a model for later researchers.

Martha Eliot's rickets project not only allowed her to live with Ethel; it also launched her career in community pediatrics and then in administrative medicine. The rickets study was funded by the Sheppard-Towner Act, a maternal and infant care bill that had been passed through the efforts of activists such as Jane Addams and her protégés. It was administered by the U.S. Children's Bureau (which also owed its existence to the persistence of Addams and her colleagues). The bureau had been established by Congress in 1912 to investigate and make recommendations on infant mortality, child labor, and all other issues pertaining to child welfare. Martha Eliot's research on rickets resulted in her being named director of the Child Hygiene Division of the Children's Bureau in 1924.

This appointment might have led to a crisis in her relationship with Ethel Dunham. The Children's Bureau headquarters were in Washington, D.C. While Ethel may have been footloose earlier in her career, in 1924 she became one of the first female professors at Yale University's School of Medicine. A couple in a heterosexual marriage with a comparable dilemma would perhaps have assumed that someone would have to sacrifice something — and it would undoubtedly have been the wife, who would have forgone her advancement for the sake of the family. As Morantz-Sanchez has shown, in the early generations of female doctors, those who married usually were constrained by the various demands of their situation to modify their careers drastically. Such a possibility did not even occur to Dunham and Eliot. They had to find a way to work it out so that they could both keep their jobs and yet remain together.

Martha Eliot's success at finding a solution was surely due in good part to luck, but pluck and determination cannot be discounted. She argued with validity that her New Haven rickets study was ongoing — she continued it for ten years, until 1933 — and that she could not give up teaching at Yale, which she had recently undertaken. (In addition to being attending pediatrician at the hospital, she eventually rose to the rank of associate professor at the Yale Medical School.) Her arguments were persuasive. She arranged with the Children's Bureau to travel to Washington once a month and stay for three or four days to give hands-on guidance to the Child Hygiene Division. The rest of her work for the division would be done at a distance, from New Haven. She and Ethel were therefore able to remain at Yale until 1935, when Martha was appointed assistant chief of the bureau and had to be in Washington full-time. In 1951, with the consent of the Senate, President Truman named her chief of the Children's Bureau.

Throughout the intervening years, both Martha and Ethel conducted intense careers that often placed them under great pressure. But they seem to have believed that their relationship gave them sustenance for the challenges and that their work and their life together were inextricably connected. For example, in 1923, just before they were to go off on a vacation to England, Martha learned that she had received funding for her rickets project. But "Excitement no. 2," as she described it in a letter, which came at the same time and was fully as important to her as "Excitement no. 1," was "the little house we were looking at, and as the owner has come across with everything we asked . . . we will probably move in!"

Martha's letters leave a close record of how the two women managed to combine the home life they needed during those years with their varying duties and long-distance commutes. For example, in the midst of committee work, lectures, administrative tasks, sick patients, travel, research, and writing, "we brought down a box full of plants from the Dunhams' garden — pansies, forget-me-nots, sweet williams, canterbury bells, English daisies — and yellow lilies. Our garden will be very superior if they all grow." They read books out loud to each other. They learned to play the piano together. They planned their professional trips together as much as possible; when Ethel visited a tuberculosis sanitarium in Minnesota for a project on infant tuberculosis, for instance, Martha visited a child welfare institute at the University of Minnesota.

They shared a phenomenal energy level and good health, which permitted them both to make remarkable accomplishments. Ethel Dunham became an expert on premature babies. In 1927 (undoubtedly in part through Martha's influence, but primarily through her own abilities), she was appointed the Children's Bureau's medical officer in charge of neonatal studies. This meant that she and Martha could travel to Washington together every month, though like Martha, she retained her position at Yale and conducted her neonatal studies in New Haven. They continued living in their little house with its flourishing garden.

When Martha became assistant chief of the Children's Bureau in 1935, Ethel was able to make her own career run parallel once again. They both gave up their Yale positions, and Ethel became director of the division of child development research in the Children's Bureau. She more than earned this promotion, establishing national standards for the treatment of premature infants, developing a model program to extend the care of infants from the hospital to the community by public health nurses and social workers, and writing a pioneering work on hospital care of newborns, which became one of the most widely distributed publications ever sponsored by the American Pediatric Association. She was made the first female member of the American Pediatric Society and in 1957 became the first woman to be honored with its highest award, the Howland Medal.

In the years following her appointment as assistant chief, Martha Eliot was especially interested in the interrelationship of child health and socioeconomic factors, and her particular concern was with obtaining better medical services for children of low-income families. She was an advocate for all children, appearing before countless congressional committees whenever legislation was proposed for child welfare. She argued tirelessly for universal health care for the young, and many of her proposals were eventually incorporated into law. She served as the chief architect of health provisions for children in the 1935 Social Security Act, which mandated that every state establish child health services.

Her interests and contributions spread beyond American children, as President Eisenhower noted when she retired. After World War II, in 1946, she served as the vice chair of the U.S. delegation to the International Health Conference and on behalf of the United States signed the constitution that established the World Health Organization. (She was the only woman to sign WHO's constitution.) She was also active in the formation of UNICEF, and in 1947 she traveled on behalf of UNICEF to central and eastern Europe to conduct a study of how best to address the needs of children in war-torn countries. From 1949 to 1951, Eliot worked as an assistant director for WHO in Geneva, where she played a major role not only in setting up the organization but in getting governments all over the world to strengthen their health services, especially with regard to children.

Almost needless to say, Martha did not go to Geneva without Ethel, who became a consultant to WHO's maternal and child health division. In that capacity she developed international interest in training personnel for work with "premies" and in doing research on the connections between socioeconomic problems and premature birth. In 1951, when President Truman named Martha Eliot chief of the Children's Bureau, the couple returned to Washington together, and Ethel began a long-term study on gestation and parturition.

What an "Unnatural Female Celibate" Might Do

Despite the contributions of women such as Martha Eliot and Ethel Dunham to the welfare of American children, they — and the few women like them who flourished as professionals during these years — were often under attack because they didn't tend to their knitting. For example, arguing against the continued existence of the Children's Bureau, James Reed, a senator from Missouri, called the women who worked for the bureau (many of whom were lesbians) "unnatural . . . female celibates." He scoffed that "it seems to be the established doctrine of the bureau that the only people caring for babies and mothers of babies are ladies who have never had babies." He missed the point that during his era, the ladies who had the babies were convinced that they must eschew a professional life. The senator claimed to believe that instead of having a Children's Bureau, America would be better off having a "Mothers' Committee . . . to take charge of the old maids and teach them how to acquire a husband and have babies of their own." Such attacks must have been hurtful not only to Eliot and Dunham but to any young women who wanted a career rather than a life of "normal" domesticity.

However, Martha May Eliot proceeded as though she were deaf to such criticisms. Her contributions went beyond the welfare of children. For example, in the 1930s she was invited often to Harvard University to lecture on child health, though Harvard had refused to accept her as a medical student in 1914 because she was a woman. Women were admitted to Harvard's School of Public Health by the 1930s, but they were not permitted to take a degree. The protest and pressure that Eliot exerted on the school made it relent and agree to give women degrees in public health. Harvard even awarded degrees retroactively to women who had completed the program before 1936.

Eliot's influence in the field of public health was manifested in other ways too. For example, in 1947 she became the first female president of the American Public Health Association. She was also the second female president of the American Pediatric Association — the first was Ethel Dunham — and from 1949 to 1950 she was president of the National Council of Social Work (later called the National Council on Social Welfare). Martha Eliot had by then certainly fulfilled her youthful ambition to "be some kind of a 'social doctor.'"

Her association with Harvard continued, and in 1957, at the age of sixty-six, she left the Children's Bureau in order to become one of the handful of women with full professorial status at Harvard, accepting an appointment as professor and head of the department of maternal and child health at the School of Public Health. Ethel, who was then seventy-four years old, moved to Cambridge with her and continued her research on gestation and parturition.

When Martha Eliot retired from her professorship, she was replaced by a man, Dr. William Schmidt. By then the tail end of the generations of women with enough stature to assume such posts — to carry on — had ostensibly long since disappeared. But though Martha was seventy years old, she had not finished working. In 1960 and 1961 she took two major trips to Africa, India, and the Far East to investigate projects that the World Health Organization was financing in developing countries.

Ethel, now on the far side of her seventies, kept the home fires burning. They exchanged almost daily letters during Martha's travels for WHO. Those letters, written when they were both old women, reveal that the relationship had kept working for them their entire adult lives. Emotionally, they ended much as they began. Ethel encouraged Martha in her WHO work and was excited with her about her travels. Nevertheless, it was still painful for them to be without each other. They wrote day after day: "Dearest, It was hard to say goodbye and I shall miss you terribly. . . . Ever and ever so much love, my darling"; "How I count the time until you do arrive. I miss you my darling"; "I do want you too. . . . I miss you so very much my dearest love."

Martha Eliot began depositing her papers in the Schlesinger Library in 1969, the year Ethel died, and continued until 1976, two years before her own death. In the beginning she culled them. She destroyed most of the letters between herself and Ethel, though she preserved her voluminous letters to her family, which recorded her medical education and early career. (It is fortunate that she preserved those letters, since they provide the best lens we have through which to view the relationship between the two women.) She also began to expurgate the greetings and closings of her letters to Ethel from the 1940s, written when she was traveling for WHO. However, she stopped those expurgations after mutilating only two of the letters, because she saw that the scissors were also destroying important details about WHO, which she thought posterity would be interested in. From the intact letters to Ethel from this period, we can see that she opened with greetings as tame but telling as "Dearest," which would suggest that by the time she was ready to begin to hand her papers over to the library, people like Senator Reed had made her well aware of homophobia and fearful that even addressing another woman as "Dearest" would be damning.

Martha's and Ethel's letters written in 1960 and 1961, including those quoted above, did not suffer from the scissors — although in the face of Martha's other bowdlerizations, it is not entirely clear why. Perhaps she thought that women in their seventies would never be suspected of having been or being in love with each other. Perhaps by the time she got to those letters, she had decided to let the future make of her and Ethel what it would. Or perhaps Martha Eliot took hope from the lesbian and gay rights movement that emerged in 1969 and grew strong in the 1970s. Perhaps she felt that a generation to come would understand and appreciate what was hinted at in those letters to the woman who had been so central in her life.

❧ 17 ❧

THE RUSH TO
BAKE THE PIES AND
HAVE THE BABIES

The time, too, has passed when girls went to college to prepare themselves . . . [for] bread-winning occupations. In considerable numbers they now seek intellectual resources and the enrichment of their private lives.

— Alice Freeman Palmer, 1900

Losing Ground in the Professions

THERE WERE NOT many Martha Eliots or Ethel Dunhams in the 1920–1970 years. The pioneers who had struggled so hard to pave the way for women in the professions must have been horrified at the signs of the turning tide. Surveys in the 1920s and '30s indicated that more and more female college graduates shared the opinion of the former president of Wellesley, now Mrs. Alice Freeman Palmer, that the purpose of female education should be enrichment rather than professional striving. In actuality, women were entering the occupational market in increasing numbers in the early decades of the twentieth century, but they were usually employed at low-paying jobs in which they could work for a limited period and which could be adjusted around their domestic responsibilities.

Women steadily lost ground in the professions. By the 1940s, as a statistician for the U.S. Women's Bureau observed, more than three quarters of the women who were listed in the census of occupations under "Professional" were in the lower-prestige, lower-salaried jobs of teachers and nurses. "The traditional learned professions of law, medicine, and theology," the statistician wrote in 1947, "accounted for almost 24 percent of the men grouped as professional and semi-professional workers, but the proportion of women in these fields was relatively so insignificant (all of them together less than 1 percent)" that she could not show them separately in her statistical summary.

As Carey Thomas and Virginia Gildersleeve had done in academia, lesbian leaders in the learned professions sought ways to encourage women who lived in heterosexual arrangements to think beyond the parameters of domestic life. Their concern was not altruistic. Emily Blackwell had understood in the nineteenth century that since she was nominally a "woman," she would be limited and tarred by whatever constrained "womankind." Lesbian professional women continued to recognize what was at stake if they could not elevate the status of women. However, they lived in a very different world from that of heterosexual women, who generally did not have the same motives to spur them in the arduous struggles toward a profession.

The gulf between the lives that professional women fashioned for themselves in the post–World War I years and the lives of most heterosexual women was vast. Dr. Ellen Potter and Dr. Martha Tracy are a case in point. The two women met at the Woman's Medical College of Pennsylvania at the start of the twentieth century and were inseparable, much like Dr. Eliot and Dr. Dunham, until Tracy's death, in 1942. Their careers and lives ran on parallel tracks: they worked together, lived together, and invariably played together. Tracy was dean of the Woman's Medical College of Pennsylvania from 1917 to 1935; Potter was a professor of medicine and in the 1940s was president of the college. During the summers, when they were not engaged in their shared profession, they ran a 370-acre camp in the Adirondacks where they could "don knickerbockers," a 1924 newspaper account quaintly phrased it, mentioning the ways in which Martha Tracy "has fallen into, naturally, social relations that develop the possibilities of women everywhere." Theirs was an all-female world, both at the college and beyond. However, they had little contact with or understanding of "woman" as she was being constructed in the post–World War I years of the (hetero)sexual revolution. Even stylistically, they and those they admired were very different from most heterosexual women. Their sincere efforts to raise the status of females were thus often frustrated.

For example, in a 1919 newspaper article, Ellen Potter was quoted as being dismayed about the postwar version of the feminine mystique that was keeping women home and making them valetudinarian, causing them (in those pre-Valium days) to "frequent[ly] resort to sanitariums and rest-cures." Potter exhorted "married women with education and brains" to strive to "perform more valuable work" than the "manual labor" of running the house. But the semiotics in the article that reported her words spoke volumes — "Don't Be a Vegetable Wife; Husbands Don't Like Them," the headline read — and the picture of Potter that accompanied the article separated her from wives of any kind. Readers undoubtedly wondered with some hostility how she could possibly know what husbands liked and didn't like. Her hair was short and without style; her glasses were rimless; her jacket and shirt were tailored; her sole ornamentation was a dark tie. Her sartorial severity was matched by the severity of her expression. The illustration announced the New Woman as dyke, 1919-style, and separated her emphatically from the married women whom Potter was attempting to address.

Martha Tracy also realized as the twentieth century wore on that most college women would marry, and that if women were going to hold their own in the professions, heterosexual women had to be encouraged to participate. However, she could not mask her ambivalence, or a conviction that the heterosexual lifestyle stood in the way of women's ability to carry out professional responsibilities. In a 1932 newspaper interview, she began by asserting that of course "a wife and mother could become a successful physician." Yet her deeper convictions soon seeped through. She felt compelled to warn of the pitfalls if women married while they were still in medical school; she complained of married interns "who expect to thoroughly disorganize hospital regime and secure for themselves unusual privileges"; and she complained about husbands who have "the take-it-for-granted attitude that when things go wrong in the home it's the wife's job (be she successful physician or artist) to straighten them out."

Her dilemma was palpable. She truly had difficulty believing that heterosexual marriage could be compatible with professional life. Yet if educated women were marrying nearly as often as the rest of the female population, how would it be possible to assure women's continuation in medicine without the participation of married women? To whom would Tracy and Potter pass the torch that — as they wrote in a 1919 article — had been given into their hands by Emily Blackwell, who so long ago "demonstrated that women were capable of distinguished ability in the practice of the art [of medicine]"? How could they even keep the Woman's Medical College of Pennsylvania going? Lesbians alone could not make up an entire student body.

Their well-intentioned but inept efforts failed to stem women's retreat to the home. Yet any attempt to counter that retreat was doomed to failure for multiple reasons. Many men continued to protest women's bid for independence virulently, just as they had in the nineteenth century. Magazine articles such as "This Two-Headed Monster — The Family" (1928) admonished that women's financial independence was driving a wedge between husband and wife and would make an increasingly high divorce rate inevitable, that when "men are married to intellectual tomboys family life lacks a certain spiritual richness," and that everyone is hurt by that impoverishment — especially the children. Women were complicit in the scheme to drive women home again. Numerous magazine articles by women held that women were losing their sex appeal by engaging in men's careers. The writer of "Still a Man's Game: Reflections of a Tired Feminist" (1929) lamented that "in forswearing our past security we have forsworn something which had a biological as well as a conventional and religious sanction." Or, as another tired heterosexual ex-feminist cried in 1931, "We're tired of our rights, give us our privileges again."

Such sentiments naturally widened the rift between heterosexual women and professional women who lived outside of heterosexual domestic arrangements. "Tired feminists" were speaking a language that was gibberish to women such as Martha Tracy and Ellen Potter — nor could the tired ones understand the tongue that the doctors employed.

Hollywood, always anxious to reflect the prevailing ethos, often dramatized the "tired feminists'" sentiments in popular movies. Actresses such as Katharine Hepburn and Rosalind Russell were featured as "strong-minded females" who learned finally to become "real women" — that is, they turned their backs on hard-won professional careers, ceased to be "intellectual tomboys," and settled down in a vine-covered cottage with a companionate hubby. The manlike professional woman was doomed, Hollywood proclaimed. In a normal female, the biological urge would win out; despite her brief delusions about the glory of a career, nature would propel her into a strong man's arms, where she would be reminded that she was a woman after all.

The pioneers who lived to see that day despaired at the ubiquitous illusions about vine-covered cottages, but they despaired even more at what they considered the terrible self-absorption of the interwar years. It seemed to Jane Addams, as she complained in *The Second Twenty Years at Hull House* (1930), that the new generation of educated women were interested only in the kind of personal gratification that the post–World War I sexual revolution promoted. They had no passion for playing public roles of the kind that had grabbed the imagination and energies of their predecessors. Addams responded with dismay to the ostensible fact that advances in birth control had created a generation of women who expended their energies in embracing sexual experimentation (which would have been impossible in earlier eras, when extramarital sex easily resulted in the shame of illegitimate births) rather than committing themselves to the more serious business of public life and human betterment. What Addams and other "intellectual tomboys" had once accomplished for women, they now feared, was being entirely vitiated by rampant (hetero)sexuality.

Their fears were not entirely groundless. The American heroine of the 1920s was no longer someone like Jane Addams (or Emily Blackwell or Ellen Potter, needless to say); rather, she was a representative of flaming girlhood — someone like Zelda Fitzgerald, who pronounced with disgust over what the pioneers had done for women, "I think a woman gets more happiness out of being gay, light-hearted, . . . than out of a career that calls for hard work, intellectual pessimism, and loneliness."

Obviously Zelda Fitzgerald did not speak for all straight women, yet she spoke for many. A survey conducted around the end of the 1920s for a book revealingly titled *New Girls for Old* reported that about 85 percent of the young women interviewed responded with an unequivocal no when asked "Do you prefer a career to marriage?" The authors proclaimed that "for the modern girl, work has lost the glamour which surrounded it when women had to struggle against the odds for this means of self-expression. It is no longer the ultimate aim in life but has taken a subsidiary place." The authors were not only observers of the mood of the times; along with many other writers of popular psychology, they helped fuel it by their repeated insistence that a "healthy" young female "develop[s] to a mature heterosexuality [in which] love will be given first place in her dreams of happiness, and she will not think of sacrificing marriage for any prize." It must have been difficult for a woman to resist the barrage of propaganda that painted those who had fought to open careers to women as misdirected, dull, and unhappy, and that propelled the "New Girls" into dating and marriage.

What was not accomplished during the 1920s in discouraging most women from imagining serious careers for themselves was accomplished during the Depression. Women with heterosexual leanings were redirected to pie- and baby-making more forcefully than ever in the 1930s. At the height of the Depression, twenty-six states had laws prohibiting the employment of married women. When a poll asked (in loaded language), "Do you approve of a married woman earning money in business and industry if she has a husband capable of supporting her?" 82 percent of the respondents answered no. Yet, ironically in view of the heterosexual im-

perative of the day, unmarried women had an advantage in pursuing careers during the Depression. For instance, as a 1930–31 National Education Association survey indicated, 77 percent of school
districts would not hire married female teachers for new positions,
and 50 percent said they were dismissing those women who were
married, under the assumption that they would be supported by
their husbands. Their jobs could be given to those who had no one
to support them. Lesbians had no one to support them.

It was thus up to lesbians and other unmarried women to continue to keep a mark for women in the career world when wives
were being forced or convinced to stay home. In 1940, twice as
many single women as married women were listed in the census of
occupations as "professional and semi-professional workers." The
persistent female representation in professional careers during
those years, as token as it was, was vital. It meant that in better
times women would not have to start all over again to fight for the
right to professional training and employment. Unmarried professional women — who often formed intimate relationships with
other professional women — were the main force in holding the
door ajar, even if only slightly.

Bad Influences: "Women Who Want Careers"

Predictably, perhaps, hostility toward such women increased dramatically during the decades when few questioned that women's
place was in the home. Psychiatrists, psychologists, and their popular disciples responded to lesbian tenaciousness in maintaining
careers by again playing a salient role in defining lesbians — and
their refusal of the usual domestic arrangements — as socially mal-
adjusted and even sick. The enormous investigation undertaken in
the 1930s by the Committee for the Study of Sex Variants (composed, significantly, of psychiatrists, psychologists, a criminal anthropologist, and a commissioner of the New York Department of
Corrections), which resulted in the 1941 book *Sex Variants: A Study
of Homosexual Patterns,* specifically connected lesbianism to an

interest in "aggressive occupations" and the movement for "social equality of the sexes." Indeed, "unusual self-assurance" suggested "sex variant tendencies." The investigators concluded that to counter potential lesbianism, a young female should be forced to perform feminine tasks, whether she liked them or not. "A girl should not only have knowledge of domestic activities but should engage in those activities until she feels secure in actually performing them and in supervising their performance," the study strongly recommended.

The attack on unmarried women who held professional positions — that is, the preponderance of female professionals — became merciless in the 1940s. In *Modern Woman: The Lost Sex*, for example, the sociologist Ferdinand Lundberg and the psychiatrist Marynia Farnham (a woman with a career who accused "careerist" women of penis envy!) recommended that unmarried female teachers be fired. Getting rid of them would serve a double purpose, for not only were unmarried women a bad influence on young girls, the authors proclaimed, but if those women could no longer support themselves, they would be forced to marry. Lundberg and Farnham associated the fight for women's rights with lesbianism in this immensely popular book, observing that "homosexual women are distorted as personalities and project their distortion onto society."

In the 1930s, mild innuendoes regarding an individual professional woman's inversion were not uncommon in the popular press, as demonstrated by an article about an Atlanta lawyer, Irma Von Nunes (who later became the first female prosecutor to participate in the German war crime trials in the 1940s). The writer observed that Von Nunes "wears her hair cut like a boy's, affects an almost masculine garb, and declares that marriage, like jail, is a good thing, but that she prefers to see other people in both." Yet though professional women were often suspected of lesbianism in these years and earlier, individuals in prominent positions were not publicly accused or fired over it. This changed after World War II, when vicious attacks on prominent "lesbians" were frequent (regardless of whether the women would have defined themselves by that term).

For example, in 1948, Marion Harron, a federal judge on the Board of Tax Appeals, who had been appointed twelve years earlier by Franklin Roosevelt, was challenged in her reappointment bid because her fellow judges had questioned her ethics and morality: her intimate relationship with the journalist Lorena Hickok (Eleanor Roosevelt's former lover) was widely suspected. As discussed earlier, the Framingham prison superintendent Miriam Van Waters also came under fire in that year and almost lost her position when she was suspected of being a lesbian. Two years later, Kathryn McHale, who had been nominated by President Truman to the Subversive Activities Control Board, came under attack. Truman was advised by Senator Patrick McCarran to withdraw McHale's name or it would be proved in public hearings that she was a lesbian.

These three women managed to survive because they denied the accusations vehemently and/or influential friends came to their defense. (Eleanor Roosevelt defended Van Waters, and the most powerful female lawyers and judges in America defended Harron.) But each of them had to suffer the terrors and shame of being under suspicion because of how they loved and with whom they lived. Indeed, any prominent professional woman who did not have proper heterosexual credentials risked coming under suspicion for what was now widely deemed to be both immoral and pathological. One wonders how many women who might have wanted a career were scared into obtaining heterosexual credentials by marrying because they felt they needed to disprove, perhaps to themselves as well as to others, their "deviance" and "masculinity complex." Once married, how many of them felt constrained to give up a career and tend to their conjugal and maternal duties?

This is not to say that women ceased working during these years. In 1950, women made up 29 percent of the labor force. By 1960, they made up 35 percent. Many women, married or not, worked simply because of economic need. For example, more than 40 percent of African-American women with small children held jobs. But few women of any race pursued serious (and well-paying) professions. Instead, they often took Avon Lady kinds of jobs — those that required little expenditure of time in training and were compatible with domestic duties. In 1950, only 14 percent of door-to-door sales-people were female. By 1960, women made up 60 percent of such workers. In 1950, 45 percent of bank tellers were female. By 1960, almost 70 percent were female.

Though women had been encouraged to fill in for men in many jobs that men had left behind during World War II, that encouragement was only for the duration. A clear demarcation between the sexes was prized more than ever in the aftermath of the war. Thus the post–World War II years marked the height of a new feminine mystique and a twentieth-century low point for women venturing away from the home or heterosexual domestic life. Women who could have been achievers, if their environment had been sympathetic to female achievement, were confirmed in diminished ambition, as is illustrated by Senator Adlai Stevenson's 1955 Commencement Day speech to Smith College graduates. "For my part I want merely to tell you young ladies," Stevenson said condescendingly, "that I think there is much you can do [regarding the world crisis] in the humble role of housewife — which, statistically, is what most of you are going to be whether you like the idea or not just now — and you'll like it!"

It is not coincidental that these postwar years, when women's retreat from extradomestic life was everywhere encouraged, also saw the height of lesbophobia in America. Why were successful professional women such as Harron, Van Waters, and McHale harassed? Surely it was in good part because they might be models for other women with professional ambitions at a time when the popular consensus was that females should have no interests beyond wifehood and motherhood. Harron, Van Waters, and McHale were remnants of those nineteenth-century pioneers who had wanted more than conventional family life and had made their own kinds of affectional and sexual arrangements to permit them to achieve their goals. Lesbians in the post–World War II years represented a threat to the domestic peace. What was truly intolerable about lesbians, as Frank Caprio admitted in his influential 1954 study, *Female Homosexuality,* was that in their pursuit of independence, they "deliberately renounce[d] marriage and motherhood," which, according to Caprio's mid-twentieth century wisdom, was a sign of their "flight from life's responsibilities." The lesbian refused to be a "real woman" — that blessed feminine creature who had survived the bad influences of the previous hundred years intact and continued to be at the exclusive service of her nuclear family.

The Bonding of the Bobbed-Hairs: Lena Madesin Phillips, Florence Allen, Pauli Murray

Joanne Meyerowitz has argued forcefully that Betty Friedan's depiction of an unequivocal feminine mystique in the postwar years and through the 1950s ignores "contradictions, ambivalence, and competing voices." She counters Friedan's work by pointing out that popular literature did not only and always glorify domesticity; in magazines directed at women, readers were often urged to greater participation in politics, and women's individual striving and nondomestic achievements were celebrated. Meyerowitz observes that African-American magazines were the most likely to highlight women's public success. (Her findings help confirm my conclusion that African-American women leaders were less touched than their white counterparts by the reaction that shooed females out of public life for a time.) But even in the primarily white media, some voices countered the feminine mystique, as Meyerowitz demonstrates. She shows, for example, that in 1953 the *Woman's Home Companion* named as the "six most successful women" in America those who had achieved national recognition in education, literature, the theater, medicine, human rights, and social betterment.

Thus, despite a feminine mystique that was very much alive, women with unusual talent, ambition, drive, and energy had some room to negotiate, even during the worst of times. Women were never again in the position of having to fight the major battles from scratch, because the Emily Blackwells and Carey Thomases had already done that for them, and the results of their early battles could not be entirely erased. Though many women did beat a retreat during those years — or they were socialized never to attempt the struggle in the first place — the path that had been marked for a future advance continued to be kept open by a few. Highly motivated women could get into colleges, graduate schools, medical schools, and law schools, and they could find a place in the professions. They could maneuver in the public world, even through the Depression, the postwar years when Rosie was sent home, the 1950s, and the prefeminist 1960s. But during most of the half-century between 1920 and 1970, those women who succeeded in nontraditional areas were isolated, made into a minority, and "queered" in a hostile (if sometimes ambivalent) milieu.

Yet who else but queers could or would carry on in significant numbers in the professions? Ronald Chester has observed in his oral history of female lawyers that most firms would not hire women in those years for jobs equivalent to those for which men were hired. A few female lawyers married male lawyers who could take them into practice, but most did not. Female lawyers were usually forced to find jobs outside the law (in areas such as real estate) or to build private practices. But as Chester declares about the women he studied who had independent practices, "None of them married. There was simply not enough household help and other support available to enable women who were not wealthy . . . to mix an active practice with marriage and children. Those who were wealthy would have little incentive to practice law under the conditions existing during that period and needed only to cement their positions as members of the establishment by marriage."

Female lawyers who were lesbians had neither the concerns nor the alternatives that Chester delineates. Their households did not distract from their work in the way that homes requiring a woman to serve as wife and mother did. They had great incentive to direct their energies toward a career that could give their lives meaning (which heterosexual women sought through motherhood). They could not cement their social standing through marriage. As unmarried women, even if they had independent financial resources, whatever position they attained as members of the establishment would generally depend on what they could achieve in a profession. As lesbians, they had to watch their backs, but they were otherwise much freer to struggle for a place in the legal profession than heterosexual women.

Because professional struggle could be very lonely, Lena Madesin Phillips, a lawyer during those years, understood the great need for a constituency of career women, and she devoted much of her life to creating one. When she entered the University of Kentucky Law School as the only woman in 1915, she met with protest from the male students, who feared that she would "retard the work," but her grades were among the highest in the class, and she received the LL.B., with honors, in record time. In 1919 she founded the National Federation of Business and Professional Women's Clubs, whose purpose was to bring together career women at all levels. One of her chief goals was to counter the dangerous notion on the part of some professional women that they had made it on their own and any women who really wanted to could do the same. She argued that the deep and still-existing discrimination against women would not be altered by "individualism" or "illusions of meritocracy."

Her concept had considerable appeal. At the first meeting she called, women from forty-eight different professions were present, lawyers being especially well represented. Within three years, there were 368 clubs in twenty-nine states. By 1931, there were 1100 clubs, and only two states had no branch of the NFBPWC. Significantly, at a time when about 90 percent of American women in the general population married, about half the members of NFBPWC were unmarried.

Through the National Federation of Business and Professional Women's Clubs, Phillips fought passionately for women's equality, even during the Depression, when female workers were widely vilified. In the 1930s her organization passed resolutions declaring, for example, "Because there can be no economic security for any class or group unless there is economic security for all, we demand for women employment, appointment, salaries and promotions on equal terms with men."

Why was Phillips so committed to professional options for women that would give them independence? Her reasons were surely personal at the start. She knew she had no wish ever to depend on a husband. As her autobiographical fragments suggest, her youth was like that of so many others who have been featured in this book. She recollected her childhood hatred of dolls and love of a hammer, saw, and lathe, her excitement about target shooting and boxing, her wish that she had been born a boy, and her terrible conflicts with her conventional and feminine mother. She called herself "queer" because she was entirely unlike girls of her age, though she had numerous crushes on other girls when she was a student at the Jessamine Female Institute.

She had been born Anna Lena Phillips, but at the age of eleven she dropped the name Anna and added Madesin, her spelling for the French *médecin*, which she aspired to become. The masculine-sounding Madesin remained her name of choice for the rest of her life. Madesin had absolutely no interest in the world her mother tried to push her into. She turned down more than half a dozen marriage proposals, claiming that they made "no impression" on her. She wished to pursue a career.

In the same year that she founded the National Federation of Business and Professional Women's Clubs, she met Marjory Lacey-Baker, an actress who was her life partner for more than three decades, until Madesin's death, in 1955. In autobiographical fragments, Madesin spoke quite openly of their relationship, admitting that she fell in love with "the most beautiful voice I ever heard" when she saw Marjory perform in a pageant. Even brief separations in the course of their years together were wrenching, as Marjory revealed, quoting *The Prophet*: "Love knows not its own depth until the hour of separation."

The relationship was central to Madesin's life — though she knew, just as her predecessors had, that she must equivocate when she performed as a spokeswoman for her cause. For example, arguing for women's professional opportunities during the 1920s, she disingenuously declared, "Of course, the ideal place for a woman is married and the [mother] of a large family," hastening to add the punchline, "but all of us can't do this and therefore we must not play seconds to men. We should be able to take our place at their sides, as equals." Perhaps by then she had already understood that there was danger in divulging too much about same-sex arrangements. Yet despite such public statements, in their personal lives Madesin and Maggie, as they were called by their friends, were a recognized couple in both national and international feminist circles.

They were not only lovers, they also fostered and polished each other. When they met, for example, Marjory had never heard of terms such as "rescind" or of "a motion being laid on the table." Madesin, who introduced her to feminism, also transformed her into a parliamentarian and eventually a women's rights leader. Marjory, a glamorous actress, had other qualities to share. For example, Phillips's biographer claims that Madesin, left to her own devices, would have been as oblivious of appearance as she had been in her tomboy days, but Marjory kept her looking stylish; Marjory's concern for Madesin's appearance may in fact have been prompted by a newspaper report on an NFBPWC convention, which described — with maliciousness like that which Anna Shaw had encountered decades before — a morning convocation of the NFBPWC leaders as a "Bobbed-Hair Breakfast."

Madesin led the bobbed-hair types internationally as well, establishing the International Federation of Business and Professional Women's Clubs in 1930 and serving as its president for almost twenty years. She also took seriously the heritage given to American women by Anthony, Shaw, and Catt. In the 1920s she was a Democratic National Convention delegate, and she was active in Roosevelt's 1932 campaign. (This was the same year that she and Marjory bought twelve acres of land in New Jersey and built Philsfolly, where they annually threw huge, all-women parties. Their friends included Mary Woolley and Judge Florence Allen.) In the years before World War II, Madesin organized regular radio broadcasts called "Women and World Peace," and she was engaged in rescuing victims of Nazi purges in Germany and Austria. After the war she was one of the few women to try to establish a political career, running (unsuccessfully) for lieutenant governor of Connecticut.

Her friend and fellow lawyer Florence Allen also recognized that in a world that was hostile to women's professional success, females could succeed only by acting as a constituency and noisily pushing for one another. With such a constituency, and with her own considerable talents, Allen got far in the judicial world at a time when most women were at home baking pies. The major mentors and supporters of Florence Allen's professional life were women who, like her, were unmarried and involved in relationships with other women.

In 1909, Allen entered the University of Chicago Law School. Miserable because of the hostility to women among the professors and male students, she interrupted her studies and went to New York, where she worked with Frances Kellor in the New York League for the Protection of Immigrants. Kellor and her life partner, Mary Dreier, remained influential supporters of Florence Allen in the years to come. There in New York, in friendlier company, Allen was able to resume her studies, and she received her law degree from New York University in 1913. Having family ties in Cleveland, however, she opted to leave New York and was admitted to the Ohio bar in 1914. Allen soon became one of Ohio's leading suffragists, arguing for women's right to vote before the Ohio Supreme Court. As Joan Organ shows in her dissertation on Florence Allen, Allen's rapid rise in the years that followed can be explained in good part by the network of unmarried female lawyers (most of them living in couples) who helped her advance from an elected common pleas judge in 1920 to the Ohio Supreme Court in 1922 and a federal judgeship in 1934.

It was Carrie Chapman Catt who first urged Molly Dewson, vice chair of the National Democratic Committee, to implore President Roosevelt to appoint Florence Allen as a federal judge. Dewson passed Catt's recommendation on to Eleanor Roosevelt, who got the trick done. FDR had no reason to regret the appointment. In 1937, Allen served as the judge in the suit by private utility companies that challenged the right of the Tennessee Valley Authority to build dams and distribute the electricity generated by the dams. Her ruling in favor of the TVA bolstered New Deal public works programs, and her decision was upheld by the Supreme Court, to FDR's satisfaction.

So popular was Allen as a federal judge that women such as Mary Woolley, Mary Dreier, and Molly Dewson thought it appropriate to urge FDR to appoint her to the Supreme Court. As much as he liked Allen, however, he could not be convinced that America was ready for a female justice in the highest court of the country. But even into the 1950s, Allen's supporters did not give up: a large group of female lawyers (most of them lesbians — since they apparently felt most deeply about the issue) continued to urge President Eisenhower to appoint Florence Allen as the first female Supreme Court justice. Joan Organ speculates that Eisenhower did not appoint her because by then she was known outside her own circle to be a lesbian.

Perhaps her lesbianism did keep her from the Supreme Court. Yet there is no question that it also made her various successes possible. Florence Allen may have been contemplating whether to commit herself to relationships with other women when she wrote in her diary in 1920 that she had discussed with a friend the subject of "Lesbianism and Marriage." Allen chose lesbianism. She lived with a fellow lawyer, Susan Rebhan, from 1922 until Rebhan's death, in 1935. She then lived with Mary Pierce until her own death, in 1966. She was helped in her career not only by a network of women but also, spectacularly, by Rebhan, who understood brilliantly how to organize supporters and manage campaigns. Susan Rebhan had her own career, first as executive secretary of the YWCA and later at the Department of Justice (a position that Molly Dewson found for her, as Allen's mate). But Rebhan was also Allen's greatest aid in her bid for election to the Ohio Supreme Court in 1922 and reelection in 1928. Thanks to both Rebhan's strategizing and the tens of thousands of women whom Rebhan organized into Florence Allen Clubs, Allen won by a huge margin.

Allen and Rebhan's social life was tied to their professional life.

Their closest friends were generally lesbian couples who worked in the law or in public policy positions. Together, they often visited Greenwich Village, where they spent time with Molly Dewson and her partner, Polly Porter, as well as with Eleanor Roosevelt's circle of lesbian friends, and they often corresponded with and visited Frances Kellor and Mary Dreier.

These women acknowledged each other's relationships with ease in the 1920s and '30s; however, in the years after World War II they were forced to become cognizant of the dangers of not being discreet about lesbianism. Allen's friend Judge Marion Harron, who had almost lost her federal judgeship in 1948 when it was suspected that she was a lesbian, was the one who led the continued campaign for Allen's appointment to the Supreme Court in the 1950s. As much as Allen was grateful that Harron encouraged and headed the group of women who persisted on her behalf, she was nevertheless worried about having a suspected lesbian push for the high advancement of another suspected lesbian. Sadly, she wrote to Judge Harron about her "concern . . . to protect You and Me," begging her to be "Anonymous" and to save them "both from possible embarrassment or worse." A fabulous network — a remnant of women who had carried the work of the pioneers into the mid-twentieth century — was thus effectively frightened and all but silenced.

The lesbians who continued to work in the public sphere during those worst of times were exceedingly covert — much more so than women who loved women had ever had to be in the past. Pauli Murray, an African-American lawyer, is an especially dramatic example of a lesbian who strongly believed that women must unite as a political force in order to take up the battle for women's advancement that had been squelched since the 1920s, but who was terrified that if her lesbianism were acknowledged, she would be unable to be of use in the necessary project of uniting large numbers of women.

Murray entered Howard Law School in 1941, one of two women in the student body. After graduating at the top of her class in 1943, she tried to get into Harvard Law School for an advanced law degree, but despite the support of her good friend Eleanor Roosevelt, Harvard refused to admit a woman. Murray finally went to Boalt Law School, in California. With a graduate degree, she returned to New York, where her circle of professional friends included many lesbians, such as the municipal court judge Dorothy Kenyon (life partner of the lawyer Dorothy Straus). Working with Kenyon, Murray helped write a successful brief for federal court which argued that jury service was one of the basic rights of citizenship and could not be abridged on the basis of gender. The federal decision had far-reaching effects in southern states such as Alabama, Mississippi, and South Carolina, where women had routinely been excluded from juries.

Murray's legal work centered on racial and sexual discrimination. In 1954, the NAACP utilized her writing on the separate-but-equal doctrine in its argument before the Supreme Court in the *Brown* v. *Board of Education* suit, which ended school segregation. In 1964, Murray wrote an influential memorandum about the Civil Rights Act, which was originally intended to make only racial and religious discrimination illegal. She argued persuasively in favor of an amendment that would outlaw sexual discrimination; African-American women were harmed by discrimination against their gender, she pointed out, as much as by discrimination against their race.

Because of her conviction that women must unite and promote women's interests, Murray was one of those responsible for the beginning of the largest feminist organization in America, the National Organization for Women (NOW). NOW was formed in 1966, when Murray went to Washington for a meeting of a subcommittee on women's civil and political rights of the Commission on the Status of Women. It was then that she, Betty Friedan (who was attending the meeting as a writer and observer), and a small group of other women convened in Friedan's hotel room to discuss the possibility of establishing a national nongovernmental organization for women's concerns. Murray's centrality to the formation of NOW makes Friedan's subsequent homophobic statements (she called lesbians in NOW "the lavender menace") particularly ironic.

In a 1983 interview, two years before her death at the age of seventy-four, Murray looked back on the pre-NOW years and observed that "feminists at that time tended to be self-supporting women who did not have to answer to anybody at home." What she could not explain, of course, was the extent to which "self-supporting women . . ." was a code phrase for "lesbians." Nor could she say that such women, herself included, did have intimate relationships, though not with men.

It is unfortunate that women like Murray had learned to regard such relationships not as contributing to the power that made their successes possible (compare Mary Woolley's "the greatest power in my life") but rather, as Murray's biographer, Sara Cable, has phrased it, as a sign of "sexual deviancy." Indeed, Murray spent seventeen tormented years, from 1937 to 1954, running to psychiatrists, psychologists, physicians, even committing herself for a time to a mental institution — all in order to be cured of her love for women and what she regarded as the "biological/medical disorder" that was manifested in her lack of femininity. As she wrote to a psychiatrist in 1940, she felt an "inability to integrate homosexual tendencies into a 'socially acceptable' pattern of living."

What had been the strength of previous generations became confusion to her. Yet Murray's avoidance of heterosexual domesticity, her emotional and erotic focus on other women, and her challenge to what was considered appropriate gender behavior permitted her to become a lawyer in the 1940s, a key feminist leader in the 1960s, and one of the first female priests in the Episcopal Church in the 1970s. In her multiple accomplishments as well as her emotional and erotic "masculinity," she was very much like Anna Shaw, though Shaw surely would not have sought a "cure" for what gave her her power.

The year 1964 saw not only the passage of the Civil Rights Act but also (far less important) the publication of *The Grapevine*, a book that purported to be "A Report on the Secret World of the Lesbian." The author of this "exposé," Jess Stearn, observed that lesbians "crowded" professions in engineering, the sciences, and publishing. His point was not, of course, that the lesbian lifestyle made it easier for women to achieve such goals. Rather, he made a woman's "active role in outside affairs" into a problem, connecting it — as well as what he called a "rise of homosexuality" — to the "unsettle[d] . . . moral climate" of the mid-twentieth century. In its hysteria, Stearn's approach to both love between women and women's extradomestic roles was representative of the attitudes that had been pervasive in America for the past few decades.

However, the passage of the Civil Rights Act prefigured a whole new era, signaling the start of an affirmation of diversity in America, which might begin to diminish not only racism but also the hysteria regarding same-sex love. By making gender discrimination illegal, the 1964 Civil Rights Act helped to herald a new mood with regard to women. Thus the space created many decades earlier by the lesbian pioneers — where women might assume what Stearn scoffingly called "active role[s] in outside affairs" — could finally begin to be inhabited by a broad spectrum of American women.

❧ 18 ❧

CONCLUSION: LEGACIES

They talked about their husbands or boyfriends with affection, but also with exasperation. The range of their goals and those of their partners did not fully coincide. "I'd love to marry someone if he could be another female student," said one. "That's what we [women law students] keep saying." They wished they could find men who had all the social and moral attributes of their female friends — . . . their purposes, their understanding of each other, their easy cooperation, and their good-natured humor about it all.

— Mona Harrington, *Women Lawyers*, 1994

Indifferent Legatees

ALL THE VARIOUS trajectories begun by the pioneers were for many years stalled. Proportionally fewer women enrolled in colleges, claimed places in professions, sought a voice in the public sphere. Most of the accomplishments of the pioneers became well-kept secrets, considered neither relevant nor significant enough to be recorded in history books. And yet American women could still benefit from what the pioneers had won for them. Though they may not have been aware of how they got those privileges, and may not have valued or wanted all of them, they still could vote, run for public office, go to college, get professional training, and have careers.

Even during the worst of the doldrum decades, abundant opportunities seemed to be open to women. Hints of those opportunities were locked into the twentieth-century American system of education, in which, with the exception of the hour each day when girls were directed into home economics classes while boys went to shop classes, girls could take the same course of study as boys, thanks to the struggles of the pioneers. Indeed, school reminded all girls that, in theory at least, they could make grand choices about who and what they would become. Why else were they offered chemistry and calculus and civics?

For most girls, however, the out-of-class social life promoted through coeducation delivered conflicting messages. Their peer group, taking a cue from the predominant culture, demanded that they become first and foremost proficient in the rituals of heterosexuality. As Dorothy Holland and Margaret Eisenhart have observed, females were soundly "educated in romance" through the unofficial instruction of school life. Such an education made requisite and all-consuming the joys and sorrows of dating and going steady. It led more directly to marriage and motherhood (where chemistry, calculus, and civics were of little use) than anywhere else. Hence, while a variety of choices seemed to be open to girls, the milieu generally dictated that they would be housewives.

Ironically, however, in spite of the feminine mystique, which taught girls that romance and then domesticity were what they should strive for, the postwar consumer sensibility that required washing machines, dishwashers, and televisions in every American home was simultaneously pulling large numbers of women out of the domestic setting. According to the 1960 census, females had made up 65 percent of the increase in the labor force during the 1950s. Of course, having a job was generally not tantamount to having a career; but because the ways that had been paved by the pioneers had not been completely obliterated, it was possible that a new and widespread women's work mentality might lead more women to real careers.

Nevertheless, if David Riesman, a prominent sociologist of the postwar years, was right in his depiction of Americans as being obsessed with approval, conformity, and "other-directedness" during that era, how could girls possibly dare to pursue serious careers in rebellion against the overwhelming demands of the feminine mystique?

My Inheritance

Yet even during the heyday of the feminine mystique, some girls and women did rebel, as I discovered when I was a teenager in the mid-1950s. It seems to me still that my own rebellion was intimately connected to my choice to be a lesbian.

What has been called in the twentieth century "sexual identity" is undoubtedly complex, and I cannot say that my professional dreams or my rebellion against the implications of womanhood as it was constructed in the 1950s can alone explain my lesbian life. But I believe those factors had tremendous weight. I recall, for example, my repulsion when I read articles like one that appeared in *Coronet* titled "I'd Hate to Be a Man," published in 1955, when I was fifteen years old. The writer began by insisting that

> I will even say it at five o'clock in the afternoon when my university-trained mind concentrates on bathing, dressing, soothing, entertaining and feeding my two tired children, and a load of diapers soaks in the tub, and three pies (two for the freezer) bubble in the oven. Fully aware that at this moment my well-groomed husband is leaving his air-conditioned, sound-proofed, carpeted office where he puts in a work day half as long as mine, I will brush my damp hair off my neck, lift my head and proclaim my preference for the status quo.

The author was so much happier and more fortunate than her husband, she concluded, because a man strains and strives and struggles and never gets the pleasure of "living intuitively," as a woman does. I understood by that time that if this was the normal woman, I was not normal.

But even when I was a child, the feminine mystique did not have the same impact on me as it apparently did on girls whose mothers had three pies bubbling in the oven. I saw that my mother, a working-class woman without a man to support her, had to work. Even my aunt, who was married to a butcher, had to work to make ends meet. Since I would have to work anyway, I believed, I might as well do work that I found fulfilling, that paid well, that carried more dignity with it than my mother's and aunt's garment-industry labors. As a twelve- or thirteen-year-old, I confided to the immigrant owner of the little house in which my mother and I rented a furnished room that I hoped someday to become a lawyer. "Poor girls don't become lawyers," she told me, albeit not unkindly. But I did not believe her, because somehow, perhaps through an occasional newspaper story about the legatees of the pioneers — a female doctor, a female lawyer, a councilwoman — perhaps through the system of equal education for which they had fought, I had gotten the notion that in America even poor girls could become anything they wanted to be.

The images in most postwar movies and magazines seemed to contradict that notion, to my confusion. Poor boys could become anything in America, they seemed to say, but girls became women, who were supposed to want to become wives and mothers. Yet my increasing teenage confusion fell away the night a young man whom I had thought of as a boyfriend told me he was gay and took me to a gay bar that was predominantly lesbian. There were undoubtedly many reasons, psychological and social, that I was excited by what I saw there. Not the least of them was that I understood that night how a girl might escape from the contradictions that led her to fantasize that she could become anything but convinced her by the time she was a teenager to believe that the only thing she should want to become was a housewife.

When I chanced into that lesbian subculture in 1956, the experience was like an epiphany. There one had to assume a lesbian identity, which did not exist among the women of the nineteenth century who have been the focus of this book. That identity brought with it the difficult baggage of understanding oneself to be "queer" (with which Addams and Catt never had to contend). Yet despite the potential pain of that status, I could see a potential of a different order: lesbians were exiles from the conventional world, but that state could be wonderfully freeing. We were liberated, as women with a heterosexual identity could not be, to pursue whatever roles we wished. We had no investment in following the rules of the feminine mystique, and we certainly had no desire for its rewards. If we identified with a group that was already considered outcast because of its gender behavior or sexual behavior, we did not have much to lose by pursuing "masculine" ambitions.

In fact, we had every incentive. Most of us who considered ourselves lesbians in the 1950s could not escape the enchantment with romance and erotic longing that has been so powerfully inculcated in the twentieth-century western female. We too had been "educated in romance." But because we chose other women as the objects of our desire, we, no less than women like Carey Thomas, were confirmed in our conviction that we would have to find a way to support ourselves. As I understood it, the more satisfying women were to me, the more important it was for me to prepare for a career, since I was forever closing the option — apparently so prized by other women — of being supported by a husband. Romantic love, which for most of the heterosexual women of my generation ended the possibility of accomplishing anything outside the home, was my greatest spur to accomplishment, just as it had been for Frances Kellor and Martha May Eliot.

Though in the 1950s I had probably never heard of any of the women discussed in this book except for Eleanor Roosevelt and perhaps Susan B. Anthony, they became my benefactors in a number of ways. It is impossible to imagine my life without them. Most wonderful in those years: because of them I could go to college. Though I was an odd girl among my peers for wanting a B.A., an M.A., and a Ph.D. instead of an Mrs., my hopes were not unrealistic. The pioneers had made a space for such odd girls, and Ozzie and Harriet and white picket fences could not obliterate that space. They had bestowed on me a right to higher education despite the fact that I was female.

And they had done even more. Unlike most of the pioneers, who came from affluent, socially elevated, white Anglo-Saxon Protestant households, I was the daughter of an unmarried Jewish immigrant from eastern Europe, a factory worker. Yet because of the pioneers' social conscience — their agitation for child labor laws and compulsory education; their union organizing for decent wages in the trades; their summer schools for working women — they had rescued me, generations later, from having to work as a child to help feed myself; they had made it possible for me to escape from the shop that held my mother for most of her life in America; they had encouraged my hopes and made them feasible.

Because I did not know of their existence, I thought I had invented the proverbial wheel through that epiphany in a lesbian bar that told me how I could construct my self so I could be who I wanted to be. I could not have imagined that without their labors, what I hoped for would have been impossible. Nor could I have imagined that the path I found was in important ways like the ones they had found generations earlier. What most of them had sought in the preceding century was the freedom to define themselves by meaningful work, an escape from what they regarded as the tedious prison of domesticity and other fetters that strapped womanhood, and personal joy through intimacies that would not make their other pursuits impossible. Those were my goals as well, and I procured them over the years with the rich coin of the inheritance they left me.

America's Inheritance

Though the feminine mystique had made it difficult for heterosexual women to enjoy the fruits of the pioneers' labors, the 1960s ushered in important changes that eventually resulted in great numbers of American women taking up where the pioneers had left off. The inclusion of sex in the 1964 Civil Rights Act, which was originally meant to address only the issues of race and religion, may have been triggered by the hostility of Howard Smith, a southern congressman who hoped through his "joke" to squelch passage of the act. Regardless, it helped to trigger new hopes, ambitions, and attitudes in a whole generation of American women, whose mothers had baked pies, had babies, and been Avon ladies and bank tellers. The feminist movement, which had been long out of fashion, was revitalized.

It was coincidental but not without impact that Americans were also changing stylistically in the 1960s, as hippies and radicals began to break the rigid dichotomy between masculinity and femininity with clothes and haircuts that were "unisex." Before World War II, only working-class lesbians dared to wear pants in public (generally only when going to a lesbian bar). During the war, female factory workers sometimes wore pants on the job. But in the postwar years, skirts alone were in fashion for heterosexual women, while lesbians of all classes, who had little interest in what was gender-appropriate, continued to prefer the comfort of pants, even if only in private. The unisex fad of the mid-1960s permitted heterosexual females to don pants once again.

The symbolism of the new style may have been more significant than it appeared to be. In earlier eras, the skirt was a symbol of woman's rootedness in "woman's place." Her clothes were an indisputable distinction from the purported transvestism of the female invert. In the 1960s, women's large-scale assumption of a comfortable fashion to which men had laid a claim made something of a dent in the bugaboo against female "masculinity" that had separated the heterosexual woman from the lesbian. Claiming the right to wear what had been a totem of masculinity must have helped free more women psychologically, as lesbians were free, to claim the right to "masculine" pursuits.

Official government acts and organized feminism helped much more, of course. Eleanor Roosevelt was once again behind important efforts. When only nine of John F. Kennedy's political appointees were women in 1960, she sent the new president a long list of women who were qualified to fill administrative slots. Kennedy did not make many more appointments of women, but at Eleanor Roosevelt's urging, he did establish the Commission on the Status of Women in 1961. Eleanor Roosevelt chaired it until her death, the following year. The commission took up the fight that had been waged by the lesbian pioneers decades before, seeking, for instance, equal-pay-for-equal-work legislation. Its power was enhanced by the 1964 Civil Rights Act.

In 1965, President Lyndon Johnson established the Equal Employment Opportunities Commission (EEOC) to implement Title VII of the Civil Rights Act. When the EEOC was slow in acting, a reawakened feminist consciousness goaded women to seek their own solutions; for example, they picketed the *New York Times* to demand that it cease classifying jobs on the basis of gender. In 1970, the Labor Department devised the first affirmative action guidelines, which were issued to all federal contractors and encouraged aggressive attempts to hire and promote women as well as racial minorities. In 1971, feminists formed the National Women's Political Caucus to take up the job that was largely laid down after the passage of the Nineteenth Amendment — to promote the genuine influence of women in politics.

The second wave of feminism was fueled by many women who were, to use terms that were current among lesbians in the 1970s feminist movement, "women-identified women" or "lesbian feminists." They often shared the ideals of the early pioneers, who had created virtually separatist institutions where women could work together. Those who were *radical* lesbian feminists even hoped to create a new variety of separatism and argued (as Jane Addams and others had) that what they sought was not the rights that men claimed but alternatives to a corrupt and brutal patriarchal system.

But lesbian feminists were different from their predecessors in that their lesbian identity was very conscious and consciously chosen. Though lesbianism continued to be pathologized and censured in many quarters in the 1970s, lesbian feminism in its many varieties captured the imagination of large numbers of women, who worked to define a new meaning of "lesbian." Love between women was an expressly political statement, lesbian feminists argued, striving to rescue it for all women from the associations with shame and sickness that had been widely imposed on same-sex love in the twentieth century. The widespread and conscious choice of lesbianism by those feminists who had had long personal histories of heterosexuality threw into further doubt the etiological explanations of female homosexuality as the result of hormonal imbalances or childhood trauma.

Perhaps the most valuable function of lesbian feminism, particularly its radical variety, was to act as the "bad cop" for feminist demands — as the Congressional Union suffragists had done in the early twentieth century. The militancy of the suffrage radicals undoubtedly hastened the vote for women by making more soft-spoken groups such as the National American Woman Suffrage Association appear totally reasonable. Similarly, lesbian feminist militants made far more dramatic demands than relatively conservative groups such as NOW, threatening in colorful language to smash patriarchy through various subversions. It was seldom acknowledged outside the movement that lesbian militancy made simple feminism look sweetly reasonable and deserving of reasonable response; but there can be no doubt that American women's rights and freedoms were enhanced synchronously with the rise of an angry, radical lesbian feminist movement.

Women who identified themselves as lesbians were also salient in the relatively conservative feminist organizations. In 1971, without the support of Betty Friedan (in whom the homophobia of the mid-century was firmly entrenched), NOW confirmed the importance of lesbian energy in its fight for women's rights: the national convention overwhelmingly passed a resolution declaring that NOW would cease to be evasive regarding lesbian issues and urging all feminists to fight against oppression of women who identified themselves as lesbians. Indeed, even Friedan felt constrained to admit publicly (though not until 1985) that some of the best and hardest-working women in NOW were in fact lesbians. (However, she hastened to add, quite missing the point, "For most women surely . . . [the demand for equal rights] had nothing whatsoever to do with lesbianism.")

Lesbians laboring side by side with heterosexual women effected terrific changes in the early years of the reawakened movement. In 1972, for example, their efforts finally resulted in the Senate's passage of the Equal Rights Amendment (which had been kept alive for the preceding half-century by a handful of women, many of them lesbians). Though the ERA failed to be ratified by the states, its passage in the Senate and the ratification campaigns all over America helped many women realize the extent to which inequality still needed to be addressed. Feminism thus gathered strength everywhere, appealing to diverse women and causing a variety of changes. For instance, the numbers of women in colleges and universities grew rapidly. By the early 1970s, women already made up 46 percent of the students, and by the end of the decade, female undergraduates outnumbered male undergraduates. Though most feminists were not aware of the extent to which their battles had been fought and won (and forgotten) generations earlier, they did not have to start from scratch — to fight the battle for education all over again, for example. They could turn their attention to other problems that limited women's choices, such as unwanted pregnancies, which were addressed in a 1973 Supreme Court ruling, *Roe* v. *Wade*, that guaranteed women the legal right to abortion.

Legal and moral victories did not guarantee linear progress, of course. Most women had been socialized by heterosexual mothers, who had been socialized to eschew the unfeminine. Pants notwithstanding, women who were invested in heterosexuality still often had a hard time assuming unfeminine responsibilities. And though as the decade progressed a broader spectrum of women defied the conventions of gender roles, other problems remained or were born. As one heterosexual woman wrote in a *Village Voice* article in the mid-1970s, she had enjoyed her career, but she gave it up after a year of "ignoring my feelings that the children and I wanted to be together more." She came to resent the "propaganda" from the feminist movement about "the dysfunctions of the nuclear family and the trap of motherhood. What was good for children seemed irrelevant," she complained with bitterness. In the years that followed, American women in ever-increasing numbers claimed a place in the world outside the nuclear family, but the ambivalence expressed in this article kept reappearing.

Heterosexual women's new conception of themselves as workers outside the home was helped in good part not only by the continuing consumer mentality, which capitalism made inevitable, but also by more serious market forces. The median income of young husbands (men from twenty-five to thirty-four) dropped 26 percent (adjusted for inflation) between 1972 and 1995. Married women's monetary contributions to the household were often vital merely to keep the family from poverty. And if they had to work, many female college graduates reasoned, it may as well be at serious and well-paying jobs. In addition, an escalating divorce rate reminded women that even if their husband's salary was high enough that they did not have to work, they could not assume that their marriage would last forever. By the end of the 1970s, about 50 percent of marriages were ending in divorce. Twenty-three percent of adults were living alone.

A combination of forces thus made a changing role for women inevitable. It is not surprising that by the time the 1970s were over, most of the old women's colleges were again headed by female presidents — or, indeed, that most of them had become coeducational, in the conviction that women's talents did not differ from those of men and that women were now strong enough to flourish outside of a single-sex institution. Major changes in college populations were taking place everywhere. Women of all colors and classes were now going to college, often becoming the first in their family to receive a higher education. Statistically, employment patterns were also improving among women of color. For example, while their working mothers had most frequently been employed as low-paid domestics, by 1980, 49.3 percent of African-American women were working in higher-paying white-color jobs, for which they had been qualified by better education.

Career aspirations rose dramatically among female students in the 1980s and continued to do so into the 1990s. Whereas most women in college during the preceding generations desired (or were convinced they must desire) only a home and husband, by the mid-1980s surveys showed that more than 80 percent of college women thought it was "very important to have a career," fewer than 19 percent could conceive of themselves as a "full-time homemaker," and only 25 percent would admit that it was "more important for a wife to support her husband's career than to have a career herself." Women's numbers in the learned professions expanded rapidly. For example, in 1963, less than 3 percent of law students were female. In 1980, the number had risen to over 33 percent, and in 1984 it was 40 percent. By the mid-1980s, more women than men were attending law school as full-time rather than part-time students. Female representation in law schools continued to increase in the 1990s. By 1996, women made up 44 percent of all students enrolled in American law schools. While in earlier eras it was all but impossible for women to establish a private practice, about a quarter of female lawyers were doing so by 1996.

Enough women of color became attorneys during the 1980s to warrant the establishment in 1989 of the Multicultural Women Attorneys Network when it was perceived that neither the American Bar Association's Commission on Women in the Profession nor its Commission on Opportunities for Minorities in the Profession adequately served the needs of female attorneys of color. Though women of all races have yet to receive full equity in the law profession, the number of women in upper-echelon law firms doubled between 1985 and 1991. The number of women who were made partners also rose steadily, so that, for example, in San Francisco women made up almost 18 percent of partners in major firms by 1995, and across the United States 26 percent of the partners in firms of more than a hundred lawyers were women. By 1997, women made up 30 percent of all full-time law professors.

The changes that have taken place in the medical profession are comparable. After generations in which only a tiny fraction of American physicians were women, their numbers grew with dizzying rapidity. In 1970, 7.5 percent of the medical profession was female. By the end of the 1980s, women made up 37 percent of the entering class in American medical schools. In 1994, women were 40 percent of all medical students around the country, and the entering class at the three top medical schools — Harvard, Yale, and Johns Hopkins — was more than 50 percent female. A 1996 study showed that young female physicians, hour for hour and patient for patient, were receiving the same salary as young male physicians. Female doctors are also looking to the future of the profession; for example, they mentor Girl Scouts with scientific aptitudes through the Physicians of Tomorrow program.

Women have made gains in the third learned profession, the ministry, as well. The African Methodist Episcopal Church, which

Rebecca Jackson left in the nineteenth century because it would not accept women in any position other than congregant, now has not only female pastors but also prominent spokeswomen who are pushing actively, as Pastor Vashti MacKenzie said in 1995, to "go beyond equal access to the ministry to leadership positions." Reformed and then Conservative Judaism began opening the rabbinate to women in the mid-1970s. By 1996, a third of all non-Orthodox rabbinical candidates were women.

In the Episcopal Church, women were not even permitted to become deacons until 1970. In 1974, in response to attitudinal changes wrought by the second wave of feminism, three retired bishops ordained eleven female deacons as priests, though most Episcopal bishops protested. Their protests were formally rebuffed when, in 1977, the church's General Convention agreed that women could be ordained to the priesthood. The lawyer Pauli Murray became the first African-American woman to be ordained at this time. Dioceses throughout America began ordinations. There were enough female priests by 1988 for them to agitate for the appointment of a female bishop. Barbara Harris, an African American who had been a prison chaplain and who was outspoken in her support of lesbian and gay rights, became the first female bishop of the Episcopal Church in 1989. By the end of 1997, there were eight female Episcopal bishops in America. In the United Methodist and the Evangelical Lutheran churches, women were also appointed as bishops in the 1990s.

The unfinished battles of the pioneering suffragists have also been taken up again, thanks to the second wave of feminism. By the 1980s, the renewed potential of the women's vote was perceived at the top. Anticipating the 1984 election, White House aides began to worry about a "gender gap." President Reagan won reelection despite polls that showed his ratings were positive among only 38 percent of female voters, but women were gradually learning how to organize for their candidates and make their wishes known. They worked on a statewide level first; for example, the first Hispanic woman ever to serve in a high-level legislative body, Gloria Molina, who was elected to the California congress in 1982, credited her victory to women — first to a small support group who convened with the specific goal of electing Hispanic women to office, and then "to all women across the state of California." Around the country, 1666 women ran for state legislatures in the early 1980s, and more than 50 percent of them won.

By the 1990s, women were even better organized and more powerful. They were indisputably responsible for reelecting Bill Clinton in 1996; while men split their vote evenly between Clinton and Dole, women voted for Clinton by a 55–37 margin (at one point, polls indicated that Clinton's lead among women was as high as 30 percent). Women had perceived that his policies were more sympathetic to their concerns than Dole's were. But as powerful as the women's vote became, it was in the pursuit of high political offices for themselves that women's gains were most impressive in the 1990s.

Success in achieving political office in significant numbers had been slow in coming, perhaps because it had been so difficult not only for the public to see women in roles of "masculine" leadership, but also because it was not easy for women to assume such roles. The danger that they would be called lesbian just for vying for office long remained. In 1986, after Barbara Mikulski of Maryland won more than 50 percent of the primary vote in a three-way race against two strong Democrats, she had to overcome lesbian-baiting in order to defeat her Republican opponent. In her election to the U.S. Senate, Mikulski became the first female Democrat who did not follow a husband into that office. By remaining carefully closeted, Congresswoman Barbara Jordan assured that lesbian-baiting would not be an issue in her election (though reputedly she was less closeted in private). Jordan was the first African-American woman from the South to be elected to the House of Representatives, where she served from 1972 until she retired in 1979. It was not until her death, in 1996, that she was outed, by an obituary in the *Houston Chronicle* that identified Nancy Earl as her "longtime companion"; they had been coupled for more than twenty-five years.

In 1992, women finally began to achieve positions of political leadership on a significant scale. The stellar showing in that year by many female candidates may have been the result of American women's annoyance as they watched on television the all-male 1991 Senate Judiciary Committee confirmation hearings on Clarence Thomas's nomination to the Supreme Court. Thomas was confirmed despite credible accusations by the lawyer and law professor Anita Hill that he had sexually harassed her. In the following year, so many women declared their political candidacy that 1992 came to be dubbed the "Year of the Woman."

As a result of the 1992 election, forty-eight women were serving in the House of Representatives, double the previous number. After a special 1993 election that took Kay Bailey Hutchinson to the Senate, the number of female senators reached an all-time high of seven, including the first African-American woman, Carol Moseley-Braun. Women of color had gained eight additional seats in Congress, for a total of fourteen. Their number now included a Chicana (from Los Angeles) and a Puerto Rican woman (from New York), as well as the first African-American congresswomen to be elected in Georgia and North Carolina. Women also received cabinet appointments in unprecedented numbers, including the African Americans Hazel O'Leary, who became secretary of energy, and Dr. Joycelyn Elders, who became surgeon general of the United States. The first woman on the Supreme Court, Sandra Day O'Connor (who had been appointed by President Reagan), was now joined by a second, Ruth Bader Ginsburg. In state executive offices as well as in state legislatures, women also enjoyed unprecedented successes in 1992, winning about 20 percent of the seats in each.

Though women did not fare spectacularly well in the 1994 elections, in 1996 their numbers in public office rose again. Women made up 22 percent of state legislators. In the forty-two states that had lieutenant governors, eighteen of those positions were held by women. In the U.S. Congress, there were now fifty female representatives and nine female senators. At the beginning of 1998, sixteen women were expected to declare their candidacy for governor.

Women had a number of remarkable successes in the 1998 election. In Arizona, for example, the top five elected positions — governor, secretary of state, attorney general, treasurer, and superintendent of public instruction — all went to women. On a national level, the first openly lesbian candidate, Tammy Baldwin, was elected to Congress.

Political women in the 1990s often brought to their candidacy and then to their office social issues of the kind that many of the suffragists had claimed would be vital to women if they could have a place in politics: women's rights, unemployment, child care, education. Indeed, political analysts of the 1992 election insisted that "a woman [candidate] who calls for educational reform or for more stringent enforcement of gender discrimination laws will be taken more seriously than a woman who calls for the death penalty or more aggressive monitoring of terrorist groups." However, with President Clinton's appointment of Janet Reno as attorney general and Madeline Albright as secretary of state, even those remaining stereotypes of political women have been significantly dented.

The extent to which women have "arrived" politically is dramatized in complaints that they have not yet gone far enough. For example, a 1997 article in the *National Law Journal*, "Still a Guy's Game," complained that while female staffers make up 39 percent (!) of Clinton's administration, "most . . . members are men," and that while staff women are respected, they are not consulted with enough regularity. A front-page article in the *New York Times* in 1998 argued that three of the women who were elected to the Senate in 1992 were facing doubtful reelections. Yet, as the writer admitted, two of those three Democrats were being challenged by Republican *women*, who were receiving the support of major Republican leaders such as Robert Dole. Clearly, the incumbents were in danger not because they were women but because other female politicians felt that they had enough experience at the state level to run for national office. Though Republicans had been slow to recognize the potential of women, by 1998 even that had changed. In Michigan, for example, three Republican women had their party's support in running for the ten congressional seats that

Democrats held, and of the five women who now head the state government in Arizona, four are Republican.

Attempts to depict women's role in politics (and the professions as well) as a flash in the pan have been regular. But over the past two decades, American women have resumed the progress that was put on hold for a half-century, taking up where the lesbian pioneers left off. The ambitions of the pioneers have spread to large numbers of heterosexual women. It would appear that too much has now changed to eradicate women's progress.

The Uses of History

And yet . . . progress seemed ineradicable after the passage of the Nineteenth Amendment also, and then women decided or were convinced that they were tired of trying to have it all and went home. A 1933 *New York Times Magazine* article proclaimed that "The College Girl Puts Marriage First" and quoted young women who said that "most of us would chuck everything for marriage" and "to work is impossible if you want to bring up children properly." A 1980 article in the *New York Times* sounded like a reprint. "Many Young Women Now Say They'd Pick Family over Career," the writer announced. The following week a *Boston Globe* article corroborated the sentiment, citing a poll of three thousand college students in which 77 percent of the women and 84 percent of the men said they believed that mothers of small children should not work.

Such opinions obviously did not affect what women did in reality over the next years. By 1998, 46 percent of the American workforce was female. That is, most women of working age were gainfully employed. However, the more successful women became outside the home in the 1980s and 1990s, the louder were the voices that told them they didn't really want such success, the price was too high. Popular magazines are now inundated with articles about dual-income families who have decided that "experiencing the formative years of our children's development, giving quality time (not just a rationalized concept of quality time) were experiences my wife needed to fill her joy quotient. Trading this for her talents at designing spreadsheets just wasn't worth the money." "Stay-at-Home Moms Are Fashionable Again in Many Communities," headlines of the 1990s proclaim, dubbing the nonworking mother "the newest status symbol," which few families who want to maintain middle-class status can afford but presumably all should want.

Women who have joyously given up high-powered positions and six-figure salaries to labor in their own kitchens and nurseries are frequent guests on television talk shows. They declare that staying home to tend a baby is "new and different and delicious." Books with titles such as *When Work Doesn't Work Anymore: Women, Work and Identity* and *Domestic Tranquility: A Brief Against Feminism* are cropping up with increasing frequency on bookstore shelves. The signs would be alarming even if there had not been very similar signs seventy years ago that put a virtual end to women's extradomestic strivings.

Are the generations of women on a roller coaster? Perhaps when women are powerless and dependent, many long for power and independence, and finally they (or their daughters or granddaughters) unite in a movement in order to achieve them. But is it inevitable that once achieved, power and independence feel burdensome, and most women who are not interested in living as lesbians can hardly wait to shed themselves of those responsibilities, as well as of the movement that loaded them on their shoulders? For her 1995 book, *Broken Patterns,* Anita Harris interviewed dozens of women (all but one expressly heterosexual) in medicine, law, science, and corporate management. She concluded that while her interviewees had had "a tremendous drive" to succeed in the predominantly male world outside the home, nevertheless they felt "deep ambivalence about that success," particularly since "success in the workplace often conflicted with the definitions of femininity they had internalized — based on their mother's examples — as children."

Do the pioneers who led lesbian lives have anything to teach heterosexual women who are today enjoying — or not enjoying, as the case may be — the fruits of lesbian labors? There is surely one lesson to be learned in the pioneers' lack of interest in traditional femininity. It is tautological that women who cannot divest themselves of feminine socialization are doomed to ambivalence about their success in fields that men have historically monopolized. It is not surprising that contemporary women who have been especially comfortable in nontraditional positions have childhood histories that would have landed them among the inverts if the nineteenth-century sexologists had been watching. For example, a study of key female leaders in *Fortune* 500 companies showed that 80 percent of them had loved sports when young and had considered themselves tomboys. Those very qualities that the sexologists regarded as pathological (and that characterized almost every one of the pioneers) may be crucial not only for a woman's professional success but also for her unambivalent pleasure in that success.

Even more important, heterosexual professional couples might do well to ponder the domestic arrangements of the lesbian pioneers. Recent writers challenge the sociologist Arlie Hochschild's 1989 assertion that working women exhaust themselves because after a full day at the office they do a second shift at home, since their husbands refuse to participate in domestic tasks. James Levine and Todd Pittinsky, for example, argue in their 1997 book, *Working Fathers,* that many men are now sharing fully in the second shift. However, as they show, men who are willing to assume domestic responsibilities still feel constrained to be closeted about it. They "live in fear [that employers] might question your loyalty if you say you're trying to figure out ways to balance work and family." Their worried perceptions about others' rigid gender expectations surely render the new domestic equality, to whatever extent it exists, fragile.

There was good reason, as Tracy Mygatt observed in 1966, that she and Frances Witherspoon, with whom she had had a more than fifty-year relationship, were "a model for married friends." The pioneering women generally had functional home lives. Many of them, such as Emily Blackwell and Frieda Miller, even raised children. They were able to do it all because their mates — professional women like themselves — were usually as fully involved in the operations of the home as they were. Gender worries rarely prevented a partner who had professional responsibilities from also taking half the responsibility for running the household.

Postmodernist lesbian scholars have claimed to wish to avoid constructions of lesbianism that might end in a futile and misguided search for historical foremothers. Such constructions, as one scholar states, reify the idea of a "natural or an authentic lesbian identity, by which we can measure and justify our existence." Indeed, a search for a single "authentic lesbian identity" is surely an exercise in absurdity. What connections can we find between the women who formed domestic partnerships with other women in the late nineteenth century and the "queer grrrl" of the late twentieth century? Yet it has seemed to me to be important to establish the facts about certain women whose roles in changing America for the better ought to be remembered — and whom women who call themselves lesbians today can, if they wish, regard as foremothers by virtue of their domestic arrangements and affections.

The recording and relating of history is always a matter of angle of vision and is seldom without some degree of chauvinism. But lesbian history has been nonexistent until quite recently. Generations of women who identified themselves as lesbians were never dignified with any history whatsoever, because it was virtually impossible to attempt to record it. Through much of the twentieth century, an admission of interest in homosexuality (apart from its legal or medical connections) was tantamount to the very perilous admission of being homosexual. Thus, even lesbians who sought them desperately had few heroes, no lessons of the past, little inheritance of wisdom that was left to us by our elders. It was long a secret that there even *were* elders whose legacies to women were the vote, higher education, entrance into the professions — whose legacy to America was a social conscience, and who can be claimed as lesbians' heroes as well as America's heroes.

Such a preservation of lesbian history is important not simply to set the record straight (or, in this case, unstraight) but also to provide for those lesbians who hunger for what Van Wyck Brooks has called (in another context) a "usable past." What are the uses of history? History is never simply a collocation of objective facts. History can provide something vital to any people who bond in a meaningful group. Among its uses are its possibilities for presenting role models to the young, giving people reasons for pride in the identities they have chosen, teaching lessons about the past that we may be able to incorporate in the present and use to plan the future.

NOTES

INDEX

NOTES

The following abbreviations are used to denote libraries, archives, and special collections.

APS   American Philosophical Society
AUHS Allegheny University of the Health Sciences Archives and Special Collections
BL   Bancroft Library, University of California at Berkeley
BMC   Bryn Mawr College Archives
CU   Cornell University Rare and Manuscript Collections
HL   Huntington Library
LC   Library of Congress
MHC   Mount Holyoke College Archives and Special Collections
NHA   Nantucket Historical Association
SC   Sophia Smith Collection at Smith College
SCPC Swarthmore College Library, Peace Collection
SL   Schlesinger Library, Radcliffe College
VC   Vassar College Special Collections
WC   Wellesley College Archives

I. INTRODUCTION

The sexologists' roles as creators and/or observers of lesbian identity have been the subject of scholarly debate for some time. See my article "The Morbidification of Love Between Women by Nineteenth-Century Sexologists," *Journal of Homosexuality* 4, no. 1 (Fall 1978): 73–90; George Chauncey, "From Female Inversion to Homosexuality: The Changing Medical Conceptualization of 'Deviance,'" *Salmagundi* (Fall/Winter 1983): 58–59, 114–46; Carroll Smith-Rosenberg, "The New Woman as Androgyne: Social Disorder and the

Gender Crisis, 1870–1936," in *Disorderly Conduct: Visions of Gender in Victorian America* (New York: Knopf, 1985); Esther Newton, "The Mythic Mannish Lesbian: Radclyffe Hall and the New Woman," in Martin Duberman, Martha Vicinus, and George Chauncey, eds., *Hidden from History: Reclaiming the Lesbian and Gay Past* (New York: New American Library, 1989); and Lisa Duggan, "The Trials of Alice Mitchell: Sensationalism, Sexology, and the Lesbian Subject in Turn-of-the-Century America," *Signs* (Summer 1993): 791–813.

In *Surpassing the Love of Men: Romantic Friendship and Love Between Women from the Renaissance to the Present* (New York: Morrow, 1981), I discuss the historical development of romantic friendship and Boston marriage.

PAGE

1 **"Not-men"**: Katherine Anne Porter, "Gertrude Stein: A Self-Portrait," *Harper's* 195 (Dec. 1947), pp. 519–27.

2 **Academic postmodernists**: Diana Fuss, *Essentially Speaking: Feminism, Nature, and Difference* (New York: Routledge, 1989), p. 100.

3 **"passionate fictions"**: Teresa de Lauretis, *The Practice of Love: Lesbian Sexuality and Perverse Desire* (Bloomington: Indiana University Press, 1994), p. xiv.

4 **"modern movement"**: Havelock Ellis, *Studies in the Psychology of Sex: Sexual Inversion* (Philadelphia: F. A. Davis, 1902), pp. 99–100. See also Edward Carpenter, *Love's Coming of Age* (London: Mitchell Kennerley, 1911), p. 72: "The women of the new movement are naturally drawn from those [who] . . . do not altogether represent their sex; some are rather mannish in temperament; some are 'homogenic,' that is, inclined to attachment of their own rather than the opposite sex."

7 **"Two business women"**: Crystal Eastman, "Now We Can Begin" (1920), in Blanche Cook Wiesen, ed., *Toward the Great Change: Crystal Eastman on Feminism, Militarism, and Revolution* (New York: Garland, 1976).
   "refusing to be yoked": Charlotte Perkins Gilman, "The Passing of Matrimony," *Harper's Bazaar* 40 (June 1906), pp. 495–98.

8 **"I am so glad"**: Susan B. Anthony to Anna Dickinson, Feb. 22, 1870, reel 6, Anna Dickinson Papers, LC.
   It is not surprising: Statistics analyzed in Andrew Sinclair, *The Better Half: The Emancipation of the American Woman* (New York: Harper and Row, 1965), p. 144.
   "and then withdrew": Aileen Kraditor, *The Idea of the Woman Suffrage Movement* (New York: Columbia University Press, 1965), p. 284.

10 **Judith Butler**: See Judith Butler, *Gender Trouble: Feminism and the Subversion of Identity* (New York: Routledge, 1990).

PAGE

"**as changeable as dress**": Smith-Rosenberg, "New Woman as Androgyne," p. 289.

Though few: The phrase "mother-heart" is from a speech by Anna Shaw; see chapter 6.

11 "**the rocking horse**": Richard von Krafft-Ebing, *Psychopathia Sexualis: With Especial Reference to the Antipathetic Sexual Instinct* (1886; rpt. Brooklyn: Physicians and Surgeons Book Co., 1908), pp. 334–35.

"**sacrificed to clean clothes**": Susan B. Anthony, "The True Woman," speech, 1857, reel 1 (microfilmed pages titled "Speeches," pp. 56–57), Susan B. Anthony Papers, SL.

2. THE LOVES AND LIVING ARRANGEMENTS OF NINETEENTH-CENTURY SUFFRAGE LEADERS

For this chapter I consulted the papers of Mary Grew, Susan B. Anthony, Elizabeth Cady Stanton, Anna Howard Shaw, Lucy Anthony, Alice Stone Blackwell, and Kitty Barry Blackwell, which can be found in the collections noted below. France Willard's papers are available on microfilm through the Woman's Christian Temperance Union in Evanston, Illinois.

In addition, the works that follow have been especially useful. Lee Chambers-Schiller, *Liberty, A Better Husband: Single Women in America, the Generations of 1780–1840* (New Haven: Yale University Press, 1984), discusses the great extent to which nineteenth-century social movements were fueled by single women who did not have domestic distractions. Obviously, this is not to say that married women contributed nothing to women's advancement. For a discussion of heterosexual married partnerships that advanced women's rights, see Barbara Kuhn Campbell, *The Liberated Woman of 1914: Prominent Women in the Progressive Era* (Ann Arbor: UMI Research Press, 1979), especially the chapter "Marriage." Sara M. Evans, *Born for Liberty: A History of Women in America* (New York: Free Press, 1989), p. 120ff., which presents a good discussion of Susan B. Anthony and Elizabeth Cady Stanton's refusal to support the Fifteenth Amendment and the consequent split with Lucy Stone, as well as a discussion of Anthony's support of African-American woman suffragists. Ellen DuBois, "The Radicalism of the Woman Suffrage Movement: Notes Toward the Reconstruction of Nineteenth-Century Feminism," *Feminist Studies* 3, no. 1–2 (Fall 1975): 63–71, delineates the unpopularity of the movement among most American women in the nineteenth century.

Two important biographies that deal with Frances Willard's role in the suffrage movement are Ruth Bordin, *Frances Willard: A Biography* (Chapel Hill: University of North Carolina Press, 1986), and Mary Earhart, *Frances Willard: From Prayer to Politics* (Chicago: University of Chicago Press, 1944), especially chapter 10.

PAGE

15 **"I shall go"**: Susan B. Anthony to Isabel Howland, Aug. 28, 1894, ms. group 78, box 1, Isabel Howland Papers, SC.

As Carrie: Mary Gray Peck, *Carrie Chapman Catt: A Biography* (New York: H. W. Wilson, 1944), p. 5.

16 **"Dear Anna"**: Susan B. Anthony to Anna Dickinson, n.d., reel 6, Anna Dickinson Papers, LC.

"as women": Quoted in Carrie Chapman Catt and Nettie Rogers Shuler, *Woman Suffrage and Politics: The Inner Story of the Suffrage Movement* (New York: Scribner's, 1923), p. 275.

17 **"unsexed"**: That "unsexed" was sometimes used to signify "lesbian" is suggested in an article in a Washington, D.C., newspaper, *The Capitol*, on Lillie Duer, who killed Ella Hearn, "her 'bosom' companion." The author comments: "The peculiar features in this remarkable history . . . present the most morbid, hideous phase of the unnatural female — of unsexed woman — ever recorded in tangible history"; "The Morbid, Unsexed Woman," June 22, 1879, vol. 9, p. 17, col. 1.

Sojourner Truth: Saunders Redding, "Sojourner Truth," in Edward James and Janet Wilson James, eds., *Notable American Women*, vol. 3 (Cambridge: Harvard University Press, 1971), p. 480

"a gathering": Quoted in Catt and Shuler, *Woman Suffrage*, p. 27.

18 **"It is a settled"**: Quoted in Theodore Tilton, "Mrs. Elizabeth Cady Stanton," in James Parton et al., *Eminent Women of the Age* (1868; rpt. New York: Arno Press, 1974).

19 **"Papa . . . has been blaming"**: Alice Stone Blackwell to Sarah Blackwell, Dec. 6, 1893, folder 689, Blackwell Family Papers, SL.

"I think any female": Susan B. Anthony, diary, Feb. 6, 1838, Susan B. Anthony Papers, SL. See also June 10 and 11, 1839.

"Not another baby": Susan B. Anthony to Antoinette Brown Blackwell, Apr. 22, 1858, Anthony Papers. Anthony urged Stanton too to stop procreating; see Ellen DuBois, ed., *Elizabeth Cady Stanton/Susan B. Anthony: Correspondence, Writing, Speeches* (New York: Schocken, 1981), p. 61.

"would bite out": Ida B. Wells, *Crusade for Justice: The Autobiography of Ida B. Wells*, ed. Alfreda Duster (Chicago: University of Chicago Press, 1970), pp. 254–55.

20 **"Your words"**: Mary Grew to Isabel Howland, Apr. 27, 1892, Howland Papers.

21 **"affection passing"**: John White Chadwick, *A Life for Liberty: Anti-Slavery and Other Letters of Sallie Holley* (1899; rpt. New York: Negro Universities Press, 1969), p. 7.

"When I say": Mary Grew to William Lloyd Garrison II, June 20, 1866, Garrison Family Papers, SC.

22 **"The largesse"**: Emily Howland to Mary Grew, Aug. 24, 1893, quoted in Chambers-Schiller, *Liberty*, p. 210.

23 **"sit up"**: Quoted in Ida Husted Harper, *The Life and Work of Susan B. Anthony*, vol. 3 (1898; rpt. Salem, N.H.: Ayer, 1983), p. 1263.

"So closely interwoven": Quoted in Katherine Anthony, *Susan B. Anthony: Her Personal History and Her Era* (New York: Russell and Russell, 1954). Stanton appears to have had romantic feelings for other women as well, including Anna Dickinson; Anthony teasingly told Dickinson that Stanton confessed that Dickinson's "charming face" presented itself to her "whenever she wakes at night — I have never seen her so wholly captivated with anyone — says Anna is a great deal more wonderful even in private than in public — said she could do nothing but look, *gaze her* in the face & admire & listen"; Susan B. Anthony to Anna Dickinson, June 19, 1867, reel 6, Dickinson Papers.

"Do you believe": Quoted in Evans, *Born for Liberty*, p. 120.

24 **Susan B. Anthony became**: Alma Lutz, "Susan B. Anthony," in James and James, *Notable American Women*, vol. 1, p. 54.

"merchantable property": Susan B. Anthony, "The True Woman," reel 1, Anthony Papers.

"a grim Old Gal": Quoted in Harper, *Life and Work*, vol. 1, p. 397.

25 **Anthony argued**: Susan B. Anthony, "The New Century's Manly Woman," *Leslie's Weekly*, Mar. 3, 1900, clipping, Anthony Papers.

"the outpourings": Elizabeth Cady Stanton, Susan B. Anthony, and Matilda Joslyn Gage, *The History of Woman Suffrage*, vol. 1 (New York: Fowler and Wells, 1881–1922), p. 678.

"I have an irresistible": Louise Brockett to Anna Dickinson, Mar. 8, 1865, reel 6, Dickinson Papers.

"Sweet Anna": Laura Bullard to Anna Dickinson, June 6 and June 8, 1872, ibid.

"I want to see": Quoted in Giraud Chester, *Embattled Maiden: The Life of Anna Dickinson* (New York: Putnam, 1951), p. 41.

26 **"speak right out"**: Susan B. Anthony to Anna Dickinson, Oct. 23, 1866; Dec. 6, 1866; Aug. 15, 1867; Nov. 28, 1867; all in reel 6, Dickinson Papers.

26 **"My Dear Chicky"**: Ibid., Feb. 19, 1868; Mar. 18, 1868; Mar. 31, 1868; Nov. [?] 25, 1868; Nov. 11, 1869.

In some: See, for example, Susan B. Anthony to Anna Dickinson, n.d., addressed to "Lovey," in which she refers to her "mother's yearning" for Dickinson; ibid.

27 **"made my life-work"**: Quoted in Ida Husted Harper, ms. of Shaw biography, reel 14 (p. 144), Anna Howard Shaw and Lucy Elmina Anthony Papers, Mary Earhart Dillon Collection, SL.

"I have *very weak*": Susan B. Anthony to Elizabeth Cady Stanton, Sept. 27, 1857, container 1, Elizabeth Cady Stanton Papers, LC.

"that I wanted": Susan B. Anthony to Jessie Anthony, Mar. 17, 1897, in Anthony Family Papers, Susan B. Anthony Collection, AF 18, HL.

"I will try": Susan B. Anthony to Lucy Anthony, Dec. 10, 1897, reel 2, Anthony Papers, SL.

28 **"I am so thankful"**: Anna Howard Shaw, diary, Sept. 30, 1893, series x, reel 17, Mary Earhart Dillon Collection, SL.

"call in Chicago": Susan B. Anthony to Jessie Anthony, Mar. 17, 1895, AF 18, box 1, Anthony Family Papers.

"I'm sure": *San Francisco Chronicle* interview, June 28, 1896, clipping, Anthony Papers. For other mentions of Emily Gross's travel with Susan B. Anthony to the West Coast, see Susan B. Anthony to Anna Dann, June 2, 1905, AF 82, and Susan B. Anthony to Maud Koehler, July 14, 1905, AF 27, Anthony Family Papers. This travel is also mentioned in series x, reel 14 (Harper ms., p. 131), Shaw and Anthony Papers. Anthony's visits to Gross in Chicago are mentioned in Anna Howard Shaw's diary, March 9 and March 26, 1901, reel 15, ibid. Their travel to Europe is mentioned in Susan B. Anthony to Cherril Wells, May 6, 1899, CC1–48, and Susan B. Anthony to Clara Colby, July 24, 1899, CC3–96, HL. Also see references to Gross and her travels with Anthony in reel 16, Dillon Collection, SL: Susan B. Anthony to Anna Howard Shaw, May 26, 1897, and Harper, *Life and Work*, vol. 3, pp. 1120, 1132, 1145, 1179, 1230, 1366, 1373.

29 **"the great Susan B."**: Katherine Anthony to Mr. Baker, Apr. 10, 1952, reel 2, Anthony Papers.

"If you could": Susan B. Anthony to Anna O., Oct. 14, 1894, ibid.

"splendid as ever": Susan B. Anthony to Jessie Anthony, Mar. 17, 1895, AF 18, box 1, Anthony Family Papers. For a discussion of the lesbian circles around Harriet Hosmer, see Faderman, *Surpassing the Love of Men*, p. 219ff.

30 **"Times are very hard"**: Lydia A. C. Ward to Anna Howard Shaw, Mar. 25 [1906], reel 16, Anna Howard Shaw Papers, Dillon Collection, SL.

"a long talk": Anna Howard Shaw, diary, Mar. 8, 1919, reel 17, ibid.

"My Dear girls": Susan B. Anthony to Isabel Howland and Harriet May Mills, Nov. 23, 1892; June [?] 9, 1894; June 11, 1894; ms. group 78, box 1, folder 4, Howland Papers.

Suffragism had long: See DuBois, "Radicalism."

32 **"No girl"**: Frances Willard, *Glimpses of Fifty Years: The Autobiography of an American Woman* (Chicago: H. J. Smith, 1889), p. 69.

"I never hung": Oct. 2, 1860; quoted in ibid., pp. 149–50.

33 **"never . . . abrupt"**: *Boston Times-Democrat*, clipping, Willard scrapbook 57, p. 63, WCTU series, reel 39, WCTU Library.

"Womanliness first": Quoted in Evans, *Born for Liberty*, p. 127.

"lovely Boston girl": Willard, *Glimpses*, pp. 641–42. Although Willard continued to live with the devoted Anna Gordon for the rest of her life, their relationship became a ménage à trois from 1892 to 1896, when Willard became involved with a wealthy British suffragist, Lady Isabel Somerset. See Bordin, *Frances Willard*, pp. 198–200, for a discussion of Willard's relationship with Somerset.

34 **"chopping kindling"**: Willard, *Glimpses*, p. 198.

"be with me": Ibid., p. 191.

"the fate of women": Frances Willard, diary, Mar. 12–13, 1869, quoted in Bordin, *Frances Willard*, pp. 44–45.

35 **"my loved and last"**: Willard, *Glimpses*, p. 342.

36 **"spoony"**: Alice Stone Blackwell to Kitty Barry Blackwell, Dec. 17, 1882, folder 688, Blackwell Family Papers, SL. According to Geoffrey Blodgett, Alice Stone Blackwell, who was involved in relief efforts after the Armenian genocide, may have had a romantic interest in 1893 in an Armenian theology student, Johannes Chatschumian, who died shortly thereafter; see Blodgett, "Alice Stone Blackwell," in James and James, *Notable American Women*, vol. 1, p. 158.

"[Collins] harps": Alice Stone Blackwell to Emily Blackwell, Mar. 27, 1885, folder 688, Blackwell Family Papers, SL.

37 **"I fell in love"**: Alice Stone Blackwell to Kitty Barry Blackwell, Nov. 30, 1884, reel 6, Blackwell Family Papers, LC.

She generally refused: See, for example, Alice Stone Blackwell to Kitty Barry Blackwell, Dec. 31, 1877, and Mar. 12, 1882 (the latter is a surprisingly hypocritical response to college "smashes"). In 1912 Alice was reading, with great ambivalence, Havelock Ellis's *Studies in the Psychology of Sex*, which included "Sexual Inversion"; Alice Stone Blackwell to Kitty Barry Blackwell, Mar. 21, 1912. All in reel 16, Blackwell Family Papers, LC.

"Dear Betrothed": Ibid., Oct. 15, 1871.

38 **"Indeed, when":** Kitty Barry Blackwell to Alice Stone Blackwell, Feb. 12, 1872, reel 56, ibid.

"forcibly possess": Alice Stone Blackwell to Kitty Barry Blackwell, Nov. 26, 1871, reel 6, ibid.

"Your stomach": Ibid., Mar. 19, 1871. Their aunt, Anna Blackwell, was a spiritualist who, Nancy Salhi says, "had discovered that Kitty was the reincarnation of the pirate William Kidd"; "Elizabeth Blackwell, M.D. (1821–1910)" (Ph.D. dissertation, University of Pennsylvania, 1974), p. 253.

"your faithful lover": Kitty Barry Blackwell to Alice Stone Blackwell, Jan. 2, 1874, reel 6, Blackwell Family Papers, LC.

"Why don't you": Alice Stone Blackwell to Kitty Blackwell, July 7, 1874, ibid.

"If I lost": Kitty Barry Blackwell to Alice Stone Blackwell, Mar. 24, 1877, reel 56, ibid.

"My dear Pie": Ibid., Feb. 18, 1883, reel 6.

"wrap you in ermines": Alice Stone Blackwell to Kitty Barry Blackwell, Feb. 7, 1911, ibid.

"I fell in love": Ibid., May 24, 1891, reel 7.

39 **"Florence says":** Kitty Barry Blackwell to Alice Stone Blackwell, Oct. 9, 1875, reel 56, ibid.

"made her home:" Alice Stone Blackwell, obit. of Kitty Barry Blackwell, [*Martha's*] *Vineyard Gazette,* June 19, 1936, folder 648, Blackwell Family Papers, SL.

3. BRINGING THE SUFFRAGE MOVEMENT INTO THE TWENTIETH CENTURY: ANNA HOWARD SHAW

40 **"The last day":** Anna Howard Shaw, journal, Dec. 31, 1901, quoted in Ida Husted Harper, unpublished ms., p. 76, series x, reel 14, Anna Howard Shaw and Lucy Elmina Anthony Papers, Mary Earhart Dillon Collection, SL.

"the strongest force": Obituary, *New York Sun,* quoted in Wil A. Linkugel and Martha Solomon, *Anna Howard Shaw: Suffrage Orator and Social Reformer* (New York: Greenwood Press, 1991), p. 3.

"measureless patience": Obituary, *New York Times,* July 4, 1919, p. 8.

"the ideal type": Obituary, *The Nation,* July 12, 1919, p. 33.

41 **"I will admit":** Anna Howard Shaw, *The Story of a Pioneer* (1915; rpt. New York: Harper and Bros., 1929), p. 240.

PAGE

The *New York World:* "An Adamless Eden of Women in Bloomers," *New York World,* Aug. 6, 1895, p. 23.

"almost libelous:" Shaw, *Story of a Pioneer,* pp. 261–68.

"no woman in public": Anna Howard Shaw, *Current Opinion,* Dec. 1915, quoted in Linkugel and Solomon, *Shaw,* p. 12.

42 "esteemed by her countrymen": Halford R. Ryan, "Foreword," in Linkugel and Solomon, *Shaw.*

"an arrangement": Shaw, *Story of a Pioneer,* pp. 32, 44, 55.

"We will never": Anna Howard Shaw to Dr. Esther Phol-Lovejoy, Mar. 12, 1914, folder 46, Anna Howard Shaw Papers, SL.

"Just think": Anna Howard Shaw to Clara Osburn, Aug. 19, 1902, reel 17, Shaw Papers.

43 "My dear little girl": Ibid., Nov. 5, 1873, reel 18.

"[Persis] brought me": Shaw, *Story of a Pioneer,* p. 90.

"coming opened": Ibid.

"I would give": Anna Howard Shaw to Mila Maynard, quoted in James R. McGovern, "Anna Howard Shaw: New Approaches to Feminism," *Journal of Social History* 3, no.2 (Winter 1969): 151.

44 "If she knows": Anna Howard Shaw, journal, Mar. 6, 1902, reel 15, Shaw Papers.

"a charge": Shaw, *Story of a Pioneer,* p. 148.

45 "You are dear": Frances Willard to Anna Howard Shaw, Nov. 22, 1888, reel 16, Shaw Papers.

The social historian: McGovern, "Shaw: New Approaches," p. 139.

"the greatest woman": *North American Magazine,* July 3, 1919.

46 "Miss Shaw": *Pomona Weekly Times,* June 19, 1895, box 1, folder 18, Susan B. Anthony Papers, Sophia Smith Collection, SC.

"invad[ing men's] prerogative": Anna Howard Shaw, "The New Man," reel 16, Shaw Papers.

47 "Now it may be": Anna Howard Shaw, "The Fundamental Principle of a Republic," unidentified newspaper clipping, July 1, 1915, box 20, Shaw Papers.

"men and women must": Ibid.

48 "fired my soul": Shaw, *Story of a Pioneer,* pp. 191, 202.

Anthony made it clear: Ibid., p. 226.

49 "So you are": Anna Howard Shaw to Lucy Anthony, Apr. 27, 1888, reel 17, Shaw Papers.

"So you could": Ibid., Feb. 11, 1889.

"I believe": Ibid., [July] 1889.

"but that cannot": Ibid., Jan. 20, 1890.

49 "Just think": Ibid., Aug. 20, 1890.

50 "I don't understand": Ibid., Aug. 1890.

"We [the Anthonys]": Susan B. Anthony to Lucy Anthony, Apr. 25, 1897, ibid.

"the keenest pleasure": Harper, unpublished ms., p. 52.

"I am thankful": Anna Howard Shaw to Lucy Anthony, Mar. 6, 1891, reel 17, Shaw Papers.

"I will teach you": Anna Howard Shaw to Harriet Cooper, Sept. 4, 1895, #1273, Sarah Cooper Papers, Rare and Manuscript Collection, CU.

51 "I wish I could": Anna Howard Shaw to Lucy Anthony, Sept. 24, 1891, reel 17, Shaw Papers.

"My dear": Ibid., Mar. 8, 1891.

"If I am": Ibid., Nov. 21, 1896.

52 "The wind whistles": Anna Howard Shaw to Lucy Anthony, 1892, quoted in Harper, unpublished ms., pp. 95–96.

"what a lonely": Anna Howard Shaw to Lucy Anthony, [New York], 1913, reel 17, Shaw Papers.

53 "I was interested": Carrie Chapman Catt to Mary Peck, Mar. 13, 1912, reel 5, Carrie Chapman Catt Papers, LC. Shaw's love letters to Harriet Cooper are in no. 1273, Cooper Papers, CU. Shaw's intimate involvements with a number of women were widely acknowledged by suffrage leaders, both nationally and internationally. See, for instance, Rachel Foster Avery to Aletta Jacobs regarding Shaw's affair with Frances Potter, who had been elected secretary of NAWSA under Shaw in 1909; in Mineke Bosch and Annemarie Klousterman, *Politics and Friendship: Letters from the International Woman Suffrage Alliance, 1902–1942* (Columbus: Ohio State University Press, 1990), p. 108.

"December 31": Lucy Anthony, Shaw's journal, Dec. 31, 1919, reel 15, Shaw Papers.

54 "I don't see anybody": Quoted in Linkugel and Solomon, *Shaw*, p. 62.

"Oh, the joy": Anna Howard Shaw, journal, Nov. 2, 1912, quoted in Harper, unpublished ms., p. 229.

55 "distinctly favorable": Ibid., p. 255.

"Votes for women": Anna Howard Shaw, "Militancy . . . ," *Trend*, Oct. 10, 1913, p. 31, A-68, #446, Shaw Papers.

56 "[Anna Shaw's] wise guidance": Obituary, *New York Times*, July 4, 1919.

57 Shaw removed the sting: The *New York Telegram*, July 4, 1914, quotes Shaw's letter to President Wilson denouncing the Congressional Union debacle; see scrapbook, folder 367, reel 14, Shaw Papers. Carrie Chapman Catt credited Wilson's conversion to suffrage to Shaw; see Elizabeth

PAGE

Cady Stanton et al., eds., *The History of Woman Suffrage*, vol. 5 (New York: Fowler and Wells, 1881–1922), p. 489. Wilson considered Shaw to be the spokesperson for American women and consulted her on a number of matters that concerned women; see, for example, Woodrow Wilson to Anna Howard Shaw, Aug. 22, 1918, reel 17, Shaw Papers: "Your counsel is good and I shall follow it. I took the liberty of writing to you because your counsel I have found to be a thing to be depended upon."

58 "for years": "Sees Death of Divine Right of Sex Fetish. . . ," *San Antonio Light*, Oct. 27, 1917, clipping, reel 17, Shaw Papers.
"There are two million": Anna Howard Shaw, "Select Your Own Principle of Life," speech, box 23, folder 546, Shaw Papers.

59 "Our country needs": "Dr. Shaw's Call to Arms," *Woman Citizen*, Apr. 27, 1918, clipping, reel 17, Shaw Papers.
"wild oats": Anna Howard Shaw to Lucy Anthony, Jan. 1, 1918, reel 17, Shaw Papers.
"if we come home": Ibid., Mar. 9, 1919.

60 "There is no other": William Short [League to Enforce the Peace] to Anna Howard Shaw, May 1, 1919, ibid.

4. VICTORY: CARRIE CHAPMAN CATT

In addition to the biographies cited in the following notes, Robert Booth Fowler's *Carrie Chapman Catt: Feminist Politician* (Boston: Northeastern University Press, 1986) has been especially helpful to my understanding of Catt.

PAGE

61 "Mollie do you know": Carrie Chapman Catt to Mary Garrett Hay, Mar. 21, 1923, reel 3, Carrie Chapman Catt Papers, LC.
In a 1923 article: Carrie Chapman Catt, "A Suffrage Team," *Woman Citizen*, Sept. 8, 1923, in Mary Gray Peck, *Carrie Chapman Catt: A Biography* (New York: Wilson, 1944), p. 60.
"the two of them": Peck, *Catt*.

62 "almost without": David Howard Katz, "Carrie Chapman Catt and the Struggle for Peace" (Ph.D. dissertation, Syracuse University, 1973), p. 29.
"beginning": Peck, *Catt*, p. 86. The evidence that Catt and Hay became friends in 1890 is suggested by the inscription on the marker over their

shared burial place, which says they were together for thirty-eight years; Hay died in 1928.

63 **"walk . . . the chalk"**: Carrie Chapman Catt to Mary Peck, Oct. 23, 1912, reel 5, Catt Papers, LC.

One biographer explains: Jacqueline Van Voris, *Carrie Chapman Catt: A Public Life* (New York: Feminist Press, 1987), p. 65.

In 1889 alone: James P. Louis, "Mary Garrett Hay," in James and James, *Notable American Women*, vol. 2, p. 164.

64 **"Any hope"**: Peck, *Catt*, p. 108.

"Mrs. Catt": Maud Wood Park, *Front Door Lobby*, ed. Edna Lamprey Stantial (Boston: Beacon Press, 1960), p. 120.

65 **"She was queenly"**: Caroline Reilly to Anna Howard Shaw, June 11, 1919, series x, reel 16, Anna Howard Shaw Papers, Mary Earhart Dillon Collection, SL.

"the enthusiasm": Peck, *Catt*, p. 96.

66 **"When she looks"**: Quoted in ibid., p. 222.

67 **"a body of opinion"**: Ibid., pp. 233–34.

"the decisive battle": Ibid., pp. 233–34, 277–80.

70 **"I was born"**: Carrie Chapman Catt to Caroline LaMonte, Mar. 8, 1930, ms. group 31, box 4, folder 29, Carrie Chapman Catt Papers, Sophia Smith Collection, SC.

71 **"I'm for Pandemonium"**: Carrie Chapman Catt to Mary Peck, Oct. 23, 1912, reel 5, Catt Papers, LC.

"I'm sorry": Carrie Chapman Catt to Mary Garrett Hay, Aug. 27, 1911, reel 3, ibid. According to Eric Partridge, *A Dictionary of Slang and Unconventional English* (New York: Macmillan, 1984), p. 1111, the sexual term "soixante-neuf" was "adopted from French . . . late c. 19–20. Orig. upper and middle classes." Catt's private humor was often bawdy, which would argue for her familiarity with the term "69" as a sexual expression. For example, she wrote to Hay from North Africa (on the course of her world suffrage tour) a racist but revealing letter that demonstrates her penchant for sexual explicitness: "Here is a kind of black man with hair about six inches long which stands straight out. It is about half wool and half hair. His ancestors got mixed up I think. They are called the fuzzy wuzzies. They loaded about 200 sheep on a neighboring ship. These sheep too had indecent ancestors for while they have the form of sheep they have hair"; ibid.

72 **"chum"**: Carrie Chapman Catt to Clara Hyde, July 7, 1914, reel 4, ibid.

"I received": Carrie Chapman Catt to Mary Peck, Aug. 8, 1911, reel 5, ibid.

PAGE

A perusal of Catt's personal correspondence reveals that she was often carried away by the appeal of others; see, for example, her correspondence with Clara Hyde and Rosa Manus, reel 4, ibid.

74 **"Mollie Dear"**: Carrie Chapman Catt to Mary Garrett Hay, July 25, 1911, reel 3, ibid.

75 **"I love you:"** Ibid., Aug. 8, 1911; Aug. 27, 1911; Mar. 13, 1912.
"So you have": Ibid., Nov. 17, 1911; Nov. [?], 1911.

76 **"I do not like"**: Ibid., [Nov. 20?], 1911; Nov. 21, 1911.
"You are excusable": Ibid., Dec. 25, 1911.

77 **"It is a great"**: Ibid., Nov. 1, 1922.
"Now don't be": Ibid., Apr. 24, 1923.
"bereavement": Peck, *Catt*, pp. 436–37.

78 **"It is impossible"**: Lucy Anthony to Carrie Chapman Catt, Oct. 11, 1928, reel 2, Catt Papers, LC. See also Catt's response, Oct. 28, 1928, ibid.

5. TWO STEPS FORWARD . . .

A seminal essay on compulsory heterosexuality during the 1920s has been Christina Simmons's "Companionate Marriage and the Lesbian Threat," *Frontiers: A Journal of Women's Studies* 4, no. 3 (Fall 1979): 54–59.

Paul C. Taylor's "Mary Williams Dewson," in Barbara Sicherman and Carol Hurd Green, eds., *Notable American Women: The Modern Period* (Cambridge: Harvard University Press, 1980), is a useful, concise supplement to Susan Ware's excellent biography, *Partner and I: Molly Dewson, Feminism, and New Deal Politics* (New Haven, Conn.: Yale University Press, 1987). Sara M. Evans includes a good discussion of how Progressive-era philosophy was brought into the New Deal in *Born for Liberty: A History of Women in America* (New York: Free Press, 1989), pp. 205–10.

In addition to the sources noted below, I found helpful the discussions about the National Woman's Party at mid-century in Leila J. Rupp, "The Women's Community in the National Woman's Party, 1945 to the 1960s," *Signs* 10 (Summer 1985), and Flora Davis, *Moving the Mountain: The Women's Movement in America since 1960* (New York: Simon and Schuster, 1991).

PAGE

79 **"There is a gay"**: Virginia Bellamy (?), "To M.G.P. and M.W.D.," reel 1, Dewson-Porter album, Molly Dewson Papers, SL. M.G.P. was Mary (Polly) G. Porter; M.W.D. was Mary (Molly) Williams Dewson.

79 **"masculinized" women:** Phyllis Blanchard, "Sex in the Adolescent Girl," in
V. F. Calverton and Samuel D. Schmalhausen, eds., *Sex in Civilization*
(Garden City, N.Y.: Doubleday, 1929), pp. 538–61.

80 **"becoming more fully":** Floyd Dell, *Love in the Machine Age* (1930; rpt. New
York: Farrar, Straus, and Giroux, 1973), p. 282.

Even by the 1940s: Paul F. Lazarsfeld, Bernard Berelson, and Hazel Gaudet,
*The People's Choice: How the Voter Makes Up His Mind in a Presidential
Campaign* (New York: Columbia University Press, 1948), p. 141.

81 **"fools":** Alice Stone Blackwell to Carrie Chapman Catt, Sept. 4, 1929,
Blackwell Family Papers, LC.

"for intelligent": Carrie Chapman Catt and Nettie Rogers Shuler, *Woman
Suffrage and Politics: The Inner Story of the Suffrage Movement* (New
York: Scribner's, 1923), p. xix.

"to get on the inside": Ibid.

Ironically, by the 1940s: See Leila J. Rupp and Verta Taylor, *Survival in the
Doldrums: The American Women's Rights Movement, 1945 to the 1960s*
(New York: Oxford University Press, 1987), pp. 48–49, and Martha May
Eliot, interview by Jeannette Barley Cheek, Rockefeller Oral History
Project, November 1973, p. 431, Martha May Eliot Papers, SL.

Two prevalent caricatures: Nancy Cott, *The Grounding of Modern Feminism*
(New Haven, Conn.: Yale University Press, 1987), p. 271.

"as quaint": Robert Coughlan, "Changing Roles in Modern Marriage,"
Life, Dec. 24, 1956, p. 110.

82 **After more than a decade:** Sophonisba Breckinridge, *Women in the Twentieth
Century: A Study of their Political, Social, and Economic Activities* (New
York: McGraw-Hill, 1933), p. 326.

For example, Anne: Two Ph.D. dissertations describe Martin's professional
life and give glimpses of her personal life: Ann Warren Smith, "Anne
Martin and the History of Woman Suffrage in Nevada, 1869–1914" (Uni-
versity of Nevada, 1976), and Kathryn Anderson, "Practical Political
Equality for Women: Anne Martin's Campaigns for the United States
Senate in Nevada, 1918 and 1920" (University of Washington, 1978).

Martin undertook the presidency of the Nevada Equal Franchise Society under the influence of Hannah Clapp, one of the state's first expo-
nents of woman suffrage. Clapp, who never married, was described by
her contemporaries as "always dressed in a severe masculine fashion"
and as "a mannish-looking woman," and she lived with Elizabeth Babcock, a "regular little lady," with whom Clapp founded a well-respected
school in the late nineteenth century. Although Martin seems to have
been less interested in obviously butch/femme-type lesbian relationships

than her mentor and model, there can be little doubt of her same-sex intimacies.

Martin's correspondence, BL, is also useful. See especially her correspondence with Mabel Vernon, in which Martin acknowledged Vernon's intimate relationships with women, and with Jane Addams and Mary Rozet Smith, whom Martin addressed as a couple. Addams and Smith responded by acknowledging Martin and Dr. Margaret Long as a couple. See also Long's correspondence with Florence Sabin, Florence Sabin Papers, APS; the Margaret Long Papers (especially correspondence of the 1940s), SC; and the correspondence between Mabel Vernon and Anne Martin and Dr. Margaret Long, in the People's Mandate Papers, SCPC.

Martin was deeply disappointed that enfranchisement gave women little political power. As Kristi Andersen points out in *After Suffrage: Women in Partisan and Electoral Politics Before the New Deal* (Chicago: University of Chicago Press, 1987), pp. 107–8, other suffragists who had had high hopes for women were also devastated by the reality of the difficulties of gaining female political representation. Emily Blair, who became vice president of the Democratic National Committee in 1924 and its only female officer, complained by 1930 that she had been deluded into thinking that women could make gains through traditional party politics. Like Martin, she called (in vain) for women "to organize as women, not only in politics but everywhere." See also Anne Martin, "Feminists and Future Political Action," *The Nation*, Feb. 18, 1925, pp. 185–86.

83 **Marion Dickerman:** See Blanche Wiesen Cook, *Eleanor Roosevelt: Vol. I, 1884–1933* (New York: Viking, 1992), pp. 321–22.

84 **"The reading of":** Quoted in Peck, *Catt*, p. 280. On Hay's political career, see also Elizabeth Cady Stanton et al., eds.; *The History of Woman Suffrage*, vol. 6 (New York: Fowler and Wells, 1881–1922).

85 **"Funny, everything":** Rodger Streitmatter, ed., *Empty Without You: The Intimate Letters of Eleanor Roosevelt and Lorena Hickok* (New York: Free Press, 1998), pp. 54, 77. See also Doris Faber, *The Life of Lorena Hickok: E.R.'s Friend* (New York: Morrow, 1980).

"introduced an alternative": Cook, *Eleanor Roosevelt*, pp. 3–4, 123. See also p. 116 for a discussion of the rampant homosexual crushes in Souvestre's school. Cook portrays Eleanor Roosevelt as bisexual. Streitmatter focuses on her lesbianism. See also Joseph P. Lash, *Love, Eleanor: Eleanor Roosevelt and Her Friends* (Garden City, N.Y.: Doubleday, 1982), and *A*

PAGE

World of Love: Eleanor Roosevelt and her Friends, 1943–1962 (Garden City, N.Y.: Doubleday, 1964). Lash, who counted himself among the first lady's friends, preferred to see her as asexual. Dorothy Bussy's autobiographical lesbian novel *Olivia* (1948; rpt. New York: Arno Press, 1975) is set in Mlle. Souvestre's school.

86 **The lesbians:** Cook, *Eleanor Roosevelt*, pp. 4–6, 13–14. For a discussion of Roosevelt's work with Nancy Cook and Marion Dickerman on women's issues, see also Joseph P. Lash, "Eleanor Roosevelt's Role in Women's History," in Mabel E. Deutrich and Virginia C. Purdy, eds., *Clio Was a Woman: Studies in the History of American Women* (Washington, D.C.: Howard University Press, 1980), pp. 243–53.

"the first independent": Eleanor Roosevelt and Lorena Hickok, *Ladies of Courage* (New York: Putnam, 1954), pp. 258–59.

"sanctuary": Cook, *Eleanor Roosevelt*, pp. 292–97. The Greenwich Village lesbian circle is also discussed in Streitmatter, *Empty*, pp. xvi–xviii.

87 **"profound influence":** Clarke A. Chambers, *Seedtime of Reform: American Social Service and Social Action, 1918–1933* (Minneapolis: University of Minnesota Press, 1963), p. 255.

"should receive": Hickok, *Ladies*, p. 278.

Because of her: Elaine M. Smith, "Mary McLeod Bethune and the National Youth Administration," in Deutrich and Purdy, *Clio*, pp. 149–77.

"gave me the opportunity": Quoted in Susan Ware, *Holding Their Own: American Women in the 1930s* (Boston: Twayne, 1982), p. 91.

88 **"one of the most":** Ware, *Partner and I*, p. xi.

89 **"the biggest coup":** Quoted in ibid., p. 217.

90 **"the way [for women]":** Quoted in George W. Martin, *Madame Secretary: Frances Perkins* (Boston: Houghton Mifflin, 1976), p. 146.

"mirrored": Ware, *Partner and I*, p. 58.

"Little danger": Ibid., p. 59.

91 **"The two women":** Ibid., p. 144.

"The overwhelming argument": Quoted in Ware, *Holding Their Own*, p. 92.

Nevertheless, she: According to O'Day's son, Perkins's primary domestic arrangement was with O'Day; see Cook, *Eleanor Roosevelt*, p. 324n.

93 **"Men and women":** In 1943 the wording of the ERA was changed to "Equality of rights under the law shall not be denied or abridged by the United States or by any State on account of sex."

When American women: Rupp and Taylor, *Survival*, p. 51.

94 **"If my marriage":** Quoted in ibid., p. 112.

"weird goings-on": Quoted in ibid., p. 106. See also Leila Rupp, "Feminism and the Sexual Revolution in the Early Twentieth Century: The Case of Doris Stevens," *Feminist Studies* 15, no. 2 (Summer 1989): 289–309. Rupp shows that Stevens too was capable of intense sensual and emotional relationships with another woman (Sara Bard Field). Stevens may in fact have been victimized by lesbian panic, which would explain her obsessive heterosexual insistences, such as her declaration in a 1927 speech that "the only fun in life is when men and women play together and men and women work together."

Alice Paul's reputation as a lesbian has long made some of her biographers exceedingly uncomfortable. A colleague recently informed me of a contemporary Paul biographer who "just called [her], with great relief, to say she has just discovered some evidence of a young man in Alice Paul's life that will counter those rumors about Paul and Lucy Burns!"

95 **The social theorist;** See Doug McAdam, *Political Process and the Development of Black Insurgency* (Chicago: University of Chicago Press, 1982).

6. MOTHER-HEARTS/LESBIAN-HEARTS

Useful discussions of the women's labor movement and relations between women in the movement can be found in Alice Kessler-Harris, "Where Are the Organized Women Workers?" *Feminist Studies* 3, no. 1–2 (1975); Ellen DuBois, "Working Women, Class Relations, and Suffrage Militance . . . ," in Ellen Carol DuBois and Vicki L. Ruiz, eds., *Unequal Sisters: A Multicultural Reader in U.S. Women's History* (New York: Routledge, 1990), pp. 176–94; Diane Balser, *Sisterhood and Solidarity: Feminism and Labor in Modern Times* (Boston: South End Press, 1987); and Nancy Schrom Dye, *As Equals and as Sisters: Feminism, the Labor Movement, and the Women's Trade Union League of New York* (Columbia: University of Missouri Press, 1980). Elisabeth Marbury, "We Are All Members of the One National Family," *American Federationist* 17 (March 1910): 21, provides an emotional articulation of the views of upper-class lesbian women about their support of working-class women in their labor struggles.

The relationship between Marbury and DeWolfe is well traced in Kim Marre, "A Lesbian Marriage of Cultural Consequence," *Theatre Annual* 47 (1994): 71–76.

I gleaned insights on Marot and Pratt from Caroline Pratt, *I Learn from Children* (New York: Simon and Schuster, 1948), and Helen Marot, *American Labor Unions* (New York: Henry Holt, 1914), as well as Sandra Adickes, *To Be*

Young Was Very Heaven: Women in New York Before the First World War (New York: St. Martin's, 1997).

PAGE

99 **"We can hardly"**: John White Chadwick, *A Life for Liberty: Anti-Slavery and Other Letters of Sallie Holley* (1899; rpt. New York: Negro Universities Press, 1969), p. 7.
  "how shall we": Anna Howard Shaw, "The Great Defect in Our Government," in Wilmer A. Linkugel, "The Speeches of Anna Howard Shaw," (Ph.D. dissertation, University of Wisconsin, 1960), vol. 2, pp. 149–78.
  "finding any wrong": Anna Howard Shaw, "God's Women," in Rachel Foster Avery, ed., *Proceedings of the National Council of Women of the United States, 1891* (Philadelphia: Lippincott, 1891), pp. 242–49.

101 **"conscience and heart"**: Quoted in Chadwick, *Life for Liberty*, pp. 181–82.
  "fashioned a full": Katherine Lydigsen Herbig, "Friends for Freedom: The Lives and Careers of Sallie Holley and Caroline Putnam" (Ph.D. dissertation, Claremont Graduate School, 1977), p. 135.
  "Oh, my heart": Quoted in Chadwick, *Life for Liberty*, pp. 186–87.

102 **"Dear Loving Heart"**: Quoted in Herbig, "Friends," pp. 86, 105, 164. See also Lee Chambers-Schiller, *Liberty, a Better Husband: Single Women in America, the Generations of 1780–1840* (New Haven, Conn.: Yale University Press, 1984).

104 **"bosom sex"**: Karen V. Hansen, "'No *kisses* is like youres': An Erotic Friendship Between Two African-American Women During the Mid-Nineteenth Century," in Martha Vicinus, ed., *Lesbian Subjects: A Feminist Studies Reader* (Bloomington: Indiana University Press, 1996), pp. 178–207.

105 **"keep women out"**: Quoted in Rosalyn Baxandall, Linda Gordon, and Susan Reverby, eds., *America's Working Women: A Documentary History, 1600 to the Present* (New York: Vintage, 1976), p. 167.

107 **Pratt became**: When birth control pioneer Margaret Sanger had to flee the country after being threatened with a forty-five-year prison term for her work, she left two of her young children in the care of Marot and Pratt; see Ellen Chesler, *Woman of Valor: Margaret Sanger and the Birth Control Movement in America* (New York: Simon and Schuster, 1992), p. 99.
  "only women of the highest": The strike, especially the Colony Club's participation in it, is discussed in Rheta Childe Dorr, *What Eight Million Women Want* (Boston: Small, Maynard, 1910), p. 172.

108 **"progress towards"**: Ibid., p. 175.

109 **But they were disappointed:** In her book *American Labor Unions*, Helen Marot is critical not only of labor union men who withheld their support of working women but also of the working women who were reluctant to fight for their rights within unions. She blames women's timidity largely on their (heterosexual) domestic arrangements, which did not encourage them to speak out boldly as workers (p. 16). See also Dye, *As Equals*, p. 75.

These relationships: Annaliese Orleck, *Common Sense and a Little Fire: Women and Working Class Politics in the United States, 1900–1965* (Chapel Hill: University of North Carolina Press, 1995), discusses the twenty-five-year partnership between two working-class female leaders in the WTUL, Rose Schneiderman and Maud O'Farrel Swartz.

110 **"fiery soapbox orator":** Pauline Newman, "Letters to Michael and Hugh Owen from P. M. Newman," box 1, folder 3, Newman and Miller Papers, SL.

"girl strikers": Ibid.

"Her need": Ann Schofield, *"To Do and to Be": Portraits of Four Women Activists* (Boston: Northeastern University Press, 1997), p. 94.

111 **"She was blonde":** Elisabeth Owen, quoted in ibid., p. 49.

112 **In Germany, Frieda:** Newman stated in a 1973 interview that Elisabeth was adopted. Ann Schofield, who interviewed Elisabeth in 1988, says that she was Miller's natural daughter; *"To Do,"* p. 166, note 53.

"Dear Girl": Pauline Newman to Frieda Segelke Miller, Aug. 23, 1927, box 1, folder 8, Newman and Miller Papers, SL. Although considerable material tracing their relationship appears in the Newman and Miller Papers at the Schlesinger Library, it is likely that important material was censored. When Miller was in London, working at the American Embassy, she wrote regularly only to Newman and expected her to share news with their friends. Newman told her in a letter of March 3, 1944, that she found it necessary to spend a good deal of time "preparing" Miller's letters for circulation: "I cannot give them to Miss B. [Miller's secretary] because I do not trust her judgement in what to leave out. So I 'edit' them, as it were, leaving out personal references"; ibid.

"I spent": Pauline Newman to Frieda Segelke Miller, June 1, 1936, ibid.

113 **"The sun is out":** Ibid., Mar. 3, 1944.

Despite Pauline's: The relationship between Newman and Miller could be stormy. In 1959, Miller, by then in her late sixties, had an affair with a man, which caused a breach with Newman. Their temporary separation did not affect Newman's role as grandmother to Elisabeth's children.

When Miller had a stroke in 1969, Newman cared for her until her death, four years later. See also Trisha Franzen, *Spinsters and Lesbians: Independent Womanhood in the United States* (New York: New York University Press, 1996), pp. 127–28.

113 **"You and Frieda"**: Vera Joseph, M.D., to Pauline Newman, Aug. 10, 1973, box 3, folder 50, Newman and Miller Papers, SL.

114 **"in the endless"**: Quoted in Ellen Fitzpatrick, *Endless Crusade: Women Social Scientists and Progressive Reform* (New York: Oxford University Press, 1990), p. xii.

Linda Gordon: Linda Gordon, *Pitied But Not Entitled: Single Mothers and the History of Welfare* (New York: Free Press, 1994), pp. 78–79. Gordon's figure of 28 percent is an underestimate too because it fails to include women such as Martha May Eliot (one of the leading reformers whom Gordon names), who lived her entire adult life with Dr. Ethel Dunham. Gordon erroneously identifies Eliot as the wife of Thomas Eliot, assistant solicitor to the Department of Labor (p. 258).

7. SOCIAL HOUSEKEEPING: THE INSPIRATION OF JANE ADDAMS

In addition to the biographies cited below, an excellent, concise account of Jane Addams's accomplishments can be found in Ann Firor Scott, "Jane Addams," in James and James, *Notable American Women*, vol. 1. Ida B. Wells's *Crusade for Justice: The Autobiography of Ida B. Wells*, ed. Alfreda Duster (Chicago: University of Chicago Press, 1970), discusses Addams's work with African Americans.

Several other researchers have considered the emotional and/or erotic relationships between women that characterized the settlement movement. Most notable are Blanche Wiesen Cook, "Female Support Networks and Political Activism: Lillian Wald, Chrystal Eastman, Emma Goldman," *Chrysalis* 3 (1977): 43–61; Estelle Freedman, "Separatism as a Strategy: Female Institution Building and American Feminism," *Feminist Studies* 5, no. 3 (Fall 1979): 512–29; and Rebecca Alpert, *Like Bread on the Seder Plate: Jewish Lesbians and the Transformation of Tradition* (New York: Columbia University Press, 1997).

115 **"My Ever Dear"**: Jane Addams to Mary Rozet Smith, Feb. 21, 1897, reel 113.3, Jane Addams Papers, SCPC.

In her account: Jane Addams, *Twenty Years at Hull House* (1910; rpt. New York: Macmillan, 1963), pp. 71–72.

"involving the use": Jane Addams, "Filial Relations," in *Democracy and Social Ethics* (1902; rpt. Cambridge: Harvard University Press, 1964), p. 87.

116 **The historian:** Jill Conway, "Women Reformers and American Culture, 1870–1930," *Journal of Social History* 5 (Winter 1971–72): 174–75.

"educated woman's": Jane Addams, "The Modern City and the Municipal Franchise for Women," speech, Feb. 1906.

"less selfish time": Addams, *Twenty Years*, p. 71.

117 **"I love your sex":** "A Voter" to Jane Addams, Jan. 17, 1898, reel 113.3, Addams Papers.

118 **the quintessential:** Allen F. Davis, *American Heroine: The Life and Legend of Jane Addams* (New York: Oxford University Press, 1973).

"No other single": Charles and Mary Beard, *The American Spirit: A Study of the Idea of Civilization in the United States* (New York: Macmillan, 1942), p. 478.

"a central figure": John C. Farrell, *Beloved Lady: A History of Jane Addams' Ideas on Reform and Peace* (Baltimore: Johns Hopkins University Press, 1967), p. 20.

"moving force": Daniel Levine, *Jane Addams and the Liberal Tradition* (Madison: State Historical Society of Wisconsin, 1971), p. 18.

119 **"social intercourse":** Jane Addams to Ellen Gates Starr, Aug. 11, 1879, box 1, folder 5A, Ellen Gates Starr Papers, Sophia Smith Collection, SC.

"I suppose": Ellen Gates Starr to Jane Addams, [1886], box 1, folder 10A, Starr Papers. In the preceding years, Ellen had been infatuated with a fellow teacher, Mary Runyan, whom she described to Jane as "so *beautiful*," confessing "how devoted I am to her"; Ellen Gates Starr to Jane Addams, Jan. 1, 1882, reel 113.1, Addams Papers. See also Apr. 9, 1882, and Jan. 12, 1883, ibid.

"She said today": Ellen Gates Starr to Jane Addams, [1886], box 1, folder 10A, Starr Papers.

"My Dear": Ellen Gates Starr to Jane Addams, Dec. 6, 1885, box 1, folder 10A, Starr Papers.

120 **"It has set me":** Jane Addams to Ellen Gates Starr, Dec. 2, 1883, box 1, folder 5A, Starr Papers.

"I am very impatient": Ibid., Feb. 21, 1885.

"Let's love": Jane Addams to Ellen Gates Starr, Jan. 24, 1889, box 1, folder 7A, Starr Papers.

PAGE

120 **"I need you"**: Jane Addams to Ellen Gates Starr, June 7, 1889, box 1, folder 7, Starr Papers.
"My Dear One": Ibid., June 14, 1889.

121 **"had our own"**: Ellen Gates Starr to Mary Blaisdell, Feb. 23, 1889, box 1, folder 3, Starr Papers.
"supplying in a radical": Kathryn Kish Sklar, "Hull House in the 1890s: A Community of Women Reformers," *Signs* 10 (Summer 1985): 658.
Hull House: See Jane Addams to Katharine Coman, Dec. 7, 1891, reel 113.1, Addams Papers.

122 **"With the exception"**: Helen Christine Bennett, *American Women in Civil Work* (New York: Dodd, Mead, 1915), p. 82.

123 **In the 1890s**: See Peter G. Filene, *Him/Her/Self: Sex Roles in Modern America,* 2nd ed. (Baltimore: Johns Hopkins University Press, 1986), pp. 16–18.
"The comfort of": Addams, *Twenty Years,* p. 87.
"College Girls": *Kansas City Journal,* clipping, box 1, folder 3, Starr Papers.

124 **"More perfect"**: Leila Bedell, *Woman's Journal,* May 5, 1889, clipping, ibid.
"More important": Davis, *American Heroine,* p. 62.

125 **"I positively feel"**: Jane Addams to Ellen Gates Starr, May 3, 1889, box 1, folder 7, Starr Papers.
"Her humanitarianism": James Weber Linn, *Jane Addams: A Biography* (New York: Appleton-Century, 1938), p. 81.
"drifted": Ibid., p. 147.
"It would give": Jane Addams to Mary Rozet Smith, [Spring 1890], reel 113.1, Addams Papers.
"I have a great": Jane Addams to Mary Rozet Smith, Dec. 19, 1890, ibid.

126 **"Jane and Ellen"**: Davis, *American Heroine,* p. 85.
"I feel uncommon": Ellen Gates Starr to Jane Addams, n.d., London, box 1, folder 10A, Starr Papers.
"My dear, I'm tired": Ibid., Oct. 10 [no year].
"Your letter": Jane Addams to Ellen Gates Starr, July 1892, reel 113.1, Addams Papers.

127 **"I can see"**: Quoted in Davis, *American Heroine,* p. 85. Ellen's emotional life did not come to a permanent end with the end of her intimacy with Jane. About 1907 she formed a romantic friendship with Frances Lillie, the wife of the dean of sciences at the University of Chicago, who was, in terms of religious enthusiasm, far more suitable to Ellen than Jane had been. Their correspondence is in box 10, folder 87, Starr Papers.

"conventional lady": Cook, "Female Support Networks," p. 47.

"so good to me": Jane Addams to Alice Haldeman, Feb. 23, 1893, reel 113.1, Addams Papers.

128 "One day I came": Quoted in Linn, *Jane Addams*, pp. 289–90.

129 "no affinity": Margaret Tims, *Jane Addams of Hull House* (London: Allen and Unwin, 1961), p. 57.

"one supremely": Alice Hamilton, *Exploring the Dangerous Trades: The Autobiography of Alice Hamilton, M.D.* (Boston: Little, Brown, 1943), p. 67.

"did not need": Davis, *American Heroine*, p. 88.

130 "I will confide": Jane Addams to Mary Rozet Smith, Apr. 6, 1902, reel 133.4, Addams Papers.

"I bless you": Jane Addams to Mary Rozet Smith, Dec. 23, 1894; Jan. 15, 1895; Jan. 27, 1895; Feb. 4, 1895; all in reel 113.1, Addams Papers.

"I came home": Mary Rozet Smith to Jane Addams, Dec. [?], 1896; Feb. 1896; Mar. 1896; ibid.

131 "a good deal": Jane Addams to Ellen Gates Starr, May 29, 1896, ibid.

"a very pressing": Jane Addams to Mary Rozet Smith, June [?] 1897, ibid.

"Bro Wood's": Ibid., Aug. 24, 1899.

132 "Dearest, It": Ibid., Jan. 11, 1900.

"You must know": Jane Addams to Mary Rozet Smith, May 26, 1902, reel 113.4, Addams Papers.

"healing domesticity": Ibid., Aug. 4, 1904.

"Our house": Ibid.

"Dearest, I had": Jane Addams to Mary Rozet Smith, Oct. 16, 1914, reel 113.7, Addams Papers.

"I suppose": Linn, *Jane Addams*, p. 408.

In 1904: See Robert H. Bremner, *From the Depths: The Discovery of Poverty in the United States* (New York: New York University Press, 1956), p. 219.

133 "an effective instrument": Linn, *Jane Addams*, pp. 292, 349.

134 "When the day": Quoted in Farrell, *Beloved Lady*, p. 214.

As early as 1897: See Jane Addams, "Social Settlements," *Proceedings* (National Conference of Charities and Corrections, 1897): 338–46, and Addams, *Twenty Years*, pp. 310–13.

135 "People listened": Levine, *Jane Addams*, p. xi. Sklar analyzes the ways in which Addams combined the power of female institutions with access to the male spheres of influence; see "Hull House."

135 **"Will you let me"**: Theodore Roosevelt to Jane Addams, Jan. 24, 1906, reel 113.4, Addams Papers.

8. SOCIAL HOUSEKEEPING BECOMES A PROFESSION: FRANCES KELLOR

For a helpful discussion of the settlement movement as a training ground for professionals, see Allen F. Davis, *Spearheads for Reform: The Social Settlements and the Progressive Movement* (New York: Oxford University Press, 1967).

No full-length biography of Frances Kellor has been published, but William Maxwell's "Frances Kellor in the Progressive Era: A Study of the Professionalization of Reform" (Ed.D. dissertation, Teachers College, Columbia University, 1968) provides a good overview of her professional contributions. Valuable chapters on Kellor can also be found in Ellen Fitzpatrick, *Endless Crusade: Women Social Scientists and Progressive Reform* (New York: Oxford University Press, 1990). For information about Kellor's work on immigration, see Edward George Hartmann, *The Movement to Americanize the Immigrant* (New York: Columbia University Press, 1948), and Edward Corsi, "Frances A. Kellor Sponsored New York State Policy Toward Immigration," *Industrial Bulletin* (newsmagazine, New York Department of Labor), Mar. 1952, pp. 14–18. See also Frances Kellor, *Immigration and the Future* (New York: Doran, 1920).

Mary Dreier's work is discussed in Nancy Schrom Dye, *As Equals and as Sisters: Feminism, the Labor Movement, and the Women's Trade Union League of New York* (Columbia: University of Missouri Press, 1980), and Ann Schofield, *"To Do and to Be": Portraits of Four Women Activists* (Boston: Northeastern University Press, 1997).

136 **"My own dear"**: Frances Kellor to Mary Dreier, [ca. 1905], box 5, folder 77, Mary Dreier Papers, SL.

"scientific skills": Jane Addams, "The Idea of a Settlement Movement," *College Settlement Association: Ninth Annual Report, 1897–98* (New York: Reynolds Press, 1898), p. 10.

137 **In 1910**: Addams, *Twenty Years*, pp. 450–51.

139 **"fearless tomboy"**: Fitzpatrick, *Endless Crusade*, pp. 17, 60.

"could whittle": Ibid., p. 60.

"never really": Ibid., p. 148.

PAGE

140 "If women are": Frances Kellor, "A Psychological Basis for Physical Culture," *Education* 19 (1898).

141 "close and intimate": Mary Dreier to Phyllis Holbrook, Dec. 16, 1961, courtesy of Holbrook's nephew, Pete Stewart, Columbia, South Carolina.

142 "will be unable": Frances Kellor to Mary Dreier, May 5, 1904, box 5, folder 77, Dreier Papers.
"The colors": Ibid., Oct. 10, 1904.
"My own dear beautiful": Ibid., n.d. [1905].
"I have this whole": Ibid., Jan.3, 1905.

143 "Sixy dear": Ibid., July 31, 1905.
"There is such": Ibid., Aug. 11, 1905.
"I'd give most anything": Ibid., Aug. 20, 1905.
As the papers: See Elizabeth Anne Payne, *Reform, Labor, and Feminism: Margaret Dreier Robins and the Women's Trade Union League* (Urbana: University of Illinois Press, 1988), p. 32. The love poems to Raymond Robins are in box 1, folder 17, Dreier Papers.
"something of a wreck": note in Dreier's hand, written on the back of a letter from Frances Kellor, Oct. 10, 1904, box 5, folder 77, Dreier Papers.
"Along with your love": Frances Kellor to Mary Dreier, Oct. 10, 1904, ibid.

144 "that beautiful mind": Ibid., n.d. [1905].
"Then it will": Ibid., July 17, 1905.

145 "always so dear": Ibid., Summer [?] 1905.

146 "I don't do Christmas": Ibid., Dec. 22, 1905.
"It is so beautiful": Ibid., Oct. 30, 1906.
In her early work: See Maxwell, "Frances Kellor," p. 139ff; Payne, *Reform*, p. 26ff; and Helen Christine Bennett, *American Women in Civic Work* (New York: Dodd, Mead, 1915), pp. 163–79.

147 For example, in her book: Kellor discusses the northern victimization of southern African-American women in *Out of Work: A Study of Employment Agencies* (New York: Putnam, 1904), chap. 3. Kellor's role in the formation of the National League for the Protection of Colored Women is discussed in Gilbert Osofsky, *Harlem: The Making of a Ghetto* (New York: Harper and Row, 1966). See also Mary Dreier to Phyllis Holbrook, Nov. 23, 1960, courtesy of Pete Stewart.

148 "did more": John Higham, *Strangers in the Land: Patterns of American Nativism, 1860–1925* (New Brunswick, N.J.: Rutgers University Press, 1955), p. 190.

151 "only tepidly": Theodore Roosevelt, *An Autobiography* (New York: Macmillan, 1919), p. 180.

PAGE

153 **"the tremendous forces"**: Frances Kellor, "Psychological and Environmental Study of Women Criminals," *American Journal of Sociology* 5, no. 4/5 (Jan.–Mar. 1900): 528.

9. POISONING THE SOURCE

The Swarthmore College Peace Collection holds the papers of most of the women discussed in this chapter, including Frances Witherspoon, Tracy Mygatt, Hannah Clothier, and Mildred Scott Olmsted; those of Mabel Vernon, Vida Milholland, and Margaret Hamilton can be found in the People's Mandate Papers (PMP).

Margaret Hope Bacon has written an excellent biography of Olmsted, which details Olmsted's relationship with Ruth Mellor: *One Woman's Passion for Peace and Freedom: The Life of Mildred Scott Olmsted* (Syracuse, N.Y.: Syracuse University Press, 1993). Information for my discussion of Olmsted was also garnered from Margaret Bacon during our meetings on January 15 and 16, 1997, at Swarthmore College, and from her letter to me of January 17, 1997.

PAGE

154 **"All, all"**: Tracy Mygatt to Frances Witherspoon, April 12, 1933, box 6, Tracy Mygatt–Frances Witherspoon Papers, SCPC.

"people the tools": Quoted in Clarke A. Chambers, *Seedtime of Reform: American Social Service and Social Action, 1918–1933* (Minneapolis: University of Minnesota Press, 1963), p. 80.

Convinced that now: On the women's peace movement after the Great War, see Nancy F. Cott, *The Grounding of Modern Feminism* (New Haven, Conn.: Yale University Press, 1987), p. 243ff, and Gertrude Bussey and Margaret Tims, *Women's International League for Peace and Freedom, 1915–1965* (London: Allen and Unwin, 1965).

155 **"family"**: Jeannette Marks to Mabel Vernon, July 13, 1950, Mabel Vernon Papers, PMP, SCPC.

"How is Mabel": Vida Milholland to Mary Gertrude [?], Oct. 27, 1939, series B, box 15, PMP, SCPC.

156 **"I pray"**: Margaret Hamilton to Mabel Vernon, Dec. [?] 1952, ibid.

"decided to share": Mary Ellicott Arnold, "A Brief Chronological Statement," ms., box 1, folder 1, Mary Arnold Papers, SL.

157 **"ladies"**: Mary Ellicott Arnold and Mabel Reed, *In the Land of the Grass-*

PAGE

hopper Song: Two Women in the Klamath River Indian Country (1957; rpt. Lincoln: University of Nebraska Press, 1980), p. 181.

"civilize the Indians": Ibid., p. 24.

"reserve and dignity": Ibid, pp. 110–11.

158 "masculine qualifications": Ibid., p. 68.

"I'd give all": [Mr.] Gussie MacDonald to Mary Arnold and Mabel Reed, Sept, 11, 1941, box 2, folder 12, Mary Arnold Papers, SL.

159 "at least": Arnold and Reed, *In the Land*, p. 163.

160 Together Mygatt and Witherspoon: See box 7, Mygatt-Witherspoon Papers, SCPC, for details of their activities. See box 1, ibid., for material on the Bureau of Legal Advice.

"It's a wonderful": Tracy Mygatt to Frances Witherspoon, May 20, 1923, box 6, Mygatt-Witherspoon Papers, SCPC.

"My own dear Darling": Ibid., Apr. 12, 1933.

161 "And I'll work": Ibid.

"Darling dear": Ibid., May 20, 1923.

"a model": Interview with Mygatt and Witherspoon, Feb. 1966, Columbia University Oral History Project, p. 26, in Mygatt-Witherspoon Papers.

162 "substitut[ing] an anti-gay": See Rosalyn Fraad Baxandall, *Words on Fire: The Life and Writings of Elizabeth Gurley Flynn* (New Brunswick, N.J.: Rutgers University Press, 1987), pp. 277n–278n. Baxandall discusses Flynn's lesbianism but doubts the apocryphal tale that Flynn came out in her first draft of *Alderson Story*. Marie Equi's lesbianism is further discussed in Nancy Krieger, "Queen of the Bolsheviks: The Hidden History of Dr. Marie Equi," *Radical America* 17, no. 5 (Sept.–Oct. 1983), and Tom Cook, "The Life of a Northwestern Original: Dr. Marie Equi of Portland," paper read at "Do Ask, Do Tell: Conference on Outing Pacific Northwest History," Tacoma, Wash., Oct. 24, 1998.

As a penologist: See Estelle Freedman, *Maternal Justice: Miriam Van Waters and the Female Reform Tradition* (Chicago: University of Chicago Press, 1996), the definitive biography of Van Waters; also see Burton J. Rowles, *The Lady at Box 99: The Story of Miriam Van Waters* (Greenwich, Conn.: Seabury Press, 1959).

163 "deeply romantic": Freedman, *Maternal Justice*, pp. xii, 161, 171, 166.

164 "The evil Hearst": Ibid., pp. 278–79.

"The Burning": Ibid., p. 280.

In her last years: Ibid., p. 332.

165 "My dear 'Little Lady'": Ruth Mellor to Mildred Scott [Olmsted], Sept. 17, 1913 [?], series II, box 3, Mildred Scott Olmsted Papers, SCPC.

166 **"You say as usual"**: Ibid., Jan. 5, 1914.
"Jewels": Ibid., Sept. 10, 1914.
"That you want": Ibid., Oct. 2, 1914.
"the conflict": Mildred Scott Olmsted to Ruth Mellor, n.d. [1927], box 7, Olmsted Papers.

167 **"Oh — Scottie"**: Ruth Mellor to Mildred Scott [Olmsted], Aug. 28, 1916, box 4, Olmsted Papers.
Ruth's solution: A number of writers have suggested in recent years that the Victorians were much sexier than was earlier recognized. However, my own research has led me to wonder whether they have not generally overstated the Victorian woman's willingness to indulge her libido. Mildred Olmsted's repression of sexuality and Ruth Mellor's sexual guilt seem to me to be characteristic of many women born in the nineteenth century.
"Passionate friendships": Mildred Scott [Olmsted] to Ruth Mellor, Nov. 10, 1919, box 5, Olmsted Papers.

168 **"friendship wasn't natural"**: Ruth Mellor to Mildred Scott [Olmsted], Sept. 22, 1920, box 6, Olmsted Papers. Information about Adele comes from my discussions with Margaret Bacon and her letter to me, cited above.

169 **"complete absence"**: Allen Olmsted to Mildred Scott [Olmsted], June 23, 1920, box 6, Olmsted Papers.
"bonds on a firmer": Bacon, *One Woman's Passion*, p. 96.
"Do you": Mildred Scott Olmsted to Allen Olmsted, May 29, 1923, ibid.

170 **"You should have been"**: Ruth Mellor to Mildred Scott Olmsted, Apr. 16, 1936, ibid.

171 **"No woman could"**: Ibid., [Oct. 1934].
"Ruth was confidante": Bacon, *One Woman's Passion*, p. 273.
"Marriage has been": Ibid., p. 330.

172 **"had several times"**: Ibid., p. 60.

10. "MENTAL HERMAPHRODITES": PIONEERS IN WOMEN'S
HIGHER EDUCATION

Useful discussions about romantic relationships in women's colleges can be found in L. R. Smith, "Social Life at Vassar," *Lippincott's Magazine* 39 (May 1889): 841–51; Lavinia Hart, "A Girl's College Life," *Cosmopolitan* 31 (June 1901): 192; Nancy Salhi, "Smashing: Women's Relationships Before the Fall," *Chrysalis* 8 (Summer 1979): 17–27; Debra Herman, "College and After: The

Vassar Experiment in Women's Education, 1861–1924" (Ph.D. dissertation, Stanford University, 1979); Patricia A. Palmieri, "Here Was Fellowship: A Social Portrait of Academic Women at Wellesley College, 1895–1920," *History of Education Quarterly* 23 (Summer 1983): 194–214; Jeanine M. Paquin, "Redefining Love, Friendship, and Sexuality: Women's Relationships at Women's Colleges, 1890–1920" (master's thesis, School of Social Science, Hampshire College, 1993), pp. 48–49; and Mary Jo Deegan, "'Dear Love, Dear Love': Feminist Pragmatism and the Chicago World of Love and Ritual," *Gender and Society* 10, no. 5 (Oct. 1996): 590–607.

Judith Schwarz has written very feelingly of the relationship between Katharine Lee Bates and Katharine Coman in "*Yellow Clover*: Katharine Lee Bates and Katharine Coman," *Frontiers* 4, no. 1 (Spring 1979): 59–67. See also Bates's poems memorializing their relationship, written after Coman's death: *Yellow Clover: A Book of Remembrance* (New York: Dutton, 1922). Vida Scudder's relationship with Florence Converse is discussed in Nan Bauer Maglin, "Vida to Florence: 'Comrade and Companion,'" *Frontiers* 4, no. 3 (Fall 1979): 13–20. Helen Hull and Mabel Robinson, who met when teaching at Wellesley and went on to teach at Columbia University, are discussed in Judith Schwarz, *Radical Feminists of Heterodoxy: Greenwich Village, 1912–1940* (Norwich, Vt.: New Victoria, 1986), pp. 36–39.

Copies of Hull's papers, held at Columbia University, can be found in the Lesbian Herstory Archives in Brooklyn, New York. A number of Sophie Jewett's lesbian poems have recently been reprinted in Paula Bernat Bennett, ed., *Nineteenth-Century American Women Poets: An Anthology* (Malden, Mass.: Blackwell, 1998), pp. 333–40.

PAGE

175 **[At Smith College]:** Alice Stone Blackwell to Kitty Blackwell, Mar. 12, 1882, reel 16, Blackwell Family Papers, LC.

As one clergyman: Carrie Chapman Catt and Nettie Rogers Shuler, *Woman Suffrage and Politics: The Inner Story of the Suffrage Movement* (New York: Scribner's, 1923), pp. 10–11.

176 **"distinctive profession":** Catharine E. Beecher, "How to Redeem Woman's Profession from Dishonor," *Harper's New Monthly Magazine* 31 (1865). See also Mae Elizabeth Harveson, *Catharine Esther Beecher: Pioneer Educator* (1932; rpt. New York: Arno Press, 1969).

In the decades: Southern women's colleges are discussed in Elizabeth Seymour Eschbach, *The Higher Education of Women in England and America, 1865–1920* (New York: Garland, 1993), chap. 3.

176 **Like Catharine:** In her *Prospectus: Mount Holyoke Female Seminary* (Bos-

ton: Perkins and Marvin, 1837), Lyon states, "It is no part of the design of this seminary to teach young ladies domestic work." She does concede that "this branch of education is exceedingly important"; however, "a literary institution is not the place to gain it"; Reel 2, Mary Lyon Papers, MHC.

177 **"the outstanding"**: Marion Lansing, *Mary Lyon Through Her Letters* (Boston: Books, 1937), p. 28. Lansing is at great pains to deny the emotional significance of the relationship between Lyon and Grant, though she admits that she omitted from this collection "unimportant and repetitive" material such as the "many personal protestations of affection and loyalty" (p. ix). Compare Sarah D. Locke Stow, *History of Mount Holyoke Seminary of South Hadley During the First Half Century, 1837–1887* (South Hadley, Mass.: Mount Holyoke Female Seminary, 1887), pp. 30–67 *passim*, which does not diminish the importance of the relationship.

"I love Miss Grant's": Quoted in Edward Hitchcock, *The Power of Christian Benevolence Illustrated in the Life and Labors of Mary Lyon* (Northampton, Mass.: Hopkins, Brigman, 1852), pp. 53–54.

"My heart": Mary Lyon to Miss White, Feb. 26, 1834, series A, subseries 3, Mary Lyon Collection, MHC.

"I have to bid": Ibid., Aug. 1, 1834.

"show at what sacrifice": Stow, *History*, p. 37.

178 **"a difference"**: Mary Lyon, *Mount Holyoke Female Seminary* (South Hadley, Mass.: Mount Holyoke Female Seminary, 1835), pp. 4–5.

"educators": Mary Lyon, "General View of the Principles and Designs of Mount Holyoke Female Seminary," February 1837, reel 2, Lyon Papers. I agree with Tiziana Rota's observation that although Lyon had to compromise on her articulated views because she believed the seminary "had to be accepted by the general public," the training she established was nevertheless "subversively masculine"; see "Between 'True Women' and 'New Women': Mount Holyoke Students, 1837 to 1908" (Ph.D. dissertation, University of Massachusetts, 1983), p. 6.

"mental hermaphrodites": Harry F. Harrington, "Female Education," *Ladies' Companion* 9 (1838): 293.

"principles and design": Quoted in Helen Lefkowitz Horowitz, *Alma Mater: Design and Experience in Women's Colleges from Their Nineteenth-Century Beginnings to the 1930s* (Boston: Beacon Press, 1984), p. 58.

"to prepare them": Katherine Lydigsen Herbig, "Friends for Freedom: The Lives and Careers of Sallie Holley and Caroline Putnam" (Ph.D. dissertation, Claremont Graduate School, 1977), p. 70. Regardless of such attempts to control women at Oberlin, their education led them to ideas that were often rebellious. For example, in the 1840s and '50s the Young Ladies Association of Oberlin College conducted debates on such subjects as "Is married life more conducive to a woman's happiness than single?" and "Is the marriage relation . . . essential to the happiness of mankind?" See Lee Chambers-Schiller, *Liberty, A Better Husband: Single Women in America, the Generations of 1780–1840,* (New Haven, Conn.: Yale University Press, 1984), p. 15.

179 **"It is a thing"**: Herbig, "Friends," p. 70.
"What can I do?": Lizzie Bates, *Woman: Her Dignity and Sphere* (New York: American Tract Society, 1870), p. 7.

181 **"my darling Hattie"**: Quoted in Florence Matilda Read, *The Story of Spelman College* (Princeton, N.J.: Princeton University Press, 1961), p. 16.
"a woman of powerful": Quoted in ibid., pp. 22–23.
"to train the intellect": Ibid., p. 192.

182 **"Who will bake"**: W. I. Thomas, "The Older and Newer Ideals of Marriage," *American Magazine* (Apr. 1909): 548–52.

183 **"when sitting"**: M. Carey Thomas, "Present Tendencies in Women's College and University Education," *AAUW Journal* 3, no. 17 (Feb. 1908): 46.
Spinsterhood was especially: See Mary Cookingham, "Bluestockings, Spinsters, and Pedagogues: Women College Graduates, 1865–1910," *Population Studies* 38 (November 1984): 360.

184 **Thirty-two percent**: Roberta Frankfort, *Collegiate Women: Domesticity and Career in Turn-of-the-Century America* (New York: New York University Press, 1977), tables 13 and 14.
Of Bryn Mawr: Statistics compiled from Barbara Solomon, *In the Company of Educated Women: A History of Women and Higher Education in America* (New Haven, Conn.: Yale University Press, 1985), table 4, and Daniel Scott Smith, "Family Limitation, Sexual Control, and Domestic Feminism in Victorian America," in Mary S. Hartman and Lois Banner, eds., *Clio's Consciousness Raised: New Perspectives on the History of Women* (New York: Harper and Row), table 1.
Women who received: Of the 229 women who attained Ph.D.'s in the nineteenth century, only 16 married; of the 1025 women who attained Ph.D.'s by 1924, only 20 percent married. See Solomon, *In the Company,* pp. 137–38; Emily J. Hutchinson, *Women and the Ph.D.* (Greensboro: North Carolina College for Women, 1930), pp. 117–18. Even by 1970, it was very difficult for women to combine serious academic work "with the spouse role." See Saul D. Feldman, *Escape from the Doll's House: Women in*

PAGE

Graduate and Professional School Education (New York: McGraw-Hill, 1974), pp. 125, 131.

184 **"It is considered"**: Lucy Salmon to the Learned Six, Oct. 16, 1887, Lucy Salmon Papers, VC.

185 **"a beautiful chapel"**: Lucy Salmon to the Learned Six, Oct. 19, 1887, ibid.
"porch covered": Elsie Rushmore, "In Memory of Lucy Maynard Salmon," *Vassar Quarterly,* July 1932, clipping, Underhill biographical file, folder 1, VC.

186 **"You . . . were"**: Margaret [cousin of Lucy Salmon] to Adelaide Underhill, Feb. 20, 1927, Salmon Papers. See also Louise Fargo Brown, *Apostle of Democracy: The Life of Lucy Salmon* (New York: Harper and Bros., 1943).
"Russian blouse and bloomers": "A Fraulein Not Forgotten," [New York] *Evening Post,* Nov. 1., 1908, clipping, Wenckebach Papers, VC.

187 **"suited her well"**: Eliza H. Kendrick, "Recollections of Miss Wenckebach's Student Days," *In Memoriam: Carla Wenckebach,* reprinted from *Wellesley Magazine,* February 1903, and *College News,* February 27, 1903.
"the center of": "Fraulein Not Forgotten."
"neat cut-away coat": Rose Chamberlin, "The True Womanly Woman," box 35, folder 3, Salmon Papers.
"she maintains": Ibid.

188 **"more or less lacking"**: Quoted in Elaine Kendall, *"Peculiar Institutions": An Informal History of the Seven Sister Colleges* (New York: Putnam, 1976), p. 128.
"My father": Quoted in Linda M. Perkins, "The Education of Black Women in the Nineteenth Century," in John Mack Faragher and Florence Howe, eds., *Women and Higher Education in American History: Essays from the Mount Holyoke College Sesquicentennial Symposium* (New York: Norton, 1988), p. 84.

189 **"I need no bells"**: Quoted in Rosalind S. Cuomo, "'Very Special Circumstances': Women's Colleges and Women's Friendships at the Turn of the Century" (master's thesis, University of Massachusetts, 1988), p. 46.

190 **"Miss Shipp"**: Quoted in Lynn D. Gordon, *Gender and Higher Education in the Progressive Era* (New Haven, Conn.: Yale University Press, 1990), p. 152.
"Like the blue": "My Lady of Dreams," *Newcomb Arcade* (Jan. 1912), quoted in Katy Coyle and Nadiene Van Dyke, "Sex, Smashing, and Storyville in Turn-of-the-Century New Orleans," in John Howard, ed., *Carryin' On in the Lesbian and Gay South* (New York: New York University Press, 1997), p. 60.

PAGE

"Can I tell you": Gertrude Jones, "To One I Love," in Cordelia C. Nevers, ed., *Wellesley Lyrics: Poems Written by the Students and Graduates of Wellesley College* (Boston: Frank Wood, 1896), p. 111.

191 **"I'm glad"**: Quoted in Ellen Fitzpatrick, *Endless Crusade: Women Social Scientists and Progressive Reform* (New York: Oxford University Press, 1990), p. 19.

"a mere forerunner": Howard Chandler Christy, *The American Girl as Seen and Portrayed by Howard Chandler Christy* (1906; rpt. New York: Da Capo Press, 1976), pp. 46–47.

"New Women": Quoted in Joyce Antler, *Lucy Sprague Mitchell: The Making of a Modern Woman* (New Haven, Conn.: Yale University Press, 1987), p. 72.

192 **"A woman needs"**: Phebe Mitchell Kendall, *Maria Mitchell: Life, Letters and Journals* (Boston: Lee and Shepard, 1896), p. 25. See also Mitchell's diary, 1854–1857, in which she observes, "I have certainly some female friends who are strangely attracted to me, and the longer I live the more I do value the love of my own sex" (Nov. 14, [?]). In a December 5, [?], entry, Mitchell distinguishes between her feeling for Susie, which is "as one loves a sister," and her feeling for Ida: "I am jealous of her regard for others — it is something like *love* and less generous than that which I have for Susie, which is affection"; Maria Mitchell Papers, APS. Patricia Palmieri discusses the term "Wellesley marriage" in "Here Was Fellowship," p. 203, and Ethel Puffer Howes in *In Adamless Eden: The Community of Women Faculty at Wellesley* (New Haven, Conn.: Yale University Press, 1995), p. 96.

"Men think": Quoted in Dorothy Burgess, *Dream and Deed: The Story of Katharine Lee Bates* (Norman: University of Oklahoma Press, 1952), p. 4.

"sternly nip[ped]": Quoted in Palmieri, *In Adamless Eden*, p. 99.

193 **"I want you"**: Katharine Lee Bates to Katharine Coman, n.d. [ca. Aug. 1898], Katharine Lee Bates Papers, Wellesley College Archives. Dorothy Burgess, who was Bates's niece, expurgated her discussion of the relationship between Bates and Coman in *Dream and Deed*. For example, she altered (pp. 88–91) the most revealing extant letter that Bates wrote to Coman (Feb. 28, 1891), in which Bates, in England, promises to return to Wellesley after a year's leave. Burgess never indicated where she expurgated telling phrases or added words that were not in the original. On the letter itself, now in the Wellesley College Archives, Burgess placed in parentheses what she would leave out [or add] when she quoted it in *Dream and Deed*: for example, "It was never very possible to

leave Wellesley, because so many (love) anchors held me there, and (it seemed least of all possible when I just found the long-desired way to your dearest heart. Besides) I knew that [President] Shafer tho't it dishonorable in a teacher not to return, if she could, after a year of leave." Burgess's obvious motive was to hide what would have been recognized in 1952 as lesbian love declarations.

193 **"The work of men"**: Quoted in Elaine M. Smith, "Mary McLeod Bethune and the National Youth Administration," in Mabel E. Deutrich and Virginia Purdy, eds., *Clio Was a Woman: Studies in the History of American Women* (Washington, D.C.: Harvard University Press, 1980), p. 149.

"marriage and family": Elaine M. Smith, "Mary McLeod Bethune," in Jessie Carney Smith, ed., *Notable Black American Women* (Detroit: Gale Research, 1992).

"The male attitude": Anonymous, "Confessions of a Woman Professor," quoted in Penina Migdal Glazer and Miriam Slater, *Unequal Colleagues: The Entrance of Women into the Professions, 1890–1940* (New Brunswick, N.J.: Rutgers University Press, 1987), p. 59.

194 **"distressed to see"**: Caroline Hazard, ed., *An Academic Courtship: Letters of Alice Freeman and George Herbert Palmer, 1886–1887* (Cambridge: Harvard University Press, 1940), p. 5.

"power / As I": Alice Freeman Palmer, *A Marriage Cycle*, ed. George Palmer (Boston: Houghton Mifflin, 1915), p. 3.

"Perhaps": Hazard, *An Academic Courtship*, p. 6.

"Then as a little girl": Ibid., p. 7.

195 **"Great love"**: Palmer, *Marriage Cycle*, p. 24.

"If I marry": Quoted in Joyce Antler, "Was She a Good Mother?" in Barbara Harris and JoAnn McNamara, eds., *Women and the Social Structure* (Durham, N.C.: Duke University Press, 1984), p. 57.

"You have lived": Antler, *Lucy Sprague Mitchell*, p. 168.

"You would not have to": Antler, "Was She," p. 58.

11. MAKING WOMEN'S HIGHER EDUCATION EVEN HIGHER: M. CAREY THOMAS

Thomas's voluminous papers, which are available on microfilm at Bryn Mawr College, are indexed with useful descriptions of the contents of each reel in Lucy Fisher West, *The Papers of M. Carey Thomas in the Bryn Mawr Col-*

lege Archives: Reel Guide and Index to the Microfilm Collection (Woodbridge, Conn.: Research Publications, 1982).

Gertrude Stein fictionalized the Thomas-Gwinn-Hodder triangle in *Fernhurst* (1904; rpt. *Fernhurst, QED, and Other Stories*, New York: Liveright, 1971). The triangle is also discussed in *The Autobiography of Bertrand Russell, 1872– 1914*, vol. 1 (Boston: Little, Brown, 1967), pp. 194–95. (Russell was Thomas's cousin by marriage.)

Useful discussions of the Bryn Mawr Summer School can be found in Rita Heller, "Blue Collars and Bluestockings: The Bryn Mawr Summer School for Women Workers, 1921–1938," in Joyce L. Kornbluh and Mary Frederickson, eds., *Sisterhood and Solidarity: Workers Education for Women, 1914–1984* (Philadelphia: Temple University Press, 1984), pp. 107–45, and Joyce L. Kornbluh, *A New Deal for Workers' Education: The Workers' Service Program, 1933– 1942* (Urbana: University of Illinois Press, 1987).

PAGE

197 **"If only it were"**: M. Carey Thomas to Mary Whitall Thomas, Nov. 21, 1880, reel 31, M. Carey Thomas Papers, BMC.

198 **"unusually good"**: M. Carey Thomas to Dr. James B. Rhoads, Aug. 14, 1883, ibid.
"solid and scientific": Ibid.

199 **"Oh my"**: M. Carey Thomas, diary, Jan. 6, 1871, reel 1, Thomas Papers.
"Min says": Hannah Whitall Smith to Mary Whitall Thomas, n.d. [Summer 1863], ibid.
If she had been: See my discussion of working-class women who passed as men in the late nineteenth and early twentieth centuries in *Odd Girls and Twilight Lovers: A History of Lesbian Life in Twentieth-Century America* (New York: Columbia University Press, 1991), pp. 41–45.

200 **"I greatly prefer"**: M. Carey Thomas, diary, Nov. 26, 1870, reel 1, Thomas Papers.
"Go ahead": Ibid., Jan. 23, 1872.
"one aim": Ibid., Feb. 26, 1871.
"I shall fail": Ibid., Feb. 22, 1878, reel 2.

201 **"and when I go"**: Ibid., Mar. 24, 1878.
"To think": Mamie Gwinn to M. Carey Thomas, Mar. [?], 1882, reel 53, Thomas Papers. Though Thomas left many papers that revealed her lesbianism, she did censor some material. For example, there is a hiatus in her journals from 1879 to early 1885. When the journal resumed, on Feb. 2, 1885, she wrote that she would describe in the pages to follow

PAGE

what she considered "an experience and a madness, a temptation and a delusion." But many of those pages were destroyed: the journal skips from p. 77 to p. 82, and then again to p. 128. See reel 2, Thomas Papers.

202 **"Yes, dear love"**: Quoted in Helen Lefkowitz Horowitz, *The Power and Passion of M. Carey Thomas* (New York: Knopf, 1994), p. 105.

She blamed herself: Thomas wrote to her aunt, Hannah Whitall Smith, that if she had not been appointed president, it would have been to her "a sign that I could set my wings for an attic in Paris and Bohemia"; Mar. 11, 1894, reel 29, Thomas Papers.

203 **"the Cause"**: Ibid.

"elegant times": M. Carey Thomas, diary, Feb. 13, 1878, reel 12, Thomas Papers.

"I am devoted": M. Carey Thomas, diary, Aug. 25, 1878, reel 2, Thomas Papers.

"take you in my arms": M. Carey Thomas to Mary Garrett, Aug. 9, 1893, reel 17, Thomas Papers.

"my lips": Ibid., [Oct. ?], 1893. After Julia's departure, Mary went to stay with Carey at every opportunity, whenever Mamie was gone from the Deanery. For many years, Carey balanced her two loves, never denying the importance of both in her life. She wrote to Mary: "To have such a charming thing have happened as our caring for each other, when my love for Mamie and hers for me is really as much as one lifetime deserves"; Mar. 5, 1893, ibid.

204 **"That chained woman"**: Mary Garrett to M. Carey Thomas, Aug. 30, 1892, reel 43, Thomas Papers.

"Whenever Miss M. Carey Thomas": Quoted in Edith Finch, *Carey Thomas of Bryn Mawr* (New York: Harper and Brothers, 1947), p. 209.

"the power and opportunities": Ibid.

205 **"'smashed' on each other"**: M. Carey Thomas, diary, Spring 1873, reel 1, Thomas Papers.

"we are carried": Ibid., Feb. 22, 1878, reel 2.

206 **"clasped hands"**: Ibid.

207 **"the materials"**: Helen Lefkowitz Horowitz, "*Nous Autres*: Reading, Passion, and the Creation of M. Carey Thomas," *Journal of American History* 79 (June–Sept. 1992): 72.

"bizarre": M. Carey Thomas to Margaret Hicks, Mar. 9, 1879, reel 32, Thomas Papers.

208 **"frenzied mirth"**: Charles Baudelaire, "Lesbos," in *The Flowers of Evil*, trans. P. J. W. Higson and Elliot R. Ashe (Cestrian Press, 1975), p. 122.

PAGE

"wretched victims": Ibid., "Delphinia and Hippolyta," p. 156.

"devotion": See M. Carey Thomas, diary, Aug. 25, 1878, reel 2; M. Carey Thomas to Mary Whitall Thomas, Nov. 14, 1882, reel 32; and M. Carey Thomas to Mary Garrett, Nov. 11, 1887, reel 15, all in Thomas Papers. More rarely, gossiping with Mary Garrett, Thomas used language that may have been more descriptive; for instance, she referred to Lady Henry Somerset and Frances Willard, who were in the throes of a relationship in England (Anna Gordon was back in Illinois), as "our lovers"; M. Carey Thomas to Mary Garrett, Feb. 13, 1895, reel 18, Thomas Papers.

"vile": Quoted in Marjorie Housepian Dobkins, ed. *The Making of a Feminist: Early Journals and Letters of M. Carey Thomas* (Kent, Ohio: Kent State University Press, 1979), p. 87.

"It is difficult": M. Carey Thomas, diary, Feb. 13, 1878, reel 2, Thomas Papers.

Through her lesbian: Among Thomas's papers is a letter to *The Woman Leader*, written probably after *The Well of Loneliness* was reviewed, that refers to "yearning" that is "the multiple and complicated need of a complex human being." Many women could satisfy that yearning, the letter states, "with equal success through man or woman"; quoted in Dobkins, *Making of a Feminist*, p. 86. Thomas reported to Mary Garrett that reading a reprint of Samuel Tissot's 1758 book *Onanism: A Treatise Upon the Disorders Produced by Masturbation* had answered for her "all questions raised by French novels." She was undoubtedly referring to Tissot's discussion of mutual clitoral masturbation and his observation that such exchanges caused "women to love other women with as much fondness and jealousy as they did men"; M. Carey Thomas to Mary Garrett, Aug. 27, 1895, reel 19, Thomas Papers.

209 "as well known": M. Carey Thomas, "Notes for the Opening Address of Bryn Mawr College, 1899," in Barbara Cross, ed., *The Educated Woman in America* (New York: Teachers' College Press of Columbia University, 1965), p. 140.

Sixty-one percent: Roberta Frankfort, *Collegiate Women: Domesticity and Career in Turn-of-the-Century America* (New York: New York University Press, 1977), pp. 75–78.

"had set out": Quoted in Horowitz, *Power and Passion*, p. 197.

210 "Women scholars": Thomas, "Present Tendencies," p. 60.

"Amazonian": G. Stanley Hall, *Adolescence*, vol. 2 (New York: Appleton, 1904), p. 595.

211 "schools of *manners*": M. Carey Thomas to Mary Garrett, Oct. 3, 1899, reel 21, Thomas Papers.

"What is the best": M. Carey Thomas, "Should the Higher Education of Women Differ from That of Men?" *Educational Review* 31 (1901): 1.

"aims": Laurence Vesey, "Martha Carey Thomas," in Edward T. James et al., eds., *Notable American Women,* vol. 3 (Cambridge, Mass.: Harvard University Press, 1971), p. 448.

"young women": Quoted in Hilda Worthington Smith, *Women Workers at the Bryn Mawr Summer School* (New York: Affiliated Schools for Women Workers, 1929), p. 4.

212 "to barter": Thomas, "Present Tendencies," p. 54.

213 Between 1909 and 1918: Frankfort, *Collegiate Women,* p. 73.

"find their greatest": M. Carey Thomas, "The Future of Woman's Higher Education," *Mount Holyoke College: The 75th Anniversary* (South Hadley, Mass., 1913), pp. 100–104.

214 "Until women": M. Carey Thomas to Mary Whitall Thomas, Oct. 8, 1881, reel 31, Thomas Papers.

"is so absolutely": Mary Garrett to M. Carey Thomas, May 1, 1894, reel 44, ibid.

215 "yearning": Quoted in Dobkins, *Making of a Feminist,* p. 86.

"there was no hope": M. Carey Thomas to Simon Flexner, July 10, 1914, M. Carey Thomas Collection, Flexner Papers, APS. Thomas's relationship with this Jewish brother-in-law, whom she loved and trusted, poses another provocative contradiction to her troubling anti-Semitism.

216 "after Mary's death": Quoted in Horowitz, *Power and Passion,* p. 409.

"strenuous intellectual": M. Carey Thomas, "The Curriculum of the Women's College — Old Fashioned Disciplines," *Journal of the Association of Collegiate Alumnae* 10 (May 1917).

"the functions": Hall, *Adolescence,* chap. 2.

"I have forgotten": Quoted in Cross, *Educated Woman,* p. 37.

12. THE STRUGGLE TO MAINTAIN WOMEN'S LEADERSHIP: MARY EMMA WOOLLEY

Valuable studies of Mary Woolley's role at Mount Holyoke College include Francis Lester Ward, *On a New England Campus* (Boston: Houghton Mifflin, 1937); Arthur C. Cole, *A Hundred Years of Mount Holyoke College: The Evolution of an Educational Ideal* (New Haven, Conn.: Yale University Press, 1940);

Mabel Newcomer, *A Century of Higher Education for Women* (New York: Harper and Row, 1959); Elaine Kendall, *"Peculiar Institutions": An Informal History of the Seven Sister Colleges* (New York: Putnam, 1976); Tiziana Rota, "Between 'True Women' and 'New Women': Mount Holyoke Students, 1837 to 1908" (Ph.D. dissertation, University of Massachusetts, 1983); Cynthia Farr Brown, "Leading Women: Female Leadership in American Women's Higher Education" (Ph.D. dissertation, Brandeis University, 1992); and Ann Karus Meeropol, "A Practical Visionary: Mary Emma Woolley and the Education of Women" (Ed.D. dissertation, University of Massachusetts, 1992).

PAGE

217 **"Oh! My dear"**: Mary Woolley to Jeannette Marks, April 1900, Mary Woolley Papers, MHC.

218 **Of the thirty-seven**: M. Carey Thomas, "Education of Women," in Nicholas Murray Butler, ed., *Monographs on Education in the United States*, vol. 1 (Albany: J. B. Lyon, 1900), 319–58.

"grounded in reality": Mary Woolley, inaugural address, May 15, 1901, *The Mount Holyoke*, inauguration no. [May 5, 1901], pp. 8–15, MHC.

"among all sorts": Ibid.

219 **"ability in leadership"**: Ibid.

220 **"a member of a sex"**: Mary E. Woolley, speech to the woman suffrage convention honoring Susan B. Anthony, Baltimore, Md., Feb. 8, 1906, Woolley Papers.

"a man would": Mary E. Woolley, "Some Results of Higher Education for Women," *Harper's Bazaar* 43 (1909): 586–89.

221 **"those coldly intellectual"**: editorial, *The Brunonian*, quoted in Anna Mary Wells, *Miss Marks and Miss Woolley* (Boston: Houghton Mifflin, 1978), pp. 38–39.

"not to 'seem'": Jeannette Marks, *Life and Letters of Mary Emma Woolley* (Washington, D.C.: Public Affairs Press, 1955), p. 39.

222 **"a good figure"**: *Springfield Republican*, Jan. 18, 1900, clipping, Woolley Papers.

223 **"young and vigorous"**: Marks, *Life and Letters*, p. 46.

"like a poet": Quoted in Mary Woolley to Jeannette Marks, Oct. 3, 1910, Woolley Papers.

"Dearest, I thought": Mary Woolley to Jeannette Marks, n.d., folder of undated letters, "1898–1900," Woolley-Marks correspondence, Woolley Papers.

224 **"my heart's great"**: Ibid., Aug. 28, 1900.

224 "to lavish": Ibid., Aug. 20, 1900.

"May, I want": Jeannette Marks to Mary Woolley, Apr. 6, 1905, ibid. Marks understood how the letters would be read when she debated whether to deposit them in the Mount Holyoke College Archives; see, for example, her letter to the Wellesley librarian Hannah French, a sympathetic friend, May 1, 1956, Special Collections, WC Library. In choosing to give the love letters to the archives, she knew very well that she was preserving a bit of lesbian history.

225 "Just think": Mary Woolley to Jeannette Marks, Aug. 18, 1900, Wooley Papers.

"As I look": Ibid., July 13, 1900. Wells (*Miss Marks and Miss Woolley*) presents Woolley's love for Marks as a tragic flaw in the life of an otherwise wholly admirable individual. Meeropol ("Practical Visionary") is far more persuasive in her reasoned observation that "Woolley and Marks functioned at a remarkably high level professionally throughout their long lives, an achievement attributable in part to the emotional sustenance of their relationship" (p. 301).

226 "The demands of the home": Mary Woolley, "The College Woman's Place in the World," Oct. 16, 1908, speech 44, Woolley Papers.

227 "Your success": Mary Woolley to Jeannette Marks, Apr. 7, 1905, Woolley Papers.

"No stone": Ibid., Oct. 3, 1910.

"one of the twelve": *Good Housekeeping*, Mar. 1931, pp. 200–204.

228 "I can picture": Mary Woolley to Jeannette Marks, Oct. 1, 1901, Woolley Papers.

"The week has been": Ibid., Oct. 3, 1901.

"with some amusement": Susan Stifler, interview by Elizabeth Green, May 1972, in *Mount Holyoke in the Twentieth Century*, transcript of oral history, vol. 10, pp. 2–3, Special Collections, MHC.

"as everyone else": Viola Barnes, interview by Elizabeth Green, ibid., vol. 3, pp. 3, 1–2.

229 "My anxiety": Mary Woolley to Jeannette Marks, Oct. 21, 1910, Woolley Papers.

230 "a feministic": Mary Woolley, "The Woman's College," quoted in Marks, *Life and Letters*, p. 80.

231 "You are the one": M. Carey Thomas to Mary Woolley, June 28, 1913, Woolley Papers.

233 "If Jeannette": See Wells, *Miss Marks and Miss Wolley*, p. 169.

"the best person": See Helen Lefkowitz Horowitz, *Alma Mater: Design and*

Experience in Women's Colleges from their Nineteenth-Century Beginnings to the 1930s (Boston: Beacon Press, 1984), p. 304.

234 **"If the college"**: Quoted in Meeropol, "Practical Visionary," pp. 341–42.

235 **"get [the college]"**: "Dr. Woolley Opposes Male Successor," *Newsweek*, Feb. 13, 1937.

"Mr. Ham's big": Quoted in "What Would Mary Lyon Say?" *Boston Sunday Globe*, Feb. 7, 1937, p. 1.

Not only did: Penina Migdal Glazer and Miriam Slater discuss the ways in which Ham changed the composition of the faculty, specifically reversing departmental nominations of women in favor of men because he felt that "there were too many older women at the college and . . . any new appointment should go to a younger man"; *Unequal Colleagues: The Entrance of Women into the Professions, 1890–1940* (New Brunswick, N.J.: Rutgers University Press, 1987), pp. 259–60n. History professor Margaret Judson, who was refused an appointment on such grounds in 1941, discusses the incident in *Breaking the Barrier: A Professional Autobiography by a Woman Educator and Historian Before the Women's Movement* (New Brunswick, N.J.: Rutgers University Press, 1984), pp. 75–76.

236 **"Jeannette writes"**: Quoted in Jeannette Marks to Martha Shackford, Oct. 1, 1955, WC.

13. THE TRIUMPH OF ANGELINA: EDUCATION IN FEMININITY

Attitudes toward women's education at mid-century may be gleaned from George Stoddard, *On the Education of Women* (New York: Macmillan, 1950); Louis W. Norris, "How to Educate a Woman," *Saturday Review*, Nov. 27, 1954, p. 40ff.; and Dorothy D. Lee, "What Shall We Teach Women?" *Mademoiselle* (Aug. 1947): p. 213ff.

The shift in views of women's education is well traced in Roberta Frankfort, *Collegiate Women: Domesticity and Career in Turn-of-the-Century America* (New York: New York University Press, 1977), and Barbara Solomon, *In the Company of Educated Women: A History of Women and Higher Education in America* (New Haven, Conn.: Yale University Press, 1985).

237 **"Nine [professors]"**: Quoted in Trisha Franzen, *Spinsters and Lesbians: Independent Womanhood in the United States* (New York: New York University Press, 1996), pp. 139–40.

237 **"Women as a whole"**: Charles W. Eliot, *Charles W. Eliot: The Man and His Beliefs* (New York: Harper and Brothers, 1926), p. 167.

238 **"equal education"**: Debra Herman, "College and After: The Vassar Experiment in Women's Education, 1861–1924" (Ph.D. dissertation, Stanford University, 1979), p. 334.

"little thought": Robert Foster and Pauline Wilson, *Women After College* (New York: Columbia University Press, 1942), p. 239.

In 1920: Jessie Bernard, *Academic Women* (University Park: Pennsylvania State University Press, 1964), p. 40, and Cynthia Fuchs Epstein, *Options and Limits in Professional Careers* (Berkeley: University of California Press, 1971), pp. 200–201. See also Susan B. Carter, "Academic Women Revisited: An Empirical Study of Changing Patterns in Women's Employment as College and University Faculty, 1890–1963," *Journal of Social History* 14 (Summer 1981): 675–95. Carter argues that the spread of coeducation opened many more jobs for women, but acknowledges that within these coeducational institutions "women's academic employment has been restricted to the lowest rungs of the hierarchy" (p. 690).

For example, at Smith: Penina Migdal Glazer and Miriam Slater, *Unequal Colleagues: The Entrance of Women into the Professions, 1890–1940* (New Brunswick, N.J.: Rutgers University Press, 1987), pp. 260–61. Anecdotal information corroborates the statistics. For example, in a 1919 article, Helen Hughes talked about her personal experiences with a department that had virtually hired her and then reversed its decision when a man became available. As the chairman admitted, "We prefer to appoint a man." See "The Academic Chance," *Journal of the Association of Collegiate Alumnae* 12, no. 2 (Jan. 1919). Roswell Ham's blatant discrimination against women at Mount Holyoke is described in Mary Woolley to Belle Ferris, Feb. 6, 1942, Woolley Papers; Woolley quotes a *New York Times* article that reported on eight hirings: four men, all in professorial ranks; four women, all in instructor rank.

239 **The decrease**: See Brown, "Leading Women," p. 15.

"prevailing view": *Radcliffe Alumnae Report, Class of 1952* (1977), quoted in Wini Breines, *Young, White and Miserable: Growing Up Female in the Fifties* (Boston: Beacon Press, 1992), p. 193.

240 **"who yearns"**: John W. Meagher, "Homosexuality: Its Psychobiological and Psychopathological Significance," *Urological and Cutaneous Review* 33 (Aug. 1929): 508.

241 **"homosexuality among women"**: Carl Jung, "The Love Problem in the Student" (1928), in John Francis McDermott, ed., *The Sex Problem in Modern Society* (New York: Modern Library, 1931), pp. 327–47.

PAGE

242 **A 1923 survey:** Cited in Regina Morantz-Sanchez, *Sympathy and Science: Women Physicians in American Medicine* (New York: Oxford University Press, 1985), p. 322.

"turned their backs": Bernard, *Academic Women*, p. 215.

"thought with the founders": Worth Tuttle, "Autobiography of an Ex-Feminist," Part I, *Atlantic Monthly*, Dec. 1933, p. 641.

243 **"handful of eager":** Quoted in Horowitz, *Alma Mater*, p. 284.

In fact: Newcomer, *Century of Higher Education*.

By the end: Ibid.

244 **But by 1930:** Patricia Graham, "Expansion and Exclusion: A History of Women in American Higher Education," *Signs* 3 (1978): 764–65. Frank Stricker has attempted to counter figures such as these by pointing out that though women failed to keep up with men proportionally, the *number* of doctorates they were awarded during these years continued to increase. See "Cookbooks and Law Books: A Hidden History of Career Women in Twentieth Century America," *Journal of Social History* 10 (Fall 1976): 1–19.

Of 1025 women: Emily J. Hutchinson, *Women and the Ph.D.* (Greensboro: North Carolina College for Women, 1930). In a mid-century study of women who won fellowship support in graduate school, the authors were surprised to discover that "the proportion of single women in [this] group is much greater than in the population as a whole" (p. 189) and that 84 percent of the single women said that they were "satisfied with [their] personal life" (p. 134); Eli Ginzberg et al., *Life Styles of Educated Women* (New York: Columbia University Press, 1966).

Fifty-five percent: Helen Astin, *The Woman Doctorate in America: Origins, Career, and Family* (New York: Russell Sage Foundation, 1969), pp. 26, 101–2.

245 **In fact, only:** Glazer and Slater, *Unequal Colleagues*, p. 254n.

"on air": Eva von Baur Hansl, "Parenthood and the College," *Journal of the AAUW* 15, no. 2 (1922): 44.

"threw off": Clarence Little, "Women in College Administration" (1928), quoted in Brown, "Leading Women," pp. 444–45.

246 **"The estate":** Lorraine Hansberry, letter to the editor, *The Ladder* 1, no. 1 (Aug. 1957): 28. *The Ladder's* editor, Barbara Grier, identified the anonymous letter as having been written by Hansberry in "Lesbiana," *The Ladder* 14, no. 5–6 (Feb.–Mar. 1970).

"I don't believe": Quoted in Anne MacKay, *Wolf Girls at Vassar: Lesbian and Gay Experiences, 1930–1990* (New York: St. Martin's Press, 1993), p. 16. Binger did not, in fact, have much to worry about with regard to the lesbian influence of Vassar's leaders. The general ethos of the era guaranteed that most students would choose heterosexual domesticity. The Mellon survey of Vassar women, which was published in 1956 (Donald Brown, *Journal of Social Studies*), concluded that Vassar students were "overwhelmingly 'future family oriented,'" and elected to take courses primarily that would "enrich family life"; quoted in Elaine Kendall, *"Peculiar Institutions": An Informal History of the Seven Sister Colleges* (New York: Putnam, 1976), p. 219.

247 **"It is of great"**: *Annual Report of Dean Gildersleeve of Barnard College* (New York: Barnard College, 1932), p. 7.

"almost always": Quoted in Brown, "Leading Women," p. 445.

248 **"There was an old maid"**: Anonymous, "Down with English," *Mount Holyoke Magazine*, Spring 1920.

College women thus chose: Clyde V. Kiser et al., *Trends and Variations in Fertility in the United States* (Cambridge, Mass.: Harvard University Press, 1968), pp. 148–49.

"whether or not": Dorothy Bromley and Florence Haxton Britten, *Youth and Sex: A Study of 1300 College Students* (New York: Harper and Row, 1938), p. 129.

In their study: Ibid., p. 117.

249 **In Davis's study**: Katharine Bement Davis, *Factors in the Sex Life of Twenty-Two Hundred Women* (New York: Harper and Row, 1929), pp. 246–48.

As a further: Bromley and Britten, *Youth and Sex*, p. 120.

"they frequently": Ibid., pp. 129–30.

250 **"I felt passionately"**: Quoted in MacKay, *Wolf Girls*, pp. 23–24.

"attraction of colleges": Milton E. Hahn and Byron H. Atkinson, "The Sexually Deviant Student," *School and Society* 82 (Sept. 17, 1955): 85.

"if I didn't": Quoted in MacKay, *Wolf Girls*, p. 16.

251 **According to a recent**: Margaret M. Caffrey, *Ruth Benedict: Stranger in this Land* (Austin: University of Texas Press, 1989).

14. "WHEN MORE WOMEN ENTER PROFESSIONS": LESBIAN PIONEERING IN THE LEARNED PROFESSIONS

Useful general histories of women in medicine include Mary Roth Walsh, *Doctors Wanted — No Women Need Apply: Social Barriers in the Medical Profession, 1835–1975* (New Haven, Conn.: Yale University Press, 1977), and Ruth J. Abram, ed., *"Send Us a Lady Physician": Women Doctors in America, 1835–*

1920 (New York: Norton, 1985). The most complete biography of Dr. Mary Walker is Charles McCool Snyder's *Dr. Mary Walker: The Little Lady in Pants* (New York: Vantage, 1962); also see Elizabeth Leonard, *Yankee Women: Gender Battles in the Civil War* (New York: Norton, 1994). S. Josephine Baker's *Fighting for Life* (New York: Macmillan, 1939) is a good autobiographical account of a female doctor in the early twentieth century, though Baker veils her lesbianism. Dr. Eliza Mosher's series for the *Medical Woman's Journal*, "The History of American Medical Women," generally acknowledged the "devoted companions" of the doctors on whom she focused. See, for instance, Jan. 1924, pp. 14–16, on Dr. Mary Smith, whose relationship with Dr. Emma Culbertson is discussed, and on Dr. Chloe Annette Buckell and her "beloved friend," Charlotte Playter; and Oct. 1922, pp. 253–59, in which Mosher discusses herself and Lucy Hall.

Ionia Whipper is discussed in Carole Ione, *Pride of Family: Four Generations of American Women of Color* (New York: Summit Books, 1991). For information about Charlotte Ray, see the *Woman's Journal*, May 25, 1872, p. 161ff.; Phebe A. Hanaford, *Daughters of America* (Augusta, Ga.: True, 1882); Sadie T. M. Alexander, "Women as Practitioners of Law in the United States," *National Bar Journal* (July 1941); and Darlene Clark Hine, *Black Women in America* (Brooklyn: Carlson, 1993), p. 965.

Karen Berger Morello's *The Invisible Bar: The Woman Lawyer in America, 1638 to the Present* (New York: Random House, 1986), is a good general history of female lawyers.

PAGE

255 **"Dr. Culbertson"**: M. Carey Thomas to Mary Whitall Thomas, Nov. 14, 1882, reel 32, M. Carey Thomas Papers, BMC.

256 **"the cult of true"**: See Barbara Welter, "The Cult of True Womanhood, 1820–1860," in *Dimity Convictions: The American Woman in the Nineteenth Century* (Athens: Ohio University Press, 1976), pp. 21–41, and Sara M. Evans, *Born for Liberty: A History of Women in America* (New York: Free Press, 1989).

"the privilege": Peter G. Filene, *Him/Her/Self: Sex Roles in Modern America*, 2nd ed. (Baltimore: Johns Hopkins University Press, 1986), p. 13.

"a woman who has": Quoted in Gloria Moldow, *Women Doctors in Gilded Age Washington: Race, Gender, and Professionalization* (Urbana: University of Illinois Press, 1987), p. 33. Carroll Smith-Rosenberg demonstrates the connection between the New Woman and the lesbian in "The New Woman as Androgyne: Social Disorder and the Gender Crisis, 1870–1936," in *Disorderly Conduct: Visions of Gender in Victorian America*

(New York: Knopf, 1985). See also my chapter "New Women" in *Surpassing the Love of Men: Romantic Friendship and Love Between Women from the Renaissance to the Present* (New York: William Morrow, 1981).

257 **"You give me":** Quoted in Agnes C. Vietor, ed., *A Woman's Quest: The Life of Marie E. Zakrzewska, M.D.* (1924; rpt. New York: Arno Press, 1972), pp. 140–41.

"with them: Ibid., pp. 7–8, 22.

258 **Even by 1900:** Marriage statistics for 1900 and 1920 in William Chafe, *The American Woman: Her Changing Social, Economic, and Political Roles* (New York; Oxford University Press, 1972), pp. 219–20, and Lynn Y. Weiner, *From Working Girl to Working Mother* (Chapel Hill: University of North Carolina Press, 1985), pp. 4, 6.

For example: Frances Bryan, "Occupations of Vassar Women," *Vassar Quarterly* (Feb. 1932), pp. 26–29. Bryan found that only 21 percent of Vassar graduates were both "married and gainfully employed."

259 **"the most distinguished":** R. W. Shufeldt, "Dr. Havelock Ellis on Sexual Inversion," *Pacific Medical Journal* 45 (1902): 201.

By 1870: See Mabel Newcomer, *A Century of Higher Education for Women* (New York: Harper and Brothers, 1959), pp. 11–15, and Mary P. Ryan, *Womanhood in America: From Colonial Times to the Present* (New York: New Viewpoints, 1979), pp. 85–89.

260 **"Well did she know":** Willystine Goodsell, ed., *Pioneers of Women's Education in the United States: Emma Willard, Catharine Beecher, Mary Lyon* (New York: McGraw-Hill, 1931), pp. 131–32.

261 **"froward females":** Quoted in Lillian O'Connor, *Pioneer Women Orators: Rhetoric in the Ante-Bellum Reform Movement* (New York: Columbia University Press, 1954), p. 32.

Antoinette Brown: The relationship between Brown and Stone is discussed in Andrew Sinclair, *The Better Half: The Emancipation of the American Woman* (New York: Harper and Row, 1965), pp. 155–58. As Sinclair phrases it, "At Oberlin, Antoinette Brown fell in love with Lucy Stone, with all the passion and sentimental license possible between women of the time, before they learned to question their subconscious motives" (p. 155). Jonathan Katz quotes from their love letters in *Gay American History* (New York: Crowell, 1976), p. 644.

"Paul said": Anna Howard Shaw, *The Story of a Pioneer* (1915; rpt. New York: Harper and Row, 1929), pp. 126, 127.

262 **"preaching a doctrine":** Joseph Hanaford to Phebe Hanaford, June 10, 1872, folder 2, Hanaford Papers, NHA.

263 **"My loved one"**: Ellen Miles to Phebe Hanaford, n.d. [early 1880s], folder 21, Hanaford Papers.

"the golden links": Marietta Holley to Phebe Hanaford, Nov. 31, 1914, folder 20, Hanaford Papers. Letters from Frances Willard and Alice Stone Blackwell are also in this collection. Hanaford and Miles's care of Anna Dickinson can be traced through letters in reel 6, Anna Dickinson Collection, Manuscript Division, LC: see, for instance, Feb. 8, Feb. 24, and Mar. 3, 1893.

264 **"both physically"**: Jean McMahon Humez, ed., *Gifts of Power: The Writings of Rebecca Jackson, Black Visionary, Shaker Eldress* (Amherst: University of Massachusetts Press, 1981), pp. 312–13.

"She was going east": Ibid., p. 261.

265 **"of all things"**: Ibid., p. 17.

"unit[ing]": Ibid., p. 252.

"crowned King": Ibid., p. 308.

"I saw Rebecca": Ibid., p. 225.

"close relationship": Ibid., p. 9.

266 **As Eula Young**: Eula H. Young, "The Law as a Profession for Women," *Publications of the Association of Collegiate Alumnae*, series III, no. 5 (Feb. 1902): 15–23.

In 1880: Ronald Chester, "Women Lawyers in the Urban Bar: An Oral History," *New England Law Review* 18, no. 3 (1983): 522. Virginia G. Drachman says there were only *seventy-five* female lawyers in the United States in 1880; *Women Lawyers and the Origins of Professional Identity in America: The Letters of the Equity Club, 1887 to 1890* (Ann Arbor: University of Michigan Press, 1993), p. 2.

"not a virtue": Young, "The Law," p. 19.

267 **"The majority"**: Quoted in Drachman, *Women Lawyers*, p. 27.

One law historian: Virginia Drachman, "'My Partner in Law and Life': Marriage in the Lives of Women Lawyers in Late Nineteenth and Early Twentieth Century America," *Law and Social Inquiry* 14 (1989).

For example: See Chester, "Women Lawyers," p. 521.

268 **When Frances Kellor**: See William Joseph Maxwell, "Frances Kellor in the Progressive Era: A Case Study in the Professionalization of Reform" (Ed.D. dissertation, Teachers' College, Columbia University, 1968), on Perry's influence on Kellor.

269 **"made a mockery"**: Regina Morantz-Sanchez, *Sympathy and Science: Women Physicians in American Medicine* (New York: Oxford University Press, 1985), p. 30.

PAGE

269 **"gain complete"**: Elizabeth Blackwell, *Pioneer Work in Opening the Medical Profession to Women: Autobiographical Sketches* (1895; rpt. New York: Source Book Press, 1970), p. 61.

"[even] if no other": Ishbel Ross, *Child of Destiny: The Life Story of the First Woman Doctor* (New York: Harper and Brothers, 1949), p. 109.

270 **"We . . . had looked"**: Lilian Welsh, *Reminiscences of Thirty Years in Baltimore* (Baltimore: Norman, Remington, 1925), pp. 32–33.

"No woman": Gertrude Baillie, "Should Professional Women Marry?" *Woman's Medical Journal* 2 (Feb. 1894): 33.

In any case: Morantz-Sanchez, *Sympathy and Science*, p. 137. Though no separate statistics have been gathered for pioneering African-American physicians, many of them also were unmarried. See Darlene Clark Hine, *Black Women in America* (Brooklyn, N.Y.: Carlson, 1993), entries for Francis Kneeland, Matilda Evans, Rebecca Crumpler, May Edward Chinn, etc.

272 **"The whole dreadful week"**: Elizabeth Clark to Ada P. McCormick, n.d. [Jan. 1914], box 1, folder 7, Ada P. McCormick Papers, AUHS.

273 **"I do not"**: Florence Converse, *Diana Victrix* (Boston: Houghton Mifflin, 1897), pp. 240–41, 339.

15. MAKING PLACES FOR WOMEN IN MEDICINE: EMILY BLACKWELL

An assessment of the Drs. Blackwell by their medical contemporaries can be found in Women's Medical Association of New York, eds., *In Memory of Dr. Elizabeth Blackwell and Dr. Emily Blackwell* (New York: Academy of Medicine, 1911). Annie Sturgis Daniel's "A Cautious Experiment: The History of the New York Infirmary for Women and Children and the Women's Medical College of the New York Infirmary," Medical Women's Journal 49 (Jan. 1942): 12–15, is an interesting mid-century account of their work.

My view of Elizabeth Blackwell is informed by Nancy Ann Salhi's "Elizabeth Blackwell, M.D. (1821–1910): A Biography" (Ph.D. dissertation, University of Pennsylvania, 1974), as well as by the sources cited below.

PAGE

274 **"I have often thought"**: Emily Blackwell, journal, July 16, 1853, reel 3, Blackwell Family Papers, SL.

PAGE

"her [professional] desires": Elizabeth M. Cushier, "In Memory of Dr. Emily Blackwell," *Woman's Medical Journal* (Apr. 1911): p. 88.

275 "strong-minded woman": Emily Blackwell, journal, Oct. 1852, reel 3, Blackwell Family Papers.

"very persevering": Ibid., June 15, 1851.

"a something sprawling": Ibid., Aug. 20, 1850.

"little womanly airs": Emily Blackwell to Elizabeth Blackwell, Oct. 1858, box 11, folder 163, Blackwell Family Papers.

"idea of studying": Emily Blackwell, journal, Dec. 15, 1852, reel 3, Blackwell Family Papers.

276 "tall, broad-shouldered": Baker, *Fighting for Life*, pp. 34–35.

"study in disguise": Emily Blackwell, journal, July 16, 1853, reel 3, Blackwell Family Papers. Until the 1870s, even in Paris a woman could not get a medical degree if it was known she was a female; see Haryett Fontage, *Les femmes docteurs en medecine* . . . (Paris: Alliance Cooperative du Livre, 1901).

"If we could": Emily Blackwell to Elizabeth Blackwell, May 15, 1854, box 11, folder 163, Blackwell Family Papers.

"more under her control": Emily Blackwell, journal, Jan. 9, 1853, reel 3, Blackwell Family Papers.

"the *nature*": Ibid., Jan. 8, 1852.

277 "If I might": Ibid., Jan. 6, 1852.

278 "They slept": Quoted in Alice Stone Blackwell, "An Early Woman Physician," *Woman's Journal*, Oct. 6, 1906, p. 158.

279 "the first practical": Elise S. L'Esperance, "Influence of the New York Infirmary on Women in Medicine," *Journal of the American Medical Women's Association* (June 1949): 258. Most historians of women in medicine have given short shrift to Emily Blackwell's role in the Women's Medical College and the New York Infirmary, since Elizabeth Blackwell captured the spotlight as the first female doctor and a founder of both those institutions. However, the Blackwells' letters make clear the extent to which Emily was the sustaining force. See also Alice Stone Blackwell's account in "An Early Woman Physician," p. 1.

280 "friends": Emily Blackwell, journal, Sept. 24, 1850, reel 3, Blackwell Family Papers.

281 "Whenever I became": Elizabeth Blackwell, *Pioneer Work in Opening the Medical Profession to Women* (London: Longmans, Green, 1895), pp. 28, 185–86.

281 "utter social deadness": Emily Blackwell to George Blackwell, June 15, 1871, box 11, folder 170, Blackwell Family Papers.

"The house would seem": Emily Blackwell to Kitty Barry Blackwell, Nov. 14, 1871, box 11, folder 182, Blackwell Family Papers.

282 "How much": Emily Blackwell to Elizabeth Blackwell, Oct. 21–24, 1881, reel 4, Blackwell Family Papers.

"As I walked": Emily Blackwell, journal, Mar. 11, 1852, reel 3, Blackwell Family Papers.

283 "it for granted": Emily Blackwell to Elizabeth Blackwell, Oct. 11, 1869, box 11, folder 164, Blackwell Family Papers.

"brought them": Ibid., June 15–24, 1870.

284 "taxes my strength": Ibid., Oct. 6, 1871.

"easy[,] indulgent": Ibid., Oct. 11, 1869.

285 "We had a delightful": Elizabeth B. Thelberg, ed., "Autobiography of Dr. Elizabeth Cushier," *Medical Review of Reviews* 39, no. 3 (Mar. 1933): 126.

"with a hop": Quoted in Elinor Hays, *Those Extraordinary Blackwells: The Story of a Journey to a Better World* (New York: Harcourt, Brace, 1967), p. 232.

"Much as I want": Elizabeth Cushier to Emily Blackwell, [n.d.], box 13, folder 187, Blackwell Family Papers.

"it might be": Emily Blackwell to Elizabeth Blackwell, Jan. 8, 1897, reel 4, Blackwell Family Papers.

"in 1887": Thelberg, "Autobiography," p. 127.

286 "marriages are so far": Emily Blackwell, journal, Feb. 18, 1852, reel 3, Blackwell Family Papers.

"What I should": Emily Blackwell to Elizabeth Blackwell, Nov. 22, 1894, box 11, folder 164, Blackwell Family Papers.

287 "What a difference": Emily Blackwell to Elizabeth Blackwell, Jan. 8, 1897, reel 4, Blackwell Family Papers.

"would carry much more": Ibid., Oct. 8, 1898.

288 "keep a certain": Ibid.

"[Emily Blackwell]": Baker, *Fighting for Life*, pp. 33–34.

"I feel": Emily Blackwell to Elizabeth Blackwell, July 3, 1899, reel 4, Blackwell Family Papers.

289 "though I did not": Thelberg, "Autobiography," p. 128.

"Dr. Emily": Alice Stone Blackwell, "Dr. Emily Blackwell," *Woman's Journal*, Oct. 6, 1906, pp. 13–14.

"We were fortunate": Emily Blackwell to Elizabeth Blackwell, July 29, 1902, reel 4, Blackwell Family Papers.

PAGE

"Thus the years": Thelberg, "Autobiography," p. 128.

290 "No woman": Women's Medical Association of New York, *In Memory*, p. 29.
"happy . . . companionship": Alice Stone Blackwell, "Reminiscences of Dr. Emily Blackwell," *Woman's Journal*, Sept. 17, 1910, p. 152.

16. CARRYING ON: MARTHA MAY ELIOT, M.D.

Jacqueline K. Parker's "Women at the Helm: Succession Politics at the Children's Bureau, 1912–1968," *Social Work* 39, no. 5 (Sept. 1994): 551–60, traces the leadership of the Children's Bureau, including Martha Eliot and her predecessor, Katharine Lenroot, who, as Parker observes, also "shared her life with a female companion." The trajectory of Eliot's career is outlined in Jessie M. Bierman, "Martha May Eliot, M.D.," *Clinical Pediatrics* 5, no. 9 (Sept. 1966): 569–78.

PAGE

291 "It is dangerous": John Meagher, "Homosexuality: Its Psychobiological and Psychopathological Significance," *Urologic and Cutaneous Review* 33, no. 6 (Aug. 1929): 518.
"You take": Quoted in Myron Wegman, "Martha Eliot and the U.S. Children's Bureau," *Pediatrics* 19, no. 4 (Apr. 1957): 656.

292 "the prime motive": Charles W. Eliot, *Charles W. Eliot: The Man and His Beliefs* (New York: Harper and Brothers, 1926), p. 167.
"to leave home": Jeannette Barley Cheek, interview with Martha May Eliot, M.D., *Rockefeller Oral History Project*, Nov. 1973–May 1974, p. 12, SL.
"Boys as a matter": Ella Lyman, "The Importance of Purpose in the Life of a Girl," May 29, 1907, scrapbook, box 1, folder 10, Martha May Eliot Papers, SL.

293 "When I announce": Quoted in Trisha Franzen, *Spinsters and Lesbians: Independent Womanhood in the United States* (New York: New York University Press, 1996), p. 75.
"thought I was": Cheek interview, pp. 20–21.
"So that year": Ibid., p. 21.

294 "We [Ethel and herself] braved": Martha May Eliot to Mary Eliot, Oct. 2, 1914, Eliot Papers.
"continued a watchful": Regina Morantz-Sanchez, *Sympathy and Science: Women Physicians in American Medicine* (New York: Oxford University Press, 1985), p. 123.

295 **Martha Eliot's letters:** For Eliot's references to Thomas at Johns Hopkins, see letters to Mary Eliot of Nov. 12, 1916; Feb. 10, 1917; and Apr. 22, 1917, Eliot Papers.

"**E. and I**": Martha May Eliot to Mary Eliot, Nov. 6, 1914; Nov. 28, 1914; Jan. 23, 1915; all in Eliot Papers.

"**Part of my reason**": Ibid., Oct. 16, 1917.

296 "**it didn't leave**": Ibid., Nov. 24, 1917.

"**You will be interested**": Ibid., Aug. 1, 1920.

"**I am not**": Ibid.

297 **They would have considered:** See Barbara Solomon, *In the Company of Educated Women: A History of Women and Higher Education in America* (New Haven, Conn.: Yale University Press, 1985), p. 133.

298 "**it was frustrating**": Cheek interview, pp. 40–41.

"**I spent the night**": Martha May Eliot to Mary Eliot, Dec. 27, 1921; June 1, 1922; Feb. 9, 1922; all in Eliot Papers.

"**Whether I shall stay**": Ibid., March 1923; Mar. 6, 1914; Feb. 12, 1915.

299 "**Those of us**": Julius B. Richmond, "From a Minority to a Majority," *American Journal of Public Health* 61, no. 4 (Apr. 1971): 681.

300 "**Excitement no. 2**": Martha May Eliot to Mary Eliot, May 10, 1923, Eliot Papers. She does not hide the fact that although the new house has two bedrooms, she and Ethel sleep in the same room; ibid., July 28, 1923.

301 "**we brought down**": Ibid., Nov. 1932.

303 "**unnatural**": Quoted in Lela B. Costin, *Two Sisters for Social Justice: A Biography of Grace and Edith Abbott* (Urbana: University of Illinois Press, 1983), pp. 141–42. When Eliot left the Children's Bureau, Katherine Oettinger was appointed to succeed her. Oettinger was the first married woman with children to head the bureau in its forty-five-year history; see Parker, "Women at the Helm."

304 "**Dearest, It was**": Ethel Dunham to Martha May Eliot, June 30, 1960, Eliot Papers.

"**How I count**": Ibid., July 10, 1960.

"**I do want**": Martha May Eliot to Ethel Dunham, July 26, 1960, Eliot Papers.

17. THE RUSH TO BAKE THE PIES AND HAVE THE BABIES

The papers of Martha Tracy and Ellen Potter can be found in the Archives and Special Collections, Allegheny University of the Health Sciences (formerly the Woman's Medical College of Pennsylvania).

Additional useful studies of women in the 1930s are Sophonisba Breckinridge, *Women in the Twentieth Century: A Study of Their Political, Social, and Economic Activities* (New York: McGraw-Hill, 1933); Susan Ware, *Holding Their Own: American Women in the 1930s* (Boston: Twayne, 1982); and Ruth Schwartz Cowan, "Two Washes in the Morning and a Bridge Party at Night: The American Housewife Between the Wars," *Women's Studies* 3 (1976).

Harron and McHale are discussed in India Edwards, *Pulling No Punches: Memoirs of a Woman in Politics* (New York: Putnam, 1977), and Joan Ellen Organ, "Sexuality as a Category for Historical Analysis: A Study of Judge Florence E. Allen, 1884–1966" (Ph.D. dissertation, Case Western Reserve University, 1998). Harron is also discussed in Doris Faber, *The Life of Lorena Hickok: E. R.'s Friend* (New York: Morrow, 1980), and McHale in Leila J. Rupp and Verta Taylor, *Survival in the Doldrums: The American Women's Rights Movement, 1945 to the 1960s* (New York: Oxford University Press, 1987).

PAGE

306 **"The time"**: Quoted in Roberta Frankfort, *Collegiate Women: Domesticity and Career in Turn-of-the-Century America* (New York: NYU Press, 1977), p. 72.

 In actuality: Frank Stricker presents a fairly rosy statistical picture of women in the professions from the start of the twentieth century to 1930. However, as he points out, "The job level which these women reached is another question. . . . Half the female professionals were school teachers. . . . Nurses [were] the second largest subcategory of female professionals"; "Cookbooks and Law Books: The Hidden History of Career Women in Twentieth Century America," *Journal of Social History* 10 (Fall 1976): 6–7.

307 **"The traditional"**: Janet M. Hooks, *Women's Occupations Through Seven Decades*, Women's Bureau Bulletin, no. 218 (Washington, D.C.: Government Printing Office, 1947), pp. 25–26.

 "don knickerbockers": Esse V. Hathaway, "Finding a Balance in Living," *Independent Woman*, June 1924.

308 **"frequent[ly] resort"**: Marguerite Mooers Marshall, "Don't Be a Vegetable Wife . . . Dr. Ellen C. Potter Warns," Oct. 1, 1919, clipping, Ellen Potter Collection, AUHS.

 "a wife and mother": Irma Benjamin, "Marriage and Fame," *Philadelphia Inquirer*, Jan. 17, 1932, pp. 1, 8.

309 **"demonstrated that women"**: Martha Tracy and Ellen Potter, "The Woman's Medical College of Pennsylvania; Its Relation to All Women in Medicine," *Woman's Medical Journal*, Oct. 1919.

309 **"men are married"**: Henry Carey, "This Two-Headed Monster — The Family," *Harper's Monthly Magazine* 156 (June 1928): 169.

"in forswearing": Lillian Symes, "Still a Man's Game: Reflections of a Tired Feminist," *Harper's Monthly Magazine* 158 (May 1929): 685.

"We're tired": Alice Beal Parsons, "Man-Made Illusions About Woman," in Samuel D. Schmalhausen and V. F. Calverton, eds., *Woman's Coming of Age* (New York: Horace Liveright, 1931), p. 23.

311 **"I think"**: Quoted in Nancy Milford, *Zelda* (New York: Avon, 1971), p. 160.

"for the modern": Phyllis Blanchard and Carolyn Manasses, *New Girls for Old* (New York: Macaulay, 1930), pp. 174–75.

When a poll: Mary P. Ryan, *Womanhood in America: From Colonial Times to the Present* (New York: New Viewpoints, 1979), p. 188.

312 **For instance**: See Ware, *Holding Their Own*, p. 12.

In 1940: See Hooks, *Women's Occupations*, p. 5.

313 **"aggressive occupations"**: George W. Henry, *Sex Variants: A Study of Homosexual Patterns* (New York: Paul B. Hoeber, 1941), pp. 1024, 1026–27.

"homosexual women": Ferdinand Lundberg and Marynia Farnham, *Modern Woman: The Lost Sex* (New York: Harper and Brothers, 1947), p. 296.

"wears her hair": Quoted in Karen Berger Morello, *The Invisible Bar: The Woman Lawyer in America, 1638 to the Present* (New York: Random House, 1986), p. 184.

314 **In 1950**: Figures on working women are from Glenda Riley, *Inventing the American Woman: A Perspective on Women's History, 1865 to the Present* (Arlington Heights, Ill.: Harlan Davidson, 1986), p. 125, and Alice Rossi, "Barriers to the Career Choice of Engineering, Medicine, or Science Among American Women," in Jacqueline Mattfeld and Carol G. Van Aken, eds., *Women in the Scientific Professions* (Cambridge, Mass.: MIT Press, 1965), p. 77.

315 **"For my part"**: Adlai E. Stevenson, address, Smith College Commencement, June 6, 1955, p. 2, Neilson Library, SC.

316 **"deliberately renounce[d]"**: Frank S. Caprio, *Female Homosexuality: A Psychodynamic Study of Lesbianism* (New York: Citadel Press, 1954), p. 11. Donna Penn has argued that "butch style" and "masculine appearance" were what raised antilesbian hysteria during these years; "The Meanings of Lesbianism in Post-War America," *Gender and History* 3, no. 2 (Summer 1991): 190–203. However, the persecution of women like Harron, Van Waters, and McHale suggests that success in professions that were deemed masculine was much more likely to incite public ire against non-working-class women than their "masculine appearance."

PAGE

"contradictions": Joanne Meyerowitz, "Beyond the Feminine Mystique: A Reassessment of Post-War Mass Culture, 1946–1958," *Journal of American History* 79, no. 4 (Mar. 1993): 1457, 1462. Meyerowitz refers, of course, to Betty Friedan's *The Feminine Mystique* (New York: Norton, 1963).

317 "None of them": Ronald Chester, "Women Lawyers in the Urban Bar," *New England Law Review* 18, no. 3 (1983): 574.

318 "retard the work": Nancy Cott, *The Grounding of Modern Feminism* (New Haven, Conn.: Yale University Press, 1987), p. 231.
At the first meeting: Ibid. See also Organ, "Sexuality as a Category," p. 100.
By 1931: Cott, *Grounding*, p. 231.
"Because there can be": Quoted in J. Stanley Lemons, "Lena Madesin Phillips," in Barbara Sicherman and Carol Hurd Green, eds., *Notable American Women: The Modern Period* (Cambridge: Harvard University Press, 1980), p. 544.

319 As her autobiographical: Lisa Sergio's *A Measure Filled: The Life of Lena Madesin Phillips Drawn from Her Autobiography* (New York: Robert B. Luce, 1972), is the most complete biography of Phillips. See also Rupp and Taylor, *Survival*.
"no impression": Rupp and Taylor, *Survival*, p. 122.
"the most beautiful": Quoted in ibid., p. 104.
"Of course, the ideal": Quoted in Sergio, *Measure Filled*, p. 54.

320 When they met: Ibid., pp. 47, 60, 62.

322 Florence Allen may have: Organ, "Sexuality as a Category," p. 148.

323 "concern": Florence Allen to Marion Harron, May 1957, quoted in ibid., p. 242.

325 "feminists at that time": Quoted in Rupp and Taylor, *Survival*, p. 96.
"sexual deviancy": Sara Cable, "Biology as Social Identity: How the Medical Discourse on Sexuality During the Early Twentieth Century Influenced Pauli Murray's Conception of Her Identity in American Society During the 1930s and '40s," unpublished ms., SL, pp. 5, 6, 23. Cable shows that Murray was so tormented by the image of lesbianism as pathology and the rigidity of gender roles that she believed herself to be a man trapped in a woman's body and actually sought testosterone implants in the 1930s, when she read that such treatments were transforming "effeminate boys" into "virile men." See also Heather Phillips, "I Feel in My Bones That You Are Making History: The Life and Leadership of Pauli Murray" (senior honors thesis, Radcliffe College, 1997), especially the section "Hiding Identity," pp. 21–25.

PAGE

325 "crowded": Jess Stearn, *The Grapevine: A Report on the Secret World of the Lesbian* (Garden City, N.Y.: Doubleday, 1964), pp. 3, 59.

18. CONCLUSION: LEGACIES

For more information on "women-identified-women," see New York Radicalesbians, "Woman-Identified-Woman," 1970; rpt. in *Lesbians Speak Out* (Oakland, Calif.: Women's Press Collective, 1974), pp. 87–89. Lesbian feminist communities and similarities between lesbian feminists and pioneering feminists are treated in my *Surpassing the Love of Men* and *Odd Girls and Twilight Lovers*.

Lesbian leadership in NOW is discussed in Sidney Abbott and Barbara Love, *Sappho Was a Right-On Woman: A Liberated View of Lesbianism* (New York: Stein and Day, 1972), and Flora Davis, *Moving the Mountain: The Women's Movement in America Since 1960* (New York: Simon and Schuster, 1991), chap. 13.

PAGE

327 "They talked": Mona Harrington, *Women Lawyers: Rewriting the Rules* (New York: Knopf, 1994), pp. 229–30.

328 "educated in romance": Dorothy Holland and Margaret Eisenhart, *Educated in Romance: Women, Achievement, and College Culture* (Chicago: University of Chicago Press, 1990).
    According to the 1960: Elaine Tyler May, *Homeward Bound: American Families in the Cold War Era* (New York: Basic Books, 1988).

329 "I will even": Elaine Whitehill, "I'd Hate to Be a Man," *Coronet* 37 (Jan. 1955), p. 27.

335 "For most women": Betty Friedan, *It Changed My Life: Writings from the Women's Movement* (New York: Norton, 1985), p. 159.

336 By the early 1970s: Sheila Rowbotham, *A Century of Women: The History of Women in Britain and the United States* (New York: Viking, 1997), p. 443.
    "ignoring my feelings": Quoted in Peter G. Filene, *Him/Her/Self: Sex Roles in Modern America*, 2nd ed. (Baltimore: Johns Hopkins University Press, 1998), p. 232.
    The median income: Marc Breslow, "Can We Still Win the War Against Poverty?" *Dollars and Sense* (July/Aug. 1995), p. 40.

337 By the end: Glenda Riley, *Inventing the American Woman: A Perspective on*

Women's History, 1865 to the Present (Arlington Heights, Ill.: Harlan Davidson, 1986), p. 141.

For example: Rowbotham, *Century of Women*, p. 441.

Whereas most women: Arlie Hochschild, *The Second Shift: Working Parents and the Revolution at Home* (New York: Viking, 1989), pp. 263–65.

For example, in 1963: Cynthia Fuchs Epstein, *Women in Law* (New York: Basic Books, 1981), p. 53; Karen Berger Morello, *The Invisible Bar: The Woman Lawyer in America, 1638 to the Present* (New York: Random House, 1986), Ronald Chester, "Women Lawyers in the Urban Bar: An Oral History," *New England Law Review* 18 (1983): 523; and "Gender Discrimination Still Alive in the Profession," *Trial* 32, no. 4 (April 1996): 76.

338 **Enough women:** See Jill Schachnen Chanen, "Reaching Out to Women of Color: Special Report Chronicles Concerns over Bias in the Profession," *American Bar Association Journal* 18 (May 1995): 105.

Though women of all races: Chris Klein, *National Law Journal* 18, no. 36 (May 6, 1996): A1.

The number of women: Julie Brienza, "Upper Echelons of Large Firms Have Few Minorities or Women," *Trial* 31, no. 6 (June 1995): 94–95, and Martha Lufkin, "How to Succeed in a (Still) Masculine World," *National Law Journal* 18, no. 51 (Aug. 19, 1996): C8.

By 1997: Deborah Rhode, "Progress for Women in Law — But No Parity Yet," *National Law Journal* 19, no. 26 (Feb. 24, 1997): A23.

In 1970: Dr. Nancy Dickey, "Our Sisters' Sickness, Our Sisters' Satchels," *Vital Speeches* 62, no. 19 (July 15, 1996): 582–83.

By the end of the 1980s: Anita M. Harris, *Broken Patterns: Professional Women and the Quest for a New Feminine Identity* (Detroit: Wayne State University Press, 1995), p. 136.

the entering class: Lisa Bennett, "Women Doctors Are Changing the Face of Medicine: Or Are They?" *American Health* 15, no. 3 (Apr. 1996): 72–73.

A 1996 study: Dickey, "Our Sisters' Sickness," p. 83.

339 **"go beyond":** "Amazing Grace: Fifty Years of the Black Church," *Ebony* 50, no. 6 (Apr. 1995): 87.

Reformed and then: "Religious Women Gain Earthly Power and Change the Faith of their Fathers," *Working Woman* 21, no. 11 (Nov.–Dec. 1996): 71.

The lawyer Pauli: See Pauli Murray, *Song in a Weary Throat: An American Pilgrimage* (New York: Harper and Row, 1987), pp. 369–435; Heather Phillips, "I Feel in My Bones That You Are Making History: The Life and

PAGE

Leadership of Pauli Murray" (senior honors thesis, Radcliffe College, 1977); and Pamela Darling, *New Wine: The Story of Women Transforming Leadership and Power in the Episcopal Church* (Cambridge, Mass.: Cowley, 1994).

339 **Barbara Harris:** "The First Female Bishop of the Episcopal Church," *Working Woman* 21, no. 11 (Nov.–Dec. 1996): 72.

President Reagan won: John McLaughlin, "The Galling Gap," *National Review* 35 (July 22, 1983): 864.

340 **"to all women":** Quoted in Ruth Mandel, "Who Won? The Women Candidates," *Working Woman* 8 (Apr. 1983): 110.

They were indisputably: Deborah Kalb, "Dole Must Close the 'Gender Gap' to Avoid Clinton Landslide," *Congressional Quarterly Weekly Report* 54, no. 43 (Oct. 26, 1996): 3085.

In 1986: Susan M. Hartmann, *From Margin to Mainstream: American Women in Politics Since 1960* (Philadelphia: Temple University Press, 1989), p. 173.

By remaining: See J. Jennings Moss, "Barbara Jordan's Other Life," *Advocate*, Mar. 5, 1996, pp. 39–45. Jordan hints at her relationship with Nancy Earl in her autobiography, *Barbara Jordan: A Self-Portrait* (Garden City, N.Y.: Doubleday, 1979).

341 **As a result:** Toni Caribillo, Judith Meuli, and June Bundy Csida, *Feminist Chronicles, 1953–1993* (Los Angeles: Women's Graphics, 1993), p. 149.

Women of color: See Kitty Dumas, "The Year of the Black Woman," *Black Enterprise* 23, no. 1 (Aug. 1992): 35.

Though women did not: The 1994 election is analyzed in Katha Pollitt, "Subject to Debate," *The Nation* 259, no. 18 (Nov. 28, 1994): 642.

in 1996: Pam Belluck, "A 'Year of the Woman' Cedes to Days of Embattled Senators," *New York Times*, Jan. 19, 1998, p. 1.

342 **"a woman [candidate]":** Shanto Iyengar et al., "Running as a Woman: Gender Stereotyping in Political Campaigns," in Pippa Norris, ed., *Women, Media and Politics* (New York: Oxford University Press, 1997), p. 97.

"most . . . members": Alexis Simendinger, "Still a Guy's Game," *National Law Journal* 29, no. 31 (Aug. 2, 1997): 1566.

A front-page article: Belluck, "A 'Year of the Woman,'" p. 1.

343 **"most of us":** "The College Girl Puts Marriage First," *New York Times Magazine*, Apr. 2, 1933, pp. 8, 9.

A 1980 article: Deena Kleiman, "Many Young Women Now Say They'd Pick Family over Career," *New York Times*, Dec. 28, 1980, pp. 1, 24.

PAGE

The following week: *Boston Globe,* Jan. 3, 1981.

"experiencing the formative": Andy Dapper, "When Less Means More," *Hemispheres,* Nov. 1997, p. 155.

344 "the newest status symbol": Alecia Swasy, "Stay-at-Home Moms Are Fashionable Again in Many Communities," *Wall Street Journal,* July 23, 1993, p. A1.

"new and different": Harrington, *Women Lawyers,* pp. 145–46.

"a tremendous drive": Harris, *Broken Patterns,* p. 16.

345 For example: Mary Brophy Marcus, "If You Let Me Play . . . A Basketball or a Hockey Puck May Shatter the Glass Ceiling," *U.S. News & World Report,* Oct. 27, 1997, pp. 88–90.

"live in fear": James A. Levine and Todd L. Pittinsky, *Working Fathers: New Strategies for Balancing Work and Family* (New York: Addison-Wesley, 1997), p. 29.

"a model": Tracy Mygatt, Feb. 1966, Columbia University Oral History Project, p. 26, box 7, Mygatt-Witherspoon Papers, SCPC.

346 "natural or an authentic": Shane Phelan, "(Be)Coming Out: Lesbian Identity and Politics," *Signs* 18 (Summer 1993): 765–90.

INDEX

AAUW. *See* American Association of University Women (AAUW)

Abolitionism, 20–22, 100–101

Abortion, 336

ACLU. *See* American Civil Liberties Union (ACLU)

Adamless Eden, 259

Addams, Jane
  and American Civil Liberties Union, 133
  awards and recognition for, 133, 134, 227
  and child labor legislation, 133
  Children's Bureau and, 299
  death of, 125
  and death of Mary Smith, 132
  in Department of Food Administration, 134
  depression following college graduation, 115
  on educated women in 1920s–1930s, 310
  education of, 115–16, 118
  end of relationship with Ellen Starr, 125–27
  and financial support for Hull House, 6, 128, 129
  friends of, 3–4
  and International Congress of Women, 134
  medicine as interest of, 270
  on municipal housekeeping, 138
  NAACP and, 133
  as NAWSA vice president, 116

Nobel Peace Prize for, 133, 134
  and Office of National Progressive Services, 151
  as pacifist, 133–34, 155, 160
  poem by, 128–29
  as president of National Conference of Charities and Corrections, 133
  as radical, 116–17
  relationship with Ellen Starr, 118–27
  relationship with Mary Rozet Smith, 115, 125–33, 365n
  religion and, 124–25
  Theodore Roosevelt and, 114, 151
  as secular humanist, 125
  and settlement house movement, 102, 116–18, 120–26, 128, 129, 133–37
  Sheppard-Towner Act and, 299
  significance of, 118, 133, 134–35
  on woman suffrage, 116
  Women's International League for Peace and Freedom founded by, 134, 155
  Women's Peace Party founded by, 134
  works
    Newer Ideals of Peace, 133–34
    Second Twenty Years at Hull House, 301
  World War I and, 134

Addy, Persis, 43–44, 51

Affirmative action, 334

AFL. *See* American Federation of Labor (AFL)

African Americans. *See also* specific African Americans
as college administrators, 239
as doctors, 188, 270
as domestic workers, 147
education of African-American women, 180–81, 188
education of freed slaves, 100–103, 180
employment of African-American women, 314, 337
as lawyers, 267, 323–26, 338
marriage of college graduates, 248
media portrayal of women's public success, 316
migration of women to North, 147
as ministers, 264–65, 325
in U.S. House of Representatives, 340
in U.S. Senate, 341
voting rights for, 23, 35, 102–03
in woman suffrage movement, 23–24

African Methodist Episcopal (AME) Church, 264, 338–39
Agriculture, 157
Albion College, 43
Albright, Madeline, 342
Alderson Story (Flynn), 162, 377n
Allen, Florence, 83, 92, 320, 321–23
Alpha, 256
"Amazonian" professional women, 195, 210, 255–60
AME Church, 264, 338–39
American Anti-Slavery Society, 21
American Association for Labor Legislation, 231
American Association of University Professors, 211
American Association of University Women (AAUW), 231, 234–35, 245
American Bar Association, 338

American Civil Liberties Union (ACLU), 133, 160, 231
American College of Surgeons, 271
American Communist Party, 162
American Federation of Labor (AFL), 105, 112
American Indians. *See* Native Americans
American Legion, 232
American Medical Association, 269
American Medical Women's Association, 271, 279
American Pediatric Association, 301
American Protective Association, 150
American Public Health Association, 303
American Woman Suffrage Association (AWSA), 22, 25, 35, 45, 54, 262
Andersen, Kristi, 365n
Anthony, Jessie, 28
Anthony, Katherine, 29
Anthony, Lucy
and Susan B. Anthony's love relationships with women, 27
and bathing suit episode, 41
and death of Anna Shaw, 60
on death of Mollie Hay, 78
plans with Anna Shaw after World War I, 59
relationship with Anna Howard Shaw, 5–6, 27, 28, 40, 44, 48–54, 59
in woman suffrage movement, 50, 51
Anthony, Mary, 27, 28
Anthony, Susan B.
abolitionism and, 22
African-American woman suffrage leaders and, 23–24
birthday of, as national holiday, 94
break with American Woman Suffrage Association, 23, 25, 35
Catt and, 62
death of, 30

Anthony, Susan B. (*cont.*)
and defense of free-love advocate
Victoria Woodhull, 54
on equality for women, 24–25
Fifteenth Amendment and, 23
friends of, 3, 214
on gender restrictions during girlhood, 11
on heterosexual marriage, 8, 19–
20, 30
lecture on "Homes of Single
Women," 185
on love relationships between
women in suffrage move-
ment, 30
love relationships of, with women,
3, 11, 15, 16, 25–30
as "manly," 24–25
National Woman Suffrage Association founded by, 35
physical appearance of, 24
on relationship between Anna
Howard Shaw and Lucy An-
thony, 49–50
relationship with Stanton, 22–23
Shaw and, 47–48, 54
on single life for women, 8
sister of, 27
on Stanton's relationship with
Dickinson, 355n
in temperance movement, 22
on "true woman," 24
in woman suffrage movement, 23–
30, 35, 47–48, 69
Anti-Enlistment League, 160
Anti-slavery movement. *See* Abolitionism
Arizona state government, 342, 343
Arnold, Mary, 156–59
Astin, Helen, 244
*Athletic Games in the Education of
Women* (Kellor), 141
Athletics, 141
Atlanta Baptist College, 181–82
AWSA. *See* American Woman Suf-
frage Association (AWSA)

Babcock, Elizabeth, 364n
Bacon, Margaret, 165, 171, 172
Baillie, Gertrude, 270
Baker, Sara Josephine, 271, 280, 288
Baldwin, Tammy, 342
Banister, Marion Glass, 92
Bank tellers, 315
Bannister, Mary, 32
Baptist Church, 262–63
Barnard College, 180, 231, 246–47
Barnett, Ida Wells. *See* Wells, Ida
Barry, Kitty, 37–39, 358n
Bates, Katharine Lee, 192–93, 196,
223, 383–84n
Bates, Lizzie, 179
Baudelaire, Charles-Pierre, 207–8
Baxandall, Rosalyn Fraad, 377n
Beard, Charles, 118
Beard, Mary, 118
Beecher, Catharine, 176, 177, 198,
260
Bellamy, Virginia, 79
Benedict, Ruth, 251
Bernard, Jessie, 242
Bethune, Mary McLeod, 87, 193, 239
Bethune-Cookman College, 193, 239
Biddle, Caroline, 155
Binger, Carl, 246, 393–94n
Bisexuality, 143, 146, 202, 251, 366n
BLA. *See* Bureau of Legal Advice
(BLA)
Blacks. *See* African Americans; *and
specific African Americans*
Blackwell, Alice Stone
on Emily Blackwell, 289, 290
and Cushier, 285
friends of, 263
on heterosexuality, 36–37, 80–81
and reading of Havelock Ellis,
358n
relationship with Kitty Barry, 37–
38, 39
relationships with other women,
38–39, 357n
on romances between college
women, 175

in woman suffrage movement, 35–
36, 39, 48, 69, 80–81
youth of, 19
Blackwell, Anna, 358n
Blackwell, Antoinette Brown. *See*
Brown, Antoinette
Blackwell, Elizabeth, 37, 257, 269,
275–79, 281, 283, 287, 289,
399n
Blackwell, Emily
adopted daughter of, 281–82, 285,
289, 345
and Alice Stone Blackwell's reaction to heterosexuality, 36–37
death of, 289
as doctor, 37, 274–90, 309
on "femininity," 275–76, 307
on heterosexual marriage, 286
loneliness of, 280–82
in medical school, 270, 275–76
and New York Infirmary for
Women and Children, 257,
268–69, 275, 277–84, 289,
399n
relationship with Elizabeth Cushier, 6, 36, 281, 284–87, 289–90
retirement of, 289
and Women's Medical College of
the New York Infirmary, 279–
80, 282–84, 286–89, 399n
Blackwell, Florence, 39
Blackwell, Henry, 18, 19, 261
Blackwell, Kitty, 175
Blackwell, Lucy Stone. *See* Stone,
Lucy
Blackwell, Nannie, 281–82, 285,
289
Blackwell, Samuel, 18, 19, 261
Blair, Emily, 365n
Blanchard, Phyllis, 79–80, 160–61
Blanding, President (Vassar Col-
lege), 246
Blodgett, Geoffrey, 357n
Boalt Law School, 324
Bohn, Frank, 110
Booth, Mary Louise, 258

Boston marriage, 6, 73, 114, 119, 159,
161, 192
Boston University, 43, 45, 261
Bourdet, Edouard, 208
Bowden, Artemesia, 239
Branch, Elizabeth, 239
Brent, Margaret, 266
Britten, Florence, 248, 249
Broken Patterns (Harris), 344
Bromley, Dorothy, 248, 249
Brooks, Van Wyck, 346–47
Brown, Addie, 103–4
Brown, Antoinette, 17, 18, 19, 39,
260–61, 396n
Brown, Cynthia, 239
Brown University, 221–22
Brown v. *Board of Education*, 324
Bryn Mawr College
bachelor's degree requirements
of, 220
compared with other women's colleges, 198, 209, 217, 218, 220
education of, 197
faculty of, 110, 196, 202, 218
faculty self-governance at, 211
founding of, 180
Garrett's financial endowment for,
6, 204
graduate program of, 202, 210
graduates of, on Mount Holyoke
faculty, 219
high standards for, 198, 210–11
as Quaker institution, 207, 209
Rhoads as first president of, 198
statistics on alumnae with children, 184
statistics on graduates with careers, 209
statistics on married college
graduates, 184, 212, 213
students at, 160, 293, 295
students going on to graduate
study from, 209
Summer School for Women Workers, 154, 211–12
Thomas as dean of, 198

Bryn Mawr College (*cont.*)
Thomas as president of, 6, 154,
160, 183, 202–4, 209–16, 218,
222
Thomas's vision for presidency of,
197–98, 207
tutorial system at, 211
Buck, Gertrude, 196
Bureau of Legal Advice (BLA), 160
Burgess, Dorothy, 383–84n
Burleigh, Margaret, 20–22, 99, 101,
172
Burns, Lucy, 55, 69, 93
Bussy, Dorothy, 366n
Butch/femme relationship, 34, 365n
Butler, Judith, 10

Cable, Sara, 325, 405n
California congress, 340
Cancer research, 271
Caprio, Frank, 315–16
Captive (Bourdet), 208
Carpenter, Edward, 352n
Carter, Susan B., 392n
Cather, Willa, 227
Catt, Carrie Chapman
Allen and, 321
Susan Anthony and, 62
bawdy nature of private humor of,
362n
burial place of, 78, 362n
career of, in education, 70
and death of Mollie Hay, 77–78
Empire State Campaign and, 66–
67
on grueling battle for woman suffrage, 15
on heterosexual marriage, 69–70
illnesses and hysterectomy of, 76
International Woman Suffrage Alliance founded by, 66
Interurban Suffrage Council
founded by, 66
League of Women Voters founded
by, 77, 81
marriages of, 61–62, 63, 64, 69–71

National Woman's Party and, 69
and NAWSA committee on organization, 62
as NAWSA president, 63–65, 68–
69
peace work by, 154–55
and People's Mandate to Governments to End War, 155
personal attractiveness of, to
women, 65, 66, 72
recognition for, 227
relationship with Alda Wilson, 78
relationship with Mollie Hay, 6,
15, 61, 62–64, 71–78, 361–62n
resignation of, from NAWSA, 65
Shaw and, 53
and voting records of married
women, 81
Woodrow Wilson and, 69, 360–61n
in woman suffrage movement, 61–
69, 71, 74
on Women's Committee of the
Council of National Defense,
69
on women's involvement in politics, 82
World War I and, 66, 68–69
Catt, George, 61–62, 63, 64, 74
Chadwick, John White, 99
Chamberlin, Rose, 187–88
Chambers, Clarke, 87
Chambers-Schiller, Lee, 353n
Chapman, Leo, 61, 70–71
Chatschumian, Johannes, 357n
Chester, Ronald, 317
Chicago School of Civics and Phi-
lanthropy, 137
Child labor, 107, 122, 123, 124, 133,
147, 299, 331
Children's Bureau, 291, 299–304,
402n
Children's health, 292, 298–302
Chinn, May Edward, 188
Civil Rights Act of 1964, 324, 326,
332, 333
Civil War, 179, 258–59, 279

Civilian Conservation Corps Act, 92
Clapp, Hannah, 364n
Clark, Elizabeth, 271–72
Clergy. *See* Ministry
Clinton, Bill, 340, 342
Coal miners, 158
College Entrance Examination
    Board, 231
College Settlement Association, 226
Colleges. *See* Higher education; *and
    specific colleges*
Collins, Wilkie, 36–37
Colony Club, 107–8
Columbia University, 196, 251
Coman, Katharine, 193, 196, 223,
    383–84n
Commission on the Status of
    Women, 324, 333
Committee for the Study of Sex Vari-
    ants, 312–13
Committee on the Participation of
    Women in Post-War Policy,
    236
Communist Party, 162
Congregational Church, 261
Congressional Union, 55–57, 69, 93,
    334–35
Conkey, Libbie, 205, 206
Conscientious objectors, 160
Consumer cooperatives, 158
Converse, Florence, 189, 196, 272–73
Conway, Jill, 116, 117
Cook, Blanche Wiesen, 85, 127, 366n
Cook, Nancy, 83, 86, 87, 88
Cooper, Harriet, 53
Cooperative movement, 158–59
Cornell Law School, 140, 268
Cornell Medical School, 286–88
Cornell University, 157, 191, 197, 202,
    205, 219
Corrections. *See* Prison reform
Council of National Defense, 58–59,
    69
Credit unions, 158
Crime by females, 152–53
Cross-dressing, 199, 259

Culbertson, Emma, 255, 271
"Cult of true womanhood," 256, 261
Cushier, Elizabeth, 6, 36, 274–75,
    280, 281, 284–87, 289–90

Daughters of the American Revolu-
    tion, 64, 134, 232
Davis, Allen, 124, 126, 129
Davis, Katharine Bement, 248–49
Dell, Floyd, 80
Democratic Party, 86, 87–89, 92,
    320, 365n
Depression, 311–12, 318
Dewey, John, 151
DeWolfe, Elsie, 107
Dewson, Molly, 87–93, 321, 322, 323
Dial, 108
Diana Victrix (Converse), 189, 272–
    73
Dickerman, Marion, 83, 86, 87, 88
Dickinson, Anna, 16, 25–27, 198–99,
    263, 355n
Divorce, 309, 337. *See also* Hetero-
    sexual marriage
Doctors. *See also* specific doctors
    African-American women as, 188,
        270
    association of medical college
        with hospital, 279–80
    Elizabeth Blackwell as, 37, 257,
        269, 277–79, 399n
    Emily Blackwell as, 37, 257, 268–
        69, 274–90, 309, 399n
    in Civil War, 259
    education of, at Woman's Medical
        College of Pennsylvania, 270,
        271–72, 284, 307
    education of, at Women's Medical
        College of the New York Infir-
        mary, 277, 279–80, 282–84,
        399n
    Martha Eliot as, 292–305
    hospitals founded by women doc-
        tors, 257, 268–69, 278–80
    lesbian domestic arrangements
        of, 271–72

Doctors (*cont.*)
  as married versus unmarried
    women, 270–71, 297, 300,
    308–9
  in 1970s–1990s, 338
  obstetrics and gynecology, 269,
    276, 280
  statistics on, 266, 307
  women admitted to medical
    schools, 45, 214, 269–70, 275–
    76, 284, 286–88, 292, 294–96
Dole, Robert, 340, 342
Domestic science, 212, 219, 230, 238
Domestic work and domestic work-
    ers, 147, 180, 210, 219
Door-to-door salespeople, 315
Dorr, Rheta, 108
Drachman, Virginia G., 397n
Dreier, Margaret, 142, 143, 147
Dreier, Mary, 321–23
  bisexuality of, 2, 83
  friends of, 323
  immigrants as focus of, 149
  and Kellor on homosexuality, 153
  labor laws as focus of, 144–47
  Progressive Party and, 151
  relationship with Frances Kellor,
    2, 139–46
  Eleanor Roosevelt and, 87, 144
  support for Allen by, 321, 322
  Women's Joint Legislative Com-
    mittee founded by, 83
Dudley, Gertrude, 140–41
Duer, Lillie, 354n
Dunham, Ethel, 293–302, 304–5,
    370n

Earl, Nancy, 340
Eastman, Crystal, 7
Eddy, Frances, 140
Eddy, Mary, 140
"Educated in romance," 328
Education. *See also* Higher educa-
    tion
  of African-American women, 180–
    81, 188

  Catt's career in, 70
  compulsory education for chil-
    dren, 107, 147, 331
  in eighteenth and early nine-
    teenth century, 175–79
  of freed slaves, 100–103, 180
  Holley School, 102–3
  of immigrants, 150
  of Native American children, 157
  New York City and Country
    School, 107
  progressive education for chil-
    dren, 107, 196, 211
  school lunches for children, 151
  and settlement house movement,
    121
  teaching as career for women,
    179–80, 307, 312, 403n
  Willard's career in, 34
EEOC. *See* Equal Employment Op-
    portunities Commission
    (EEOC)
Eisenhart, Margaret, 328
Eisenhower, Dwight, 111, 291, 302
Elders, Joycelyn, 341
Eliot, Charles, 210–11, 212, 237, 292
Eliot, Martha May
  as American Pediatric Association
    president, 303
  as American Public Health Asso-
    ciation president, 303
  at Children's Bureau, 299–300,
    302, 304
  "coming-out" letter to mother,
    296–97
  death of, 92
  as doctor, 292–305
  education of, 293, 294, 295
  on Harvard faculty, 303–4
  internship following medical
    school, 295–96
  in medical school, 292, 293, 294–
    96
  relationship with Ethel Dunham,
    293–302, 304–5, 370n
  rickets research by, 298–300

as social worker, 294
UNICEF and, 302
World Health Organization
(WHO) and, 302, 304, 305
on Yale faculty, 292, 298, 300
youth of, 292–93
Ellis, Havelock, 4–5, 32, 37, 42, 72,
139, 240, 357n
Empire State Campaign, 66–67, 84
Employment agencies, 141, 142
Employment of women, 314–15, 328,
336–37, 343–45. *See also* Professions
Episcopal Church, 325, 339
Equal Employment Opportunities
Commission (EEOC), 333–34
Equal pay legislation, 111, 112
Equal Rights Amendment (ERA),
93, 112, 236, 335, 366n
Equal Rights Association, 262
Equi, Marie, 162
Equity Club, 267
ERA, 93, 367n
Essentialist arguments, on women's
special gifts, 10–11, 82, 99–100
Evangelical Lutheran Church, 339
Evans, Sara M., 353n
Evening Dispensary for Working
Women and Girls, 269

Fair Labor Standards Act, 92
Fairchild, James, 179
Farming. *See* Agriculture
Farnham, Marynia, 313
Federation of Women's Clubs, 57,
64, 74, 123
Feminine mystique, 242, 243, 308,
315, 316, 328–29, 332
Femininity. *See* Womanhood
Feminism. *See also* Woman suffrage
movement
caricatures of, 81
lesbian feminists, 334–35
National Woman's Party and, 69,
92–95
second wave of, 334–37

Femme (Michelet), 183
Fernhurst (Stein), 384–85n
Field, Michael, 125
Field, Sara Bard, 367n
Fields, Annie, friends of, 4
Fifteenth Amendment, 23, 35
Fighting for Life (Baker), 288
Filene, Peter, 256
Fishermen, 158
Fitzgerald, Zelda, 311
Fitzpatrick, Ellen, 139
Flexner, Simon, 215, 388n
Flynn, Elizabeth Gurley, 162, 377n
Free love, 54
Freedman, Estelle, 164
Freedman's Bureau, 102
Freedman's Relief Association, 103
Freedmen. *See* African Americans
Freedmen's Hospital, 270
Freeman, Alice, 187, 194–96, 227, 306
French, Hannah, 390n
Freudianism, 80, 168–69, 240, 245,
251, 313
Friedan, Betty, 316, 324, 335
Frost, Robert, 226

Garfield, James, 214
Garrett, Mary
financial endowment for Bryn
Mawr, 6, 204
financial endowment for Johns
Hopkins medical school, 214,
287, 292, 294–95
last illness and death of, 215
relationship with Carey Thomas,
6, 201, 203–4, 213–15, 386n
and Thomas's sexual identity, 208
in woman suffrage movement,
214–15
Garrison, William Lloyd II, 21–22
Gautier, Théophile, 207
"Gender gap," 339–40
Gender inversion. *See* Homosexuality; Lesbians; "Sexual inverts"
Geneva College, 269
Georgia Female College, 176

German war crime trials, 313
Gildersleeve, Virginia, 231, 246–47, 307
Giles, Harriet, 180–82
Gilman, Charlotte Perkins, 7
Ginsburg, Ruth Bader, 341
Girlhood, 11, 19, 32, 42, 139–40, 146, 148, 183, 198–200, 292–93
Glazer, Penina Migdal, 391n
Glimpses of Fifty Years (Willard), 33, 35
Gordon, Anna, 6, 33–35, 357n
Gordon, Linda, 114, 370n
Gorman, Harry, 199
Grant, Zilpah, 176–78, 380n
Grapevine (Stearn), 325–26
Great War. *See* World War I
Grew, Mary, 20–22, 69, 99, 101, 172
Gross, Emily, 3, 27–30
Gummere, Frank, 201
Gwinn, Mamie, 201–2, 203, 207, 215, 386n

Hall, G. Stanley, 210, 212
Hall, Lucy, 271
Hall, Radclyffe, 125, 163, 387n
Ham, Roswell, 235, 391n, 392n
Hamilton, Alice, 129
Hamilton, Peg, 155, 156
Hanaford, Joseph, 262–63, 264
Hanaford, Phebe Coffin, 262–63, 264
Handbook of Labor Literature (Marot and Pratt), 106
Hansberry, Lorraine, 245–46
Hansen, Karen, 103–4
Harper, Ida Husted, 50, 55
Harper's Bazaar, 258
Harrington, Mona, 327
Harris, Anita, 344
Harris, Barbara, 339
Harron, Marion, 314, 315, 323, 405n
Hartford Female Seminary, 176
Harvard Law School, 323–24
Harvard Medical School, 286, 292, 338

Harvard University, 194, 210, 237, 292, 303–4
Hay, Mary (Mollie) Garrett
    burial place of, 362n
    death of, 77, 362n
    Empire State Campaign and, 66–67, 84
    illness of, 76
    League of Women Voters and, 77
    relationship with Carrie Catt, 6, 15, 61, 62–64, 71–78, 208, 361–62n
    in Republican Party, 83–85, 89
    in woman suffrage movement, 62, 63–68, 74, 76
    Woman Suffrage Party and, 66, 67–68
Health insurance, 145
Hearn, Ella, 354n
Hepburn, Katharine, 310
Herbig, Katherine, 101
Herman, Debra, 238
Hermaphrodites. *See* "Mental hermaphrodites"
Heterosexual marriage
    of African-American college graduates, 248
    Susan B. Anthony on, 8, 19–20, 30
    Alice Stone Blackwell on, 36–37
    Emily Blackwell on, 286
    of college graduates, 184, 212, 213, 237–47
    companionate marriage, 241, 252
    compared with female-female relationships, 7, 191–96, 226, 227, 252, 345–46
    divorce rates and, 309, 337
    of doctors, 270–71, 297, 300, 308–9
    of faculty women, 192, 245
    Gilman on, 7
    Grew on, 21–22
    higher education as preparation for, 237–47
    of lawyers, 267–68, 317
    married women in woman suffrage movement, 18–20, 31–32

in 1920s–1930s, 309–11
in 1950s, 315
in 1980s–1990s, 343–45
Paul on wife's obedience to husband, 261–62
Ph.D.'s earned by married women, 184, 244, 381–82n
Powell on, as detrimental to pursuit of women's rights, 94
of professional women generally, 258, 267, 270–71, 396n
property law for married women, 22–23
refusal to take husband's name ("Lucy Stoners"), 36
Shaw on, 42–43
statistics on, 184, 212, 213, 244, 248
"tired feminists" on, 309–10
voting records of married women, 80–81
and wife's employment outside home in 1920s–1930s, 309–12, 343
and wife's employment outside home in 1970s, 336–37
Hibbard, Laura, 196
Hickok, Lorena, 85–87, 314
Hicks, Margaret, 205, 206
Higham, John, 148
Higher education
academic freedom in, 220
of African-American women, 188
and "Amazonian" female scholar, 195, 210
Bryn Mawr Summer School for Women Workers, 154, 211–12
coeducational universities, 184, 212, 221–22, 337, 392n
domestic science program in, 212, 219, 238
educated women as "mental hermaphrodites," 178–79, 187–88, 255–60
and educating women for "woman's life" by mid-twentieth century, 237–42

effects of heterosexual imperative on, 242–47
Charles Eliot on women's education, 210–11, 237
and fear of "unsexing" of women, 182–83, 188
graduate fellowships for women, 393n
homophobia in, 237, 247–52
importance of, for women, 203, 204
married women faculty in, 192, 245
in 1970s, 336
in 1980s, 337–38
opportunities for college-educated women in nineteenth century, 104–5, 115–16, 183–84, 256
Ph.D.'s earned by women, 184, 244, 381–82n, 393n
in post-Civil War period, 179–82
professor-student romantic relationships in, 185, 188–89, 222–23, 251
protests against and fears about, for women, 178–79, 182–83, 187–88
"race suicide" and, 182–84
romances between female students in, 189–91
"sexual inversion" and, 187–88, 240–41
single versus married women college graduates, 184, 212, 213
statistics on children of women college graduates, 184
statistics on number of women as graduate students, 244
statistics on number of women in, 243, 336
stigma against unmarried women faculty and administrators during twentieth century, 245–47
Thomas's contributions to, 209–17

Higher education (*cont.*)
Wellesley marriage and, 185, 191–96
women college administrators, 239, 246–47
women faculty in, 184–89, 191–96, 238, 245, 245–46
Woolley on, as "feminist movement," 230
Woolley's contributions to, 218–22
Hill, Anita, 341
Hillyar, Dr., 270
Hispanic women, 339–40, 341
Hochschild, Arlie, 345
Hodder, Alfred, 202
Holland, Dorothy, 328
Holley, Marietta, 263
Holley, Sallie, 101–3, 157
Holley School, 102–3
Home economics, 212, 219, 230, 238
Homeopathic New York Medical College for Women, 284
Homophobia, 161–72, 229, 237, 244–51, 303, 305, 312–16, 335, 404n. *See also* Homosexuality; "Sexual inverts"
Homosexuality. *See also* Homophobia; Lesbians; "Sexual inverts"
Caprio on, 315–16
Ellis on women's movement and, 5
as hereditary neurosis, 5, 139, 152–53
investigation of, by Committee for the Study of Sex Variants, 312–13
Jung on, 240–41
as label, 4
Meagher on, 240, 291
media's portrayal of, 17–18, 162–63, 164
as pathological, in twentieth century, 156, 161–64, 244, 325, 334, 405–6n
statistics on women's same-sex love experiences, 248–49
in women's penal institutions, 152

Hoover, Herbert, 232
Horowitz, Helen, 207
Hosmer, Harriet, 29
Housing conditions, 147, 158
Howard Law School, 323
Howard Medical School, 270
Howard University, 267
Howes, Ethel Puffer, 192
Howland, Emily, 22
Howland, Isabel, 20–21, 28, 30
Hughes, Charles, 148–49
Hughes, Helen, 392n
Hull, Hannah Clothier, 155
Hull House. *See also* Settlement house movement
Addams and, 116, 118, 120–26, 128, 129, 133, 134–37
funding for, 6, 128, 129
Kellor at, 138, 146
Humez, Jean, 265
Hutchinson, Anne, 260
Hutchinson, Kay Bailey, 341

ILGWU. *See* International Ladies Garment Workers Union (ILGWU)
Illinois Supreme Court, 267–68
Immigrants, 104–6, 110, 121–24, 133, 141, 148–51, 169, 182. *See also* Settlement house movement
Immigration Restriction League, 150
In the Land of the Grasshopper Song (Arnold and Reed), 159
Indian Service, 157–59
Inter-Municipal Committee on Household Research, 147
International Congress of Women, 134
International Congress of Working Women, 112
International Federation of Business and Professional Women's Clubs, 320
International Federation of University Women, 231

International Health Conference, 302

International Labor Organization, 111

International Ladies Garment Workers Union (ILGWU), 108, 110

International Woman Suffrage Alliance (IWSA), 66

Interracial councils, 152

Interurban Suffrage Council, 66

Inverts. *See* "Sexual inverts"

Irwin, Elisabeth, 29

IWSA. *See* International Woman Suffrage Alliance (IWSA)

Jackson, Rebecca, 264–65, 339

Jacobi, Mary Putnam, 271, 280

Jewett, Sarah Orne, 4, 208

Jewett, Sophie, 196, 223

Joan of Arc, 199

Johns Hopkins University
    faculty of, 298
    Garrett's financial endowment for women's admission to medical school, 214, 287, 292, 294–95
    statistics on women in medical school in 1990s, 338
    Thomas as student at, 197, 201, 202

Johnson, Lyndon, 333–34

Jordan, Barbara, 340

Judaism, 339

Judges, 83, 92, 314, 320, 321–23, 324

Jung, Carl, 240–41

Juvenile court, 122

Keller, Elizabeth, 271

Kellor, Frances
    characteristics of, as "sexual invert," 138–41
    domestic workers as focus of, 147
    early jobs of, 140
    education of, 140–41
    on employment agencies, 141, 142
    on female criminality, 152–53
    friends of, 323
    at Hull House, 138, 146
    immigrants as focus of, 148–51, 321
    and Inter-Municipal Committee on Household Research, 147
    on interracial councils, 152
    labor legislation supported by, 146, 147
    law degree for, 140, 268
    National League for the Protection of Colored Women founded by, 147
    New York State Bureau of Industries and Immigration headed by, 149–51
    Office of National Progressive Services directed by, 151–52
    relationship with Mary Dreier, 139, 140–46
    relationship with Gertrude Dudley, 140–41
    silence on lesbianism, 152–53
    social science research by, 138–41, 146–49, 152–53
    working-class background of, 139
    works
        Athletic Games in the Education of Women, 141
        Out of Work: A Study of Employment Agencies, 141, 147, 148
    youth of, 139–40, 146, 148

Kennedy, John F., 333

Kenyon, Dorothy, 324

Kerwinieo, Ralph, 199

Keyser, Frances Reynolds, 193

Kinsey, Alfred, 248

Kraditor, Aileen, 8

Krafft-Ebing, Richard von, 11, 41, 139, 206

Ku Klux Klan, 150

Labor laws
    child labor, 107, 122, 123, 124, 133, 147, 299, 331
    Dreier and Kellor's work on, 144–47
    eight-hour day, 145

Labor laws (*cont.*)
  forty-eight-hour work week, 146
  minimum wage law, 89, 111, 151
  social security, 89, 92, 151
  unemployment insurance, 111, 151
  workmen's compensation, 151
Labor movement, 92, 105–12, 122,
  124, 137, 144, 146, 331, 369n
Lacy-Baker, Marjory, 319–20
Ladd, Carrie, 205
"Ladies' Brain Trust," 87–93
Ladies' Companion, 178
Land settlement movements, 158
Lansing, Marion, 380n
Lape, Esther, 86–87
Lash, Joseph P., 366n
Latinas. *See* Hispanic women
Lawyers, 140, 258, 259, 266–68, 307,
  313, 317–26, 337–39, 397n
League of Nations, 60, 111, 231
League of Women Voters, 39, 77, 81,
  86
Lee, Dorothy, 239
Lees, Edith, 72
Legal profession. *See* Lawyers
Lehman, Governor (New York), 111
Lenroot, Katharine, 401n
Lesbians. *See also* Boston marriage;
  Homophobia; Homosexual-
  ity; "Romantic friendships";
  "Sexual inverts"; *and specific
  women*
  "aggressive occupations" and, 313
  Baudelaire on, 207–8
  before "lesbian identity," 2–5
  Caprio on, 315–16
  children adopted by, 112
  conscious choice of lesbianism by
    heterosexual feminists, 334
  criminality of women associated
    with, 152
  definition of, as adjective, 3
  denial of lesbianism by, 156, 161–
    65, 172, 247, 314
  domestic and affectional arrange-
    ments among, 5–9

  Faderman and, 329–32
  gender roles and, 9–12
  importance of preservation of his-
    tory of, 346–47
  internalization of homophobia by,
    164–72
  media's portrayal of, 17–18, 162–
    63, 164
  in 1950s, 314–16, 330–32
  in 1970s, 252
  pants as clothing for, 333
  as pathological in twentieth cen-
    tury, 156, 161–64, 244, 325,
    334, 405–6n
  postmodernist argument against
    reclaiming women of the past
    as lesbians, 2–3, 346
  in professions in early twentieth
    century, 137–38
  in professions in 1930s–1970s, 313–
    26, 405n
  radical lesbian feminists in sec-
    ond wave of feminism, 334–35
  self-consciousness and lesbian
    identity, 249
  statistics on same-sex love experi-
    ences, 248–49
  among suffragists in nineteenth
    century, 4–9, 80
  "unsexed" sometimes used to re-
    fer to, 354n
  as "woman-identified women," 9,
    334
Lesbienne, 4
L'Esperance, Elise, 279–80
Levine, Daniel, 135
Levine, James, 345
Library science, 185
*Life and Letters of Mary Emma Wool-
  ley* (Marks), 223, 236
Lillie, Frances, 372n
Lindsay, Vachel, 226
Linn, James, 125, 132
Little, Clarence, 245
Livermore, Mary, 8
Lockwood, Belva, 259

Lombroso, Cesare, 152
Long, Margaret, 4, 83, 365n
Love poems, 128–29, 189, 190, 203, 224
Lowber, Edith, 215–16
Lowell, Amy, 226
Loyalty oath, 231
"Lucy Stoners," 36
Lundberg, Ferdinand, 313
Lutheran Church, 339
Lutz, Alma, 94
Lyon, Mary, 176–78, 179, 217, 219, 233, 380nn

MacKenzie, Vashti, 339
Marbury, Elisabeth, 107
Marks, Jeannette, 94, 155, 189, 217, 222–30, 232–33, 236, 390n
Marot, Helen, 106–9, 144, 368n
Marriage. *See* Boston marriage; Heterosexual marriage; Wellesley marriage
Marriage Cycle (Palmer), 195
Martin, Anne, 4, 82–83, 155, 364–65n
Martin, Ellen, 268
"Masculinized" women, 79–80, 333
Massachusetts Women's Reformatory, 162
The Masses, 108
Masters, Edgar Lee, 226
Masturbation, 387n
McAdams, Doug, 95
McCarran, Patrick, 314
McCarthyism, 94
McGovern, James, 45
McHale, Kathryn, 314, 315, 405n
Mead, Elizabeth, 217–18
Mead, Margaret, 251
Meagher, John, 240, 291
Media
    on African-American women, 316
    attack on Van Waters as lesbian, 162–63, 164
    portrayal of suffragists by, 17–18
    recognition of women in 1950s, 316

recognition of Woolley in, 227, 231, 232
Medicine. *See* Doctors
Meeropol, Ann Karus, 390n
Mellon Foundation, 246
Mellor, Ruth, 156, 165–72, 378n
Ménage à trois, 170–71, 384–85n
"Mental hermaphrodites," 178–79, 187–88, 255–60
Methodist Church, 261–62, 339
Meyerowitz, Joanne, 316
Michelet, 183
Michigan Association Opposed to Woman Suffrage, 16
Midwives, 269
Mikulski, Barbara, 340
Miles, Ellen, 263
Milholland, Vida, 155–56
Miller, Elisabeth, 112, 113, 369–70n
Miller, Frieda, 110–13, 345, 369–70n
Mills, Harriet May, 30
Minimum wage law, 89, 111, 151
Ministry, 44, 49, 259, 260–65, 307, 325, 338–39
Mitchell, Lucy, 196
Mitchell, Maria, 192, 238, 383n
Mitchell, Wesley, 195–96
Modern Woman: The Lost Sex (Lundberg and Farnham), 313
Molina, Gloria, 339–40
Morantz-Sanchez, Regina, 269, 294–95, 300
Morello, Karen, 266
Moseley-Braun, Carol, 341
Mosher, Eliza, 271
"Mother-heart"
    abolition and, 100–101
    and education and voting rights for freed slaves, 101–4
    labor movement and, 104–9
    Shaw on, 99–100, 108, 114
    and women in public sphere, 10–11
Mott, Lucretia, 20
Mount Holyoke College
    academic freedom at, 220

Mount Holyoke College (*cont.*)
   bachelor's degree requirements
      of, 220
   compared with other women's col-
      leges, 217, 218, 220
   faculty of, 196, 217–20, 226–29,
      234, 391n, 392n
   founding of, 177–78, 217, 233
   Ham as president of, 235, 391n,
      392n
   loss of female succession battle
      at, 233–35
   Mead as president of, 217–18
   name change to, 217
   need for academic improvements
      at, 217–18
   romantic rituals at, 191
   Woolley as president of, 155, 189,
      215, 218–22, 225, 228–35
   Woolley's problems with trustees
      of, 230, 232–33
   Woolley's retirement plans at, 233
Mount Holyoke Female Seminary,
      177–78, 180, 217
Müller, Margarethe, 187
Multicultural Women Attorneys Net-
      work, 338
Municipal housekeeping, 100, 138
Murray, Pauli, 323–26, 339, 405n
Musson, Emma (Noel), 271–72
Mygatt, Tracy, 6, 154, 156, 159–61, 345

NAACP. *See* National Association
      for the Advancement of Col-
      ored People (NAACP)
National American Woman Suffrage
      Association (NAWSA)
   Addams as vice president of, 116
   Alice Stone Blackwell's founding
      of, 35–36, 39
   Catt as president of, 63–66, 68–69
   Catt's resignation from presidency
      of, 65–66
   compared with Congressional Un-
      ion, 335
   Dewson and, 90

and founding of League of
      Women Voters, 81
   funding for, 214–15
   Porter and, 90
   Shaw as president of, 48, 51, 54–
      57, 68, 116
   standing committee on organiza-
      tion for, 62
   Woman's Journal of, 36, 39, 123–24
National Association for the Ad-
      vancement of Colored People
      (NAACP), 106, 133, 324
National Association of Deans of
      Women, 245
National Child Labor Committee,
      133
National Civil Liberties Bureau, 160
National College Women's Equal
      Suffrage League, 215, 230
National Conference of Charities
      and Corrections, 133
National Conference of Social
      Work, 133
National Consumers' League, 88–
      89, 91, 92, 108
National Education Association,
      312
National Federation of Business and
      Professional Women's Clubs
      (NFBPWC), 318–19, 320
National Organization for Women
      (NOW), 324, 335
National Progressive Services
      Office, 151–52
National Recovery Administration,
      91
National Urban League, 147
National Woman Suffrage Associa-
      tion (NWSA), 23, 54
National Woman's Party (NWP), 69,
      92–95, 236
National Women's Political Caucus,
      334
National Youth Administration, 87,
      239
Native Americans, 157–59

Nativism, 150
NAWSA. *See* National American Woman Suffrage Association (NAWSA)
Neilson, William, 243
Nevada Equal Franchise Society, 82, 364n
New Deal, 87–93, 141, 239, 322
New England Female Medical College, 270, 284
New England Hospital for Women and Children, 257, 269, 271
New Haven Hospital, 296
New York Child Labor Committee, 107
New York City and Country School, 107
New York Compulsory Education Act, 107
New York Equal Suffrage League, 74
New York Federation of Women's Clubs, 74
New York Industrial Commission, 91
New York Infirmary for Women and Children, 257, 268–69, 275, 277, 278–84, 289, 399n
New York League for the Protection of Immigrants, 321
New York Republican Party, 83–85
New York School of Civics and Philanthropy, 144
New York State Assembly, 83
New York State Bureau of Child Hygiene, 280
New York State Bureau of Industries and Immigration, 149–51
New York State Department of Corrections, 312
New York State Factory Investigating Commission, 144
New York State Labor Department, 111, 149
New York State Minimum Wage Board, 112
New York Times, 334
New York University, 321

New York Woman Suffrage Party, 67–68
New York Women's City Club, 144
New York Women's Joint Legislative Committee, 83
New York Women's Municipal League, 142
New York Women's Trade Union League, 110, 144, 146
Newer Ideals of Peace (Addams), 133–34
Newman, Cardinal, 209
Newman, Pauline, 110–13, 369–70n
NFBPWC. *See* National Federation of Business and Professional Women's Clubs (NFBPWC)
Nightingale, Florence, 281
Nineteenth Amendment, 15, 24, 35, 36, 59, 60, 69, 81, 343
NOW. *See* National Organization for Women (NOW)
Nurses, 259, 279, 280, 307, 403n
NWP. *See* National Woman's Party (NWP)
NWSA. *See* National Woman Suffrage Association (NWSA)

Oberlin College, 101, 178–79, 184, 260–61, 380–81n
O'Connor, Sandra Day, 341
O'Day, Caroline, 88, 91
Oettinger, Katherine, 402n
Office of National Progressive Services, 151–52
Ohio Supreme Court, 83, 321, 322
O'Leary, Hazel, 341
Olivia (Bussy), 366n
Olmsted, Allen, 165, 168–72
Olmsted, Mildred Scott
 and anxieties over sexuality, 166–68, 378n
 marriage of, 2, 165, 168–72
 ménage à trois and, 170–71, 384–85n
 relationship with Ruth Mellor, 2, 156, 164–72

Oread Collegiate Institute, 181
Organ, Joan, 321, 322
Osburn, Clara, 43
Out of Work: A Study of Employment
    Agencies (Kellor), 141, 147,
    148
Owen, Ruth Bryan, 92
Oxford University, 192

Pacifism, 57, 68, 133–34, 154–56, 160,
    231–32, 320
Packard, Sophia, 180–81
Palmer, Alice Freeman, 187, 194–95,
    196, 227, 306
Palmer, George, 194–95, 227
Palmieri, Patricia, 192
Park, Maud Wood, 64
Patterns of Culture (Benedict), 251
Paul, Alice, 55, 69, 93, 94, 236, 367n
Peace movement. See Pacifism
Pearce, Louise, 271
Pearson, Drew, 87
Peck, Mary, 53, 61–65, 71, 72–73, 75,
    76, 77–78
Pediatrics. See Children's health
Pegler, Westbrook, 94
Penis envy, 313
Penn, Donna, 405n
Pennsylvania Anti-Slavery Society,
    21
Pennsylvania Woman Suffrage Asso-
    ciation, 22
Penology. See Prison reform
People's Mandate to Governments
    to End War, 155, 232
Perkins, Frances, 88–92, 107, 111,
    137, 144, 163, 234
Perot, Rebecca, 265
Perry, Mary, 268
Peter Brigham Hospital, 295–96
Phi Beta Kappa, 210, 231
Phillips, Lena Madesin, 318–23
Physical education, 140, 141
Physicians. See Doctors
Pierce, Mary, 322
Pike, Clara, 221

Pioneer Work in Opening the Medi-
    cal Profession to Women
    (Blackwell), 281
Pittinsky, Todd, 345
Poems. See Love poems
Political appointments, 85–93, 111–
    13, 299, 300, 321–22, 333, 341,
    342
Politics. See also Democratic Party;
    Republican Party
    "gender gap" and, 339–40
    National Woman's Party (NWP),
        69, 92–95, 236
    Progressive Party, 113–14, 135, 151,
        152
    Woman Suffrage Party, 66, 67–68,
        144, 160
    women as political candidates, 82–
        83, 321, 340–43
    women's involvement in, 82–85,
        339–40
    Women's Peace Party, 134
Porter, Katherine Anne, 1
Porter, Polly, 88, 90, 92, 323
Postmodernism, 2–3, 346
Potter, Bessie, 29
Potter, Ellen, 271, 307–8, 310
Potter, Frances, 360n
Powell, Rose, 94
Pratt, Caroline, 106–9, 368n
Premature infants, 301, 302
Prentice-Tully Bill, 147
Primus, Rebecca, 103–4
Prison reform, 162–64
Professions. See also Education;
        Higher education
    attacks on lesbians in, 313–14
    college administrators, 239, 246–
        47
    college teaching, 184–89, 191–96,
        238, 245–46, 392n
    law profession, 140, 258, 259, 266–
        68, 307, 313, 317–26, 337–38,
        397n
    lesbians' choice of, in twentieth
        century, 137–38, 313–26

library science, 185
married versus single professionals, 258, 309–12, 317–18, 396n
medicine, 45, 188, 214, 257–59, 268–305, 307–9, 338
ministry, 44, 49, 259, 260–65, 307, 325, 338–39
movie stereotypes of, 310
for municipal housekeeping, 100
new professions for New Women
    in early twentieth century, 136–38
    in 1970s–1990s, 337–39
    in 1990s, 344–45
    in nineteenth century after Civil War, 258–60
nurses, 259, 279, 280, 307, 403n
penologists, 162
professional women as "Amazons" and "mental hermaphrodites," 195, 210, 255–60
science, 231
settlement house movement and, 136–37
social scientists, 122, 136, 138–41, 146–49, 152–53
social work, 135, 294
teaching, 179–80, 307, 312, 403n
women's loss of ground in, from 1920s–1970s, 306–12, 337
Progressive Party, 113–14, 135, 151, 152
Property law for married women, 22–23
Public health, 271, 303
Public Health Service, 112
Public libraries, 123
Pugh, Sarah, 99
Putnam, Caroline, 101–03, 157

Quakers, 207, 209

"Race suicide," 182–84
Radcliffe College, 180, 184, 191–92, 204, 239–40, 293, 294
Ray, Charlotte, 267
Rank, Otto, 170–71

Ray, Charlotte, 267
Read, Elizabeth, 86–87
Reagan, Ronald, 339
Rebhan, Susan, 83, 322–23
Red Cross, 90
Reduction and Limitation of Armaments Conference, 232
Reed, James, 303, 305
Reed, Mabel, 156–59
Reform. *See* Child labor; Immigrants; Labor laws; Labor movement; Settlement house movement
Religious Magazine, 178
Reno, Janet, 342
Republican Party, 83–85, 89, 103, 342–43
Republican Women's National Executive Committee, 84
Reyes, Consuelo, 94, 155–56
Reynard, Elizabeth, 246
Rhoads, James, 197, 198, 202
Rickets, 298–300
Riesman, David, 328
Riis, Jacob, 151
Rivington Street College Settlement, 138
Robins, Raymond, 143
Rockefeller, John D., 181
Rockefeller, Laura Spelman, 181
Rockford College, 115, 118–19, 121
Rockford Female Seminary, 118–19
Roe v. *Wade,* 336
Rogers, Julia, 201, 203
"Romantic friendships," 20–23, 33–34, 44, 73, 156, 159, 161, 166–68, 205–6
Roosevelt, Eleanor
    on Addams, 134
    bisexuality of, 365–66n
    and Commission on the Status of Women, 333
    in Daughters of the American Revolution, 232
    death of, 333
    Dreier and, 87, 144

Roosevelt, Eleanor (*cont.*)
    and FDR's appointment of women
        to political office, 87, 321
    and Kennedy's appointment of
        women to political office, 333
    and "Ladies Brain Trust," 87–92
    lesbian friendships and relation-
        ships of, 85–92, 107, 114, 314,
        323, 366n
    Murray and, 324
    prominence of, 331
    relationship with Lorena Hickok,
        85–87, 314
    on Thomas, 154
    Van Waters defended by, 163, 314
Roosevelt, Franklin D., 86–90, 163,
    314, 320, 321–22
Roosevelt, Theodore, 114, 135, 148,
    151
Ross, Nellie Taylor, 92
Rota, Tiziana, 191, 380n
Rumsey, Mary H., 91, 107
Runyan, Mary, 371n
Rupp, Leila, 367n
Rush Medical School, 275–76
Russell, Rosalind, 310

Sacco and Vanzetti executions, 112
St. Louis Children's Hospital, 296
St. Philip's College, 239
Salhi, Nancy, 358n
Salmon, Lucy, 184–86, 188–89, 192,
    196, 238
Sandburg, Carl, 226
Sanger, Margaret, 276, 368n
Schmidt, William, 304
Schneiderman, Rose, 369n
Schofield, Ann, 110, 369n
Schools. *See* Education; Higher edu-
    cation
Science, 231
Scott, Adele, 168
Scudder, Vida, 189, 196, 223, 272–73
Second Twenty Years at Hull House
    (Addams), 301
Seneca Falls convention of 1848, 20

Settlement house movement, 88, 92,
    102, 105, 116–18, 120–26, 128,
    129, 133–37, 138
Sewall, Lucy, 271
*Sex Variants: A Study of Homosexual
    Patterns*, 312–13
Sexologists, 4–5, 11–12, 32, 37, 42,
    72, 80, 139, 152–53, 160–61,
    206, 240, 259, 358n
Sexton, Lydia, 260
Sexual harassment, 341
"Sexual inverts." *See also* Homopho-
    bia; Homosexuality; Lesbians
    Alice Blackwell's response to la-
        bel, 37, 358n
    college professors as, 186–88
    crime by women associated with,
        152
    hereditary cause of, 5, 139, 152–53
    higher education and, 187–88,
        240–41
    Kellor as, 138–41
    Lees as, 72
    in professions, 137–38
    sexologists on, 4–5, 11–12, 37, 42,
        72, 80, 139, 152–53, 160–61,
        206, 240, 259, 358n
    Shaw as, 42
    Mary Walker as, 259
    Willard as, 32
    Zakrzewska as, 257–58
Shackford, Martha Hale, 189, 196,
    223, 236
Shakers, 264–65
Shaw, Anna Howard
    anomie and exhaustion of, 51–52
    Susan B. Anthony and, 47–48, 54
    and bathing suit episode, 41
    as chair of Woman's Committee
        of the Council of National
        Defense, 58–59
    characteristics of, as "sexual in-
        vert," 42, 325
    death of, 40, 60
    and death of Susan B. Anthony,
        30

Distinguished Service Medal for, 59
as doctor, 45, 270
dress and appearance of, in public, 41–42
early lesbian relationships of, 43–44
education of, 43, 44–45
"feminine charm" of public persona of, 40–42
friends of, 3–4, 45, 208, 214
on heterosexual marriage, 42–43
infidelities of, with other women, 52–53, 360n
as minister, 44, 49, 261–62
on "mother-heart," 99–100, 108, 114
as NAWSA president, 48, 51, 54–57, 68, 116
on New Woman and New Man, 46–47
as orator, 45–47, 48, 54
plans with Lucy Anthony after World War I, 59
on relationship between Susan B. Anthony and Emily Gross, 28
relationship with Lucy Anthony, 5–6, 27, 28, 40, 44, 48–54, 59
WCTU and, 45, 48
Woodrow Wilson and, 56–57, 58, 60, 69, 361n
in woman suffrage movement, 40–42, 45–49, 54–60, 69
on women's participation in government, 99–100
World War I and, 57–59
youth of, 42
Sheppard-Towner Act, 299
Sherwood, Margaret, 189, 196, 223, 236
Sherwood, Mary, 269, 271
Shirtwaist Employers Association, 108
Simmons, Christina, 241
Skinner, Joseph, 232
Sklar, Kathryn Kish, 121, 374n

Slater, Miriam, 391n
Slavery. *See* Abolitionism
Sleeping sickness, 271
Smith, Elaine, 87, 193
Smith, Hannah, 199, 386n
Smith, Howard, 332
Smith, Marguerite, 94
Smith, Mary, 255, 271
Smith, Mary Rozet, 3–4, 6, 118, 125–33, 365n
Smith College
compared with other women's colleges, 198, 217
faculty of, 238
female-female romantic relationships at, 175, 189, 190
founding of, 180
marriage following graduation from, 315
students at, 165, 243
Smith-Rosenberg, Carroll, 10
Social constructionism, 152–53
Social reform. *See* Child labor; Immigration; Labor laws; Labor movement; Settlement house movement
Social scientists, 122, 136, 138–41, 146–49, 152–53
Social security, 89, 92, 151
Social work, 135, 294
Somerset, Lady Isabel, 357n, 387n
Sophie Newcomb College, 190
Souvestre, Marie, 85–86, 365–66n
Spelman, Laura (Rockefeller), 181
Spelman College, 180, 181–82, 189
Sprague, Julie, 258
Sprague, Lucy, 195–96
Spurgeon, Caroline, 231, 246
Stanton, Elizabeth Cady
on Susan B. Anthony's involvement in suffrage movement, 25
and Susan B. Anthony's love relationships with women, 27
and defense of free-love advocate Victoria Woodhull, 53–54

Stanton, Elizabeth Cady (*cont.*)
  marriage and children of, 18, 23, 30
  National Woman Suffrage Association founded by, 35
  relationship with Susan B. Anthony, 22–23
  relationship with Anna Dickinson, 355n
  and Seneca Falls woman's rights convention of 1848, 20
  in woman suffrage movement, 18, 22–23, 35
Stanton, Ellen, 221
Starr, Ellen Gates, 118–27, 371n, 372n
State legislatures, 82, 339–40, 341
Stearn, Jess, 325–26
Stein, Gertrude, 384–85n
Stevens, Doris, 94, 367n
Stevenson, Adlai, 315
Stone, Alice. *See* Blackwell, Alice Stone
Stone, Lucy, 18–19, 35, 36, 45, 261, 396n
Straus, Dorothy, 324
Stricker, Frank, 393n, 403n
Strikes, 107–08, 124, 144. *See also* Labor movement
Subversive Activities Control Board, 314
Suffrage movement. *See* Woman suffrage movement
Swartz, Maud O'Farrel, 369n
Sweet, Thaddeus, 83, 84
Swinburne, Algernon, 207
Syracuse University, 269

Taft, William Howard, 60
Teachers. *See* Education
Temperance movement, 22, 30–32, 34–35, 48
Tennessee and Alabama Female Institute, 176
Tennessee Valley Authority (TVA), 322
Terrell, Mary Church, 24
Theology. *See* Ministry

Thomas, Clarence, 341
Thomas, M. Carey
  aspirations for becoming Bryn Mawr College president, 197–98, 207
  as Bryn Mawr College president, 6, 154, 160, 183, 202–4, 209–16, 218, 222
  as dean of Bryn Mawr College, 198
  education of, 197, 201, 202, 244
  on female-female love relations, 197, 255
  friends of, 208
  heterosexual feelings of, 200–201, 205
  and heterosexual imperative, 247
  and last illness and death of Mary Garrett, 215
  on male-female relations, 205–6
  medicine and medical education as interest of, 270, 287, 292, 294–95
  prejudices of, 211, 388n
  as Quaker, 207
  relationship with Mary Garrett, 6, 197, 201, 203–4, 213–15, 386n
  relationship with Mamie Gwinn, 201–2, 203, 207, 215, 386n
  relationship with Edith Lowber, 215–16
  sexual identity and, 205–9, 247, 251–52, 385–86n, 387n
  Shaw and, 3
  on stereotypes of inferiority of women, 183, 199–200, 307
  woman suffrage movement and, 214–15, 230
  on Woolley, 231
  youth of, 183, 198–200, 205
Thomas, Mary, 197
Thompson, Geraldine, 6, 163
Thompson, Lenore, 250
Tillotson College, 239
Tissot, Samuel, 387n

Toynbee Hall, 120
Tracy, Martha, 271, 307–9, 310
Tresca, Carlo, 162
Triangle Shirtwaist Company, 110, 144
Troy Female Seminary, 175–76
"True Womanly Woman" (Chamberlin), 187–88
Truman, Harry, 300, 302, 314
Truth, Sojourner, 17, 101, 103
Turner, Eliza Sproat, 38
Tuskegee Institute, 270

UCLA, 250
Underhill, Adelaide, 185–86, 188–89, 196
Unemployment insurance, 111, 151
UNICEF, 302
Unionization. *See* Labor movement
"Unisex" fad, 333
United Brethren Church, 260
United Methodist Church, 339
U.S. Army, 112
U.S. Attorney General, 342
U.S. Children's Bureau, 291, 299–304, 402n
U.S. Department of Food Administration, 134
U.S. House of Representatives, 82, 340, 341
U.S. Indian Service, 157–59
U.S. Industrial Commission, 106
U.S. Justice Department, 322
U.S. Labor Department, 91–92, 111, 137, 147, 334
U.S. Senate, 82–83, 340, 341, 342
U.S. State Department, 342
U.S. Supreme Court, 322, 323, 341
U.S. Surgeon General, 341
U.S. Women's Bureau, 111, 112, 113, 306–7
Universalist Church, 262
Universities. *See* Higher education; *and specific colleges*
University of California at Berkeley, 195–96

University of Chicago
    graduates and faculty of, at Hull House, 121
    graduates of, on Mount Holyoke faculty, 219
    Kellor at, 138, 139, 140–41, 146, 152
    Law School of, 321
    Miller at, 111
    social scientists trained at, 122, 138, 139, 140–41, 146
    women faculty at, 196
University of Kentucky, 318
University of Leipzig, 197, 198
University of Michigan, 184, 268
University of Minnesota, 301
University of Zurich, 202, 244, 271
"Unsexing," 17–18, 24–25, 84, 182–83, 188, 354n
Uprising of the Twenty Thousand, 107, 144

Valentine, Ruth, 251
Van Waters, Miriam, 6, 156, 162–63, 314, 315, 405n
Vassar College
    Blanding's retirement as president of, 246
    compared with other women's colleges, 198, 217, 220
    domestic science program in, 212, 238
    faculty and staff of, 184–85, 192, 196, 238, 246
    founding of, 180, 217
    graduation requirements of, 220
    homophobia at, 250
    marriage as goal of students at, 242, 394n
    married versus single professionals among alumnae of, 258
    student advising at, 246
Vernon, Mabel, 94, 155–56, 365n
Volunteer work, 100, 105, 136–37
Von Nunes, Irma, 313
Voting records of married women, 80–81

Voting rights for African Americans, 23, 35, 102–3

Wadsworth, James, 85
Wald, Lillian, 116, 155
Walker, Mary, 259
Walling, William, 106
Ware, Susan, 90, 91
Warner, Charles, 199
Watervliet Shakers, 265
WAVES, 246
WCTU. *See* Women's Christian Temperance Union (WCTU)
Well of Loneliness (Hall), 163, 387n
Wellesley College
    Bates's return to, 383–84n
    compared with other women's colleges, 198, 209, 217
    faculty of, 187, 189, 192, 196, 222–23
    founding of, 180
    Freeman as president of, 187, 194–95
    married faculty women at, 192
    and romances between female students, 190
    statistics on graduates with careers, 209
    statistics on graduates with children, 184
    statistics on married graduates, 184
    students going on to graduate study from, 209
    Wellesley marriage and, 185, 191–96
Wellesley Lyrics, 190
Wellesley marriage, 185, 191–96, 225–26, 252
Wells, Anna Mary, 390n
Wells, Ida B., 19–20, 24, 122
Welsh, Lilian, 269, 270, 271
Wenckebach, Carla, 186–87
Western Reserve University, 270, 276
Wheaton Seminary, 221

Whipper, Ionia, 270
WHO. *See* World Health Organization (WHO)
Wilde, Oscar, 125
Willard, Emma, 175–76
Willard, Frances
    career of, in education, 34
    characteristics of, as "sexual invert," 32
    Frank persona of, 32, 33, 34
    friends of, 45, 208, 263
    Gordon's books on, 35
    relationship with Anna Gordon, 6, 33–35, 357n
    relationship with Kate Jackson, 34
    Shaw and, 45
    Lady Somerset and, 357n, 387
    as WCTU leader, 31, 34–35, 45
    in woman suffrage movement, 31, 69
    womanly, motherly public image of, 32–33
    on women's love for each other, 33
    works
        Glimpses of Fifty Years, 33, 35
        Woman of the Century, 8
    youth of, 32
WILPF. *See* Women's International League for Peace and Freedom (WILPF)
Wilson, Alda, 78
Wilson, Woodrow, 56–57, 58, 60, 69, 151, 360–61n
Winslow, Caroline, 256
Witherspoon, Frances, 6, 154, 156, 159–61, 345
Wollstein, Martha, 280
Woman Citizen, 39, 61
Woman of the Century (Willard), 8
Woman suffrage movement. *See also* specific leaders and organizations
    Addams on, 116
    Susan B. Anthony in, 22–30, 35, 47–48
    beginnings of, 22–30

Alice Stone Blackwell in, 35–36, 39, 48, 69, 80–81
Catt in, 61–69, 71, 74
divisions within, 23, 25, 35
Empire State Campaign and, 66–67, 84
female antisuffragists on "real" women, 16–20
as frightening to women in nineteenth century, 30–31
Garrett in, 214–15
Grew in, 22
as grueling battle, 15
Hay in, 62, 63–68, 74, 76
leaders of, labeled as "sexual inverts," 4–5, 80, 352n
lesbian relationships among nineteenth-century suffragists, 6–9, 15–39, 80
married women's involvement in, 18–20, 31–32
media portrayal of suffragists, 17–18
men's support of, 18, 61
reasons for lesbians as early leaders in, 6–9, 15–16
Theodore Roosevelt on, 151
Shaw in, 40–42, 45–49, 54–60
Stanton in, 18, 22–23, 35
state votes for, 54
suffragists accused of being "unsexed" or "manly," 17–18, 24–25
Thomas in, 214–15, 230
WCTU's endorsement of, 31–32
Willard in, 30–35
Woodrow Wilson and, 56–57
Woolley in, 230
Woman Suffrage Party (New York), 66, 67–68, 144
Womanhood
Anthony on "true woman," 24
antisuffragists on "real" women, 16–20
Emily Blackwell on femininity, 275–76

"cult of true womanhood," 256, 261
educated women as "mental hermaphrodites" and "semiwomen," 178–79, 187–88
feminine mystique of 1920s–1930s, 242, 308
feminine mystique of 1950s, 243, 315, 316, 328–39, 332
"masculinized" women, 79–80, 333
"moral superiority" of women, 10–11, 82, 99–100
"mother-heart" of women, 99–100
movie stereotypes of, 310
New Women, 165–67, 191, 256–57, 259, 308
Shaw on new woman, 46–47
"unsexing," 17–18, 24–25, 84, 182–83, 188, 354n
"Woman-identified women," 9, 334
Woman's Christian Temperance Union (WCTU), 6, 31–32, 34–35, 45
Woman's Hospital of Philadelphia, 272
Woman's Journal, 36, 39, 123–24, 289
Woman's Medical College of Chicago, 284
Woman's Medical College of Pennsylvania, 270, 271–72, 284, 307
Woman's Suffrage Party (Penn.), 160
Women's Bureau, 111, 112, 113, 306–7
Women's Clubs. *See* Federation of Women's Clubs
Women's Committee of the Council of National Defense, 58–59, 69
Women's Committee on Defense Manpower, 113
Women's International League for Peace and Freedom (WILPF), 134, 155, 165, 169–70
Women's Medical College of the New York Infirmary, 277, 279–80, 282–84, 286–89, 399n
Women's Municipal League, 142, 145

Women's Peace Party, 134
Women's rights convention of 1848,
    20
Women's Trade Union League
    (WTUL), 86, 87, 88, 106–12,
    124, 144, 146, 369n
Wood, Robert, 131
Woodhull, Victoria, 54
Woolley, Mary Emma
    as AAUW president, 231
    academic freedom and, 220
    biography of, 223, 236
    death of, 236
    education of, 221–22
    on equality for women, 230
    feminist causes supported by,
        236
    friends of, 208, 320, 322
    on gender differences, 220–21
    loss of female succession battle at
        Mount Holyoke, 233–35
    as pacifist, 231–32, 236
    as president of Mount Holyoke
        College, 155, 189, 215, 218–22,
        225, 228–35
    problems with Mount Holyoke
        trustees, 230, 232–33
    recognition for, 227, 231, 232
    relationship with Jeannette
        Marks, 94, 155, 189, 217, 222–
        30, 232–33, 236, 250, 321, 390n
    retirement of, 233, 235

    social reform efforts by, 231–32
    on Wellesley College faculty, 222–
        24
    woman suffrage movement and,
        230
Working Fathers (Levine and Pittin-
    sky), 345
Working-class women. *See also* La-
    bor laws; Labor movement
    Bryn Mawr Summer School for
        Women Workers, 154, 211–12
    Faderman's mother as, 329–30
    Kellor's mother as, 139–40
Workmen's compensation, 151
World Health Organization (WHO),
    302, 304, 305
World War I, 57–59, 66, 68–69, 90,
    134, 160, 232, 295
World War II, 81, 92–93, 113, 246,
    315, 320
World's Anti-Slavery Convention, 20
Wright, Anne, 258
WTUL. *See* Women's Trade Union
    League (WTUL)
Wylie, Laura, 196

Yale Medical School, 298–301, 338
Yale University, 133, 219, 235, 292
Young, Eula, 266
YWCA, 322

Zakrzewska, Marie, 257–58, 269